Mass Media and Free Trade:
NAFTA and the Cultural Industries

Emile G. McAnany

Kenton T. Wilkinson

EDITORS

MASS MEDIA AND FREE TRADE

NAFTA and the Cultural Industries

UNIVERSITY OF TEXAS PRESS

AUSTIN

Requests for permission to reproduce material from this work should be sent to
Permissions, University of Texas Press, P.O. Box 7819, Austin, TX 78713-7819.

⊗ The paper used in this publication meets the minimum requirements of
American National Standard for Information Sciences—Permanence of Paper
for Printed Library Materials, ANSI Z39.48-1984.

Library of Congress Cataloging-in-Publication Data

Mass media and free trade : NAFTA and the cultural industries / Emile G.
  McAnany and Kenton T. Wilkinson, editors. — 1st ed.
      p.   cm.
    Includes bibliographical references and index.
    ISBN 0-292-75198-2 (alk. paper). — ISBN 0-292-75199-0 (pbk. : alk. paper)
    1. Mass media and culture—North America.   2. Mass media—Economic
  aspects—North America.   3. Canada.   Treaties, etc.   1992 Oct. 7   4. Free
  trade—North America.   5. Culture diffusion—North America.   I. McAnany,
  Emile G.   II. Wilkinson, Kenton T. (Kenton Todd)
    P94.65.N7M38   1886
  302.23′097—dc20   96-10222

Contents

Preface

THE PRESENT BOOK EMERGED from a three-way conversation among academics, policymakers, and cultural-industry representatives who gathered at a conference at the University of Texas in Austin in March 1994. The conversation was promoted by conference organizers out of the conviction that past cultural-industry debates were often dialogs of the deaf rather than fruitful opportunities to learn from one another. As new technologies and rapidly growing markets push the products of cultural industries into a growing number of homes of audiences around the world, problems of culture shock, national identity, and threats to cultural sovereignty become part of politics and public discourse.

The conference was organized around a carefully prepared agenda that brought the three groups together for seminars and roundtables as well as common meals where more informal discussion could continue. Each of the groups had an important perspective to provide, even when these perspectives clashed, as they did in several of the sessions. Academics are used to the long-term and more theoretical concerns that are necessarily abstracted from many of the constraints of politics and the market that face the other two groups. But academics often do not have access to market data nor to the considerations of the policy process. Policymakers, on the other hand, are faced with making policy decisions whose future viability is at best only an informed guess; furthermore, these people are under intense pressure from a variety of interests in the public and private sectors. The industry was in a state of major change in the first half of this decade, with new technologies raising both opportunities and threats and with new trade agreements pulling more and more industries into the international market. Yet each of these three groups has an important realm of experience that helps to illuminate the dynamic nature of the cultural industries in an increasingly global economic and political context. Our hope was that by having the opportunity to talk, participants and audiences could learn from one another. And, indeed, the conference experience seemed to bear this out.

The resultant book well reflects the conference presentations of participating academics from Australia, Canada, Mexico, and the United States, but it was difficult to capture some of the rich interchange in the two roundtable discussions of policymakers and industry representatives. Fortunately, the entire conference was videotaped and edited, with the result that summaries of these two key groups were available; they are to be found in Appendixes A and B.

For the editors, this book is the fruit of a dialog that promises to continue with the expansion made possible by new technological and economic developments and with expanded trade among regional trading blocs. Thus, we consider this the first step in a much longer and more complicated process of analysis and action.

EMILE G. MCANANY
AUSTIN, TEXAS

KENTON T. WILKINSON
MONTERREY, MEXICO

Acknowledgments

WE ARE INDEBTED TO Roger de la Garde, of the Université Laval in Québec, for coming up with the original idea for the conference and book in a conversation we had over coffee in Brazil at a conference in 1992. In the same conversation Roger suggested Austin as a logical meeting place between Canada and Mexico to discuss the then-planned North American Free Trade Agreement (NAFTA) among the three countries. A year and a half later, in early March 1994, after much labor in Austin and not a little help and advice from Roger, we were able to gather some thirty or forty academics, policymakers, and industry representatives in a conference at the University of Texas at Austin for three days of intense conversations about the cultural industries under the already-operative NAFTA.

Our grateful acknowledgment goes to Roger for the original stimulus and to many others who helped make possible the conference and the book that emerged from it. The list is too long and complicated to include all who helped realize both accomplishments, but some effort to note many of those who helped is necessary at the beginning of this book. For important sources of support of the conference, we wish to gratefully acknowledge: the Canadian Embassy in Washington for an Institutional Research Grant, which allowed a basic fund to promote the conference and especially to bring some of our Canadian colleagues (special thanks to Rosalind de Rolon of the Canadian Consulate in Dallas); the Ford Foundation (through Peter Ward and Henry Selby of the

Center for Mexican Studies at the University of Texas); the College of Communication (Dean Ellen Wartella); the Department of Radio Television Film (John Downing, Chair) at the University of Texas; the French Cultural and Scientific Service (through the French Consulate in Houston); the Mexican Consulate in Austin (Daniel Hernández, vice-consul); and the Research Foundation at the Université Laval, which was responsible for the presence of the five academic participants from Québec.

In addition to financial support, there were numerous people who, through their gracious help in innumerable ways, made our conference and this subsequent book possible. They include Lillian Respress and Susan Dirks (Department of Radio Television Film's administration office) and Judy Lister (Center for Research on Communication Technology and Society). Among graduate students, Chris Patterson made possible the complicated task of getting the conference on video and later edited complete and summary versions; Carol Wilkinson helped arrange communal meals so that the conference could carry on uninterrupted from sunrise to well into the night; Geektika Pathania, Teresa Páramo-Ricoy, and Raul Tovares helped in keeping the conference running smoothly; Rafael López-Islas provided Spanish-to-English translation for two presentations. Finally, for intellectual support for the idea, we wish to thank Henry Selby and William Glade at the University of Texas. To those whose names deserve to be mentioned here but are not, we apologize for cutting this list short!

Contributors

Robert C. Allen is James Logan Godfrey Professor of American Studies, History and Communication at the University of North Carolina at Chapel Hill. He is the author of *Speaking of Soap Operas* and *Horrible Prettiness: Burlesque and American Culture* and the editor of *Channels of Discourse* and *To be Continued . . . : Soap Operas Around the World*, among much other writing on American media and popular entertainment.

Keith Acheson is Professor of Economics at Carlton University in Ottawa. He has published extensively in the area of the economics of cultural industries, with a particular focus on Canadian industries. Current interests include the economics of organizations, rights structures, shopping, retail and wholesale activities, and cultural economics.

Eduardo Barrera is a researcher at the Colegio de la Frontera Norte in Ciudad Juárez and Assistant Professor at the University of Texas at El Paso. He is also a member of the National Researchers System of Mexico. His research interests are telecommunication policy, the political economy of telecommunications, and discourse analysis about borders. His articles have appeared in *Journal of Communication, Media Development, Diálogos de la Comunicación, Ciudades*, and other journals.

Roger de la Garde is Professor in the Department of Communications at the Université Laval in Québec City. He is co-founder (in 1975) and editor of the French-language journal *Communication*. He is currently engaged with other colleagues in a funded research project on three of Québec's main cultural industries—books, television, and recorded music—with special attention to the social construction of the best-sellers in each.

ADAM FINN is a Professor in the Department of Marketing and Economic Analysis, Faculty of Business, at the University of Alberta. Recent research has focused on the characteristics of successful international joint ventures in television program production. He has also been looking at the marketing components, product development, and financial characteristics of successful feature films and television series. His research has appeared in the *Journal of Marketing Research, Marketing Science,* and the *Journal of Retailing.*

NÉSTOR GARCÍA CANCLINI is the Director of the Program of Studies of Urban Culture in the Universidad Autónoma Metropolitana Iztapalapa in Mexico City. He has taught at Stanford University, the University of Texas at Austin, and the universities of Barcelona, Buenos Aires, and São Paulo. His extensive writing on culture and communication has earned wide recognition and in 1992 he received the Iberoamerican Prize Book Award of the Latin American Studies Association for his book *Hybrid Cultures.*

LINE GRENIER is Associate Professor in the Department of Communication at the University of Montréal. She has published in such journals as *New Formations, Popular Music,* and *Ethnomusicology* and is preparing a book on popular music in Québec. Her current research focuses on the emergence of the *chanson* as a distinct social format of musical communication and its role in the development of local music-related industries in French-speaking Québec.

COLIN HOSKINS is Professor in the Department of Marketing and Economic Analysis, Faculty of Business, at the University of Alberta. He is a co-author, with Stuart McFadyen and David Gillen, of *Canadian Broadcasting: Economic Structure and Market Performance,* which examines the economic determinants of firm conduct and industry performance in the Canadian broadcasting industry. He has also looked at issues of market segmentation and other competitive strategies for Canadian television producers to employ to combat American dominance. Currently he is focusing on international joint ventures and new product development in feature film and television production in Canada.

STEVE JONES is Associate Professor and Chair of the Department of Communication at the University of Tulsa. His scholarly interests are in the area of new technology and mass communication, with a focus on social history. He is the author of *Rock Formation: Technology, Mass Communication and Popular Music* and *CyberSociety: Computer-Mediated Communication and Community*, as well as of numerous published articles and chapters.

JACQUES LEMIEUX is Professor in the Department of Information and Communication at the Université Laval and is a member of the Research Center on Quebecoise Literature. His areas of scholarly research are in the sociology of mass media and popular culture, and in particular in the relations between messages and audiences in best-selling books, television fiction, and the news media. He has published two books and many articles in Québecois and Canadian journals on these topics.

JOSÉ CARLOS LOZANO is Professor in the Department of Communication at the Technical Institute of Higher Studies in Monterrey, Mexico. He is the editor of the yearbook of communication research of the National Council of Schools of Communication of Mexico. His research interests focus on the analysis of both content and reception of foreign messages in Mexico and Latin America.

CLAUDE MARTIN is Professor in the Department of Communication at the University of Montréal. As an economist, he has researched the economic aspects of the cultural industries in Québec. Recent work has concentrated on analysis of news media, best-seller books, regulation policies for children in Québec, and regional development of the cultural industries.

CHRISTOPHER MAULE is Professor of Economics and International Affairs at Carleton University in Ottawa. His research interests are in the areas of industrial organization, international trade and investment, and government policy toward business. In recent years his published work with Keith Acheson has dealt with various domestic and international aspects of cultural industries in Canada and other countries.

EMILE G. MCANANY is Ben F. Love Professor of Communication in the Department of Radio Television Film at the University of Texas at Austin. He has written and edited a number of books on communication and social change, with special focus on Latin America. Recent research has focused on the cultural industries and their response to global competition and free trade, as well as on the more long-term impact of exposure to television in Brazil.

STUART MCFADYEN is a Professor in the Department of Marketing and Economic Analysis, Faculty of Business, at the University of Alberta. He is the co-author, with Colin Hoskins and David Gillen, of *Canadian Broadcasting: Economic Structure and Market Performance.* Recent work has focused on the development of competitive strategies for Canadian broadcasters operating in an increasingly competitive global environment and the assessment of regulation and subsidy in audiovisual industries. He is currently examining the use of international joint ventures and new product development for the feature film and television production industries in Canada.

CARLOS MONSIVÁIS is a well-known Mexican essayist and journalist. He is the author of numerous books, including *Días de guardar, Amor perdido,* and *A ustedes les consta.* He writes editorial columns for the newspaper *Reforma* in Mexico City and for a variety of journals on Mexican politics.

HORACE M. NEWCOMB is the F. J. Heyne Centennial Professor of Communication in the Department of Radio Television Film at the University of Texas at Austin. He is also curator of the Museum of Broadcast Communication in Chicago. He is currently editing the Museum's *Encyclopedia of Television.* His major interests focus on television and culture.

DENIS SAINT-JACQUES is Professor in the Department of Literature at the Université Laval and the Director of the Research Center for Quebecoise Literature. His main fields of research are in comparative literature, semiotics, and socionarratological analysis, particularly in the popular literature of best-sellers and romance and spy/detective novels. He has published four books and many articles in Québecois, Canadian, and European journals.

JOHN SINCLAIR is Associate Professor on the Faculty of Arts at Victoria University in Melbourne, Australia, where he teaches international communication, sociology and cultural studies. He also is a Senior Research Associate at the Centre for International Research on Communication and Information Technology. He has a long-standing research interest in the internationalization of the television industry, with special focus on the Spanish-speaking world. He is editor of *Media International Australia,* author of *Images Incorporated: Advertising as Industry and Ide-*

ology, and co-editor of the forthcoming *New Patterns in Global Television: Peripheral Vision.*

KENTON T. WILKINSON is Assistant Professor in the Communication Program at the University of Texas at San Antonio. His principal research interests are in cultural-linguistic markets for audiovisual products, the historical development of electronic industries in Spanish- and Portuguese-speaking countries, and language and identity issues surrounding new interactive technologies.

Mass Media and Free Trade:
NAFTA and the Cultural Industries

Part One

. . . .

Overview

1

Introduction

EMILE G. MCANANY AND KENTON T. WILKINSON

SINCE THE END OF THE COLD WAR, trade has taken over from ideology as the focus of global attention. In fall 1993 two major trade agreements were concluded among nations. In North America, Canada, Mexico, and the United States ratified the North American Free Trade Agreement (NAFTA) after a contentious fight in the U.S. Congress at the end of November. The next month, on December 15, 117 nations finalized a seven-year-old debate on the General Agreement on Tariffs and Trade (GATT). In both agreements the issue of culture emerged as a possible spoiler to the unhindered flow of products and services. In NAFTA there was a clear exception of the Canadian cultural industries[1] from the terms of the treaty, an exception that had been agreed to by the United States in the previous Free Trade Agreement (FTA) with Canada in 1988. The GATT was less amicable. France, with the backing of its European Union (EU) partners, faced down the United States at the last minute on the inclusion of the audiovisual industries in the GATT (Cohen 1993). The U.S. negotiator, Mickey Kantor, agreed to sign the accord without the cultural industries being included but made it clear that the United States intended to include them in future GATT negotiations.

The disagreements over culture and free trade center around the understanding of how cultural products and services fit into such trade regimes as NAFTA and GATT. At the heart of the debate are two issues, one a practical reality and the other a value position. The reality is the overwhelming presence in most countries of the products of the U.S.

cultural industries, from MTV to Disney characters, and from CNN to "The Cosby Show." There is a demonstrable trade imbalance between the United States and most other countries in products of popular culture. In fact, next to aerospace, the cultural industries comprise the largest export surplus area of the United States. The value position is whether culture is something that should be subject to free-trade principles in the same way as automobiles, textiles, or agriculture. The issue is not easily resolved. But it is further complicated by the belief that the presence of foreign (often American) cultural products causes the erosion of cultural values and identities in the receiving societies. If a nation asserts its right to restrict trade in the cultural area (by quotas, taxes, or tariffs) in order to protect citizens and to promote its own creative expression within its cultural industries, should this be considered the same as other forms of trade protectionism, or should it be seen as a valid "cultural exception" within the larger trade regime? The U.S. position is very peculiar in this regard because, on the one hand, it accepted Canada's position in 1988, but on the other, it was unwilling to extend the same recognition to France and the EU in 1993. Is this only a temporary situation that will resolve itself over time when Canadians and Europeans recognize that they are strong enough in their own cultural production and export not to need protection? But then, however, will not weaker countries—those dependent on France, for example—invoke the same principle regarding cultural imports from Paris? Or will not the distribution of new technologies make all protectionist strategies impossible anyway? The answer is not clear. In asserting that *either* free trade *or* cultural exception will win the day, we may be posing the question the wrong way. Rather, we foresee the continuing global flow of cultural products and expect a variety of cultural protests and efforts at protection—short of open cultural warfare breaking out—to continue in a variety of forms.

▪ ▪ The Debate on Culture and the Cultural Industries

In Chapter 2 of this book Sinclair provides an analysis of the debate over cultural industries that has preoccupied academics for decades. We might be inclined to dismiss these debates as irrelevant for the real world, had not the issues become political and economic and begun to affect the trade of goods and services. It is not proposed here to reprise the discourse started with the Frankfurt School in the 1930s and continued by Sinclair and de la Garde in the present volume. What would be more useful as a context for subsequent discussion of free trade agreements would be a more synoptic view of several key policy debates that have affected present policies and current political sentiment in a variety of countries.

To begin with the Frankfurt School is historically correct, for it was its members who first critiqued the emergent cultural industries such as radio, film, and recorded music. Their critique had a double problematic: the bastardized artistic values of industrialized culture compared with the European elite canon that these writers accepted without question; and the procapitalist content of the products and their commercialized structures of creation and distribution to markets instead of audiences. The debate begun by the Frankfurt School has continued until today as cultural critics, whether of film, television, or music, argue over "standards of quality" or fret about the inroads made by commercialization in their respective cultural arenas, and as government policymakers in Canada or Europe try to provide political and financial support for public television and national film industries.

Another debate almost two decades later provides a continuation of a number of the concerns voiced by Frankfurt writers during the 1930s and 1940s. The introduction of communication satellites at the beginning of the 1960s quickly created an international global system of satellite communication by the end of the decade through a Western organization called INTELSAT. Although neither primarily intended nor used for broadcasting television programs, the new global satellite system generated more than academic debate around the issue of television. In the United Nations' committee on uses of outer space, the former Soviet Union, together with a number of third world countries, raised questions about the danger of unwanted television programs emanating primarily from the United States (Laskin and Chayes 1974). The nub of the issue was that these opponents wanted international agreements on the control of unauthorized satellite television transmissions across national borders, but the United States did not. In a symbolic test in the United Nations in November 1972, the United States tried to quash the debate. The result was the worst defeat suffered in that body by the United States, which lost by a count of 101 to 1, abandoned by even its staunchest Western allies in this matter. It was argued later that part of the reason for lack of Western support in this challenge was that in the area of culture, U.S. dominance was as feared by Europeans and Canadians as it was by those in the former Soviet Union and third world (McAnany 1974). The matter was never formally resolved, neither side conceding defeat, but the outcome was that in common international practice countries requested formal authorization to broadcast into another's territory—that is, until 1991, when, without any recourse to the United Nations, the Hong Kong–based STAR-TV began broadcasting with five channels into 40 countries with a population of 2.2 billion people (Scott 1991).

The United Nations' debate on direct broadcasting satellite services (DBS) led into the wider and even more acrimonious debate within UNESCO over the New International Information Order in the mid-to-late 1970s. Centered on how third world countries saw their role in a new information age, the debate was also focused on the pervasive presence of U.S. cultural products on a global scale. Much of that part of the debate was driven by the striking findings of a study by Nordenstreng and Varis about global trade in television programs, in which the researchers showed that the United States accounted for about 75% of all exports (Nordenstreng and Varis 1974; Varis 1984). Even though the debate within UNESCO has long since subsided, the issues regarding imbalances in the distribution of information and entertainment remain unresolved and always threaten to emerge in some other venue.

Many of the themes of cultural domination by U.S. cultural industries that were first introduced in the UNESCO debates of the 1970s re-emerged in Europe in the 1980s. As the EU was moving toward greater integration, new communication technologies such as satellites and cable were shaking up national broadcasting organizations and cultural policies among EU members and forcing a reconsideration of the public monopoly (Negrine and Papathanassopolous 1991). Beginning with a green paper in 1984 called "Television Without Frontiers," the EU opened a debate with far-reaching consequences. During the next five years EU members promoted changes in deregulating and privatizing their television systems, debating the role and financial structures for public service broadcasting, and developing policies aimed at promoting and protecting their cultural industries (Siune and Treutzschler 1992). The passage of the Television Directive in October 1989 confirmed the controversial policy on television quotas as politically binding for EU members and symbolically prepared for the GATT debate four years later.

Meanwhile, as Europeans argued over how to keep the Americans at bay, Canadians had been engaged for some years in a debate about the same matter. What brought the discussions out of the universities and policymakers' offices and into the glare of politics was the proposal by the Reagan administration in the later 1980s to promote a free trade agreement between the two nations. One of the most contentious points of the negotiations was Canada's insistence that its cultural industries not be a part of the agreement. This was not a sudden decision, nor was it based on political whim. There was a tradition of research about Canadian cultural industries that went back to at least the early 1970s. One of the best economic studies of these industries was Audley's 1983 book *Canada's Cultural Industries,* which summarized the exact contours of Canadian dependence on U.S. cultural products. The fact that the United States agreed to this cultural exception in the FTA of 1988 was to become an important arguing point for the French and the rest of the EU in future GATT negotiations.

When the Clinton administration got NAFTA passed in Congress in November 1993, the hope was that the momentum would carry over to the GATT the following month. To a large extent this was the case. Many long-standing disagreements in areas such as agriculture and textiles were resolved and the important trading blocs both gave and received concessions. In the matter of culture, however, there was an impasse that nearly derailed all the rest. On the side of the United States was Mickey Kantor, chief negotiator, who had been an important Hollywood lawyer before taking a job with the Clinton administration. But opposed to the United States were not only lobbies for the European cultural industries but a political movement in France that made concession difficult. The fact that the United States backed down on the issue does not mean that the debate is over—far from it. What the event did for the EU was to reinforce the validity of existing quotas and taxes, but it challenged the American government to try harder to reintroduce the issue in the next round of international trade negotiations. For the NAFTA agreement, it reminds us that the debate on culture and trade is not over but simmering on back burners of policy negotiators, industry lobbyists, and, not least of all, academics.

▪ ▪ NAFTA and the Future of Trade in Culture

This book is about the North American Free Trade Agreement and the cultural industries and trade of the three signatory nations, Canada, Mexico, and the United States. It asks whether NAFTA is likely to have an impact on trade in the area of cultural products and services and in foreign investment among the partners and what the agreement is likely to mean for the cultures of the three nations. It also asks how the likely extension of NAFTA to include other Latin American and Caribbean countries might affect the flow of cultural products, what difference it will make in the internal cultural dynamics of each nation, and how it will affect their ability to compete even for their own national audiences.

In order to answer these questions, the following series of basic issues needs to be addressed.

Size and Dominance of U.S. Cultural Industries[2]

The size of U.S. cultural industry exports is growing on a global basis. The Motion Picture Association of America cites an almost doubling of revenues for film and television exports on the eve of NAFTA, from $3.5 billion in 1987 to over $7 billion in 1991 (U.S. Department of Commerce 1993, p. 20). By comparison, in Chapter 3 of this book Hoskins, Finn, and McFadyen show that Canada had a total cultural industry (not just film and television) export of about $280 million in 1991, or less than one half of one percent of U.S. film and television export revenues. Mexico's Televisa, the giant cultural conglomerate, reported export revenues of $20 million in 1992 (Bear and Stearns 1992)—less than 10% of Canadian exports and only a tiny fraction of the U.S. equivalent. The U.S. Spanish-language sector is an important export market for Televisa, while anglophone Hollywood is the largest exporter of television and film to Mexico. In Canada the United States dominates in most categories, but does so most prominently in film and television, to the extent that in English-speaking television markets some assert that more than 95% of prime time is U.S. dominated (Starowicz 1993). One could cite other statistics about the dominance of U.S. cultural products in Europe (Siune and Treutzschler 1992) or in other parts of the world, but two points will suffice. First, the United States enjoys a growing trade surplus in the cultural arena and is unlikely to make further concessions that would limit its expansion. Second, the increase in revenues from these industries is likely to continue as new technologies of distribution and increasing concentration of transnational cultural industries tend to favor the first mover in this area—namely, the United States. Further, with a worldwide trend toward deregulation and privatization in the audiovisual area in other nations and the expansion of distribution channels, the demand for cultural products has increased over the past decade and the United States is the source of choice for satisfying this demand.

What Real Difference will NAFTA Make in Cultural Trade?

The text of the NAFTA agreement paid relatively little attention to the cultural industries in particular; furthermore, as we have seen, the

Canadians maintained their cultural exception for their own industries; and finally, there was already a widespread presence of U.S. cultural products in both Canada and Mexico and comparatively few of Canada's or Mexico's products in the United States. So what difference might NAFTA make in this area, and to whose benefit? There are two concrete changes that can be observed, and these are magnified within the context of an expanded Latin American trade liberalization and the increased global access to cultural products and services brought on by a rapid diffusion of new electronic distribution technologies.

First, the NAFTA section on cultural industries emphasized copyright and intellectual property rules. In this area Canada already had a set of laws that were largely comparable to those of the United States. The major change was in Mexico. In anticipation of NAFTA, in 1991 Mexico passed significant changes in its copyright and intellectual property laws. This meant that Mexico not only enacted the laws but made the necessary changes in its judicial system to ensure enforcement. This in turn meant that licensing agreements for film and television, for example, would be on a firmer legal footing, and that piracy in Mexico should decrease and revenue flows to U.S. corporations increase.

Second, because NAFTA is a treaty agreed to by the U.S. Congress, it places trade in a much more stable political atmosphere than was previously the case. Even though there are escape clauses in the treaty, each nation is politically committed to more stable trade relations and mechanisms for negotiating and settling disputes. This stability has the important consequence of attracting more foreign investment among the signatory nations than by those outside the pact. It also has the added consequence that each country will necessarily be more closely involved in the economy of the others and will be more concerned with events in their partners' societies that in some way threaten the well-being of those economic ties. It is not implausible that the heightened international attention to the Mexican presidential elections in August 1994 and the peso devaluation the following December were outcomes of the NAFTA agreement of 1993.

The passage of NAFTA means more of a boom in foreign investment in Mexico than in Canada or the United States simply because Mexico has more competitive space in which to grow in the area of cultural production. With more than 80 million people relatively underserved by even the giant Televisa, Mexico seems a good place in which to invest in some sort of cultural production or distribution services. Four recent examples may be cited to illustrate this:

1. In May 1994 the new national private television network (and com-
    petitor to Televisa), Televisión Azteca, announced a co-venture with
    NBC in which the latter would acquire up to 20% of Azteca and
    provide management, programming, and marketing direction for
    the Mexican corporation.
2. Blockbuster announced in spring 1994 that it would increase its
    presence in Mexico with a $280 million expansion, to become Mex-
    ico's second-largest video chain.
3. Fox Broadcast and Televisa began collaborating in 1994 to produce
    telenovela scripts in both English and Spanish.
4. A U.S. cinema chain announced in June 1994 its intention to invest
    $50 million in building modern cinema complexes in Mexican ur-
    ban areas.

The significance of NAFTA to other Latin American countries is also
substantial. Not only has trade liberalization been on the increase and
trade among these countries on the rise, but a number of countries have
indicated an interest in joining NAFTA itself. One consequence is that
many Latin American countries are now examining their copyright and
intellectual property laws. An improvement in copyright would in turn
increase the attraction of foreign investment in the cultural industries in
the region by the three NAFTA partners. It will increase investment in
new television technologies such as cable, satellite, and pay-per-view and
it will increase demand for programming to fill these new channels. In
short, the ripple effect of NAFTA will augment international trade and
investment in this area and will most likely increase a U.S. cultural presence in these countries.

Dominance or Cultural Imperialism?

The cultural issues related to the present and future expansion of
trade in cultural products in Canada, Mexico, and elsewhere are by no
means dead with the passage of NAFTA. Canada held a bitter political
debate over the cultural industries prior to the FTA in 1988 and the issue
is still present there, even with the cultural exception it achieved. Mexico
did not choose to raise the cultural issue in NAFTA (certainly it would
not have served the purposes of Mexico's major cultural exporter, Televisa), but like Canada, Mexico's sensitivity to American influence, cultural or political, lies just below the surface and could flare up quickly
in the future. With the likely increase in the availability of new distribution technologies and the increase in U.S. products on these channels,

the issue could be quickly raised to political status, especially in a post-PRI era of electoral politics. Mexico could, in this scenario, argue for parity with Canada in its cultural industries, although this seems unlikely in the near future for several reasons. First, Mexico and most Latin American countries are less dependent on U.S. television programs, where most of the cultural debate is often focused. Second, language seems to be a natural protective barrier and English is only a relatively weak second language in Mexico and the rest of Latin America, compared with its position in Canada and many European countries. Third, the thoroughly commercialized media systems of Latin America not only are philosophically less inclined to call for protection, they also produce more popular programs for their national and regional markets than do those of Canada, for example. The U.S. domination may grow in Latin America, but it has not yet reached the level of representing cultural imperialism as it has been commonly identified by Canadian and European writers.

Cultural Trade and Cultural Resistance

In the cases of Canada and Europe there are a variety of possible responses to the perception of cultural imperialism. It is not, as NAFTA and GATT both indicate, a choice of *either* free trade *or* cultural resistance. In both cases, but especially in NAFTA, policymakers wanted the promotion of free trade as well as some form of cultural protection. The European members of the EU already have in place a series of rules that provide a tax on foreign films that goes to funding their own national industries and a quota on imports of non-European television programs, that are not to exceed 50% of total programming. The Canadian rules are similarly disposed to protect audiences from the dominance of U.S. programs and products in a number of areas. But cultural protection provided by trade rules must be distinguished from cultural resistance that resides in audiences. The case of Canada may be particularly instructive. While Canada has made it clear that its cultural industries are not held by the same rules as other industries, this in no way means that U.S. products are banned, as is clear above in the case of film and television, where U.S. products have an overwhelming presence, especially in English Canada. Canada has attempted to create a space for its cultural industries and an incentive structure that will encourage production, if only for its national market. More importantly, as one Canadian writer and television producer put it, there is a problem when one of the nation's most important public media such as television cannot function properly. Starowicz (1993, p. 95) suggests that "a country which does not have the basic tools to conduct even routine national debate on its airwaves clearly has a . . . dilemma which diminishes every group's ability to arbitrate affairs, and help set the national agenda."

The assessments of the success of the strategy of cultural protection for Canada seem to differ even among the Canadian authors in this volume. Hoskins, Finn, and McFadyen provide a somewhat sobering picture for Canada as a whole, but especially so for anglophone Canada, when it comes to the presence of U.S. cultural products. On the other hand, Martin, de la Garde, Lemieux and Saint Jacques, and Grenier seem to argue that Québec has managed to hold its own and yet adapt to international competition better than its English-speaking counterpart in Canada. One conclusion might be that it is simply a matter of the protective barrier of language, but this alone does not seem to explain all the difference. As all the francophone authors point out, there is an increasing presence of international (both U.S. and French) products in their markets. The success of cultural survival in the free and competitive markets seems due in part to the historical legacy of resistance that francophone audiences have felt long before the era of NAFTA. The authors in Part Four make the argument that Québécois identity is closely tied to, and perceived as dependent on, the survival of its cultural expression within the cultural industries. This illustrates the difference between cultural protection, tied to rules and laws, and cultural survival or resistance, that more closely relates to historical audience identities.

Mexico, like Québec, has a natural protective barrier of language. More than this, however, it has a large domestic market of more than eighty million people and a strong, though heavily concentrated, set of cultural industries. As in Canada, so in Mexico there is a large presence of U.S. cultural products in its markets, but it has not been so thoroughly dominated as certain parts of Canada. However, as the Mexican authors in this book assert, there are problems. García Canclini points out that the Mexican government has handed over much of its cultural policy role to the private sector (primarily to Televisa), with the consequence that a commercial enterprise identified with free trade makes important decisions for Mexican culture. Lozano provides evidence of a cultural resistance along the Mexican border, yet indicates a major gap where Mexican film is concerned. Barrera and Monsiváis, while critical of government policy, do not raise questions about cultural survival. In brief, though these authors seem to confirm cultural resistance and adaptation, they do not see the Mexican state providing the leadership in cultural policy that they would like.

New Distribution Technologies and Industry Structure

Communication industry analysts and academics alike have argued recently that developed societies are entering a new era with the introduction of broadband technologies and the improved information infrastructure such as a "superhighway" would entail. Entertainment services would be delivered to consumers through various interconnections of the telephone industry, cable television, and an extensive computer network such as the Internet. Although many of the predictions seem to be based as much on hype by parties making deals or on technological determinism as on theories of significant changes in society, the general consensus within broadcast and pay-TV industries is that serious transformations are under way. These transformations will have important implications for the NAFTA signatories and for future international partnerships in the cultural industries.

One example of such change is the increased foreign investment in television systems and services in Mexico and other nations of Latin America that has occurred so far during the 1990s. Technological as well as market-related factors have stimulated the investments; neither would have occurred without important contextual changes in the region. During the 1960s, the three U.S. television networks held substantial interests in commercial Latin American television concerns (Cardona 1977). In the early 1970s, whether voluntarily or under pressure, they divested of direct ownership, concentrating instead on supplying programs, equipment, technical support, and the like. The emergence of elected democracies and economic restructuring programs in many countries during the late 1980s and early 1990s combined with resolution of the debt crisis (at least from the lending institutions' perspective) to create a favorable climate for investment. Movements toward freer trade through agreements such as the Andean Pact, Mercosur, the Caribbean Basin Initiative, and, of course, NAFTA, also boosted investor confidence.[3]

Consequential developments were occurring simultaneously in the area of satellite communication. In 1988 PanAmSat launched over the Western Hemisphere the first satellite that was privately owned and operated (President Reagan had deregulated that market in 1984). As a welcome alternative to INTELSAT and government-owned satellites in the region, PanAmSat leased its transponder space quickly, has begun offering digital signal compression service (to permit up to six signals per transponder rather than two), and plans to launch a second satellite over the region in early 1996 (it already has a worldwide system in place [Satellite Journal International 1995]).[4] This increased capacity to distribute television programs over large distances was paralleled by a change in the program dissemination environment. Pay-TV systems[5] emerged in numbers in the larger Latin American television markets: Mexico, Brazil, Venezuela, and Argentina. While only 7.5% of Latin America's television households had subscribed to a pay service in early 1994, the number of new subscribers was estimated to be growing at a rate of 100,000 per month (Scheck 1994). What pay-TV systems offer besides more channels and revenues from subscriber fees is access to audiences with disposable income and audience segmentation, whereby advertisers may concentrate their efforts on a single demographic group. Yet another technological incentive for television program suppliers to enter the Latin American market has been the adoption of integrated receiver decoders (IRDs), a signal encryption system which allows multiple audio tracks to accompany a video signal. Program services' IRDs may offer pay-TV system operators (or, in some cases, viewers) the option of selecting audio in English, Spanish, or Portuguese.

Despite these impressive technological advances, our position is that changes in the industry structure are key to understanding the relationship between television and free trade. Such changes are rooted in shifts in the U.S. market which, along with "globalization" as a corporate growth strategy, pushed the sidelines for many television industry players beyond U.S. borders. The cabling of U.S. television during the 1970s and 1980s shifted the industry's power structure to place program services, such as Turner, and cable system operators, such as Tele-Communications Inc. (TCI), on a par with the big three networks. The maturation of these and other cable competitors and the upstart Fox Network coincided with a saturation of the cable market; viewers desiring the service—and who could be profitably reached—had already subscribed. An obvious place to seek growing markets was overseas. Theodore Levitt (1983) and his globalization groupies attracted the attention of television industry executives at an opportune moment; global programs could hawk global products and services to worldwide audiences.

This time around, however, direct ownership looked less appealing. Previous experience and the arguments posed by detractors from Levitt's advice to "ignor[e] superficial regional and national differences" (1983, p. 92) engendered a strategy change: partnerships to produce, distribute, and disseminate programs were entered into with local partners who understood the markets and shared the risks. While most of the nearly two dozen U.S.-based program services targeting Latin American pay-TV audiences in the mid 1990s merely dubbed or subtitled programs from their libraries, a few were co-producing with partners in the region.[6] During the Cable Co./Telephone Co. merger mania in the fall of 1993, TCI and Televisa agreed to jointly develop pay-TV systems in Latin America, but complications with Bell Atlantic and its telephone interests in Mexico eroded the deal. In the area of broadcast, the Televisión Azteca/NBC co-venture has already been alluded to. These brief examples suggest the range of agreements entered into, but also illustrate the important role of local partners in the internationalization efforts of U.S. cultural industries in the 1990s.

▪ ▪ Cultural-Linguistic Media Markets and NAFTA

The foregoing sections have outlined some academics' and policy-makers' fears of cultural homogenization, fears heightened by the global expansion efforts of cultural industry players. The concerns of both camps have diverted attention away from an issue of mutual consequence: the very real power of locally produced media materials to appeal to regional and national markets. Attention to regional markets does not change U.S. dominance or the overall expansion strategy of U.S. cultural industries, but it does reveal limitations to that dominance (and strategy) in the areas of culture and language. The fact is that Hollywood has long catered to diversity through its pricing structure to culturally and linguistically distant markets, as Hoskins, Finn, and McFadyen point out in Chapter 3. The effect of NAFTA's likely expansion to other Latin American countries in the future has implications for two major cultural-linguistic markets, English and Spanish/Portuguese.[7] As suggested in the discussion above, industries in both the United States and Latin America are recognizing this and adopting various strategies to take advantage of increasing trade ties among nations of the Western Hemisphere. It is important that academic researchers recognize the implication of change as well.

The earliest and most sustained attention given to the role of culture and language in media market formation has focused on Europe. That is where the possibilities of reaching a diverse audience with a single marketing campaign for a single consumer product were first discussed (Elinder 1961), and where the problem of integrating a collection of national media markets into a regional one was first confronted. Our contention is that Europe does not constitute a cultural-linguistic market, but rather a geographic concentration of a number of single-language markets, many but not all of which spill across national boundaries. Cultural-linguistic markets are constituted by several factors. Audiences share the same or similar languages as well as intertwined histories and overlapping cultural characteristics. Cultural products are exchanged among participants; these products reflect cultural and linguistic commonalities among their producers and audiences, and the most popular (and lucrative) of them may be native to a market, such as the *telenovela* in Latin America. Lastly, the cultural industries operating within these markets are characterized by significant co-production, cross-national ownership, and a fluid exchange in personnel as well as in cultural products (Wilkinson 1995). The nature of cultural-linguistic markets and their relevance to the cultural homogenization problem, industry globalization, and free trade is explored in the next few pages through discussions centered on language and the markets that have formed around English, French, and Spanish/Portuguese.

Language and Language Conversion

European efforts during the 1980s to foment a more vigorous regional trade in film and television coincided with a general deregulation of broadcast industries and reduced government support for state-run film and broadcast enterprises, some of which were privatized. These developments increased the demand for media products, many of which originated in the United States. A twofold problem emerged: How could language transfer be executed so that more European products would circulate within the region? And, concerning the imported material, how could it be made most appealing to audiences? Research conducted to address these questions yielded interesting insights into the role of language in international television markets, and limitations to the European regional project.

While the larger European countries tended to be "dubbing markets," language transfer between the minor languages and between one minor and one major language was typically achieved through subtitling. The resulting disparity of audience preference for different transfer techniques and the nonstandardization of products greatly complicates the operation of a linguistically diverse regional market.

Another important finding was that European television is characterized by single-language markets that may include viewers in a number of countries, such as francophones in areas of Belgium and Switzerland as well as France, or in only one country, such as Denmark, Greece, the Netherlands, and Norway (Biltereyst 1992). Not surprisingly, multilingual countries such as Switzerland and Belgium tend to import more programs than do countries with one dominant language, where a high percentage of locally produced programs are aired. This situation mitigates against the creation of a regional market based on language transfer, and the failure of unilingual, pan-regional projects such as the U.K.'s BSkyB satellite service affords little optimism for overcoming linguistic barriers (Collins 1990). Recognition of these barriers led scholars and policymakers in France to propose projects for the formation of alternative markets, one based on shared culture, the other on the French language.

Shared-Culture and Single-Language Market Proposals by France

Mattelart, Delcourt, and Mattelart (1984) offered an intriguing suggestion for resisting cultural homogenization while at the same time stimulating production and exchange of film, television, and other materials among kindred nations. The creation of a "Latin audiovisual space" among the Latin nations of Southern Europe and Latin America would deter U.S. dominance while "developing an alternative form of universality" based on shared cultural and linguistic traits. The authors recognized the problem of contextual differences (e.g., in audience taste, industry structure, and level of technological development) among these nations, and expressed concern that homogenization based on U.S. popular culture not be replaced by French cultural imperialism.[8] The proposal, which was commissioned by the French government, recognized the linkage between cultural issues and the significance of export markets to the competitive standing of non-English cultural industries. It also threatened the EU unification efforts by suggesting that the nations of Southern Europe ally themselves with Latin America rather than with Northern and Eastern Europe, at least in the audiovisual sphere.

The French government has also promoted more vigorous exchange in cultural products among the francophone nations of the world. As Mahamdi (1992) points out, one strategy has been to offer French programs free of charge or at low prices in Africa to ensure that they are aired. Satellite services have also been extended to many areas of the world, including some areas where French is the national and/or native language of very few people. In explaining the reasoning behind a French-only satellite service beamed by TV5 (a public-service broadcaster) to Latin America, a manager pointed out that many South Americans know French as a second language because it is taught in many schools there ("TV5 compresses," 1992).

A major concern of francophones in countries other than France is cultural domination from Paris. As pointed out in the chapters in Part Four of this volume, the Québecois fight a two-front battle, against Hollywood and anglophone Canada on one side and France on the other. The issue is economic as well as cultural—as the wealthiest francophone market, France executes the language transfer for cultural products moving in and out of the international francophone market. Thus France operates as an international producer, distributor, and translator, while smaller markets such as Québec function more as national markets. The smaller markets are caught in the non-U.S. cultural domination trap that Mattelart, Delcourt, and Mattelart warned against. Meanwhile, Hollywood maintains a strong international presence.

The English-Language Market and Reasons for its Dominance

Explanations for Hollywood's privileged position in film and television markets have been explored through applications of microeconomic trade theory. As Sinclair explains in fuller detail in the next chapter, Wildman and Siwek (1988) argued that the following factors have been key to international dominance by the United States: a "natural" advantage in the domestic U.S. market deriving from the productions' close cultural-linguistic fit with their domestic audience; high-quality production values which travel well; and a large and wealthy domestic market together with well-to-do, accessible English-language markets in Australia, Canada, the U.K., and New Zealand. Hoskins and Mirus (1988) added two other factors contributing to U.S. power: a long history of pursuing audience maximization through efforts to create a single mass audience in a culturally diverse nation, and a domestic market closed to film and television imports because of audiences' supposed disinterest in such material for cultural and linguistic reasons. To elucidate this final point, the authors discuss "cultural discount," which asserts that audiovisual cultural products rooted in one culture will have diminished appeal in others because they portray nonnative values, behaviors, institutions, and the like. Therefore, the imported products are sold at a discounted price in order to compete with more popular local productions. The more substantial the language barrier crossed, the heavier the discount imposed; thus a U.S. television program that costs $20,000 in anglophone Canada may cost only $200 in Central Africa.

Not surprisingly, the economic focus of the trade-theory studies has alarmed some critical scholars who reject the studies as apologetic for U.S. domination (see Sepstrup 1989). In spite of its limited treatment of culture and language, the trade-theory perspective does provide insight into why English-language products so dominate world markets. The perspective would be more useful if applied to other language markets that have begun to export their cultural products on a global level.

The Spanish/Portuguese Market

In Latin America a handful of commercial television networks have progressed from national producers to regional producers/distributors and, more recently, global exporters. Mexico, Brazil, and Venezuela, the principal television-exporting nations of Latin America, have culturally diverse national audiences and have established viable production and export industries even while importing large quantities of dubbed U.S. programs. The fact that these potentially rich research issues have not been explored by the trade-theory economists or communication scholars points to an Anglo/Euro-centrism that has characterized much of the existing work on international film and television markets. It also reveals a lack of attention paid to culture and language as significant factors shaping cultural-product flow.

The technological advances and changes in television industry structure enumerated earlier are two recent factors that influenced a boom in Spanish- and Portuguese-language television in the early 1990s. Other factors, such as the maturation of national television markets and the formation of audience taste for programs produced within the region, built up over several decades. The language factor spans centuries. The two dominant languages of Latin America share grammatical structure, cognates, and other important elements in common. This diminishes the conversion problem confronting Europe, and has facilitated the formation of a cohesive regional market which, in turn, serves as a solid stepping-stone to global markets for the large producers.

The major television producing networks in Latin America in 1995 were Televisa (Mexico), TV Globo (Brazil), and Venevisión and Radio Caracas Televisión (Venezuela). All were initiated, and continue to be run, by influential families having ample political connections in their respective countries, and all benefited from substantial upswings in the economies of their home countries at the time they were consolidating their national markets.[9] While those national economies soured during the "lost decade" of the 1980s, the producers continued to develop their national markets as well as regional ones within the cultural-linguistic area. Early efforts to export beyond the region were also initiated at this time.

Televisa began its U.S. efforts by setting up the first full-time Spanish-language station there in 1961. Although the network that was subsequently established did not turn a profit until the late 1970s, those returns on its investment did help the company weather a grossly devalued peso in the early 1980s. Following a brief FCC-imposed hiatus, Televisa is back in the United States as a partner, along with Venevisión, in the Univisión network. TV Globo concentrated its *telenovela* export efforts on Europe during the 1980s and held a substantial share of TV Monte Carlo, which covered markets in Southern France and most of Italy, up to 1993. The Venezuelan companies also concentrated their efforts on export by engaging in co-productions, setting up distribution operations, and maintaining a strong presence at international programming trade shows. The international presence that these producers now enjoy, we contend, was built upon a regular demand for their programming within the Latin American cultural-linguistic region (including the United States).

Just as the U.S.-based producers and programmers entering the Latin American market are motivated by a growing Spanish-speaking sector within the United States, so Latin American producers are reinforcing their presence in the south while looking north. Both foreign investors in the U.S. Univisión Network—Televisa and Venevisión—have purchased substantial shares in television stations in other nations (including Argentina, Chile, and Peru), and are partners in *Cadena de las Américas* ("Americas Network"), a project among broadcast networks in Latin America to pool their advertisers in long-term commitments which must be paid for in advance, but offering discounts as high as 75% on normal advertising rates (Reyes 1994). (Besides the discounted advertising rates, advertisers benefit by airing their messages in a number of national markets through a single contract.) Televisa has challenged the FCC's rule limiting foreign ownership of U.S. broadcast stations to 25% (Darling 1992), and announced in 1994 that its U.S. cable network since 1979, Galavisión, would offer four channels (Katz 1994). Venevisión has been producing programs in English as well as Spanish in the United States (the 1993 Emmy Awards, for example).

These and other developments lead us to see an increasingly regional character to Spanish/Portuguese television in the Western Hemisphere. It is not that national media markets are in decline, but rather that the ties between them in terms of technology, business, and audience are closer than ever before. As players in international television maneuver to take full advantage of freer trade in the Western Hemisphere, they do so within the larger cultural and linguistic confines of the English versus Spanish/Portuguese split, but in the process seek to minimize the differences among local dialects and cultures within the Latin sphere. This may lead to situations in Latin America similar to those confronted by Québec, with a two-front battle being waged against cultural homogenization from Hollywood on one side and the large Latin American producers on the other. Thus, non-English cultural-linguistic markets, while challenging U.S. domination of international markets, pose threats of their own.

▪ ▪ Chapter Summaries

The authors of this volume (except Finn, McFadyen, and Maule) took part in a conference on which this book is based. What is reported in the present chapter and the ones to follow is from the academic participants, yet many of the concerns voiced by industry representatives and policymakers are also reflected in the treatment by chapter authors.[10]

Sinclair in Chapter Two provides an analysis and critique of the cultural imperialism thesis, while building an analytical model based on his notion of cultural industries. The concept of national culture is critiqued as well, but his conclusion is not simply a retreat to postmodernist pluralism, as the author points out:

> Thus, while it might be true that the defense of national culture is a project in the interests of the dominant sectors of a given nation-state, it is also in the interests of the subordinated groups for there to be a national culture against which to define themselves . . . as well as to form an intermediate line of defense against amorphous global cultural influences.

He concludes that a cultural-industries approach allows a focus on unique historical circumstances as well as global forces that affect the way cultural products are both produced and assimilated by national audiences.

In Part Two, the authors describe the ways in which different countries have dealt with the reality of U.S. dominance in the area of culture. Hoskins, Finn, and McFadyen provide an economic analysis of trade in cultural goods and services, with special emphasis on why the U.S.

dominates in film and television trade. A central question raised by the authors concerns whether there is an "external benefit" in trade of such products. They believe that "indigenous [television] programming and film [possessing] desirable attributes can make viewers better citizens [and] is at the heart of the 'cultural' argument." In other words, as economists, they believe that popular cultural products may be more than mere entertainment and should, where markets fail, be promoted by government intervention. A major section of the chapter argues that some cultural policies of the Canadian government do not work and should be abandoned, while others are critical to the external-benefit argument and need to be strengthened. Overall, the chapter is a careful economic argument about market forces as well as national cultural benefits from government policies.

Newcomb's chapter begins with the premise that "*culture* cannot be protected by treaty or agreement" but that "*culture industries* can be." His interest is in understanding the "relationship between the particular formation of a culture industry and the expressive material it produces." The author describes a project in which he helped members of Finnish television invent for themselves a form of serial fictional programming that could benefit from Hollywood production techniques but be adapted to current Finnish experience. The serial form allows a powerful type of storytelling while fulfilling important needs for national prime-time programming. Newcomb recounts how a teenage serial was successfully developed by young Finnish writers and producers and helped contribute in some small way to attracting audience attention to local versus imported prime-time fare. He ends with a reflection on why in some cases cultural industries may need temporary protection in order to develop the institutional capacity to produce their own entertainment programming.

Allen argues in his chapter for the centrality of the domestic drama serial in many countries' television systems, but concentrates his attention on two examples—U.S. daytime soap opera and the Latin American prime-time *telenovela*. His analysis of the narrative structure, appeal, and production history of soap operas shows a powerful genre spanning radio and television for the past sixty years. But the dynamics of international television markets today suggest to him that the Latin American *telenovela* is a stronger competitor than U.S. soaps, which, for a variety of reasons, have never had export success and, in fact, are in critical decline with domestic audiences. The fact that the *telenovela* has captured a significant portion of Hispanic audiences in the United States is an indication that this form of cultural product has wide international appeal and provides an example of countries other than the United States being successful in the international export competition.

Part Three includes four chapters on Mexican cultural industries and NAFTA. Monsiváis begins with an analysis of what nationalism means in the era of NAFTA. Arguing that Mexicans cannot return to the Mexican Revolution of the beginning of the twentieth century, the author acknowledges that changes in the economy of Mexico have made the old myths harder to maintain. On the other hand, he does not fall into the easy affirmation of the Salinas administration that economic liberalism will not threaten national culture and character. Rather, Monsiváis argues that the notion of nationalism must be redefined, by recognizing the deep influences of the U.S. culture and economy in Mexican society without surrendering the regional and national identities that have helped define Mexican peoples in the past. The author suggests that the current democracy movement begun in Chiapas in January 1994 at the very beginning of the NAFTA era is one of the unexpected manifestations of the agreement and will play an important part in redefining national culture and identity in the future.

García Canclini begins his chapter with the hypothesis that a Mexican perspective on NAFTA "should include interactions with other North American countries and with Latin America, as well as with other processes of regional integration." He goes on to reformulate the notion of national identity from several theoretical considerations: the historically constructed nature of that identity; the multicultural and hybrid composition of specific identities; and pervasive transnational conditioning. He concentrates his remarks on Mexican cultural policy, trying to redefine the role of the state in our times as a critical reaction against a heavy-handed interference and as a defense of outmoded traditions, yet with some support for national creativity through national cultural institutions. Using Mexican film and its precipitous decline in the 1980s and 1990s as an example, García Canclini argues for the protection of this institution's role in helping to redefine national cultural identity in an era of multiculturalism and transnational influences.

Lozano's work reports audience research on the cultural identity of Mexican border youths heavily exposed to U.S. cultural products. The chapter reports a rare attempt to ask the straightforward question of how exposure to foreign cultural products affects young peoples' perception of themselves. Four results are underlined in the chapter: most Mexican adolescents in the study preferred Mexican products even when U.S. products were available in Spanish; most adolescents affirmed strong national identity despite a considerable exposure to U.S. cultural products; nevertheless, upper-class boys seemed to be more affected in their self-perception and identification with U.S. culture, though even among this group, the number thus affected was not close to a majority; finally, in the area of film, U.S. products so dominate that all youths chose the majority from U.S. imports. The results do not argue that there is no reality to cultural influence, as many Mexican border youths do use imported U.S. products, but the study gives some detail as to how this process takes place and what it may mean for audiences.

In the final chapter concerning Mexico Barrera suggests that the border region may be the best laboratory for testing the effects of NAFTA, but not in the way most Mexican scholars have discussed it. The border is, of course, the site of much economic growth, with its *maquiladoras* and transnational presence. It is the area of heaviest economic and cultural exchange and therefore an appropriate location for the study of NAFTA effects. Barrera reviews how the border has been conceived of by a long tradition of Mexican scholars, but he critiques many of their efforts as not reflecting the combined influence of economics and culture in Mexican self-definitions. His analysis of the binational border television in El Paso and Ciudad Juárez attempts to include both the cultural and the economic aspects of this key cultural industry. Finally, he critiques the Salinas rhetoric of strictly economic consequences of NAFTA while disregarding the cultural impacts.

In Part Four, Québec authors in turn explain the importance of cultural industries for their identity in a NAFTA era of free trade. Martin begins with the strong assertion that the cultural industries in Québec, although fragile compared with Hollywood, are a vital reason for the continued cultural existence of the francophone population of Canada. This seems to be a central tenet of all the authors represented here. In contrast to the Mexican writers, who (except Lozano) largely concentrate on the more theoretical view of identity, Martin and his colleagues operate from the perspective that their cultural industries are a key to their cultural survival. Martin provides a synoptic view of all of these industries, their economic significance in terms of jobs and revenues, and the important role that both federal and provincial governments play in supporting them. His analysis of each cultural industry indicates the relative strength in terms of audience support each enjoys. Although fragile, the cultural industries enjoy an advantage over their competitors from outside, whether from English Canada, the United States, or even

France, because of an historically based sense of distinctness in the Québécois cultural identity.

Television for de la Garde is not simply an entertainment medium but a public forum where society's agendas are worked out. If that is true in Québec society, his synchronic analysis of how francophone audiences use television is an important measure of how they define themselves as a people. The NAFTA and FTA are incorporated into the design of the study as the author takes two audience surveys done in 1987 and 1993 (on the eve of each agreement) and tracks change over time to see how audiences used television and watched local, national, and foreign programs. His conclusion is that although francophone audiences have access to an increasing number of U.S. television channels in English and that even on French-language channels the amount of dubbed U.S. programming increased, they still were largely loyal to their own locally made programs. While recognizing the presence and attractiveness of U.S. materials, the author does not confirm the cultural-imperialism hypothesis that he discusses and critiques at length in his chapter.

Lemieux and Saint Jacques argue quite convincingly that the bestseller book is as much a part of the cultural industries in Canada as film or television. In their study of this industry over two decades (1970–1990), they show a variation in the loyalty of Québec audiences toward local authors but conclude that after a low point in the early 1980s the presence of these authors on Québec best-seller lists has stabilized at about 40%. U.S. best-sellers, at about 33%, represent the most significant competitor, their success being due in part to the recent practice of publishers in France of translating U.S. best-sellers into French and then distributing them to Québec audiences along with their own hits. This, as the authors point out, is a kind of double imperialism from both the United States and France. English Canada, on the other hand, has a small market in Québec and even in its own market is far outstripped by U.S. best-sellers.

Grenier offers an analysis of the Québec music industry that echoes some of the conclusions of her colleagues. The history of the francophone music industry in Canada from the early 1960s to the mid-1990s is a struggle to define itself within the changing politics of Québec separatism and the changing musical tastes of audiences. Her work is a study of how Québec music audiences are discursively constructed within music-related industry practices. The author gives both a historical analysis of the industry and an institutional analysis of how music producers, distributors, broadcasters, and performers have redefined themselves within a competitive global marketplace. Grenier argues for a better understanding of how Québec, much like other small or minority nations, works out the conundrums of language, ethnicity, locality, and nationhood in the context of increased liberalization of trade and its concomitant global vying for markets and audiences.

Part Five consists of two chapters on copyright and intellectual property as important mechanisms for defining the practices of cultural industries in international markets. Jones points to the practices of U.S. music industries to indicate the changes that make copyright and trade practice in this industry difficult to pin down. Changes in technologies, for example, make "traditional copyright protection obsolete." But the one constant, according to Jones, is that "NAFTA continues the evolution of copyright as publisher's right and largely overlooks the author." The contradiction inherent in the copyright and trade relationship is that copyright is a mechanism to circumscribe the market and yet promote the product. How copyright will be defined in the future of NAFTA and other trade rules will depend on how courts decide on interpretations of these rules in a global marketplace.

Acheson and Maule provide a detailed study of the interaction of copyright law and contracts in cultural industries. They point out the enormous complication in coordinating the creative efforts in such industries as filmmaking and how contracts are a key mechanism to legally ensure both coordinated creative effort and the fair reimbursement for creativity. Copyright law carries the cultural work beyond the present into the future, sometimes forty or fifty years into the future. The authors demonstrate the detail in which NAFTA defined copyright and intellectual property in order to harmonize the trade in cultural products and services. They, like Jones, see the gradual harmonization of these rules among all trading nations of the world so that both the creation and the protection of these products will be assured and more trade promoted. They end their chapter with the question of whether the new interactive technologies might not mean an end of copyright, but they argue that for people to continue efforts of creativity, some form of legal protection of intellectual property will have to be worked out.

NOTES

1. Usually included in this category are radio, television, film, video, cable, recorded music, and some forms of print.

2. It is true that since the mid-1980s foreign interests have acquired a number of U.S. cultural industries (Sony purchased Columbia and CBS Records, and News

Corp [Murdoch] purchased Fox, for example), but those industries still operate within U.S. cultural space and produce essentially U.S. cultural products (see Mc-Anany and Wilkinson 1992).

3. Venezuela, Colombia, Ecuador, Peru, and Bolivia are member-states of the Andean Pact. Mercosur consists of Brazil, Argentina, Uruguay, and Paraguay. The Caribbean Basin Initiative includes the Central American nations (minus Panama) and the larger Caribbean nations (minus Cuba).

4. In late 1993, 66% of PanAmSat's business was from broadcasting, 31% from business communications, and 3% from long-distance telephone service. One industry analyst believes the mere presence of the service stimulated business that would not have otherwise existed (Cooper 1994).

5. These include cable television as well as multichannel multipoint distribution systems (MMDS, or "wireless cable"). Direct broadcasting satellite services (DBS) have also been initiated.

6. For example, in 1994 Time Warner had two projects under way, TV Marte, a *telenovela* and TV-movie production enterprise based in Venezuela, and Tropix, a company developing programs for two of the conglomerate's Spanish- and Portuguese-language program services, HBO Olé and Cinemax Olé.

7. The principal participant nations in the English cultural-linguistic market are the United States, anglophone Canada, the U.K., Australia, and New Zealand. The prominence of English as a widely spoken second language throughout the world is an important contributing factor. The Spanish/Portuguese cultural-linguistic market consists principally of Latin America, Spain, Portugal, and the U.S. Spanish-language market.

8. The conceptual limitations of the proposal are treated thoughtfully by Philip Schlesinger (1987).

9. In the cases of Mexico and Venezuela, oil wealth was the main stimulant during the 1970s; in the case of Brazil, loans and private investment during the so-called Brazilian miracle of 1969–1974 were the main factors responsible.

10. Readers are referred to Appendixes A and B for further detail on discussions of the industry and policymaker groups.

BIBLIOGRAPHY

Audley, P. 1983. *Canada's Cultural Industries.* Toronto: Lorimer.
Bear Stearns & Co. 1992. *Grupo Televisa S.A. de C.V.* (company report). June 24.
Biltereyst, D. 1992. "Language and culture as ultimate barriers? An analysis of the circulation, consumption and popularity of fiction in small European countries." *European Journal of Communication* 7: 517–540.
Cardona, E. 1977. American television in Latin America. In *Mass Media Policies in Changing Cultures,* ed. G. Gerbner. New York: John Wiley.
Cohen, R. 1993. "A Realignment Made Reluctantly." *New York Times,* December 15, p. C19.
Collins, R. 1990. *Television: Policy and Culture.* Boston: Unwin Hyman.
Cooper, J. 1994. "PanAmSat closes in on global goal." *Broadcasting and Cable,* February 7, pp. 38, 40.

Darling, J. 1992. "New focus on TV stations' foreign ownership." *Los Angeles Times*, April 10, p. D3.

Elinder, E. 1961. "How international can advertising be?" *International Advertiser*, December, pp. 12–16.

Hoskins, C., and R. Mirus. 1988. "Reasons for the U.S. dominance of the international trade in television programmes." *Media, Culture, and Society* 10: 499–515.

Katz, R. 1994. "Galavision plans four new U.S. nets." *Multichannel News*, May 23, p. 2.

Laskin, P., and A. Chayes. 1974. "A Brief History of the Issues." In *Control of the Direct Broadcast Satellite: Values in Conflict*, ed. R. Wills. Palo Alto, Calif.: Aspen Institute Program on Communications and Society.

Levitt, T. 1983. The globalization of markets. *Harvard Business Review*, 61(3), May–June, pp. 92–102.

Mahamdi, Y. 1992. Television, globalization, and cultural hegemony: The evolution and structure of international television. Ph.D. diss., University of Texas, Austin.

Mattelart, A., Delcourt, X., and Mattelart, M. 1984. *International Image Markets: In Search of an Alternative Perspective*, trans. D. Buxton. London: Comedia.

McAnany, E. 1974. "Reflections on the International Flow of Information." In *Control of the Direct Broadcast Satellite: Values in Conflict*, ed. R. Wills. Palo Alto, Calif.: Aspen Institute Program for Communication and Society.

McAnany, E., and K. Wilkinson. 1992. "From Cultural Imperialists to Takeover Victims? Questions on Hollywood Buyouts from the Critical Tradition." *Communication Research* 19(6): 724–748.

Negrine, R., and S. Papathanassopolous. 1991. "The Internationalization of Television." *European Journal of Communication* 6: 9–32.

Nordenstreng, K., and T. Varis. 1974. *Television Traffic—A One Way Street?* Paris: UNESCO Reports and Papers on Mass Communications.

Reyes, M. 1994. Changes in U.S. competitors' Latin American marketing strategies. Talk given at *The New Americas: Agency and client perspectives*, advertising department symposium chaired by M. Tharp. University of Texas at Austin. April 29.

Satellite Journal International 3(15), August 15, p. 2.

Scheck, E. 1994. "Latin America: The advertising stakes are high." *International Cable*, April, pp. 28–33.

Schlesinger, P. 1987. "On national identity: Some conceptions and misconceptions criticized." *Social Science Information*, 26(2): 219–264.

Scott, M. 1991. "News from Nowhere." *Far Eastern Economic Review*, November 28, pp. 32–34.

Sepstrup, P. 1989. "An economic approach." *Journal of Communication* 39(4): 49–50.

Siune, K., and W. Treutzschler, eds. 1992. *Dynamics of Media Politics: Broadcast and Electronic Media in Western Europe*. Newbury Park, Calif.: Sage.

Starowicz, M. 1993. "Citizens of Video-America: What Happened to Canadian Television in the Satellite Age?" In *Small Nations, Big Neighbor: Denmark and*

Québec-Canada Compare Notes on American Popular Culture, ed. R. de la Garde, W. Gilsdorf, and I. Wechselmann. London: John Libbey.

"TV5 Compresses for Cheap Latin Launch." 1992. *Satellite TV Finance*, October 1.

U.S. Department of Commerce. 1993. *Globalization of the mass media*. Washington, D.C.: National Telecommunications Information Administration.

Varis, T. 1984. "The International Flow of Television Programs." *Journal of Communication,* 34(1): 143–152.

Wildman, S. S., and S. Siwek. 1988. *International Trade in Films and Television Programs.* Cambridge, Mass.: American Enterprise Institute / Ballinger Publications.

Wilkinson, K.T. 1995. Where Culture, Language and Communication Converge: The Latin American Cultural Linguistic Television Market. Ph.D. diss., University of Texas, Austin.

2

. . . .

Culture and Trade: Some Theoretical and Practical Considerations

JOHN SINCLAIR

▪ ▪ The Sacred and the Profane

In the beginning, the juxtaposition of the concepts "culture" and "industry" was a deliberate contradiction in terms. For Theodore Adorno and his colleagues at the Frankfurt School who coined the term, "culture industry" was an oxymoron, intended to set up a critical contrast between the exploitative, repetitive mode of industrial mass production under capitalism and the associations of transformative power and aesthetico-moral transcendence that the concept of culture carried in the 1940s, when it still meant "high" culture. This view, though often with rather more romantic, aristocratic, and other conservative inflections, is familiar to us from the general critique of "mass culture" as it emerged in the 1950s, in which the industrialization of cultural production was viewed as an intrinsic debasement of cultural values, particularly through the process of "standardization." We are left in no doubt that that the core meaning of the concept is the industrialization of cultural production, but also that this process is intended to be viewed in a critical light.

As members of a cultivated elite, Adorno and Horkheimer bewailed what they saw to be the loss of the sublime power of creative works in the face of the industrialization of culture, or what Benjamin called "the decay of the aura" (1977, p. 388)—the sacred reduced to the profane. However, as Marxists, their critique was motivated by their perception that the standardized mass manufacture and marketing of cultural goods was as much an ideological as an industrial process, which had the "function" of stabilizing capitalism: "The machine rotates on the same spot . . . the universal triumph of the rhythm of mechanical production and reproduction promises that nothing changes, and nothing unsuitable will appear" (p. 359). In this metaphor can be seen the model for Marcuse's concept of "one-dimensional" capitalist culture, Althusser's "ideological apparatuses," and, indeed, the whole "dominant ideology thesis" which became the most influential theoretical paradigm in communication and cultural studies throughout the 1970s and beyond (Collins 1990).

At a later stage in this chapter, we will return to acknowledge the insights and consider the limitations of the dominant ideology paradigm. It is sufficient to suggest here that one of the reasons for its ultimate exhaustion was the abstract homogeneity with which it subsumed all the cultural industries into the singular category "culture industry." As Mattelart and Piemme have observed, because Adorno and Horkheimer's analysis was "too closely connected with nostalgia for a cultural experience untainted by technology," they could never come to terms with cultural production "as a diversified and contradictory collection of specific economic components occupying a given place in the economy" (1982, pp. 52–53). That is, because industry and commerce are seen as a stigma upon all mass culture and there is no attempt to distinguish between its various genres and forms, the Frankfurt School concept of "culture industry" offers a critical stance, but of dubious value, not the least because it provides no framework in which the actual cultural industries can be analyzed.

If the "dominant ideology thesis" was an idealist legacy from Marx on the side of "culture," there has also been a materialist tradition on the side of "industry" which can be characterized as the "political economy" approach. This also has its continuities with the Frankfurt School, notably in the contention that consumers of cultural commodities are "working" for capitalism. This rather functionalist proposition was put forward by Adorno and Horkheimer as part of their "culture industry" argument, but is more familiar to those in the English-speaking world from the development it was given by Dallas Smythe (1977) in his "blindspot" debate with Graham Murdock (1978), a definitive exchange within the formulation of "political economy" positions. It should be noted in passing that Smythe was just as contemptuous as the Frankfurt School had been of the meanings that the variety of cultural products might hold for their audiences, but such conceptual and theoretical issues will be reserved for discussion in the last section of this chapter.

More important for the emergence of "cultural industries" as a category of analysis as well as criticism has been the work of Nicholas Garnham, who is explicit in theorizing a "political economy" point of view:

> It sees culture, defined as the production and circulation of symbolic meaning, as a material process of production and exchange, part of, and in significant ways determined by, the wider economic processes of society with which it shares many common features.
>
> Thus, as a descriptive term, "cultural industries" refers to those institutions in our society which employ the characteristic modes of production and organization of industrial corporations to produce and disseminate symbols in the form of cultural goods and services, generally, although not exclusively, as commodities (1990, pp. 155–156).

Garnham develops his formulation of the concept in a number of useful ways. First and foremost is the important step he has taken in pluralizing "industry" and rendering "culture" into its adjectival form. This is more than a grammatical refinement. Instead of the abstract category of "culture industry," we have in "cultural industries" a concept that can distinguish between different forms of symbolic production, and that opens the way for a more empirical approach to understanding them, which, while still critical, is less denunciatory. Ironically, it is Adorno who must be acknowledged as having first drawn the distinction between two historically different modes of the industrialization of culture: on the one hand, preindustrial cultural forms that have been transformed by subsequent industrial and institutional processes (as in book publishing), and on the other, forms that were industrial in their very origins, notably television. The processes through which the industrialization of culture is said to occur are

> capital-intensive, technological means of mass production and distribution, highly developed divisions of labour and hierarchical modes of managerial organization, with the goal, if not of profit maximization, at least of efficiency (pp. 156–157).

Finally, the heuristic gains made with Garnham's "descriptive" formulation of the concept are not made at the expense of Adorno and Horkheimer's initial critical intent. He also posits an "analytic" use for "cultural industries"—namely, that of focusing upon the effects of commodification under capitalism, but in a way which sets aside the Frankfurt School's functionalist problematic (p. 158).

Bearing in mind this distinction between the descriptive and analytic uses of the concept of "cultural industries," and recalling Lazarsfeld's classic distinction between "administrative" and "critical" research, we can now look at how it has been applied in communication and cultural policies at the international and national levels. From there we can move on to how these industries have been dealt with in trade agreements.

In 1978, UNESCO initiated a comparative research program "on the place and role of cultural industries in the cultural development of societies." UNESCO explained its attraction to an explicit cultural industries approach, saying that culture was not "spontaneous and unconditioned," but subject to economic and technological factors, and that the impact of these had to be known if the content and values of cultural works were to be assessed (UNESCO 1982, p. 12). However, UNESCO defined the commercial purposes of cultural industries as antagonistic to cultural development, and expressed concern over both the concentration and internationalization of ownership and control in the cultural industries and "the subordination of creative artists to market forces or to more or less overtly dictated consumer demand" (p. 21).

Without looking here at its subsequent activities in the area of cultural development, which include the declaration of the years 1988–1997 as a World Decade for Cultural Development and, most recently (in 1993), the establishment of a World Commission on Culture and Development, it is clear that UNESCO's explicit concern wth cultural industries was framed within the New World Information and Communication Order debate of the 1970s and 1980s. In that debate, the protection of national cultural integrity against foreign influence was a major issue, and third world countries were encouraged to develop their own communication and cultural policies. UNESCO thus brought forward the concerns then being voiced in many countries about "cultural imperialism," and lent its legitimation to the principle of national cultural sovereignty and hence to policies supportive of domestic cultural industries. It was believed that individual national governments could thus affirm their own identities and resist what would otherwise be the inexorable attraction that foreign cultural products held for their people.

UNESCO's interest in these matters has been significant in the establishment and elaboration of the concept of "cultural industries." For example, UNESCO advisers began to lay the basis for an analysis in such terms, pointing out at an early stage that cultural products included services as well as goods—advertising at least as much as books, for example (Girard 1982); that marketing and distribution were an integral part of the industrialization process; that the cultural industries had their own distinct forms of marketing themselves, as seen in film genres and the "star system"; that both vertical and horizontal integration were advantageous strategies in the cultural industries (Breton 1982); and also that not all cultural industries were equal—rather, some determined the development of others (Mattelart and Piemme 1982).

Above all, the UNESCO discussion broached the question of just which industries ought to be included under the rubric of "cultural industries," an issue for cultural and communication policy as much as theory. Although the term was already in use in Europe by 1980, and was even then "a means of barter or an export item in international forums," its scope was not clear. During the 1970s in the French-speaking world (through which the concept also appears to have diffused to Canada around this time), the concept of "industries culturelles" had become an "eminently respectable" and unproblematic way to refer to the media in particular; but while there was a consensus to include film, radio, and television, there remained the question of other such leisure and entertainment industries as tourism (Mattelart and Piemme 1982, p. 51).

More obvious omissions from the list of media industries just mentioned are newspaper, magazine, and book publishing. However, these, together with sound recordings, were included without question in a Canadian policy study of the cultural industries in the early 1980s (Audley 1983). Garnham also includes all of these, together with "commercial sports organizations, etc.," in his study of public policy and the cultural industries in London, and distinguishes them from libraries, museums, galleries, and other facilities provided out of "public cultural expenditure" (1990, p. 156). By contrast, a more recent Australian policy document embraces public-funded performing and visual arts, "heritage" institutions and sites, and national libraries and galleries under a single "cultural industry" heading. This also covers subsidized activities in film and television, but not the private audiovisual sector as such nor the print media, since they receive no direct public assistance (Australia: Department of the Arts, Sport, the Environment and Territories 1992).

The conflict evident here is about the use of "cultural industries" for different policy objectives, not just disagreement over which kinds of activities fall under the heading. On the one hand, there is an apparent need for flexibility in the scope of the concept so as to express the different geopolitical concerns, relations of public to private sectors, policy priorities, and portfolio responsibilities which apply in different national settings. On the other, the concept has to have some defined limits if it is to retain even any descriptive denotation, let alone analytic value. The story is told of one UNESCO committee which, after reviewing hundreds of definitions of the concept, commented that "culture" could easily be confused with life itself. In a similar vein, there is a case to be made for an "anthropology of consumption"—that is, seeing all goods and services as "cultural" in the sense that they form a set of semiotic relations which are meaningful for societies (Sinclair 1987, pp. 52–57). Again, any institutionalized activity which draws on inputs such as skilled labor (in singing or dancing, for example) and produces outputs for which audiences are charged admission (such as opera and ballet), or commodities of a cultural kind (such as art and crafts), might be called an industry. This is consistent with the emergence of "cultural economics" as a field within applied economics (Towse and Khakee 1992). However, if the concept of "cultural industries" is to be meaningful, there must be some boundaries drawn between those industries that are distinctively "cultural" and those that are not, and between those cultural forms that are distinctively industrialized and those that are not. In the present context, it is not appropriate to attempt to resolve this problem philosophically; rather, we should look for more pragmatic resolutions relevant to international and national practice and policies in culture, industry, and trade.

▪ ▪ Tradeable Culture and the Nation

A helpful definition that both affirms the common core of meaning in the concept and opens the way to the analysis of the cultural industries in an international context comes from the Canadian Institute of Economic Policy's 1983 study cited earlier:

> the common element which justifies dealing with these industries
> within a single framework is the fact that in all of them the process
> of individual or collective creation and expression leads to the
> manufacturing or electronic diffusion of the resulting product. . . .
> A natural result of the characteristics of these industries is a ten-
> dency towards increasing flows of such products and programs
> among nations and a tendency for those flows to be primarily from
> large nations to small ones.

> Recent technological innovations in the distribution systems for
> cultural products and programs, and the evolution of large multi-
> national conglomerates, have intensified the pressure towards un-
> balanced international cultural trade. . . . Any move to alter the
> present imbalance, however, is predicated on government action in
> some form. The focus of a very heated debate has set those in fa-
> vour of intervention against those in favour of a free flow. (Audley
> 1983, pp. xxii–xxiii)

What are the special characteristics of cultural products that have allowed them to emerge as what a British government report of the same
year (cited in Schiller 1986, p. 13) called "the tradeable information
sector"? Although we must take account of the durable consumer goods
or "hardware" that consumers require for cultural consumption—CD
and cassette players, VCRs, radio and television sets—these are best
thought of in the present context as the technical means with which to
gain access to the "software" or cultural content that they can reproduce
or receive. That is not to say that the consumer durables are inconsequential in themselves; on the contrary, as Silverstone, Hirsch, and
Morley (1992) have so elaborately argued, they are "doubly articulated,"
meaningful as objects in themselves, as well as being the carriers of
meaningful content. However, from a cultural exchange point of view,
there is a fundamental difference between watching television on a
Japanese set and watching a Japanese television program: the cultural
industries are not so much about the *stock* of goods that consumers
hold as they are about the *flow* of contents that the goods carry (Breton
1982, p. 41). Audiovisual goods—television and radio programs, prere-
corded audio and video cassettes, and CDs—these are the paradigmatic
products of the cultural industries.

It was mentioned in the first section of this chapter that Nicholas
Garnham had based his analysis of cultural industries upon the particular characteristics that cultural products exhibit as commodities. In
the first place, cultural products are distinct from other commodities
in that one of their use values lies in the ephemeral appeal of novelty
or difference, so the consequent continuous development and production of new cultural products has high fixed costs. However, the costs
of reproduction are marginal. The daily newspaper is a traditional example. This characteristic favors larger producers and distributors who
have economies of scale as well as economies of scope (a range of out-

put over which risk can be spread), which in turn motivates them to maximize their audiences.

However, a second characteristic is that cultural commodities are not used up in the act of consumption—other members of the household or colleagues at work can read the same copy of the newspaper; new generations of viewers can be introduced to "I Love Lucy." Broadcasting in particular is a kind of "public good," in that simultaneous access to a radio or television service is in technical terms both "non-rival" and "non-excludable"; that is, my watching of a television program does not prevent any other person with a set from watching it (Collins, Garnham, and Locksley 1988, pp. 6–19; Garnham 1990, pp. 160–161). For this reason, cultural providers under capitalism have instigated various strategies to limit access to their products, and hence secure their exchange value. These are: copyright; the box-office mechanism and other forms of monopolization of distribution channels and reception conditions; built-in obsolescence; state subsidization; and the selling of audiences to advertisers (Garnham 1990, p. 40). Garnham goes on to conclude that "it is cultural distribution, not cultural production, that is the key locus of power and profit" (pp. 162–163). Book publishing would be the most evident example of this, but television is more instructive: the big money is in the control of networks and the consequent capacity to sell audiences to advertisers rather than in the selling of programs to networks. Of course, profitability is maximized to the extent that production and distribution can be vertically integrated under the one conglomerate. Similarly, horizontal integration enables the exploitation of copyright from a book to a film, a film to a sound-track recording, and so on.

These commodity characteristics do not apply equally across the whole range of activities that have been designated as cultural industries. In particular, in the case of the performing arts, what one pays to see is the singularity of a particular theatrical production, finite in time and space. The acquisition of a ticket is more a private than a public good, and the production is not reproducible—unless it becomes a video, film, or broadcast program. In this sense, the arts are more "cultural," in the older and narrower sense of the term, than "industrial." Furthermore, although there are several forms in which international commercial exchange can be carried out in both performing and visual arts, they clearly are not as amenable to international commercial and technological exploitation, and hence not "tradeable" in the same sense as audiovisual commodities. For this reason it is unhelpful in the present context to include them under the rubric of cultural industries.

As Philip Schlesinger points out, "the 'audiovisual' is both a symbolic arena and an economic one" (1987, p. 228), and in the context of international trade, it can be taken theoretically as the "ideal type" of the cultural industries, and pragmatically as the referent of what cultural industries means in actual trade agreements. However, if the arts are more cultural than industrial, it does not follow that audiovisual commodities are therefore more industrial than cultural. In fact, it is the cultural significance that certain countries see as being inherent in their cultural industries that is the rationale for their demand that these industries be given special recognition in trade agreements. Nations also ascribe significance to the cultural products of other nations, so that the central issue for most national governments concerning the cultural industries in trade agreements becomes their power to maintain controls over the importation of foreign cultural products and, at the same time, to foster domestic cultural industries as an expression and defense of their "national culture." One familiar instance of this, of course, is the Canada–United States Trade Agreement (FTA, also referred to as CUSTA) of 1988, which secured a general exclusion for audiovisual goods and services, as well as print media, but not the performing and visual arts. This was at the cost of conceding the right to the United States to take retaliatory action against "unfair trade restrictions in the cultural industries" (Kesten 1992, pp. 164–165). A similar arrangement was retained when this agreement was superseded by the North American Free Trade Agreement (NAFTA) in 1993. Another well-known recent instance is the success of the European Union (EU) in retaining its systems of quotas and subsidies for its audiovisual industries, even in the face of considerable U.S. opposition, in the final negotiations that concluded the Uruguay round of the General Agreement on Tariffs and Trade (GATT).

The rhetoric in support of claims for "cultural exemptions" in trade agreements is that of national cultural sovereignty, one of the key issues in the "cultural imperialism" debate of the 1970s and 1980s referred to above. For example, in his campaign to win the support of the world's forty-six French-speaking countries for the French position on the audiovisual industries and GATT, Mitterand (then president of France) asked them: "Who could be blind today to the threat of a world gradually invaded by Anglo-Saxon culture, under the cover of economic liberalism?" (Bremner 1993).

We shall see that there are now sound reasons to question the assumptions upon which the discourse of cultural imperialism has rested, but more immediately, it is useful to consider a trend in which the concept of national culture itself has become problematized by a number of communication theorists. In an important critique, Philip Schlesinger has argued not only that the concept of a common European culture is a suspect ideological construction, but also that the concept of national culture subordinates the actual diversity of ethnic cultures to the purposes of the nation-state. In both cases, he sees the cultural concepts as rationalizations for political and economic objectives. Because the inherent ambiguities of the dual character of audiovisual cultural industries "allow one to make a cultural and economic argument at one and the same time" (1987, p. 228), Schlesinger deduces that "'culture' is clearly there to serve economic ends. It functions as a discrete synonym for the protection of domestic production capacities and employment" (p. 222).

This is a simplistic inference, however, and uncomfortably close to the "free flow" position that the United States has held for some years now, an inversion of the Mitterand view cited earlier. That is, where the French see trade liberalization as a camouflage for cultural invasion, the United States challenges the national cultural expression argument as an excuse for continued economic protection of cultural industries. There will be reason to return to this issue, too, later in the chapter.

Yet it is ever more difficult to find intellectual justification, as distinct from visceral sentiment or intuition, to support the belief that a nation's audiovisual products can somehow be an authentic expression of the culture of that nation, and so affirm that culture among its recipients. It is clearly the notion of national culture that is the weakest link in the argument. "National culture" glosses over not only ethnic cultural differences within a nation, but also other basic kinds of social difference, such as gender and class. As Quijano has pointed out, a national culture might not be the culture of the dominant class, but it is a culture supportive of its domination (1971). For Richard Collins, national culture is "a contradiction in terms" and "a mystifying category error" (1990, p. 199), in that there is no necessary or even desirable relationship between the political order of a nation-state and its "symbolic" (as distinct from "anthropological") culture. While he has taken the critique of the "European culture" concept even further than Schlesinger, he is better known for his application of this heretical thesis to Canada.

In the field of cultural studies, there is similar negative support for the notion of "national culture"; that is, it is not just that such support is absent, there is a critical movement against the concept. This has been greatly accentuated as cultural studies has shifted into its present post-Marxist, postmodernist, and postcolonialist phase. In Australia, for example, when broadcast regulators looked to cultural theory for arguments in defense of the Australian content quotas that they were reviewing during the 1980s, they found instead a denunciatory discourse that not only equated national culture with the Anglo masculinism of *Crocodile Dundee,* but that also was undermining the rationale for public broadcasting as an institution and the principle of foreign-ownership regulation. In this respect, cultural theorists have yet to reflect on the degree to which their drift into postmodernism is lending theoretical legitimation to global capitalism in its drive for the deregulation and privatization of the cultural industries. Similarly, the emergent international cultural studies literature on media representations of gender as well as of ethnic and indigenous minorities in a postcolonial context gives one cause to wonder whether the critique of dominant national cultures is not destabilizing the capacity of nation-states to act in benign and positive ways in the defense of minorities against globalizing forces. Certainly, to take the Australian case again, national policies have been instrumental in establishing ethnic and Aboriginal broadcasting institutions which, while not beyond criticism, have given effect to a more plural system that is unlikely to have eventuated without the support of the nation-state (Cunningham 1992; Sinclair 1992b, 1994). Even in the absence of social democratic government, "national culture" can be a progressive force, if we think of the albeit uneven role of nation-states in fostering the national cinemas of Latin America (King 1990). As Raquel Salinas and Leena Paldán observed some time ago (1979), national culture is "inherently contradictory": "On the one hand, it is an expression of the basic relations of domination as they exist in the cultural sphere . . . On the other hand, national culture provides the site for the subordinated social groups to struggle against the dominant culture." Thus, while it might be true that the defense of national culture is a project in the interests of the dominant sectors of a given nation-state, it is also in the interests of the subordinated groups for there to be a national culture against which to define themselves and as a ground of struggle, as well as to form an intermediate line of defense against amorphous global cultural influences. It is in this sense that we still can think usefully of national culture as expressive of the nation, rather than as a particular set of common narratives and images.

▪ ▪ Market Forces and Natural Protection

If national culture is worth defending, then, how much and what kind of defense is appropriate in an era of trade liberalization? Before raising the issue of how national protectionist measures can be reconciled with an international free-trade regime, it is useful to assess "natural" protective barriers against foreign cultural influence, considered in the context of "comparative advantage" theory as it applies to the cultural industries.

As one prominent Australian producer has put it, "if it were only economics at stake, it would make sense for all English-speaking film and television to be manufactured in Los Angeles and for the rest of the English-speaking world to watch it" (Edgar 1993, p. 15). This sets national culture against the *reductio ad absurdum* of comparative advantage theory. An approach that goes back to Ricardo in classical economics, comparative advantage in recent years has been renovated by neoliberal economists, particularly by Michael Porter with his variant of "competitive advantage," which he has developed within an "industrial organization" framework (1986). No doubt it would surprise Ricardo, but these concepts have usefully been applied to the analysis of cultural industries by a diverse range of communication economists (Collins 1990; Hoskins and McFadyen 1991; Wildman and Siwek 1988).

The broad facts of U.S. preeminence within the world audiovisual trade are as familiar as the concerns that its perceived cultural influence has generated. Historically, in the field of television programs, quite apart from Hollywood's traditional dominance of world cinema screens, the United States exports more than three times the combined total of the next three largest exporting countries, or, in other words, is responsible for an estimated 75% of all television program exports. It is easily overlooked that this world-market dominance is an issue for the United States as well as for the countries affected by it: foreign markets have made up about half of all sales by U.S. film and television producers for the last few decades, and the size of U.S. entertainment exports is second only to that of its aerospace industry (Hoskins and McFadyen 1991, p. 207; Wildman and Siwek 1988, p. 1). However, we shall see in this section that there are significant changes in the world environment that has allowed the United States its dominance in the past, and these help explain the U.S. government's active, albeit unsuccessful, protagonism for a free-trade regime in audiovisual products and services under GATT.

Hoskins and McFadyen (1991, pp. 209–211) use Porter's competitive advantage framework to identify the factors with which they explain traditional U.S. dominance in the audiovisual sphere—namely, economies of scale, "first-mover" advantages, and various specific comparative advantages. The theoretical significance of economies of scale, and of scope, in the cultural industries has already been remarked upon in the previous section, with regard to their inherent trends toward concentration and audience maximization. First-mover advantages are those that accrue due to the kind of technological and organizational innovations with which cultural forms have become industrialized in the United States and then internationalized: commercial radio and television, the studio system, distribution networks (Hoskins and Mc-Fadyen, p. 214).

As the Australian producer's remark suggests, one of the most salient factors in comparative advantage in the cultural industries is language and, by extension, cultural similarities and differences in general. Richard Collins has drawn attention to English in particular as "the language of advantage" and has argued:

> Linguistic and cultural barriers limit the extension of markets for information in ways that markets for textiles, grains, steel and many manufactured products are not [limited]. . . . Works in English enjoy enormous advantages, for not only are anglophones the largest and richest world language community . . . but English is the dominant second language of the world. But it is important to recognize that this is a *potential* advantage which may or may not be realizable. (1990, p. 211)

Wildman and Siwek use the concept of "domestic opportunity advantage" to encapsulate the opportunities the United States enjoys as the largest domestic market for audiovisual products in English, but recognize that a similar situation applies in certain other countries in relation to what we can call their "geolinguistic region"—that is, all the countries throughout the world in which the same language is spoken. Just as the United States dominates the English-speaking world, so there are other notable instances where the country with the largest number of speakers of a particular language in its domestic market is also the source of most audiovisual exports in that language. Hence, "producers in countries that belong to large natural-language markets, have a financial incentive to create larger budget films and programs that generally have greater intrinsic audience appeal, a clear advantage in international competition" (Wildman and Siwek 1988, p. 68). Hoskins and McFadyen (1991, pp. 211–212) refer to a similar phenomenon with their concept of "unique access to the largest market."

Before considering some of the other geolinguistic regions, it is worth noting some other characteristics, both quantitative (economic) and qualitative (cultural), of the U.S. domestic market relative to the English-speaking world. Wildman and Siwek anticipate Collins' observation about the contingent nature of linguistic advantage in the emphasis they give to two factors—the demographics of geolinguistic regions, especially with regard to income, and the regulatory environment of the export target countries. The point need not be labored that it is not just the absolute size that is decisive, but also the wealth of a geolinguistic region, otherwise the language of advantage would be Chinese. It follows that the growth of the English geolinguistic region as a market for U.S. audiovisual products also required the basic institutional structures of capitalism, so as to favor the spread of the commercial model of social communication, and its practice of creating audiences to sell to advertisers. This is a cultural as well as an economic similarity, seen also in the regulatory regimes that have evolved in the various English-speaking countries. Without playing down the importance of their relative differences, particularly in the kind and degree of regulatory constraint applied (even including impediments to trade), it can be said that these regimes are all basically functional for the health of the commercial system.

As well as being the largest and wealthiest market in the wealthiest geolinguistic region and the least constrained system among the most liberal regulatory regimes in the world, the U.S. domestic market is said to have a comparative advantage in its diversity: "The variety of populations immersed in the melting pot of the United States gave US producers a kind of microcosm of the developed world's population as a home market," Collins argues, and this enabled "their invention of a cultural form that is the closest to transnational acceptability of any yet contrived" (1990, pp. 214–215). For those of us schooled in the critical traditions of "cultural imperialism" and related manifestations of "the American hegemony paradigm," these points might stick in the craw. Where Collins sees diversity, the critical tradition has seen homogenization, or the assimilation of difference, and rather than even acknowledging, let alone trying to understand, the appeal that U.S. programs might have for various audiences at home and abroad, the critical tradition has seen only manipulation. This is one major area in which a "cultural industries" approach might instead allow more attention to be given to the cultural meanings that films and television programs carry for their audiences, without losing sight of their economic significance. In the present instance, it is crucial to appreciate that linguistic and cultural factors are determinants in the formation of audiences or markets, both domestic and export, and hence have to be considered as having their own level of economic effects. To use the discourse of contemporary economics, language and culture have to be taken account of as "market forces." As such, they are influential factors in the facilitation of trade, and in the erection of barriers against it, as it is hoped this discussion will demonstrate. At the same time, a cultural industries approach needs to be alert to differences between media. In this respect, U.S. films are evidently more universal in their appeal than U.S. television programs have proven to be, an important qualification to the present analysis.

Whatever the explanations that might emerge in time for the apparent universality of appeal of U.S. audiovisual products, and whatever the differences among them, one final and consequential cultural characteristic of the U.S. domestic market is its resistance to imported material. As with the universality-of-appeal question, this is an enigmatic cultural issue that has not been theorized or researched, and so at present it can only be accounted for by speculation. Perhaps the United States does find sufficient cultural diversity within its own borders and popular cultural traditions to continuously generate new films, television programs, and music, or perhaps the phenomenon has more to do with culturally formed attitudes toward the world outside, and the place of the United States in it. For their part, Hoskins and McFadyen (1991, p. 217) suggest that the historical lack of exposure to foreign material becomes a cause in itself, so that audiences are intolerant of dubbing and subtitling, and even of accents in non-American English. Furthermore, they say, foreign programs are less "commercial" in their style and packaging, and this becomes another kind of cultural barrier which ensures that the access that U.S. cultural producers enjoy to their domestic market remains "unique."

This line of observation brings us, of course, to the flip side of language as a comparative advantage: that is, language is also a "natural" barrier to trade in cultural products such as television programs. Colin Hoskins has contributed on this score also, with the concept of "cultural discount," which is the diminished market appeal that a television program has for audiences who speak a different language or who "find it difficult to identify with the style, values, beliefs, institutions and behavioural patterns of the material in question" (Hoskins and Mirus 1988, p. 500). Thus, all foreign programs carry some measure of cultural discount in the U.S. market but, as Collins observes, the converse is that the cultural discount which non-English-speaking markets apply to programs in English is not so great as for programs in other languages. Historically, in most non-English-speaking markets, the United States has been the preferred source for such material, particularly for films. Collins goes on to argue that language is a comparative advantage (or disadvantage) factor independent of domestic market size, and that English-language production is particularly advantaged, citing the relatively strong export performance of the U.K. and, more strikingly, Australia (1990, p. 55). One further point in this connection is that it is useful to distinguish between language and culture as variables, since linguistic similarities or differences seem to be a more decisive basis for comparative advantage or disadvantage than the more secondary role played by whatever cultural characteristics of the source nation might be discernible in its programs. It is perhaps for this reason that many Americans find it difficult to distinguish between a British and an Australian accent, or that English-speakers tend to confuse the cultural signifiers of Spain with those of Mexico and South America.

The role of the comparative advantage of English and of linguistic and cultural "screens" or "membranes" as barriers to trade in television programs has implications for the partners in NAFTA, and warrants some mention at this stage. While French-speaking Canadians in Québec form a market with "natural" protection against English-language cultural products of whatever origin (Martin 1992, pp. 6–7), English Canada is distinguished from the United States by much more permeable cultural differences, and is in fact the world's biggest market for U.S. films and television programs (Johnson, Calhoun, and Bruno 1992, p. 32). Canada's concerns about this situation provide the rationale for its insistence that its cultural industries be exempt from its obligations under the FTA and NAFTA, so that it would not have to abandon the subsidies to domestic cultural production with which it seeks to protect its national culture. There is an argument that Canada is in a good position to cultivate certain comparative advantages it has over other foreign producers in the U.S. market, both linguistic and commercial (Kesten 1992, pp. 167–169). However—and this is a dilemma also familiar to Australian producers in a comparable, although geographically remote, situation—the tradeoff is that in order to maximize its international appeal, it is necessary to suppress the "look and feel" with which a film or television program might otherwise express its national origins. To the Canadian government, these are questions of sovereignty on which they are determined to hold the line.

The Mexican case is quite distinct. "Protected by an ancient and vigorous cultural identity and a rich language of its own which had survived North American penetration," Mexico did not regard national culture as being on the negotiating table (de Maria y Campos 1992, p. 5). However, NAFTA critics in Mexico are concerned about the degree of integration between U.S. and Mexican media, seeing an unequal dependence not offset by Mexican access to the important Spanish-speaking market of the United States (Sánchez Ruiz 1994). The Mexican situation is considered further in the next section.

▪ ▪ From Cultural Imperialism to Globalization

While the analysis so far has been oriented toward explaining the undisputed preeminence of the United States over the world's trade in audiovisual products, we can now acknowledge that, at least with the television industry in particular, similar factors have been conducive to the growth of certain other nations as market leaders within their own geolinguistic regions. Indeed, this has been taking place within a broader trend toward the "internationalization" or "globalization" of television. The most impressive and relevant case is Mexico, a country that bears a comparable relationship to Spain and the world that speaks its language as the United States does to the U.K. and the English-speaking world. That is, Mexico's history as a former colony of Spain has come to be overshadowed by the fact that it is home to the greatest number of Spanish-speakers of any country in the world. Furthermore, Mexico is the home base of Televisa, the private audiovisual conglomerate that has built itself into the world's largest exporter of Spanish-language programs on the strength of its "domestic opportunity advantage," its more-or-less "unique access to the world's largest domestic market" in that language.

Televisa's transformation into an international television network operator and satellite service provider has been partly based on geographic contiguity: on one side, there is the Spanish-language market in the United States (which Televisa and its predecessors built into a national market during twenty-five years of operation there, a "first-mover advantage"); and on the other, there is Central and South America.

However, Televisa has also made a notable incursion into the television industry in Spain, and its exploitation of worldwide satellite delivery opportunities has been decisive in enabling it to bring all these zones into a single geolinguistic region. In doing so, it has compensated for the relative poverty of the Mexican domestic market by drawing in the world's richest Spanish-speaking markets—the United States and Spain. Finally, Televisa has taken full advantage of the relative absence of regulatory constraints upon it in Mexico, particularly in maximizing the benefits of the vertical integration of production and distribution which it is allowed there (Sinclair 1992a).

A comparable but distinct instance is TV Globo in Brazil, in that Globo is the market leader in Brazilian television and the most active producer and exporter of television programs in Portuguese. Brazil is the largest Portuguese-speaking country in the world, so Globo is based to some extent on a similar kind of domestic opportunity advantage to that which Televisa enjoys in Mexico. Again in parallel to Televisa, Globo is a participant in the television industry of Portugal, and at home benefits from a permissive regulatory environment which, among other things, also permits it to integrate production with distribution. Unlike Televisa, however, Globo does not command an international satellite service, and since Portuguese-speaking countries are much fewer and poorer than those in which Spanish is spoken, it has to rely more on dubbing its programs for export markets that are culturally related to, but not members of, its own geolinguistic region—notably, Italy and France, as well as its Spanish-speaking Latin American neighbors (Sinclair, in press).

In respect of the Brazilian case, Joseph Straubhaar and his collaborators have made a helpful contribution to the present discussion with their concept of "cultural proximity," which is a comparative advantage factor based on cultural similarities that go beyond language to include such elements as dress, nonverbal communication, humor, religion, music, and narrative style. Drawing a useful distinction between the national, regional, and global levels at which television programs circulate, Straubhaar et al. (1992, p. 5) argue that

> audiences will tend to prefer that programming which is closest or most proximate to their own culture: national programming if it can be supported by the local economy, regional programming in genres that small countries can afford. The United States continues to have an advantage in genres that even large Third World coun-

tries cannot afford to produce, such as feature films, cartoons, and action-adventure series.

While acknowledging that the United States remains hegemonic in film and at the level of the big-budget, globally distributed television genres, we need to assess how far the growth of geolinguistic and culturally proximate markets outside the English-speaking zones demands a revision of the U.S.-centric worldview constructed by cultural imperialism theory in the 1970s and 1980s. There has been much recent debate about the theoretical basis of "cultural imperialism" (Schiller 1991; Tomlinson 1991), but as early as 1977 Jeremy Tunstall was questioning the empirical grounds on which the paradigm was based. In particular, he argued that the high levels of U.S. television imports into Latin American countries in the 1960s had been a temporary phase rather than the permanent condition that Herb Schiller and Alan Wells assumed it to be in their "television imperialism" thesis. Tunstall argued that, if anything, the dominance of the world film industry by Hollywood was a much more convincing case of "media imperialism." Tunstall also pointed out that some of the heaviest importers of U.S. television programs, including Mexico, India, and Egypt, were also emerging even then as "strong regional exporters" (p. 62). Finally, he discerned the growth from these new centers of "hybrid" media genres, such as the Latin American *telenovela,* and predicted that they would come to occupy an intermediate level of television scheduling throughout the world, between the local on the one hand, and the global—which Anglo-American production would continue to dominate—on the other (p. 274).

A further challenge to the empirical basis of the cultural imperialism paradigm came in the 1980s, with the publication of research on Latin American *telenovelas* by Everett Rogers and Livia Antola. Although exaggerated in their conclusions, particularly in the absurd claim that Televisa's operations in the United States constituted "reverse media imperialism" (1985, p. 33), their research confirmed the "trend towards greater regional exchanges" found by Tapio Varis also at that time (1984), as well as the pivotal role played by Mexico (Televisa) and Brazil (Globo) within a broad shift in the region away from U.S. programs and toward Latin American *telenovelas.*

By the 1990s the blindspots in "the American hegemony paradigm" of cultural imperialism and its variants were clear (Sinclair 1992a), and attention had shifted to Europe, where, as a result of the privatization and deregulation of the 1980s and the spread of satellite and cable delivery systems, a process of "internationalization" of television was under way. However, this was a code word for European anxieties about the prospective influx of American programs and the adoption of the commercial model—demonized as "wall-to-wall *Dallas*" and "Coca-colonization" (Collins 1990, pp. 151–152), respectively. Negrine and Papathanassopoulos's book, *The Internationalisation of Television* (1990), is concerned with Europe alone, while Dunnett, in *The World Television Industry: An Economic Analysis*, of the same year, condenses the huge geolinguistic markets of "The Developing World" into one chapter. Thus, "internationalization" means the "Americanization" of Europe, and this process includes the "horizontal . . . restratifications of national cultural communities," in which dominant national cultures are seen to be subverted by the popular audiences created by foreign programs (Collins 1990, p. 214). At least in the U.K., some theorists interpret this as a positive experience for the subordinate classes affected by it (Morley and Robins 1989), while others, both inside and outside Europe, have been concerned that the fragmentation of audiences intensifies social divisions, creating an informed minority and an entertained majority (Martín-Barbero 1993, p. 26).

A more comprehensive concept that it is now fashionable to apply to, among other things, international dealings in television programs and services is "globalization." To take Michael Richards' albeit European-flavored list, manifestations of globalization in television include

> the increasing number of channels, the increasing length of television schedules, changing patterns of global ownership, the increasing wealth potential of local television markets, the increasing massification of television markets, the changed economic base of broadcasting systems, changes in the technology of reception and pressure upon established regulatory regimes. (1993, p. 1)

However, in spite of serious efforts to develop the globalization concept for theoretical analysis (Featherstone 1990), it is still very much a buzzword. It carries several meanings and can express quite different attitudes toward the phenomena it seeks to describe, and there is not even universal agreement as to what these are. Richards suggests a convenient categorization of the various usages of the concept. The initial category is that in which "globalization" refers to the "supranational" level at which corporations are owned and controlled, and at which national governments and international organizations provide the "operative conditions" to facilitate business at this level (1993, p. 1). The first point here in turn refers to the ascendancy of the supranational corporation over the nation-state as the basic organizational unit of world power, and the ever more complex and decentralized international structures that these organizational units assume. This trend can be associated with the cognate concepts of "flexible accumulation" and "post-Fordism" (Grossberg 1992, pp. 340–344), and with a more internationalized pattern of ownership in the cultural industries, seen in the advent of foreign ownership in core U.S. media industries (Carveth 1992; McAnany and Wilkinson 1992) and in the international growth of corporations based in the erstwhile third world, such as Televisa and Globo. The latter aspect, "operative conditions," would include both international and regional trade agreements, GATT and NAFTA in particular, which can be regarded as an integral part of the globalization process, neither cause nor effect, but both.

The second category includes the more ideological uses of the term, particularly the notion that there is a common "global culture" developing, regardless of whether that is seen as a positive or a negative trend. This is the usage upon which Marjorie Ferguson has mounted her important critique of the "myths" of globalization (1992) and pointed to the "mounting evidence of counter-globalisation" at the level of cultural identity (1993, p. 4).

The third category is that in which globalization is treated as an empirical process, and it is in this respect that research on cultural industries has much to contribute to current theoretical understanding of worldwide change, particularly concerning those trends in ownership and control noted above, but also with respect to the question of transformation of identities. This is a theoretical issue, but there has been a premature foreclosure of debate among postmodern theorists who, like the cultural imperialist theorists just decades before, have assumed that the "internationalization of dominant imagery" (Golding 1993, p. 4) has a homogenizing effect on subjectivities across cultures, "taking as given precisely what should be the object of study" (Martín-Barbero 1993, p. 24). Accordingly, a cultural industries approach to this object would articulate ownership and control studies with ethnographic studies of actual audiences, rather than inferring the social impacts from superficial observations of media content alone. "The question is not abstract: it is a matter of the relative power of different groups to mobilise these definitions through their control of cultural institutions" (Morley and Robins 1989, p. 15).

Even more concretely, and in relation to trade, Ferguson comments, in her discussion of the global cultural homogenization thesis, that

> For national cultural policy-makers and film and TV producers, such seemingly arcane issues translate into pragmatic questions of market access, industry control, product demand and supply, where relevant legal and economic questions are those of copyright law, import regulation, foreign ownership, production support and audience preference. At the level of bi-lateral and multi-lateral trade negotiation . . . McLuhan's global village vision dissolves into hard bargaining about who wins and who loses from cultural trade deals. (1993, p. 7)

In this respect, it would be quite exaggerated to pronounce the demise of the nation-state, to paraphrase Mark Twain. While we might be able to discern an emergent "New World Order" of immense trading blocs (Varis 1993, p. 18), it is evident that each nation-state is concerned to pursue its own interests, and that certain nation-states are dominant in each of the blocs—the United States in NAFTA, Japan in Asia, and, particularly so far as the cultural industries are concerned, France in the EU. Furthermore, these same nation-states have been foremost in establishing their positions at an international level in the course of the negotiation of the various agreements that constitute the recently concluded GATT round, and in exerting pressure on less powerful nations to fall in line. For example, in response to an EU agreement to establish television program quotas, the U.S. trade representative Carla Hills threatened that the United States would "take a crowbar" against them (Collins 1990, p. 208). Again, the United States maintains a "Priority Watch List" of alleged trade transgressors: Australia has occupied a place on this list because of its regulations on domestic quotas for television programs and advertisements (Levy 1993, p. 11). The right of the United States to take retaliatory action as a tradeoff for the Canadian "cultural exemption" under the FTA and NAFTA has already been noted. Hence also the reluctance of the United States to concede that other nations indeed do have bona fide concerns about their cultural identities, and that these are not just rationalizations put forward in order to justify continued protective measures for their domestic audiovisual industries.

Even though the audiovisual sector was excluded from the GATT services agreement at the last moment, the conclusion of the round was otherwise a triumph for the beneficiaries of an international free-trade regime, which, "with its presumption of liberalization in all sectors over time will institutionalise pressure on domestic assistance arrangements" (Given 1993, p. 10). It may be that just as Canada can be made to suffer for the privilege of its cultural exemption, so the EU will have cause to regret the tough stand it has taken over its quotas if the United States now goes on to raise the stakes and exert bilateral pressures on a range of matters beyond that which was being contemplated under the multilateral agreement. Perhaps instead the EU might have negotiated to retain its quotas and subsidies within the normal limits of the general obligations and using the specific derogations possible within the framework of the services agreement—that is, to keep the audiovisual industries in the agreement, but without any need for a cultural exemption. Certainly, that was the strategy being pursued by Australia (Given, pp. 8–9). In any event, "offending" countries can expect to experience continued, even intensified, U.S. pressure on local content quotas, foreign ownership restrictions, the scope of public broadcasting activities, and communication and cultural development policies.

Some mention should be made about intellectual property. Although this is an issue that bears on several industries beyond the cultural and so outside our present scope, the agreements that have been made under both NAFTA and GATT are very much in the interests of U.S. audiovisual producers, allowing the mechanisms of copyright control to be extended and strengthened in foreign markets, where piracy has been a considerable problem for them. As was noted earlier in the discussion of Garnham's work, copyright is a fundamental strategy in the commodification of culture, and in such markets, achieving effective enforcement is at least as important to U.S. interests as demolishing trade barriers.

A final consideration is the technology that has made the globalization of markets possible. International satellite delivery systems in particular have made possible the instant delivery of global television services, a relatively new phenomenon that overshadows the traditional export-import trade in programs. To hark back to Garnham once again, distribution has eclipsed production as the real center of power and profit in the cultural industries. Hoskins and McFadyen emphasize the qualitative leap in the capabilities of new television technologies of transmission and reception, but also of production, and the decreased costs that have enabled the wider diffusion of television in Latin America and other third world regions, notably the geolinguistic regions mentioned earlier, based on India and Egypt, and now also "Greater China." At the same time as production in these regions has thus become more

competitive and domestic market sizes have increased, overall world demand for programs has expanded with the multiplication of available
channels, the U.S. audience has become more fragmented, and foreign
producers have been gaining access to the U.S. market through copro-
ductions or other new kinds of venture, including U.S. production of
Spanish-language programs for the world market. Hoskins and Mc-
Fadyen conclude that the United States will continue to lead in the kind
of global genres in which it has its traditional strength, and will remain
in command of the "North American / West European /Australasian market," but that within overall world output, U.S. production "will constitute a smaller share of an expanding market" (1991, p. 221). In distribution, there is the unprecedented circumstance of Televisa's involvement
in the private international satellite system PanAmSat, even though its
own Galavisión service now competes with U.S. services in Spanish from
CNN and Time-Warner on that system (Sinclair, in press; Wilkinson
1992). Whatever new patterns emerge, it is clear that whereas cultural
imperialism theory saw U.S. television dominance as a necessary determinant of the world system, the analysis of globalization must see it as
contingent.

▪ ▪ "Cultural Industries": Not Quite a Paradigm

Once again, this is to allude to the limitations of the "dominant
ideology thesis," insofar as the critical discourses of cultural imperialism
and dependency were applications of that thesis on an international
scale—"the American hegemony paradigm" (Schement, Gonzalez, Lum,
and Valencia 1984, p. 163). Indeed, its status as a paradigm and its durable
appeal were due at least in part to its totalizing power, its explanation of
the "big picture," and the revisionist critiques that have appeared since
its heyday have not been articulated into a systematic paradigm that
could replace it (Collins 1990, pp. 4–5).

However, in the era of post-Marxism and postmodernism, not only
have such "grand narratives" of the past been discredited, but totaliza-
tion itself has been rejected as an objective of theoretical effort. That is,
we should not now expect to find a new paradigm in which we can take
up the same kind of secure and familiar positions that we once occupied
in the old. Rather, we need to climb down to do our work at lower levels
of abstraction, and act without the former certitude afforded by a deterministic Weltanschauung that always told us what we would find.

This is not just a concession to intellectual fashion or a reaction to the collapse of Marxism as an intellectual and political movement over the last few years. A decade ago, some mainstream theorists were urging a shift toward Merton's "middle range" rather than "grand" theory as an appropriate level at which specific empirical studies of processes could be pursued without abandoning an understanding of their structural context (Schement et al. 1984, pp. 177–179). At the same time, there were critical theorists who were beginning to unpack cultural imperialism and cultural dependency from what one of them, Emile McAnany, then called a "cultural industries approach" which

> places more emphasis on the economic structures of cultural production . . .
> Instead of trying to create a theory suited to all countries and having arguments raised about the generalizability of results and the validity of the theory, the study of the growth and impact of cultural industries within each country is more appropriate. (1984, pp. 205–206)

A cultural industries approach of the kind argued for here has strong continuities with the political economy of mass communication tradition alluded to earlier in the chapter, insofar as it concentrates upon the media as industries, but is quite distinct to the degree that the cultural industries approach problematizes the meaning and the appeal which the content of television programs have for their audiences and, as we have seen, recognizes this to be a factor in the formation of audiences as markets. In the more hardline formulations of the political economy approach, the appeal that television has for audiences has just been taken for granted (Smythe 1977), or simply assumed to be manipulative of them. Furthermore, there is a refusal to acknowledge the differences between types of media content, such as the U.S. soap opera compared with the *telenovela*, so the cultural clues in content that might explain links between particular kinds of programs and their audiences are ignored on principle (Schiller 1991, p. 22).

The cultural industries approach advocated here also gives major attention to the structural formation of the audiovisual industries under capitalism—their ownership and control, and the role of the state in conditioning their development. Of particular interest are the effects of regulatory regimes, modes of direct and indirect industry assistance, and trade policy, and, similarly, the effects of the absence of such intervention. However, the cultural industries approach pursues its interest in these areas in a more specific and empirical and less deterministic manner than is customary in the hardline political economy tradition. Furthermore, it is more "cultural" in the sense that it does not assume the social impact of the media a priori from their structural conditions. Rather, it takes seriously Stuart Hall's dictum for the related "cultural studies" school of thought: "the level of economic determination is the necessary but not sufficient condition for an adequate analysis" (1978, p. 239). On the other hand, cultural industries refuses to follow cultural studies on its subsequent deviations from this, neither into the thicket of ideological, representational, and discursive analysis of media "texts," nor down the cheerful cul de sac of autonomous "active" audiences in subversive search of their pleasures.

It should not be thought that this cultural industries approach is seeking merely to stake a claim by default in the spaces that separate the economic and the cultural determinisms of political economy and cultural studies, respectively—that is, that it is able to define itself only by what they are not. More than looking for a mere balance between the industrial and the cultural, it takes account of their interaction. Of course, the media sell audiences to advertisers, but they can only do so on the basis of the irreducibly cultural relationships that are established between certain types of program and the audiences for whom they are meaningful. This dynamic is seen in turn to operate at the distinct but connected levels at which cultural products circulate—the local, the national, the regional, and the global.

> This approach to cultural industries recognizes the limits placed on many nations' media systems by operating within subordinate positions within the world economy, but also recognizes and gives analytical emphasis to the distinct dynamics of each nation or industry's historical development. Key national issues include conflicts between domestic and transnational elites, interests of key national elites, entrepreneurial competition, the agendas and actions of key production personnel, the effects of state intervention, particularly as policy-maker, provider of infrastructure and advertiser. (Straubhaar et al. 1992, p. 12)

The era of globalization demands more than ever that theorists seek to understand the continuities and the contradictions between these levels. The "geolinguistic regions" identified in this chapter are a major case in point where communication technologies have allowed the major producers in the largest "natural language" markets to cultivate markets wherever there are linguistic and cultural similarities beyond their own national boundaries, thereby creating new "imagined communities" which restratify and transcend the nations in which they are located. Yet the individual nation-state has to remain the definitive unit of analysis, not just for the sake of the unified "relations of force" which each nation presents to the theorist and researcher, but because the nation-state is still the most effective level at which theory and research can make an input to policy, whether national (communication and cultural development), or international (trade).

Attention to specific national realities, taken in the context of their relation to global forces, allows researchers to understand the historical development of communication media within particular social formations, and to see the difference between what is determinant and what is contingent, what is general and what is particular in that process. The Mexican and Brazilian cases referred to in this chapter provide significant examples of how relationships of dependence can provide the motivation and opportunities for media entrepreneurs in subordinate countries to initiate their own push toward internationalization, at least in those regions where they have some comparative advantage to pursue. These cases do not permit the conclusion that their ascendance marks a permanent change in the international patterns of media flows, or that the era of U.S. domination in the audiovisual sphere has passed, as its NAFTA partners are well aware, but the cultural industries approach which brings such cases to light provides us with a more detailed and complex picture than the former critical orthodoxies could ever have given us.

BIBLIOGRAPHY

Adorno, Theodor, and Max Horkheimer. 1977. "The Culture Industry: Enlightenment as Mass Deception." In *Mass Communication and Society,* ed. James Curran, Michael Gurevitch, and Janet Woollacott. London: Edward Arnold.
Audley, Paul. 1983. *Canada's Cultural Industries.* Toronto: James Lorimer & Co./ Canadian Institute for Economic Policy.
Australia. Department of the Arts, Sport, the Environment and Territories. 1992. "The Role of the Commonwealth in Australia's Cultural Development: A Discussion Paper." Canberra.
Benjamin, Walter. 1977. "The Work of Art in the Age of Mechanical Reproduction." In *Mass Communication and Society,* ed. James Curran, Michael Gurevitch, and Janet Woollacott. London: Edward Arnold.
Bremner, Charles. 1993. "Mitterand Musters Troops to Defend the Culture Cocoon." *The Australian,* October 20, p. 9.
Breton, Albert. 1982. "Introduction to an Economics of Culture: A Liberal Ap-

proach." In *Cultural Industries: A Challenge for the Future of Culture*, ed. UNESCO. Paris: UNESCO.

Carveth, Rod. 1992. "The Reconstruction of the Global Media Marketplace." *Communication Research*, 19(6): 705–723.

Collins, Richard. 1990. *Television: Policy and Culture*. London: Unwin Hyman.

Collins, Richard, Nicholas Garnham, and Gareth Locksley. 1988. *The Economics of Television: The UK Case*. London: Sage.

Cunningham, Stuart. 1992. *Framing Culture: Criticism and Policy in Australia*. Sydney: Allen & Unwin.

de Maria y Campos, Mauricio. 1992. "Las Industrias Culturales y de Entretenimiento en el Marco de las Negociaciones del Tratado de Libre Comercio, México, Estados Unidos, Canadá." Discussion paper, Fundación Nexos, México DF.

Dunnett, Peter. 1990. *The World Television Industry: An Economic Analysis*. London: Routledge.

Edgar, Patricia. 1993. "Cultural Industries: National Policies and Global Markets." In *Cultural Industries: National Policies and Global Markets*, ed. Marcus Breen. Proceedings of a CIRCIT Conference. Melbourne: Centre for International Research on Communication and Information Technologies.

Featherstone, Mike, ed. 1990. *Global Culture: Nationalism, Globalization and Modernity*. London: Sage.

Ferguson, Marjorie. 1992. "The Mythology about Globalisation." *European Journal of Communication* 7(1): 69–93.

———. 1993. "Globalisation of Cultural Industries: Myths and Realities." In *Cultural Industries: National Policies and Global Markets*, ed. Marcus Breen. Proceedings of a CIRCIT Conference. Melbourne: Centre for International Research on Communication and Information Technologies.

Garnham, Nicholas. 1990. *Capitalism and Communication*. London: Sage.

Girard, Augustin. 1982. "Cultural Industries: A Handicap or a New Opportunity for Cultural Development." In *Cultural Industries: A Challenge for the Future of Culture*, ed. UNESCO. Paris: UNESCO.

Given, Jock. 1993. Cars, Culture and Comparative Advantage. Paper presented at seminar, Australian Content: New Rules and Policies. Centre for Media and Telecommunications Law and Policy, Melbourne.

Golding, Peter. 1993. "The Communications Paradox: Inequality at National and International Level and the Communications Media." Paper presented at conference, Communication and Development in the Postmodern Era: Re-evaluating the Freirean Legacy. University of Sains, Penang.

Grossberg, Lawrence. 1992. *We Gotta Get Out of This Place*. New York: Routledge.

Hall, Stuart. 1978. "The TV Feuilleton and the Domestication of the World: Some Preliminary Critical Notes." In *The Feuilleton in Television*, vol. 1, ed. Secretariat of Prix Italia. Turin: Edizione RAI.

Hoskins, Colin, and Stuart McFadyen. 1991. "The U.S. Competitive Advantage in the Global Television Market: Is it Sustainable in the New Broadcasting Environment?" *Canadian Journal of Communication* 16(2): 207–224.

Hoskins, Colin, and Rolf Mirus. 1988. "Reasons for the US Dominance of the International Trade in Television Programmes." *Media, Culture, and Society* 10(4): 499–515.

Johnson, Craig, Julia Calhoun, and Susan Bruno, eds. 1992. "The United States and Canada: The Hidden Borders of Telecom." Summary report. Center for Strategic and International Studies, Washington.

Kesten, Myles. 1992. "The Canada-U.S. Free Trade Agreement: Provisions Directly and Indirectly Affecting Trade in Cultural Product." In *Cultural Economics*, ed. Ruth Towse and Abdul Khakee. Berlin: Springer-Verlag.

King, John. 1990. *Magical Reels: A History of Cinema in Latin America.* London: Verso.

Levy, Jonathan. 1993. "Australian-US Trade in Audiovisual Products." *CIRCIT Newsletter* 5(9): 11–13.

Martin, Claude. 1992. The Economics of Quebec's Cultural Industries. Paper presented at International Association for Mass Communication Research XVIII Conference, São Paulo.

Martín-Barbero, Jesús. 1993. "Latin America: Cultures in the Communication Media." *Journal of Communication* 43(2): 18–29.

Mattelart, Armand, and Jean-Marie Piemme. 1982. "Cultural Industries: The Origin of an Idea." In *Cultural Industries: A Challenge for the Future of Culture*, ed. UNESCO. Paris: UNESCO.

McAnany, Emile. 1984. "The Logic of Cultural Industries in Latin America: The Television Industry in Brazil." In *The Critical Communications Review. Volume 11: Changing Patterns of Communications Control*, ed. Vincent Mosco and Janet Wasko. Norwood, N.J.: Ablex.

McAnany, Emile, and Kent Wilkinson. 1992. "From Cultural Imperialists to Takeover Victims? Questions on Hollywood's Buyouts from the Critical Tradition." *Communication Research* 19(6): 724–748.

Morley, David, and Kevin Robins. 1989. "Spaces of Identity: Communications Technologies and the Reconfiguration of Europe." *Screen* 30(4): 10–34.

Murdock, Graham. 1978. "Blindspots About Western Marxism: A Reply to Dallas Smythe." *Canadian Journal of Political and Social Theory* 2(2): 109–119.

Negrine, Ralph, and Stylianos Papathanassopoulos. 1990. *The Internationalisation of Television.* London: Pinter.

Porter, Michael, ed. 1986. *Competition in Global Industries.* Boston: Harvard Business School Press.

Quijano, Aníbal. 1971. "Cultura y Dominación." *Revista Latinoamericana de Ciencias Sociales* 1–2: 39–56.

Richards, Michael. 1993. Questioning the Concept of Globalisation: Some Pedagogical Challenges. Paper presented at conference, Communication and Development in the Postmodern Era: Re-evaluating the Freirean Legacy, University of Sains, Penang.

Rogers, Everett, and Livia Antola. 1985. "*Telenovelas*: A Latin American Success Story." *Journal of Communication* 35(4): 24–35.

Salinas, Raquel, and Leena Paldán. 1979. "Culture in the Process of Dependent Development: Theoretical Perspectives." In *National Sovereignty and International Communication*, ed. Kaarle Nordenstreng and Herbert Schiller. Norwood, N.J.: Ablex.

Sánchez Ruiz, Enrique. 1994. "The Mexican Audiovisual Space and the North American Free Trade Agreement." *Media Information Australia* 71: 70–77.

Schement, Jorge, Ibarra Gonzalez, Patricia Lum, and Rosita Valencia. 1984. "The International Flow of Television Programs." *Communication Research* 11(2): 163–182.

Schiller, Herbert. 1986. "Electronic Information Flows: New Basis for Global Domination?" In *Television in Transition*, ed. Paul Drummond and Richard Paterson. London: British Film Institute.

———. 1991. "Not Yet the Post-Imperialist Era." *Critical Studies in Mass Communication* 8: 13–28.

Schlesinger, Philip. 1987. "On National Identity: Some Conceptions and Misconceptions Criticised." *Social Science Information* 26(2): 219–264.

Silverstone, Roger, Eric Hirsch, and David Morley. 1992. "Information and Communication Technologies and the Moral Economy of the Household." In *Consuming Technologies: Media and Information in Domestic Spaces*, ed. Roger Silverstone and Eric Hirsch. London and New York: Routledge.

Sinclair, John. 1987. *Images Incorporated: Advertising as Industry and Ideology*. London: Croom Helm.

———. 1992a. "The Decentering of Cultural Imperialism: Televisa-ion and Globoization in the Latin World." In *Continental Shift: Globalisation and Culture*, ed. Elizabeth Jacka. Sydney: Local Consumption Publications.

———. 1992b. "Television and Australian Content: Culture and Protection." *Media Information Australia* 63: 23–28.

———. 1994. "Communication Media and Cultural Development." In *Enhancing Cultural Value: Narrowcasting, Community Media and Cultural Development*, ed. Marcus Breen and Elaine Wightman. Proceedings of a CIRCIT Conference. Melbourne: Centre for International Research on Communication and Information Technologies.

———. In press. "Mexico, Brazil and the Latin World." In *Peripheral Vision: New Patterns in Global Television*, ed. John Sinclair, Elizabeth Jacka, and Stuart Cunningham. Oxford: Oxford University Press.

Smythe, Dallas. 1977. "Communications: Blindspot of Western Marxism." *Canadian Journal of Political and Social Theory* 1(3): 1–27.

Straubhaar, Joseph, C. Campbell, S.-M. Youn, K. Champaigne, L. Ha, S. Shrikhande, and M. Elasmar. 1992. Regional TV Markets and TV Program Flows. Paper presented at International Association for Mass Communication Research XVIII Conference, São Paulo.

Tomlinson, John. 1991. *Cultural Imperialism: A Critical Introduction*. Baltimore: Johns Hopkins University Press.

Towse, Ruth, and Abdul Khakee, eds. 1992. *Cultural Economics*. Berlin: Springer-Verlag.

Tunstall, Jeremy. 1977. *The Media Are American: Anglo-American Media in the World.* London: Constable.

UNESCO, ed. 1982. *Cultural Industries: A Challenge for the Future of Culture.* Paris: UNESCO.

Varis, Tapio. 1984. International Flow of Television Programs. Paper presented at International Association for Mass Communication Research XIV Conference, Prague.

———. 1993. "Cultural Industries and the Post Cold War World." In *Cultural Industries: National Policies and Global Markets,* ed. Marcus Breen. Proceedings of a CIRCIT Conference. Melbourne: Centre for International Research on Communication and Information Technologies.

Wildman, Steven, and Stephen Siwek. 1988. *International Trade in Films and Television Programs.* Cambridge, Mass.: American Enterprise Institute/Ballinger Publications.

Wilkinson, Kenton. 1992. Southern Exposure: U.S. Cable Programmers and Spanish-Language Networks Enter Latin America. Paper presented at International Association for Mass Communication Research, XVIII Conference, São Paulo.

Part Two

Dominance and Resistance

3

Television and Film in a Freer International Trade Environment: U.S. Dominance and Canadian Responses

COLIN HOSKINS, ADAM FINN, AND STUART MCFADYEN

IN THIS PAPER WE BEGIN by considering the international trade environment in television and film, international trade flows, and the treatment of cultural industries under the FTA, NAFTA, and GATT. We identify important trade issues arising from negotiation of these international agreements and, after examining the characteristics of television and film that are relevant to trade, analyze these issues. The implications for Canadian public policy and the competitive strategy of Canadian corporations are then examined.

▪ ▪ The International Trade Environment

A major change in the international television environment in the last decade or so has been the transformation from a situation of spectrum scarcity to one of program scarcity. This has been due to innovations in distribution and compression technology which permit expansion of channel capacity and the coincident political acceptance that some degree of deregulation is desirable on efficiency and choice grounds. In Western Europe in the early 1980s, only the U.K. and Italy had commercial television; now the commercial sector dominates there. A similar change appears to be under way in Asia. The consequence is a growing international demand at the same time as traditional domestic buyers are suffering from audience fragmentation and a decreased ability to pay as much as they have previously paid for programming.

The pattern of feature-film release has been transformed during the last twenty years. Pay-per-view, movie pay-channel, and video have been added to the theatrical release and broadcast television exhibition windows. One of these new windows, video, now generates more revenue than theatrical box office.

Another significant change has been the emergence of vertically integrated media conglomerates. These conglomerates are able to control film and TV program libraries to exploit program shortages and ensure availability of software for hardware innovations, and to benefit from economies of scale or scope. Videotron provides an interesting Canadian exemplar (see Tremblay and Lacroix 1991).

▪ ▪ International Trade Flows

Although official government statistics are often unreliable or nonexistent, several research studies have tracked trade flows (see, e.g., Varis 1974, 1984; Larson 1990) and have clearly established that the United States dominates a very extensive trade. The United States accounts for at least 75% of all television program exports and the current account trade balance of the broader U.S. entertainment industry is second only to that of aerospace. U.S. features generate more gross box office abroad than at home. For audiovisual products alone, in 1992 the United States enjoyed a surplus with the European Union (EU) of $3.4 billion[1] (of which about 45% was attributable to TV programs, 32% to video, and 23% to theatrical movie releases), an increase of $1.4 billion since 1989 (IDATE estimates). Most of this jump is due to increased U.S. exports of television programs to new channels, such as the satellite channel BSkyB in the U.K. (Godard 1993, pp. 14–17). Although there was little change in U.S. theatrical film receipts between 1989 and 1992, it is reported that the U.S. share of the French box office has doubled in the last ten years to 60%. Paul Kennedy (1988) argues that the United States is a declining great power, but there is no evidence of this in the audiovisual sector.

Canada is a minor player in this league. Exports of Canadian cultural industries amount to about $280 million (Government of Canada 1993, p. 34) and Canada is a substantial net importer. Canadian television programs are increasingly finding export markets and Canada is a significant player in the expanding international co-production mode. Canadian feature films, particularly English-language ones, have rarely made an impression abroad (the English-language movies rarely make an impression in the Canadian domestic market, either).

In addition to official trade there is also cross-border reception of television signals. In the case of Canada and the United States this has, in most cases, been unintentional, the exceptions being a few U.S. border stations, such as that in Bellingham, Washington, targeted at a Canadian market. Even though largely unintentional, the effects have been significant, as U.S. stations attract around 15% of the Canadian English-language market. Winners include Canadian cable systems that have attracted subscribers by further distributing these signals (although as a consequence of the 1988 FTA they have recently begun to pay a royalty) and some PBS stations near the U.S. border with Canada that attract significant donations from Canadian viewers (KSPS [Spokane, Washington] attracts over half of its donations from Alberta). Losers have been the Canadian broadcasters and cable channels that have had to compete for viewers against these U.S. signals. They have raised the alarm against the next generation of cross-border signal delivery—U.S. direct broadcasting satellite (DBS) services to be marketed in Canada.

▪ ▪ The FTA, NAFTA, and GATT and Some Trade Issues Arising

Exemptions for Cultural Industries

Trade in cultural products has long been controversial. Canada succeeded in exempting cultural industries from the Free Trade Agreement (FTA), although a "notwithstanding" clause was included which permits the United States to take countermeasures of equivalent commercial effect if Canada introduces a cultural measure that would (but for the exemption) be inconsistent with the provisions of the FTA. Canada successfully fought to maintain this exemption under NAFTA, "to prevent the cultural standardization of content and the complete foreign control of distribution" (Government of Canada 1993, p. 33).

The importance of trade issues related to cultural industries became particularly apparent in the closing stages of the Uruguay round of GATT. Contrary to expectations, the item that came closest to causing the Uruguay round to fail was not trade in agriculture but trade in cultural goods. At the last moment the United States acceded to EU (effectively French) demands that culture be exempted. There are reports that Canadian officials advised French officials behind the scenes and there is no doubt that the Canadian precedent was exploited (Conlogue 1993, p. A12). As Le Monde is quoted as asking, "Why refuse the Europeans what one has already accorded the Canadians?" (quoted by Ross 1993, p. B1).

Thus, although we are in a freer trade environment, no officially negotiated move to freer trade in cultural goods has taken place, to the chagrin of the United States. The big increase in the trade of audiovisual products that has occurred has instead been related to the technological innovations and partial deregulation noted earlier.

Trade Issues Arising

The debates over trade in cultural goods associated with the FTA, NAFTA, and GATT have raised three important issues: Are products of the cultural industries merely entertainment goods? Is the United States guilty of dumping? And why does the United States dominate?

With respect to the first issue, there is a fundamental difference in philosophy between the United States, which regards cultural industries as entertainment industries producing a commercial product no different from any other, and most other countries, that regard the products of cultural industries as essential to the preservation of distinctive values and hence to the well-being of the nation-state.

French negotiators at the GATT talks accused the United States of dumping television programs and movies and hence of practicing unfair price competition. Such an allegation has been made before by Schiller (1969) and others. Dumping is usually defined as selling in a foreign market at a price below that in the domestic market or below production cost. When queried about the French accusations, Gordon Ritchie, who negotiated the cultural exemption clause on behalf of Canada in the FTA, said that the application of dumping to cultural goods is a new development, but that "the dumping argument is one I would muster" (as quoted by Conlogue 1993).

In explaining why the United States dominates trade in audiovisual products, the French negotiators at the GATT talks are reported to have stressed the significance of nontariff barriers to the U.S. market. In an open letter dated October 29, 1993 and sent to U.S. directors Martin Scorsese and Steven Spielberg, a group of European directors wrote, "Ask yourself who is really 'closing the frontiers' and who is truly 'not welcome' in the other's country. . . . do you seriously think that our European films are so bad that they reach only one per cent of the American public?" The complaints about access to the U.S. market seem to take two tacks. One is that the alleged aversion of U.S. viewers to dubbing is just an excuse and that the United States has never given dubbing a chance or attempted to make it work. French stars often dub U.S. films, adding to their box-office appeal, and Jean-Marie Poiré, director of the recent French hit *Les Visiteurs,* asks, "Why don't we see great American actors (doing the dubbing)? Why not Dustin Hoffman or Tom Cruise?" The other tack is a conspiracy theory. Alain Terzian, producer of *Les Visiteurs,* states, "The truth of the matter is that the cartel of large American (film) companies has no desire to see French films succeed in the U.S. market" (quoted by Conlogue 1993). The specific complaint of the director and producer of *Les Visiteurs* is that their U.S. distributor, Miramax, is resisting demands for the simultaneous release of the film in 200 U.S. theaters.

We will analyze these issues after laying the groundwork by examining some characteristics of television programs and film that are relevant to trade.

▪ ▪ Characteristics of Television and Film Relevant to Trade

Audiovisual products have several unusual characteristics: there may be external benefits associated with consumption, the incremental costs associated with increasing supply to reach additional markets is very low, and there is a cultural discount associated with exporting. An understanding of these characteristics is necessary not only to an analysis of trade issues but also to a consideration of appropriate public policies and competitive strategies.

External Benefit

In economic terminology an externality is a cost or a benefit arising from an economic transaction that falls on a third party and that is not taken into account by those party to the transaction. External costs, in the form of pollution and associated environmental problems, are quite common, but external benefits are less so. The issue in the philosophical debate between the United States and most other countries is whether or not external benefits are associated with cultural goods. For a given television program or film to be adjudged as providing an external benefit, viewers must bring benefits to others through social interaction. In effect, consumption of a cultural good must be similar in this regard to education, a product that is commonly agreed to meet this criterion.

Low Incremental Cost of Supply

Television programming is essentially a "public good," as the cost of supplying is largely unaffected by the number of viewers. In a given broadcast or cable market, an additional viewer for a television program has no effect on cost. Viewers are not rivals in consumption, as viewing by one consumer does not use up the product (as a consequence, it is sometimes described as a joint-consumption good), nor does it detract from the experience enjoyed by other viewers. Even when an extra copy of the program is necessary to reach viewers in other markets, the cost of replication is insignificant compared with the original production cost.

With respect to theatrical distribution of a feature film, the cost of supplying a "print" is, similarly, unaffected by the number of people in the theater, the same print can be used later by other theaters, and the cost of supplying additional prints to reach other markets is low. Even though a video of a film or television program is not a public good, the incremental cost of another copy is again very low relative to the original production cost.

This cost structure, which permits access to additional markets at very low incremental cost, makes international trade particularly attractive. An export sale is worthwhile at any price that covers this incremental cost.

Cultural Discount

In most countries television viewers prefer to watch domestic programs when given the choice (see Berwanger 1987). As Hoskins and Mirus (1988) explain, a particular program rooted in one culture, and thus attractive in that environment, will have diminished appeal elsewhere, as viewers find it difficult to identify with the styles, values, beliefs, institutions, and behavioral patterns of the material in question. If the program is produced in another language its appeal will likely be further reduced by dubbing or subtitling. Even if the language is the same, accents or idioms may still cause problems. Hoskins and Mirus denoted the consequent reduction in the value of a foreign program, which will be reflected in the price the broadcaster is willing to pay, as the "cultural discount." The concept applies equally to feature films and videos.

The cultural discount tends to reduce the value of trade. U.S. or Canadian consumers are typically indifferent to the origin of their VCR—no characteristic of the product is likely to provide a clue to its Japanese origin (in recent years this is usually even true of the accompanying instruction booklet). The same would certainly not apply to a Japanese television program or movie.

The extent of the cultural discount varies with the genre and thus explains why trade is concentrated in a few categories. Action drama typically hurdles cultural barriers (including those of language) relatively unscathed and it is not surprising to find that it is the most traded television program type (see Chapman 1987). Consistent with this is the prevalence of action movies in the theaters. Situation comedy, on the other hand, does not export as well, since national tastes in humor differ and language subtleties are lost in translation. Indeed, so great is the discount that sometimes the format of the program, rather than the program itself, is exported. For example, Thames Television's "Man about the House" in the U.K. was developed into "Three's Company" in the United States. Not surprisingly, very few of the Canadians tuned to U.S. stations are watching U.S. network or local news although the success of CNN and the BBC World Service has demonstrated that a significant global market segment is willing to watch foreign-based international news.

As we will explain later, the cultural-discount concept is the key to explaining the competitive advantage conferred by market size. Also, any country that manages to minimize the discount for its exports, or that applies a particularly large discount to imports, has a trade advantage.

▪ ▪ Examination of Trade Issues

Are Cultural Goods Merely Entertainment Goods?

Pure entertainment goods would not result in external benefits. Are television programming and film merely entertainment goods or do viewers bring benefits to others through social interaction? For illustrative purposes we examine this question from a Canadian perspective. Canadian drama programming and feature films may provide external benefits in the form of an increased sense of Canadian identity and greater awareness of Canadian themes and values. Current affairs and news programming and documentary programs or films may promote a population more informed on Canadian institutions, events, and issues as well as a Canadian perspective on foreign affairs. The crucial question is whether the content of audiovisual products affects social behavior (the current debate on violence indicates a common belief that it does). The belief that indigenous programming and films possessing desirable attributes can make viewers better citizens is at the heart of the "cultural" argument. We tend to believe that this is the case, although we consider that the case is often exaggerated.

If cultural goods do provide external benefits, there is market failure because program and film producers, distributors, and exhibitors do not receive any compensation for the provision of such external consumption benefits. Government intervention is thus justified to the extent that it compensates for this failure.

Is the United States Guilty of Dumping?

Taken at face value it would seem that allegations of U.S. dumping are justified, as programs are certainly sold below production cost. The U.S. production cost of an hour of drama programming is some $1.2 million, but such a program is sold to the Caribbean island of Aruba for a mere $80–$100, to the Canadian Broadcasting Company (CBC) or CTV networks in Canada for $10,000–$60,000, and to the BBC or ITV in the U.K. for $20,000–$100,000 ("The Global TV Program Price Guide" 1992). However, we would argue that the relevant reference cost is not the production cost of the original but the incremental cost of supplying the additional market. For most traded products this is not an important distinction, but for audiovisual products it is crucial. The production cost quoted is always for the "first copy," but the relevant cost is the low replication cost (for some small markets, such as those in the Caribbean, even this is avoided by "bicycling" the same copy from market to market) plus the distribution cost. We know of no evidence that the United States sells in any export market at a price below the incremental cost of supplying that market.

If the United States is not guilty of selling below cost, is it guilty of exporting at prices below its own domestic price? A U.S. network pays around $800,000 for an hour of U.S. drama programming. The highest export price charged (typically to a U.K. network) for the same program will be about one-eighth of this. Hoskins, Mirus, and Rozeboom (1989) developed a quasi-public good model for explaining the price of U.S. television programs on the international market and found that prices could be explained solely in terms of demand characteristics, such as number of TV sets, gross national product (GNP), language, and presence of buyer competition. The fact that the U.S. market is much the largest and wealthiest of the world's TV markets thus explains the higher U.S. domestic prices.

To summarize, we consider that the allegation of dumping on the basis of selling below cost is misguided, as it is based on the wrong reference cost. The case for dumping based on selling in export markets at prices below that charged in the domestic market is more soundly based.

However, if the United States is guilty of dumping audiovisual products, so are its competitors. The U.K., France, Italy, Brazil, and others all sell to most export markets at prices below that in their domestic market. Given the cultural discount, this is to be expected unless the foreign market is significantly bigger and richer. We thus find the allegation of dumping to be largely meaningless in the context of quasi-public goods. However, we do not deny that the low prices of imported programming make it difficult for indigenous programming to compete.

Why Does the United States Dominate?

In this section we examine the reasons for U.S. dominance of the audiovisual sector and consider whether nontrade barriers are as significant as they are alleged to be. Our explanation is based on Hoskins and Mirus (1988) and Hoskins and McFadyen (1991b).

THE LARGEST DOMESTIC MARKET

Because of the cultural discount associated with imported television programs and movies, U.S. producers are in a superior position to supply the U.S. market, a market large enough to enable them to recover a substantial proportion of production cost. In 1990 the United States had 203 million television receivers, distantly followed by the former Soviet Union with 95 million and Japan with 77 million (UNESCO 1992); comparable numbers for Canada and Mexico are 13 million and 12 million, respectively. Thus the size of the U.S. market provides U.S. producers with the solid domestic base from which to pursue foreign sales.

A numerical example illustrates the interaction between cultural discount and market size and the consequent competitive advantage bestowed by having the largest domestic market. Assume a two-country world comprised of the United States and Canada, with the U.S. market being eleven times larger than the Canadian. Suppose it costs $1.15 million to produce comparable one-hour drama programs in both countries and that in the absence of a cultural discount both programs could recover $1.1 million in the U.S. market and $100,000 in the smaller Canadian market. If there were no cultural discount, no advantage would be conferred upon the United States by its larger market (in effect, this is the situation with a culture-free product such as a VCR). However, if a cultural discount of, say, 25% applies to trade in both directions, the revenue earned by the two producers would be as follows:

U.S. producer: $1,100,000 + (1 − 0.25) 100,000 = $1,175,000
Canadian producer: $100,000 + (1 − 0.25) 1,100,000 = $925,000

Assuming the cost of reproduction for export to be insignificant, the U.S. production would make a profit of $25,000, while the Canadian producer would make a loss of $225,000. Domestic market size is important: only the U.S. program would get made.

PRODUCES IN ENGLISH

U.S. sales are facilitated by the fact that U.S. TV programs and feature films are produced in English. The GNP of the English-language market is several times that of the Japanese- or German-language markets, the next largest language markets. Language is an important component of the cultural discount and hence English-language producers enjoy a lower discount when accessing other English-language national markets. In addition, English is the world's major second language and hence English-language productions are often more acceptable than other foreign-language productions in non-English-language markets.

Of course, U.S. producers are not the only ones with the advantage of producing in English. Collins (1989) argues that the U.K. and Australia are, given their domestic market size, relatively successful. Historically this has not been true of Canada, although recently there has been evidence that this is changing in television, though not in film. Wildman and Siwek (1988) consider language so important that in their model of trade in film and television programs, they define markets by language rather than by political boundaries.

CHARACTERISTICS OF THE U.S. INDUSTRY AND MARKET

The U.S. television and film industry is a competitive industry based on the Hollywood studios. In the case of television programs, they are sold to U.S. networks, sophisticated and demanding buyers who, in the early 1980s, had $40 million riding on a single ratings point (Gitlin 1983). These characteristics are consistent with those that Porter (1990) suggests provide a desirable global platform. It should not be surprising that many programs that are successful in the competitive, polyglot U.S. domestic market have also been successful in the world market, where, until recently, much of the competition has been from in-house production by public broadcast monopolies. In effect, "the format and type of drama originated by the American entertainment industry have in the most recent era created a new universal art form which is claiming something close to a worldwide audience" (Meisel 1986). Hence U.S. programs and films enjoy a relatively small cultural discount in most foreign markets.

Another feature of the U.S. domestic market is the very high cultural discount applied to foreign films and programs. The evidence suggests that U.S. viewers are unusually insular and intolerant of foreign programming or films, perhaps partially because historically they have been exposed to very little. Renaud and Litman (1985) report that not only will U.S. viewers not accept dubbing or subtitling, they are also averse to British accents. The fact that audiences for those foreign movies that do get theatrical exhibition in the United States are so limited suggests that this characteristic of the U.S. market is real and is not simply used as an excuse to keep out foreign films.

THE HOLLYWOOD SYSTEM

The United States has enjoyed first-mover advantages in television production largely as a result of economies of scope (synergies) with the Hollywood movie industry. The movie industry provided an infrastructure of skilled technicians and actors, a worldwide distribution system, and the Hollywood "star" system. The United States was the first country to switch from live television drama to film (an innovation that made export possible in a pre-satellite era) and the first to move from an artisanal mode of production where products are strongly marked by an authorial signature, whether that of director or scriptwriter, to series production in which it hardly makes sense to ask who is the author of, for example, "Dallas" (Collins, Garnham, and Locksley 1988, p. 56).

In film, the star system and the huge promotion budgets have helped the United States maintain dominance of movies produced for theatrical exhibition. Success in the cinema has fueled demand for the same U.S. films in the video, pay-TV, and broadcast television markets. The significance of large promotion budgets has been enhanced by a change in exhibition pattern away from a gradual rollout, beginning in a few key markets, to a blanket exhibition strategy. This new strategy makes it difficult for non-U.S. films to stay in the cinema long enough for word-of-mouth promotion, which tends to be more important for these films, to be effective.

MARKET POWER AND CONTROL OF DISTRIBUTION

In some countries U.S. domination of distribution is claimed to be a major factor contributing to the prevalence of U.S. movies in domestic theaters. In the case of Canada, a particular bone of contention is the bundling of the Canadian market together with the U.S. market in the North American rights for distribution of independently produced foreign films. Given the relative size of the U.S. and Canadian markets, U.S. distributors, who likely have greater expertise and knowledge with respect to their domestic market, have an advantage over Canadian distributors when competing for North American rights.

The National Film and Video Product Bill, which was introduced into the Canadian Parliament in 1987, proposed separating Canadian from U.S. distribution rights for independently produced foreign films; under U.S. pressure, however, it was first watered down and then allowed to lapse. Although culture was exempted from the FTA, it is widely believed that the demise of the bill was related to those negotiations. However, even if inclusion of Canadian rights in North American rights has hindered development of a Canadian-owned distribution industry, it does not follow that Canadian films are disadvantaged. Harcourt (1989, p. 81) expresses the predominant view that Canadian films have not done well because they were released within an economic infrastructure controlled by American interests and designed to favor the American product. However, this contention has not gone unchallenged. Globerman (1991, p. 191) argues that foreign (U.S.) film distributors act in an efficient and competitive fashion, with no bias against distributing commercially promising Canadian films.

A similarly based argument is the contention, made at the GATT negotiations, that there is a conspiracy among the major U.S. players to keep foreign films out of the U.S. market. While it may be true that the United States has not gone out of its way to increase film imports, we know of no reason why, if profitable opportunities to distribute and exhibit foreign films exist, independent distributors would fail to exploit them. Conspiracy is unlikely under competitive conditions and Globerman and Vining (1987) find evidence of quite aggressive rivalry among the majors in the form of substantial year-to-year variations in market share and in the form of profit margins only slightly higher than those for smaller distributors.

SIGNIFICANCE OF NONTRADE BARRIERS

We consider that U.S. dominance of trade in audiovisual products is attributable to its domestic market size, use of the world's main language, characteristics of its domestic market and industry that make it an ideal global platform, and exploitation of the star system. Evidence is weak that a U.S. conspiracy or U.S. control of distribution excludes foreign products from the U.S. market or limits the access of producers in other countries to their own market. In addition, this argument only applies to theatrical exhibition of movies and can in no way explain U.S. dominance in trade in television programs. U.S. viewers' reluctance to watch dubbed, subtitled, or even non–North American English films or programs is a problem, but not one for which the U.S. industry is responsible or where accusations of unfair trading practices make sense.

▪ ▪ Canadian Public Policy

Approximately 75% of Canadian viewing of television programming and 95% of Canadian viewing of movies in theaters is devoted to U.S. productions. In this section we examine the public policy responses, both in terms of regulation and subsidies, that have been followed and comment on their effectiveness and appropriateness. With respect to broadcasting, we have recently addressed this issue elsewhere (Hoskins and McFadyen 1994), and much of the remainder of the section is based on that study. Although it is presented in the Canadian context, we consider much of the discussion and many of the recommendations to be widely applicable. However, before we can assess public policy we must first examine the rationale for government intervention.

Rationale for Government Intervention

As noted earlier, where audiovisual goods do provide external benefits, there is market failure because producers, distributors, and exhibitors do not receive any compensation for the provision of such benefits. Government intervention is thus justified to the extent that it provides this compensation or has an effect of equivalent value.

Other rationales are often put forward for intervention. One put forward with respect to television is that because of spectrum scarcity and advertiser financing, "collective provision and regulation of programmes does provide a better simulation of a market designed to reflect consumer preferences than a policy of laissez-faire" (Peacock Committee 1986, p. 133). While not disputing the historical validity of this argument, we believe that technological developments are rapidly overcoming impediments to effective competition.

The infant-industry argument is another justification sometimes given for intervention. The argument is that the television and film production industry needs protection while it is young and vulnerable. Only if given this protection will it grow into a mature, internationally competitive industry. The essence of this argument is that the protection should be temporary and withdrawn once the industry has matured. We do not consider that this rationale can justify Canadian government intervention today, since this is no longer an infant industry in Canada.

Government support is sometimes justified on the grounds of economic development and creating employment. We are opposed to this rationale on philosophical grounds, but note that Canada's deficit and debt problems make such an argument particularly weak. We suspect that the industry lobby, which has most to gain from government support, often has this in mind even when couching its arguments in cultural terms.

In summary, we consider the external-benefits argument to be the only one justifying government intervention at this time. Even in this case, intervention should only compensate for these benefits. Indigenous programming that does not provide external benefits should not get preferential treatment.

The Experience with Regulation

Television broadcasting has been subject to extensive regulation, but theatrical exhibition of feature films has not. However, Canadian feature films are also affected by broadcasting regulations, as much of their revenue is earned through pay-TV and commercial broadcast exhibition. In fact many Canadian feature films are never released theatrically.

The primary vehicle for promoting Canadian programming has been via the CRTC's Canadian content regulations. These require private broadcast stations to show 60% Canadian programming on a full-day basis and 50% (60% for CBC) on a prime-time basis (6 P.M. to midnight), averaged over a year. The spirit of these regulations has regularly been thwarted by bunching Canadian programming in the early or late evening (thus leaving the peak period for audience-maximizing U.S. programs) and the summer off-season, and producing low-cost programming to minimize the possible loss from satisfying the Canadian-content quota.

A common theme of a number of regulations has been protection of Canadian broadcasters. Thus we find that a new Canadian station is given a broadcast license only if it can be demonstrated that the market can absorb a new station without financial harm to incumbents. The CRTC gives local Canadian broadcasters priority carriage on the basic cable tier, while cable's carriage of U.S. channels is strictly regulated. Bill C-58 discourages placement of advertising aimed at Canadians on U.S. border stations (by denying tax deductibility). Simultaneous substitution requires a cable company to substitute the Canadian signal (including commercial messages) for the U.S. signal when both are showing the same U.S. program.

The Experience with Subsidies

One subsidy approach involves parliamentary appropriations to a public broadcaster and public film producer. We have estimated that the annual direct subsidy to CBC mainline television services amounts to some $530 million (Hoskins and McFadyen 1992). However, the CBC also benefits, in the form of reduced license exhibition fees, from Telefilm Canada subsidization of much of the independently produced Canadian programming it exhibits. The National Film Board receives an annual appropriation of around $64 million, primarily for film production and distribution.

An indirect subsidy approach adopted has been to fund Telefilm Canada, a government agency created in 1983. Telefilm Canada invests on a project-by-project basis in television programming and feature films. In the financial year 1992–1993 it received a parliamentary appropriation of $116 million (Telefilm Canada 1993) and invested $102 million in television programming and feature films. This investment is a subsidy in the sense that Telefilm only recoups a fraction of its investment (about 14%) and allows its investment to be subordinate to that of other investors.

Through its Canadian Broadcast Development Fund, Telefilm committed to investing $53 million in eighty television program projects during the financial year 1992–1993 (*Telefilm Annual Report* 1992–1993). This investment comprised 33% of the projects' budgets. The fund is confined to investment in drama, children's programming, variety, and documentaries made by private Canadian production companies. To be eligible, producers must obtain a letter of intent from a broadcaster, pay-TV, or specialty channel to exhibit within two years of completion, and the program must qualify as Canadian. It is difficult to know how many of these television projects would have gone ahead in the absence of the Telefilm investment, but a comparison between the current fairly healthy independent production industry and the almost nonexistent one in 1983 suggests that the impact of Telefilm Canada has been substantial. NGL Consulting, in a 1992 study undertaken for Telefilm, claims that "the Fund has virtually created an independent supply system."

Through its Feature Film Fund, Telefilm Canada invested $19 million in 23 feature films in 1992–1993, an average of 36% of the total production budgets for these films. When other government sources of funding (the National Film Board, provincial government funding agencies, and the Quebec Tax Credit) are included, we find that the public sector contributed more than 80% of the funding of French-language features and over 60% of the funding of English-language features. Even these figures understate the case, however, as they "do not take account of Telefilm Canada's participation in minimum guarantees paid by Canadian distributors, which also contribute to production financing" (Telefilm Canada 1993, p. 31). In contrast, external private investors contributed about $1.5 million, a mere 3% of the total.

The Feature Film Distribution Fund was launched in 1988 with the long-term goal of "reinforcing the sector by encouraging a consolidation of companies and improving cooperation between distributors and producers, and thus to ensure a more effective marketing of Canadian films, especially to commercial movie theatres." In 1992–1993, fifteen Canadian distributors received a total of $11 million from the fund. Of this, 74% was spent on minimum guarantees for Canadian films to acquire distribution rights and 17% was spent on marketing Canadian films.

Recommendations Regarding Canadian Public Policy toward Television

1.   Deregulate broadcasting.

Canadian content rules classify a program as qualifying if it scores six points or more on a ten-point scale based on the nationality of the inputs. However, external benefits can only result if the program produced is distinctly Canadian. Some Canadian drama, *Top Cops* being a recent example, certainly does not qualify; in some instances the program's Canadian origin is deliberately obscured in the hope of facilitating a U.S. sale.

Regulations that protect Canadian broadcasters seem to be based on the naive belief that if, as a consequence of protection, broadcasters are very profitable, these profits will be spent on Canadian programming. We know of no evidence that this is the case, and indeed it would be inconsistent with the economic incentives that favor exhibition of U.S. programming. We consider that such protection is best explained by the capture theory of regulation, which argues that the regulator is "captured" by the industry and that its regulations protect the interests of the regulated industry rather than those of the public (Stigler 1971).

We thus consider that regulation has largely been ineffective in promoting Canadian programming consistent with an external-benefits rationale. Even if such regulation had been successful in the past, it would become increasingly irrelevant as new delivery technologies, in conjunction with digital compression, bypass the regulatory process. In the U.K. the Peacock Committee (1986, p. 124) made the analogy of King Canute trying to control the waves. Technology permits distant television signals to be delivered by satellite or by telecom, while video can also deliver programs (BBC Video World, a compilation of programs shown in the U.K., is express delivered in this way). Regulation is powerless against video delivery and seems destined to be impotent against DBS delivery. Given its past ineffectiveness and increasing irrelevance, we advocate deregulation of private broadcasting and signal delivery.

2. Maintain subsidies to Canadian programming through Telefilm Canada.

A deregulated television broadcasting sector would still have a place for Canadian programming. Canadians will always demand national and local news and current affairs. As television becomes more transactional, through pay-per-channel and pay-per-view, it will become increasingly economic to target niche markets for Canadian programming. However, if the external-benefits argument is accepted, the availability and reach of Canadian programming should nevertheless be extended through subsidy. As an externality can occur only if the program is watched, ideally it is the viewing of the program that should be subsidized. As this currently appears to be impractical, the best alternative is to continue a direct subsidy to production through Telefilm Canada. The externalities argument would suggest, though, that the emphasis for eligibility should be changed from the nationality of the inputs to the nature of the resulting program. Eligibility should depend on the "Canadianness" and likely audience appeal of the program.

3. Revise and reduce the role of the CBC.

The current CBC subsidy is not cost-effective. However, some continuing role is justified, as the Telefilm investment approach is not suited to the provision of programming with a short lead time, such as news magazines and current affairs. In addition, it is prudent not to put all the nation's eggs in one basket. We have recently expanded on the appropriate role and structure of the CBC elsewhere (Hoskins and McFadyen 1992), and will highlight a few of the conclusions we reached:

The CBC should concentrate on distinctive Canadian programming (that, in the absence of a public broadcaster, would not be exhibited) consistent with the externalities rationale and deliver this programming nationally as efficiently as possible. Except for news and current affairs, programming should be bought from independents. Program exchanges between the English and French networks should be increased in the hope that this will improve understanding and tolerance. The CBC should withdraw from programming areas plentifully supplied by the private sector, as the incremental external benefit of additional programs in such areas will be low (this follows from the economic law of diminishing marginal utility). As well as sports and foreign programming, this includes locally produced programming for a local audience; consequently, the nationwide infrastructure of owned-and-operated stations is not needed.

Recommendations Regarding Canadian Feature Films

While we have examined broadcast policy issues for many years, we have only recently begun to consider feature-film policy, beginning with an examination of distribution issues and an analysis of determinants of film performance. Thus these "recommendations" are tentative and indicate preliminary views rather than firm conclusions on the directions policy should take.

1.   Reconsider improving access to rights and financial support to distribution.

The National Film and Video Product Bill, which would have required international film producers to give Canadian distributors the right to bid for separate Canadian distribution rights for films not being distributed by their original producer or a company with world rights, can be supported on grounds of "leveling the playing field" (passage of such distribution legislation would mean that the United States could invoke the "notwithstanding" clause under the 1988 FTA). It would certainly improve the access of Canadian distributors to independently produced foreign films and may stimulate the distribution sector. But we do not believe this will be a panacea for the Canadian feature-film industry. Globerman (1991) argues that it is not distribution and access to theaters that is the problem, but rather the nature of the Canadian films themselves. A comparative study of the performance characteristics of Canadian, Australian, British, and U.S. movies found considerable support for this contention, as Canadian movies consistently received the lowest critical acclaim (Finn, Hoskins, and McFadyen 1993a).

The Feature Film Distribution Fund appears to have been intro-duced as a consolation prize after the demise of the National Film and Video Product Bill. It appears to have doubtful merit because little in-centive is provided to promote and market the film aggressively to try to ensure the movie is a box-office success. Posner (1993) reports: "As of July 1993, three-quarters of the distributor's advance for a Canadian fea-ture is covered by Telefilm's Distribution Fund, using taxpayer money; the distributor is therefore at risk for only 25 percent, which is normally recouped through sales of video rights and broadcast licenses" (p. xvi). Ellis (1992, pp. 101–102) reports an estimate, based on *Statistics Canada* data, that only 5% of distributors' revenues on Canadian films are de-rived from their performance at the box office.

2. Reconsider the effectiveness of production subsidies.

While the Feature Film Fund, in conjunction with the Feature Film Distribution Fund, has had some success in inducing production of films, many of these films do not obtain theatrical exhibition and, when they do, the box office is often disappointing. Only two English-language Canadian movies have exceeded $800,000 (Ellis 1992, p. 100). External private investors would be willing to contribute more than 3% of the total budget if the films being produced were considered com-mercially attractive. Again we have the impression that an incentive problem has been created where movies are produced for fees rather than profits. There is little financial risk or reward. As one producer we recently interviewed put it, "We have developed a mentality of how to get our film financed instead of how to get our film seen." External benefits can only result from viewing of Canadian films. With Canadian films obtaining only a 3% share of the Canadian box office, it is difficult to believe that the external benefits from theatrical exhibition can justify the extent of public sector financing received.

In addition, the Telefilm funding may be distorting the type of film produced. In interviews with several producers and distributors there seemed to be a commonly held view that Telefilm encourages pro-duction of art-house style movies rather than those reflecting popular Canadian culture. It is noteworthy that the largely unsubsidized U.K. feature-film industry has recently sired such commercial and artistic successes as *The Remains of the Day, The Crying Game,* and *Four Wed-dings and a Funeral* and enjoyed a record surplus of £131 million in 1992 (Godard 1993).

Even if a subsidy is justified, it is not clear that a production subsidy is the optimal approach. The externalities rationale suggests it should be consumption of the product, rather than its production, that is subsidized. One possibility would be to make vouchers or coupons available for Canadian movies judged likely to result in external benefits. A decade ago the Ontario government did try a scheme like this—losing lottery tickets became $1-off coupons for Canadian movies or books. However, most industry participants we interviewed are dubious about this approach, doubting whether the demand for movies is sensitive to relative prices. They argue that going to the movies is an entertainment event and that often the price of admission is a small proportion of the total evening's expense, that might include such items as baby-sitting costs. An alternative would be to subsidize exhibition of domestic films. For example, the exhibitor could receive $2 for each person attending a Canadian movie. It would be up to the exhibitor whether some or all of this were passed on to the theatergoer in the form of lower prices for qualifying films. The advantage of this approach is that there is an inducement to produce and promote films that will be seen. A variant, and one that has been employed at various times and in various places, is to tax foreign-film box office. This could be considered an alternative or else could be combined with a subsidy for Canadian films.

Ellis (1992) makes a convincing case that the emphasis on the theatrical distribution and exhibition of Canadian films is misplaced. His case is based on a comparison of the sizes of audiences reached in the various exhibition windows. Using NGL estimates, a Canadian movie attracting 30,000 in cinema attendance would attract about 100,000 on pay-per-channel TV (although pay-TV is found only in 10% of Canadian cable homes), about 150,000 on home video, and 1 million on broadcast television (two showings of 500,000 each). Ellis goes on to argue that the discrepancy between cinema and other audiences is likely to grow as cinema attendance continues to fall (in Canada it fell 22% during the 1980s), as pay-per-view becomes established, and as non-broadcast technologies continue to develop.

One factor that Ellis fails to consider is the extent to which theatrical exhibition, and the marketing and publicity surrounding it, create a demand for the film in later exhibition windows. But it is noteworthy that made-for-TV movies or miniseries often do very well on broadcast television without this boost—in fact, they usually do better than movies that have previously been released theatrically. English-language Cana-

dian miniseries typically attract over one million viewers for a first showing on network television (Ellis 1992, pp. 100–101).

▪ ▪ Competitive Strategies for Canadian Producers

Porter (1985) contends that firms should select a well-defined
"competitive strategy" in order to achieve "competitive advantage" that
will permit sustained superior profitability. Three generic strategies are
available: cost leadership, differentiation, and focus. Through a cost-
leadership strategy a firm tries to achieve superior price-cost margins by
providing basic products, with similar features to those of rivals, at less
cost. Through a differentiation strategy a firm tries to achieve superior
price-cost margins by providing product attributes that increase the
value to the customer (and hence the price that can be charged) more
than the cost to the producer. A focus strategy is a cost-leadership or
differentiation strategy applied to a segment of the market rather than to
a broad product line.

In this section we examine the cost-leadership, differentiation, and
focus strategies available to Canadian television and film producers. We
also examine a particular mode of production—that of international co-
production or co-venture—that is increasingly being used to pursue
these strategies.

Cost-Leadership Strategy

To be successful in competing directly against U.S. producers by
making program or film types that they supply adequately, some comparative advantage is necessary. For much of the 1980s, with a cheap
Canadian dollar and a skilled workforce that did not have the restrictive
work practices of Hollywood, Canadian producers could produce action-
adventure drama considerably more cheaply than U.S. producers. Much
of that advantage was lost in the late 1980s and early 1990s with the
Canadian dollar worth U.S. $0.85, but it has recently been regained with
the fall back to the $0.70–$0.75 range.

English Canada is close to the United States in terms of popular
culture, topography, architecture, and, perhaps most important of all, a
North American accent that in most cases is virtually indistinguishable
from that of neighboring U.S. states. Canadian producers have exploited
this situation by producing American-style drama (similar value) at less

cost. An early example, in the mid-1980s, was *Night Heat,* which was pre-sold to CBS. The story line was American, Toronto was made to look like any big U.S. city, and differences between Canadian and U.S. legal systems were blurred. Most U.S. viewers probably did not realize they were watching a foreign production. *Night Heat* was produced for about $650,000 an hour and shown on the 11:00 P.M. late-evening time slot, a time when the potential audience is insufficient to justify the $1 million-plus budget associated with making a U.S. drama. To ensure a comparable product, a marketing approach was adopted by involving the U.S. buyer at all stages of development and production.

This unique ability to produce programs that are similar to those of the country with the largest domestic market and the dominant world exporter makes Canadian producers ideal co-production partners for producers in countries such as France who want to access the U.S. market. French producers state approvingly that "Canada adds a modern air" and "the flavour is North American" (Sherman 1987, p. 14). While wanting this North American flavor, French producers are reluctant to partner U.S. producers because such co-ventures do not qualify as treaty co-productions and are looked upon as unequal, with the French partner having little control (Hoskins and McFadyen 1993, p. 231).

Porter emphasizes that comparative advantage exists at the activity rather than the industry level. Canada's cost advantage has centered on shooting. As a consequence, Vancouver and Toronto have become important centers for shooting runaway U.S. television and film productions such as "MacGyver."

Differentiation Strategy

A differentiation strategy is to produce programs and films with a distinct national orientation. In terms of pursuing this strategy, the closeness to the United States makes it difficult for English-Canadian producers to differentiate significantly from U.S. productions, although some programs and films do succeed in this regard, a recent example being the miniseries *The Boys of St. Vincent,* set in Newfoundland and Montreal.

In a recent empirical study we found that English-Canadian movies with a distinct national orientation received more critical acclaim but lower North American box-office rentals than those without such an orientation (Finn, Hoskins, and McFadyen 1993b). This suggests that this differentiation strategy is not commercially promising. Interestingly, Australian movies with a distinct national orientation did better than those without at the North American box office.

Focus Strategy

Aiming for a market niche will often be more promising than meeting U.S. producers head-on by competing in the more competitive mass market. Producers should consider nonentertainment programming that is cheaper to produce and where U.S. competition is limited. The type of informational programming should be selected to minimize cultural barriers and problems with censorship. As Hoskins and McFadyen (1991a, p. 45) point out, cultural and censorship barriers tend to be particularly high for national and local news and current affairs programming, but are likely to be very low for wildlife/nature/outdoors programming.

The Government of Canada (1993, p. 33) claims that "Canadian firms are meeting with success in such global niche markets as docudramas and children's programming." Most of the recent successful Canadian miniseries have been of the docudrama ilk. Examples include *Love and Hate,* which achieved top rating in its time slot when it ran on NBC, and *Conspiracy of Silence.* Canadian producers have had considerable success providing family drama, such as *Anne of Green Gables* and *Danger Bay,* to specialty channels such as the Disney Channel. As U.S. specialty channels do not have the audience to support big-budget U.S. programming, sales to specialty channels have become a good way to access the U.S. market.

Canadian producers, often in co-productions with France, are also becoming increasingly successful in animated productions. The cultural discount is minimal, as the language of choice can be added after production.

A niche that Canada has exploited in films has been 70-mm films shot for IMAX theaters, IMAX itself being a Canadian innovation. A recent example of such a film is the international co-production *Titanica.*

Another possible niche is for offbeat low-budget movies that need little box office to be profitable. An example is *I've Heard the Mermaids Singing,* made in 1986–1987 for an incredibly low $362,000. The movie went on to make money (Posner 1993), an event almost without precedent for English-Canadian films.

International Co-production or Co-venture Mode

An increasingly important strategy adopted to produce big-budget television programs and feature films with a chance of succeeding on the international market is to form a coalition with a foreign partner. Canada distinguishes between official international co-productions, which are undertaken under the auspices of a treaty, and international co-ventures, which are not. Canada has co-production treaties with some twenty-four countries; this number includes Mexico [2] but not the United States. Official co-productions are recognized as national productions for each partner. In Canada they qualify as Canadian content for quota purposes and are eligible for Telefilm Canada and provincial government agency financing, while Canadian private investors are eligible for tax incentives.

The importance of this mode of production has been examined by Hoskins and McFadyen (1993). For the years 1983–1991 official international co-productions in television programming accounted for between 21% and 38% of the total budgets of all television projects with Telefilm Canada funding; good data is not available for international co-ventures, but they are probably of similar importance. The most noticeable distinguishing characteristic of international co-productions consists of their large budgets—on a per-hour basis, 2.6 times greater than those of purely domestic projects. English-language and English-French double-shoots with France, much the most important treaty co-production partner, have particularly large budgets: the thirteen English-language projects with France have a combined budget exceeding that of the seventeen French-language projects.

Survey evidence has been gathered from sixty-four participants in Canada-Europe co-productions/co-ventures. This indicates that pooling of financial resources, access to foreign government subsidies, and improved access both to the partner's market and to third-country markets are the major benefits, while the drawbacks include the transactions costs associated with coordination with the partner, increased shooting costs, and loss of control and cultural specificity (Hoskins, McFadyen, Finn, and Jackel 1995). In another recent study, a statistical analysis of the performance of international co-productions/co-ventures as a mode of production suggests that their performance is less extreme than that of purely domestic productions (Finn, Hoskins, and McFadyen 1993b). International co-productions/co-ventures are less likely to be complete failures and hence can be viewed as a less risky approach to competing in the international market.

▪ ▪ Conclusion

In this paper we examined the international trade environment in television and film, international trade flows, and the treatment of cultural industries under the FTA, NAFTA, and GATT. Cultural industries are actually exempted under each of these agreements, so there is no negotiated move to freer trade in the audiovisual sector. Nevertheless, new distribution technologies and widespread partial deregulation have resulted in a proliferation of TV channels, the rise to predominance of the private sector in important markets in Europe and elsewhere, and increased demand for, and trade in, television programs.

Trade in audiovisual products is dominated by the United States, which strove to have them included under the provisions of the international trade treaties. However, Canada successfully fought to have cultural goods excluded under the FTA and NAFTA, while the EU (led by France) was successful in getting them excluded from the Uruguay round of the GATT talks. Three important questions involving trade issues arose from negotiation of these international agreements: Are the products of the cultural industries merely entertainment goods? Is the United States guilty of dumping television programs and feature films in export markets? And why does the United States dominate? After examining the characteristics of television and film that are relevant to trade, these questions were analyzed. We concluded that cultural goods are not merely entertainment goods because external benefits can result, that the charge of dumping was largely meaningless for such quasi-public goods, and that there are many reasons for U.S. dominance, and U.S. nontariff barriers are not a major factor. In effect, we find against the U.S. position on the first issue and for it on the other two.

We then examined the implications of U.S. hegemony for Canadian public policy and corporate competitive strategy. We found that regulation has been largely ineffective in promoting Canadian programming consistent with an external-benefits rationale and that it is becoming increasingly irrelevant as new delivery technologies, in conjunction with digital compression, bypass the regulatory process. Telefilm Canada financial assistance to production of television programs can be supported in cases where it is reasonable to suppose that this compensates for external benefits. The decision should depend on the nature of the program produced rather than on the nature of the inputs used. Preliminary examination suggests that financial assistance for the production or distribution of Canadian feature films is questionable. We doubt that the results justify the expenditure, while a perverse incentive structure appears to have been created. Many of the films supported do not receive theatrical release, and when they do, the audiences reached are often disappointing. The National Film and Video Product Bill, separating Canadian from U.S. rights for independently produced foreign films, can be supported on grounds of "leveling the playing field."

We examined three generic competitive strategies: cost leadership, differentiation, and focus. English-Canadian producers have both the disadvantage and the advantage of being close to the United States in terms of popular culture, topography, architecture, and, perhaps most important of all, a North American accent that in most cases is virtually indistinguishable from that of neighboring U.S. states. This makes it difficult to differentiate significantly from U.S. productions, although some programs and films do succeed in this regard. However, the advantage is that Canada is uniquely positioned to produce U.S.-style action drama at lower cost. In some cases this advantage has been exploited by persuading U.S. film and television producers to shoot in Canada. In television there are a number of examples of Canadian productions that appear simply as North American and that have been successful in the U.S. market. This ability makes Canada a very attractive co-production partner for producers in countries such as France who wish to access the U.S. market.

The preeminent feature of trade in audiovisual products is the extent of U.S. dominance, but is this likely to continue? Technological advances and the trend toward deregulation in broadcasting may be undermining the U.S. advantage in television program production. With the rise of cable channels, independents, and the Fox Network, the U.S. economies-of-scale advantage is threatened by audience fragmentation of its domestic market. Paramount and Warner have decided to launch their own networks. If this occurs it will further fragment the audience and, as independent stations become affiliated, undermine the syndication market (Brown 1994). Deregulation in many other broadcast markets is increasing competition and may result in the creation of domestic global platforms that rival that of the United States. There has already been a trend toward regional markets where producers in a country within a region dominate trade (Berwanger 1987). One increasingly used strategy for competing—the use of an international co-production mode—may be undermining the U.S. market-size advantage as joint ventures pool finance and aid access to foreign markets.

However, there are also factors tending to perpetuate U.S. dominance. The growth of commercial channels in Europe and elsewhere has led to an increased demand for programming, particularly for escapist action drama, which the United States, with its large output and huge library of programs and films, is uniquely equipped to supply. The increased demand is reflected by increases in prices being paid. With respect to television, we have concluded elsewhere that "the most likely scenario is one where sales of U.S. programming will increase in value and volume but nevertheless will constitute a smaller share of an expanding market" (Hoskins and McFadyen 1991b, p. 221).

It is difficult to foresee any lessening in U.S. dominance of theatrical-release feature films. However, video and pay-TV will provide increasing opportunities to non-U.S. producers, including access to ethnic, minority-language, and other niche markets.

NOTES

1. All currency amounts are expressed in U.S. dollars. Where necessary, the following exchange rates were used: Canadian $1 = U.S.$0.80; £1 = U.S.$1.60.

2. For an examination of the Canada-Mexico Co-production Agreement, see Hoskins, McFadyen, and Zolf 1992.

BIBLIOGRAPHY

Berwanger, D. 1987. *Television in the Third World: New Technology and Social Change.* Bonn: Friedrich-Ebert-Stiftung.

Brown, L. 1994. "Hurricane of Change." *Television Business International,* January, p. 4.

Chapman, G. 1987. "Toward a Geography of the Tube: TV Flows in Western Europe." *Intermedia* 15(1): 10–21.

Collins, R. 1989. "The Language of Advantage: Satellite Television in Western Europe." *Media Culture and Society* 11(2): 351–371.

Collins, R., N. Garnham, and G. Locksley. 1988. *The Economics of Television: The UK Case.* London: Sage.

Conlogue, R. 1993. "Taking a stand for the cinematic national soul." *Globe and Mail,* December 21, p. A12.

Ellis, D. 1992. *Split Screen: Home Entertainment and the New Technologies.* Toronto: Friends of Canadian Broadcasting.

Finn, A., C. Hoskins, and S. McFadyen. 1993a. Empirical Foundations For Public Policy: What Makes For Successful Canadian Feature Films? Working paper.

———. 1993b. The International Success of Nationally Oriented and International Joint-Venture Products/Services. Working paper.

Gitlin, T. 1983. *Inside Prime Time.* New York: Pantheon.

Globerman, S. 1991. "Foreign Ownership of Feature Film Distribution and the Canadian Film Industry." *Canadian Journal of Communication* 16(2): 191–206.

Globerman, S., and A. Vining. 1987. *Foreign Ownership and Canada's Feature Film Distribution Sector: An Economic Analysis.* Vancouver: The Fraser Institute.

Godard, F. 1993. "Gatt Real." *Television Business International,* November/December, pp. 14–17.

Government of Canada. 1993. *International Trade Business Plan, 1993–94.* Ottawa: Minister of Supply and Services.

Harcourt, P. 1989. "Canadian Film Policy: A Short Analysis." In *Cultural Economics 88: A Canadian Perspective,* ed. H. Chartrand, W. Hendon, and C. McCoughey, pp. 79–86. Akron, Ohio: University of Akron.

Hoskins, C., and S. McFadyen. 1991a. "International Marketing Strategies for a Cultural Service." *International Marketing Review,* 8(2): 40–52.

———. 1991b. "The U.S. Competitive Advantage in the Global Television Market: Is It Sustainable in the New Broadcasting Environment?" *Canadian Journal of Communication* 16(2): 207–224.

———. 1992. "The Mandate, Structure and Financing of the CBC." *Canadian Public Policy* 18(3): 275–289.

———. 1993. "Canadian Participation in International Co-Productions and Co-Ventures in Television Programming." *Canadian Journal of Communication* 18(2): 219–236.

———. 1994. "Public Policy Toward Television Broadcasting in Canada." *Policy Options* 15(1): 4–7.

Hoskins, C., S. McFadyen, A. Finn, and A. Jackel. 1995. "Survey Evidence on the Benefits and Drawbacks Associated with Canada/Europe Co-productions." *European Journal of Communication* 10(2): 221–243.

Hoskins, C., S. McFadyen, and D. Zolf. 1992. "Canada-Mexico Co-production Agreement on Film and Television Programming." In *North America Without Borders?* ed. S. Randall, H. Konrad, and S. Silverman. Calgary: University of Calgary.

Hoskins, C., and R. Mirus. 1988. "Reasons for the U.S. Dominance of the International Trade in Television Programmes." *Media Culture and Society* 10(4): 499–515.

Hoskins, C., R. Mirus, and W. Rozeboom. 1989. "US Television Programs in the International Market: Unfair Pricing?" *Journal of Communication* 39(2): 55–75.

Kennedy, P. 1988. *The Rise and Fall of the Great Powers.* New York: Random House.

Larson, P., ed. 1990. "Import/Export: International Flow of Television Fiction." UNESCO Reports and Papers on Mass Communication, No. 104. Paris: UNESCO.

Meisel, J. 1986. "Escaping Extinction: Cultural Defence of an Undefended Border." In *Southern Exposure: Canadian Perspective on the United States,* ed. D. Flaherty and W. McKercher, pp. 149–156. Toronto: McGraw Hill Ryerson.

NGL Consulting. 1992. *Evaluation of the Feature Film Distribution Fund.* Report prepared for Telefilm Canada.

Peacock Committee. 1986. *Report of the Committee on Financing the BBC*. London: HMSO.

Porter, M. 1985. *Competitive Advantage: Creating and Sustaining Superior Performance*. New York: Free Press.

———. 1990. *The Competitive Advantage of Nations*. New York: Free Press.

Posner, M. 1993. *Canadian Dreams: The Making and Marketing of Independent Films*. Vancouver: Douglas and McIntyre.

Renaud, J., and B. Litman. 1985. "Changing Dynamics of the Overseas Marketplace for TV Programming." *Telecommunications Policy*, 9(3): 245–261.

Ross, V. 1993. "U.S. doesn't get the picture." *Globe and Mail*, December, p. B1.

Schiller, H. 1969. *Mass Communication and the American Empire*. New York: Augustus M. Kelley.

Sherman, D. 1987. "US Films Sweeping Over France." *Playback*, November 16, pp. 14, 23.

Stigler, G. 1971. "The Theory of Economic Regulation." *Bell Journal of Economics and Management Science* 2(1): 3–21.

Telefilm Canada. 1993. *Annual Report 1992–1993*. Montréal: Telefilm Canada, Communications department.

"The Global TV Program Price Guide." 1992. *Television Business International*, October, pp. 99–100.

Tremblay, G., and J. Lacroix. 1991. *Télévision: Deuxième Dynastie*. Québec: Presse de la Université du Québec.

UNESCO. 1992. *Statistical Yearbook 1992*. Paris: UNESCO.

Varis, T. 1974. "Global Traffic in Television." *Journal of Communication* 24(1): 102–109.

———. 1984. "The International Flow of Television Programs." *Journal of Communication* 34(1): 143–152.

Wildman, S., and S. Siwek. 1988. *International Trade in Films and Television Programs*. Washington, D.C.: American Enterprise Institute for Public Policy Research.

4

················

Other People's Fictions: Cultural Appropriation, Cultural Integrity, and International Media Strategies

HORACE NEWCOMB

In this essay I address a question central to any discussion of "culture industries": What happens to one nation's "culture" when it adopts and adapts aspects of another nation's mode of producing, creating, shaping, and representing that culture? This question has been at the core of debates over media imperialism, cultural hegemony, and the exercise of economic, industrial, and cultural power, but the presentation of the question begs a cluster of related concerns. Where does culture "reside"? Is it located in the cultural products—in film or television, for example—produced by citizens of a nation or a region? Is it located in the formal aspects of those movies or television programs, or in the content, the subject matter, that they reshape and present to audiences? Is this distinction between form and content a false distinction, as most critics and theorists would suggest? What role do industrial organization, technological resources, and the structure of financial arrangements play in determining cultural significance? Clearly these questions indicate, more than anything else, that however we define culture, we must take into account an interactive process involving many, if not all, of these factors. We might call the arrangement of these elements the cultural formation, and this formation is the central issue to be addressed.

Here I approach these very complex matters with a case example. The case I describe focuses on a television program developed by the Finnish Broadcasting Company, Ylesradio (YLE), and resulted from a training program developed jointly by YLE and professors in the Department of Radio Television Film at the University of Texas at Austin. The case can be examined from many perspectives. My analysis will not focus on policy or economic determinants. Rather, I wish to consider briefly what we mean by culture and culture industries and how they relate to and interact with one another as aspects of a larger cultural formation.

First, I do not use the term "culture" in an evaluative sense, one in which it refers only to artifacts residing in museums or to activities requiring special privilege or education focusing on certain traditions. Rather, I use the term in its more anthropological sense, a definition that would include diet and food preparation, clothing styles and costume, the decoration of domiciles, child-rearing practices, medical practices, religion, and the myriad other aspects of lived experience. Such a definition would, significantly, also include the organization of power within the group studied. It is this more anthropological sense of the term that has guided its applications in media studies for more than a decade.

The case study at the center of this analysis involves broadcast television, an aspect of contemporary lived experience that is related to "popular culture," "entertainment," or, in some instances, "art." Here I will refer to all these forms of communication and the artifacts produced within them as "expressive culture." As with other aspects of cultural experience, we should focus on expressive culture in the context of struggle—the application and implementation of enormous economic, political, social, and personal power. In broadcasting, perhaps as nowhere else at the moment, huge sums are at stake. Industries and government agencies, careers in business and politics, national pride and identity are all involved. But so too are language, vision, personal expression, the very meanings we offer to the world and record for other people now and in later times. Because we seem now so closely bound together by electronic communication systems we tend to see this as a new problem. But it is far older than our technologies.

Throughout the history of conquest and subjugation, immigration and refugee movement, evangelism and education, issues have often focused on matters of expressive culture, on meaning, on art and entertainment. The reasons for this should be clear. Artists—and here I include makers of entertainment—serve as one type of powerful voice that speaks for larger groups. Out of the welter of lived experience they select and re-present, so that others can consider what it is to live more fully. The makers of expressive culture focus, organize, collect, and intensify. They also modify and alter. They challenge our ordinary ways of seeing the world, offer bizarre possibilities, probable and improbable, for doing things differently. They establish dangerous pleasure and allow us the license to participate—vicariously, of course—in intrigue, adventure, violence, passion, solitude, contemplation, fear, and great joy. No wonder, then, that when their activities are threatened by other influences, some sort of alarm is raised.

Consider, for example, the following statement about cultural influence and imposition, a statement that challenges many received notions about the value of art and particular artists:

> this absolute and unconditional adoration of Shakespeare has grown to be a part of our Anglo-Saxon superstitions. The Thirty-Nine Articles [of the Anglican Creed] are now Forty. Intolerance has come to exist in this matter. You must believe in Shakespeare's unapproachability, or quit the country. But what sort of belief is this for an American, a man who is bound to carry republican progressiveness into Literature, as well as into Life? Believe me, my friends, that men not very much inferior to Shakespeare are this day being born on the banks of the Ohio. And the day will come when you shall say; who reads a book by an Englishman that is modern? The great mistake seems to be that even with those Americans who look forward to the coming of a great literary genius among us, they somehow fancy that he will come in the costume of Queen Elizabeth's day. . . . Let America then prize and cherish her writers; yea, let her glorify them. They are not so many in number as to exhaust her good will. And while she has good kith and kin of her own, to take to her bosom, let her not lavish her embraces upon the household of an alien. For believe it or not, England, after all, is, in many things, an alien to us.[1]

This small diatribe against British cultural imperialism was published in 1850 by Herman Melville as part of a review—actually a puff piece—regarding new work by Nathaniel Hawthorne. Both Melville and Hawthorne remain central in the accepted classification of "great" American writers. Indeed, Melville is often still considered America's greatest literary genius and is, interestingly, often compared to Shakespeare. This is no off-hand linkage. Extensive scholarly work has demonstrated Melville's reliance on Shakespearean motifs, characterizations, and themes.

From a present-day perspective this is a clear example of cultural interaction, cultural influence. In some way, however, Melville considered such an exchange a matter of cultural conflict. As part of a much larger movement in the first half of the nineteenth century to establish a fully American character, identity, voice, and literature, Melville spoke for many other Americans who felt their culture was not truly their own.

Moreover, consider Melville's own enormous influence on French literature, or that of nineteenth-century French literature on American realism and naturalism, or that of nineteenth-century Russian literature on both. Would we have had Henry James without Flaubert, Faulkner without Joyce, Camus without Faulkner? The answer is clearly yes, but they would have been different writers without those influences.

To take a more pertinent example, would American popular music be the same without the "British invasion"? Would British rock 'n' roll have been the same without earlier American rock 'n' roll? And would American rock 'n' roll have been the same without jazz and blues?

Closer still, would the French New Wave of filmmaking, Fellini, or New German Cinema have been the same without Hollywood? Would Hollywood movies have been the same without German expressionism? Would Eisenstein have been the same without Griffith, or Griffith without Dickens? And so we return to the literary fictions of the last century.

These examples illustrate that there is no way to monitor or, finally, restrict exchange and influence in the realm of expressive culture. If borders are to be protected, artists, the creators of expressive culture, will create their own black market. So, too, will audiences, the users of this material. Both groups will seek out the art house theater in the United States in order to experience international film culture or the forgotten history of their own films. American films will be viewed in Paris, Madrid, and Helsinki. Audiences will record off the air while abroad and smuggle cassettes to friends. All this, if necessary, in order to discover how others are making meanings, expressing passion, representing fear and adventure and humor.

I refer to these uses, by creators—and by audiences who seek out varied experiences of new and different material—as *cultural appropriation*. They are forms and activities of resistance in some cases, when works are modified, rejected, or re-coded into a variety of meanings. But they are also forms of pleasure, instruction, information, and enlightenment. Without such exchange, I argue, cultures become stagnant, xenophobic, hostile, repressive. They "cleanse" themselves of other cultural interactions or repress those among them whose forms of expression they deem inferior.

How, then, does a political arrangement such as NAFTA affect the processes of cultural expression and appropriation? How can we compare the contemporary film and television industries, massive sites of industrialized production of culture, to the literary wars of another century, or even to national film industries of an earlier moment in our own time?

The key here lies in the root term, *industry*. Much of what is under discussion in the NAFTA, or the GATT, negotiations is not "culture" in the sense I have used the term, but the culture industries. While meanings and forms of expression are at times invoked, it is investment, forms of taxation, and protection of industrial structure that are often at stake. The agreements may mention pleasure and enlightenment, but they also imply profit and market expansion. The issue, then, must focus on the ways in which culture and culture industries *interact*. It is the *process* that is central. And the new technologies of satellite broadcasting, cable transmission, and home-video cassettes not only amplify the easy experience of expressive culture created in other contexts, they also create a demand for "product" that exceeds all but the largest production and market interactions. In such a situation it is the industrial structure that both alters and is altered by changes in policy, economics, and technology. Those changes in turn alter modes of cultural expression.

The larger idea, the idea of culture as lived experience, will survive all these changes. Culture cannot be totally destroyed, even when a nation-state is obliterated. The record of that culture, if nothing else, will remain and will in fact continue to influence others who draw on its expressive elements. In short, *culture* cannot be protected by treaty or agreement. *Culture industries* can be. The question we face here is how those changes in industrial structure, changes emerging from attempts to guide and protect, might also be seen to alter patterns of expression and cultural significance. In a sense the issues might be described as problems in the political economy of expressive culture.

This returns us to a fundamental question: What is the relationship between the particular formation of a culture industry and the expressive material it produces? Culture industries at the infrastructural level may decline or flourish or even be altered to other uses. But they can also be altered and modified to take into account new forms of cultural interaction. The ways in which cultural expression is actually produced in new industrialized settings can be changed, even if the changes require shifts in formal policy. Such a shift in policy, and the consequent changes in a specific culture industry, are exemplified in the following case study.

The Finnish Broadcasting Company's "Austin Project" began out of necessity. Ylesradio has been, since the beginning of television broadcasting in Finland, a mixed system combining state-supported public service broadcasting and advertiser-supported broadcasting. The advertiser-supported portion of the system, Meinos TV (MTV), leases broadcasting facilities from the state company and pays back to YLE a portion of its advertising profit. Both forms of payment contribute a portion of the funding for the entire system. Until 1993 YLE operated with two channels. Advertiser-supported programming was dispersed throughout the schedules of both in the leased time periods. Much of this "commercial" television is imported, much of it American.

In January 1993 a third channel went on the air. All advertiser-supported material was then shifted to that single channel, still leased from the state, still providing revenue for YLE. But the change in transmission altered programming strategy. The public service system was clearly in more direct competition with commercial programming. Moreover, when MTV moved to the third channel, nearly 1,000 "empty" hours per year appeared on TV I and TV II, the state channels. About 400 of these hours were designated for dramatic programming.

In 1989 I was invited to Finland by Ismo Silvo, then head of the Staff Training Institute, to help design a program to train potential television writers in a more "Americanized" approach to the medium. The focus of the program was twofold. First, from an economic perspective, it was deemed necessary to attract and hold audiences with television narratives that could be more economically produced than was currently possible in the YLE production structure. Second, it was necessary to illustrate that "popular television," even a detective series or a serialized narrative such as "Dallas," could serve as a primary site for the exploration and negotiation of serious and complex social and cultural issues.

Prior to this time the state-supported Finnish television industry had placed fictional programming of all sorts at a low priority. Official policy had dictated that television was to be centered on information—educational, political, rhetorical. These forms were deemed to deal with "serious" matters. "Serious" fiction could, of course, be produced, and outstanding single plays, miniseries, and adaptations of literary classics were given a high priority and substantial budgets. Series television, comprising the genres common to much of the imported material, was considered to be distraction, culturally inferior. Little consideration was given to how such entertainment might deal with significant matters. Policymakers, programmers, producers, and a well-tutored audience were always alert to the distinctions between "high" and "low" forms of expression, as they are in almost every culture.

In the 1980s, however, the situation changed to some degree. Facing competition not only from imports aired by the commercial broadcasting company in Finland but also from satellite and cable television that brought "foreign" programs to audiences, YLE policy shifted slightly. More emphasis was to be placed on popular dramatic programs, and the introduction of more series was seen as part of this shift. While series television had been sporadically produced in Finland, most projects were one-off, stand-alone productions or short miniseries. The concept of the series was clearly associated with "American Television," with commercially supported broadcasting, and as a consequence, with inferior forms of expression.

Significantly, for the argument here, the entire mode of production at YLE was organized to support stand-alone projects and was inimical to series production. The Austin Project was designed to assist Finnish broadcasters and potential new writers in mastering the techniques for producing serious work in a form previously rejected for such a purpose. The first four-week seminar, for two YLE staff teachers and ten students, met in Austin, Texas and Los Angeles, California in the summer of 1990. A follow-up one-week seminar was held in Helsinki in April 1991 and the second seminar for ten new students and a number of YLE producers met in Helsinki in the summer of 1991.

In some ways the project was not unusual. As the face of world television continues to change, more and more exchange of information, technique, and practice is occurring in the television industries. Already several countries have invited American professional writers to instruct writers, producers, directors, and other creative personnel in American techniques. Moreover, as we know from the experience of professionals involved in international co-productions, much exchange of this sort is occurring "on the job," and is developing through trial and error. And additional "tutoring" is available to creative individuals merely by applying keen analysis to the American (or British, or Australian, or Venezuelan, or German) material appearing on the air in many countries.

The YLE Austin Project was carried out on a different premise from that of many other consulting opportunities and is different from the random learning that occurs in co-productions or by observation. While the concern throughout placed a major emphasis on technique, there was an equal concern for defining a theoretical basis underlying and supporting that technique. In the training program, as in research and teaching in the university context, our seminars began with an analysis of the relationships between television and culture and encouraged strong criticism of technique as well as appropriation and application.

We did not assume, then, that "American Television" is an appropriate model for "World Television." But neither did we assume that "American Television" is inferior television, a model to be avoided. Instead, the seminars began with a set of questions that take the concept of "American Television" as a motivating problem, a set of governing issues to be continually addressed. Keeping in mind that our mandate was to deal with television *fiction,* some of these questions can be framed as follows:

What is the role of television in culture? How does television relate to the history of other forms of popular culture, particularly those disseminated by mass media? How does television relate to other forms of cultural expression considered to be "high culture"?

How did American television develop? What were its relations to other forms of American popular entertainment? In particular, how did television relate to broadcasting (radio) and other visual entertainment (movies)? More specifically, what aspects of the broadcasting and film *industries* influenced television, and what aspects of broadcasting and film *content and technique* influenced television? How did the economic base of American television, its very conception as a "commercial medium," shape and direct its growth and change, and how does its commercial base affect technique, form, and content?

How can we best explain the popularity of American television throughout the world? What roles do narrative styles and techniques, as well as technological (production values) and marketing factors, play in that popularity? What is the relation of advertising to television's structure and appeals, particularly when that advertising is diffused in worldwide print and product culture as well as in broadcasting? How must we consider the factor of "the exotic" as an appeal of American culture generally?

What aspects of American television can be thought of as inherently "televisual," applicable in any cultural context? Why, for example, are American programs popular as *narratives,* even without the advertisements they were designed to contain? By contrast, what aspects of American television result from the organization of the American television industry, with its reliance on market-driven, advertiser-supported programming?

How are Finnish (and other worldwide) broadcasting systems changing? What is the role of competition from cable, satellite, and VCR sources in shaping the central role of broadcast television?

What is Nordic television, Euro-television, or world television? Will Finnish television, or other national systems, play a role in those larger concepts? If so, what is the role of television in Finnish culture?

How can cultural integrity be defined and preserved in a world-television system made inevitable by technological innovations? What is the role of language in preserving cultural integrity? What is the role of narrative style, structure, and strategy in such an endeavor? How does *series* television play a role in these changes, forcing certain industrial and organizational alterations? And finally, are there elements of American television that can be adopted and/or adapted and/or appropriated for use in a specifically Finnish (or other) context without sacrificing or compromising cultural integrity?

Few of these questions have easy, specific answers. Indeed, the answers are different in different cultural, social, technological, economic, and political contexts. Policy and regulation alter the formulation of the questions and the potential answers from country to country. Still, the seminars in the Austin Project required that such questions be addressed throughout our discussions of technique, narrative strategy, and programming histories. In most cases the questions emerged from the participants, often in the form of objections to the adoption or use of American models. Most seminar participants came with assumptions of their own about the role of television. Some saw it as an inherently inferior medium. Some saw it as a necessary evil. Some saw it simply as misused, popularized when it should have been used for high-culture purposes. Many saw these failings as caused or led by the influence of imported American television.

By contrast, some participants loved American television and saw it as a highly appropriate model for their own work. All of them knew a great deal about American television and most made distinctions among the familiar programs, citing some as excellent and some as useless as either expressive culture or models for future work. In all instances the goal of the seminar was to have participants question their own assumptions as fully as they questioned those underlying the instruction.

The seminar made a strong case for a particular perspective. The central approach argued that American television, developed in the American social and economic context, has established or discovered or polished certain aspects of the medium that can be applied in any particular cultural or social setting. The seminar presented American television as a form of storytelling unavailable in other media. In other words, we presented "TV" (American television) as an option for creating expressive culture in exceptionally powerful ways.

Actually, the complex narrative structures of television serials (described in more detail by Allen in Chapter 5 of this volume) are styles often appropriated by American television from European sources. They have then been highly developed to offer storytellers new ways to explore characters, ideas, and social and cultural issues. The global popularity of these styles and structures, their adaptation in other societies and broadcasting systems, suggests that television may offer new ways of communicating cultural expression, establishing an intimate relationship with audiences that is more difficult to establish in other media. Central to this process is the notion of seriality, the possibility of continuing a fictional construct through time. While there are varying degrees of seriality—some are truly open-ended, others more episodic, closed in narrative form—American television depends on some degree of continuation within its story structures. This allows audiences to become engaged with characters in an intimate manner, concerned with their problems, the choices they make, and the potential consequences of their choices. As often put in our seminars, this form of television breaks the Aristotelian imperative that all stories have a beginning, middle, and end. Television, potentially, allows for a perpetual middle, a perpetual second act in which audiences and characters are suspended, waiting and watching for human choices that may or may not be the "right" ones. And in almost every case the audience knows more than the characters involved, leading to a form of social, cultural, moral, or political judgment on what happens next. These advantages in narrative structure, however, are directly related to industrial structures, and our seminars were designed to address both and to demonstrate the complex interactions among them.

▪ ▪ *Sixteen:* A Case Example

One project that emerged from the Austin Project deserves special attention because it stands as a potential model of how such instruction might be applied. In the second phase of the project, in the summer of 1991, we learned that a television series, *Sixteen,* was to be produced by two members of the first-year seminar and was already in development. Even at this stage the project demonstrates some of the shifts in production practices that exemplify the close links between mode of production and mode of expression.

"Development" is a phase of television production central to the American industry but not often a part of other, smaller, state-supported broadcasting systems. It involves producer-writers in long-term planning for a potentially long-running project. In development, a project moves from an originating concept, to treatment, to scripts, to script revision, to first-episode production, to revision of that episode, to series—with the possibility of cancellation of the work at any time. The central concern is with assembling a team of writers, producers, directors, technical staff, and actors who will remain with the project throughout its production. Collaborative, negotiated work is central to this creative process.

In many other broadcasting systems work proceeds on a basis defined by the role of "the author" as traditionally understood in literary culture. A writer or director conceives an idea for a television production. He or she then convinces a programming executive, sometimes called a producer, that the project is worthy of support. The project is given permission to proceed and is produced without evaluation until completion, essentially as the work of an individual. Support staff are considered necessary but coincidental to the structure and content of the work, and may often change from day to day.

Sixteen was the idea of two writer-producers employed in the Swedish section of YLE. The two had worked together on other projects, and their concept was patterned, to some extent, on various American television programs that featured high-school youths as the central characters and a school as the primary setting. Examples include *Fame, Hull High,* and the then-new *Beverly Hills 90210,* which had not been seen by the producers when they began their planning. Both *Fame,* which was a relatively successful American program, and *Hull High,* which failed after only a few episodes, included music as part of the production in an obvious attempt to appeal to youth audiences.

Sixteen uses several of the same elements. It features a group of young people as its central characters. It adds musical elements that are, significantly, produced separately and can be excerpted and aired as music videos. It follows the young people through the daily problems of their lives, drawing on series television's special facility to focus on character as a central narrative and aesthetic device. It uses specific social problems—teen pregnancy, drug use—as topics for plots, even while it introduces us to more ordinary aspects of the lives of the cast members. It involves the families of some of the characters, so we may contrast youth culture with family culture. All these dramatic premises and techniques offer a solid basis for a television series.

More to the point, however, the producer-writers conceived of the program from the beginning *as a series.* Ten episodes of *Sixteen* were developed as scripts prior to production and careful attention was given to the development of characters, multiple continuing and intersecting story lines, the introduction of new characters for short-term participation, and so on. The program was not designed as a miniseries, with a planned ending that would conclude the series. Rather, the possibility for extension was always present. And while each episode offers closure on certain elements of the story, it continues others in a more serialized fashion, offering what can be termed the "cumulative narrative," one of television's strongest contributions to storytelling technique. Problems with one character ripple throughout the constellation of other characters. Small moments reveal enormous amounts of information because audiences are aware—more aware than some of the characters—of the implications of actions and choices.

As a single example, *Sixteen* demonstrates a number of significant differences between the system of American series-television production and the organization of production at YLE. From an industrial perspective, the production of series television enables producers to set out certain production problems and address them prior to the actual moment of production "on the ground." They are also able to plan, in very specific and long-range terms, such technical matters as set design, locations, and shooting schedules. These techniques have specific financial advantages in large-scale production.

By comparison, these strategies were, until recently, relatively uncommon in Finnish television production, and costs reflected the practice of mounting each new production as a major new investment. In the Finnish system producers were considered primarily as administrators of unit budgets—drama, sports, documentary, and so forth— rather than as the creative force behind particular programs. Directors or writers presented ideas for projects to producers, who decided which projects would be made, and funds were set aside. But sets, auxiliary personnel, crews, and other elements of the production were not assigned to specific projects. Instead, they were scheduled according to the needs of the producer's entire range of projects. This meant, for example, that a director might have different camera operators on different days. A floor manager assigned to one project in the morning might be assigned to another in the afternoon, and the new (afternoon) floor manager could appear on the set unfamiliar with the project, the cast, the crew. Equipment could be unavailable because it had been assigned to another project on a specific day.

These factors were not the result of economic constraint. On the contrary, until quite recently, YLE was well funded and supported with equipment, studios, and personnel. The production processes described here were the result of an entire mode of industrial production that conceived of every project as a one-time, stand-alone endeavor, that conceived of creativity on the model of the single author, and that equated other industrial patterns of production with inferior art.

The producers of *Sixteen* also faced other obstacles and overcame them in ways that would not be necessary or even available to American producers. They created a group of new, young actors by making their production an event in Finnish youth culture. They conducted a talent search throughout high schools, selected their cast members, and trained them during the year prior to the beginning of production. The point here is that series television is often seen as impossible in Finland or other smaller countries because of a limited number of trained actors. The producers of *Sixteen* not only overcame the problem, they also contributed to creating a talent pool that will be available for other productions.

The program was also planned to take advantage of locations rather than studio settings, with shooting taking place in a school during holiday periods. The intention was to assemble a technical crew that would be affiliated with the program throughout its production in order to maintain a uniform, recognizable "look." Because some aspects of the mode of production were intractable, however, this was not always possible.

The adoption of these production techniques, however, was merely one step in the appropriation process. The producer-writers of *Sixteen* used these techniques in order to tell the stories they found important, significant for contemporary Finnish culture. They used a focus on specific social problems to attract financial support for their project from social service agencies. And while many aspects of what might be called an "international youth culture" are present (dress, music, social behavior), special attention was given to Finnish social settings, social agencies, and the problems of changing social attitudes. In short, the appropriation of influential international aspects of television can be seen as a deep subject matter explored in the series itself.

In formal terms these blended aspects are quite evident. The pace is often slower than that of a typical American program, but quicker than that of many Finnish programs. The use of stand-alone music-video inserts in a dramatic program is common in neither cultural formation. The performances are uniformly competent and, in some cases, outstanding. There is a strong Finnish sensibility to the program, even while it is familiar enough to be appreciated in other cultural contexts.

Sixteen represents the most direct outcome of the Austin Project. But other Finnish television programs have begun to assume some characteristics focused on in those seminars. *Metsulat* (*The Metsulat Family*), a family melodrama with all the characteristics of American soap opera, became in 1994–1995 one of the most popular series ever programmed in Finland. Produced by TV II in Tampere, the series focuses on two generations and the move away from a family farm, a powerfully compelling topic in Finland because of its shift from a rural agricultural to an urban industrial society in the single generation following World War II. The program captured exceptionally large audiences of all ages and spoke to specific issues often discussed in other forms of cultural expression—education, film, historical writing, literature, and so forth.

Other multiple-episode series are currently in development and, in what may be the more significant change, budgeting procedures have been altered to a unit-production model in which producers of specific television series are given specific sums that must be applied as they see fit in the creation of television content. These producers are held accountable for the expenditures and are allowed to "purchase" services from other areas of the company. This makes it possible to assemble creative personnel who work primarily with single productions on more precise schedules. These shifts have not emerged in an attempt to model other systems of production. Rather, they are adaptations of strategies that have been successful in other contexts. The adaptations are a consequence of financial constraint resulting from a severe recession that began in 1992 and has continued until recent upturns in the economy.

There remains the question of what such examples and programs have to do with the difficult policy questions, the hard economic choices that must be made within and among Canada, the United States, and Mexico under NAFTA. Fundamentally, they suggest certain cultural considerations that are often overlooked in the context of more practical discussions of economics and policy. If, however, such considerations are taken into account, those more pragmatic matters might be conceived differently.

First, policymakers should be aware of the never-ending cultural exchanges that occur *without* official markets and market regulations, the exchanges sought out by those who appreciate and those who create expressive cultural materials. It might be argued that pointing to the near-universal influence of Shakespeare, or even of the great novels of a previous century, is too easy. One of the major concerns in matters of cultural exchange is the evident one-way flow of that exchange, which makes the influence of Finnish culture on American culture difficult to detect. Nevertheless, it is the case that Henry Wadsworth Longfellow was involved in a lengthy dispute over his use ("appropriation," "plagiarism") of Finland's great folk-epic *The Kallevala* in his famous poem *Hiawatha*. And the significance of Finnish design is evident to anyone who has ever flown into or out of Dulles International Airport.

Still, the counter could be made that television is another matter, that there are few cross-cultural influences here. This is indeed more the case. As indicated above, however, it must be acknowledged that the British miniseries played a major role in the development of that form in the United States. And from the miniseries it is but one more step to "Dallas," and from "Dallas" only another to "Hill Street Blues."

At this point the arguments become more subtle. Old debates regarding quality and value emerge, debates deeply embedded in cultural formations, but always open to change. If, for example, central cultural value is placed on the autonomous, solitary artist, the American system of industrialized collaboration will be taken as inferior and the cultural expressions emerging from such a system devalued. But the notion of single authorship bears its own cultural baggage. As a fundamental aspect of many public service broadcasting systems, focused as they are on one-off, stand-alone productions, the notion of the solitary artist-creator is as much a part of an industrial system as it is an ideally defined mode of creativity. Here then are the equations.

Author = Individual Work = Public Service = Culturally Valuable
    Production.
Collaboration = Series = Commercial Sponsorship = Inferior
    Cultural Product.

The first model is historically European, the second historically American. Any shift to a new form, then, can be seen to equal cultural imposition. But what I have argued here is that just as the adoption of European "realism" or "stream of consciousness" did not destroy the American novel, neither must American television and film technique be viewed as destroying European or Canadian or Mexican television and film. There is, I am arguing, no cultural "essence" in these forms, if such a quality exists anywhere. Culture *is* adaptive process and what is central to cultural integrity must transcend such technical bounds. But the adaptive process is always conducted in the context of unequal distributions of *power*.

These claims lead to the nub of the matter, the core of the issues surrounding the production of expressive culture and the attempts to "regulate" those processes. If we cannot legislate the protection of "culture," does the same argument hold for culture *industries*? Put differently, what is the relation of culture industries to the adaptive process referred to here as culture? Quite simply, this is where, in our age, the adaptation primarily occurs. While novelists and poets, singers and painters still do their work, we cannot deny that the media industries occupy the most pervasive and powerful positions in the maintenance and dissemination of cultural materials—including novels and poems, songs and paintings. Nor can we deny that the arrangements of power, expressed in terms of financial arrangements, policy formations, and technological control, have everything to do with the adaptive process.

Jaques Attali, former aide to President Mitterand and founding president of the European Bank for Reconstruction and Development, has argued these issues in terms echoed throughout this essay. He began with the following brief historical analogy:

> When the printing press was invented in the 15th century, it was widely believed that it would ensure the universalization of the Latin language at the expense of the local dialects used by the various European peoples. In fact, the opposite happened. Through the use of this new information technology, each culture was able to flourish.
>
> This lesson will also hold for the media industry of the future, despite high anxiety displayed on this side of the Atlantic during the GATT talks that English-language Hollywood is destined to suffocate European civilization. And it will hold for the American

side, despite their seeming conviction that nothing is sacred but
market access, which, if they had it completely, would guarantee
triumph in the worldwide cultural market place. It is in this context that the future of cultural trade must be considered.[2]

Attali goes on to point out that in the future, media will be closer to "a
collection of libraries than a set of networks."[3] In that setting it "will
therefore be as untenable to tax or place a quota on every pay-per-view
connection or video rental as it is to ration access to foreign books in
the public library."[4] Until this future arrives, however, Attali argues, and
I agree, that *industries* must be afforded some type of protection. This is
necessary because it is the industries that create the products that make
cultural competition, cultural influence, cultural exchange, and adaptation possible. Industry here must be understood as encompassing the
recruitment and training of creative personnel, the informal learning
structures that occur when young men and women watch films expressing their own cultural concerns rather than those of American "blockbuster" films, and the sense of a shared cultural past filled with multiple
forms of cultural expressivity, adaptation, and influence. In this sense,
the notion of "media culture industry" is utterly central to, in our day
almost synonymous with, the idea of the "cultural formation."

Without these fully realized culture industries to produce the "libraries" of material, choice will indeed be restricted to a narrower range
of cultural options. With the coming of new technologies, and with vital,
healthy culture industries in place, the options will be greater than ever
before. The choice to subsidize an industry, Attali points out, is finally a
cultural choice. European countries *choose* to subsidize their culture industries because of the value placed upon them. The United States
chooses to subsidize defense industries. This, too, is an expression of cultural value.

At this moment, it is difficult to define a single appropriate path
regarding culture and culture industries. In the context of these large
concerns the YLE Austin Project was modest. Its aim was to explain how
certain forms of television fiction manage to create deep bonds with
audiences. These bonds then make it possible for writers to explore serious and powerful social and cultural issues within the context of popular drama. This is one way in which American television has been central
to American and world cultures for many years. If television drama's
appeal to diverse and divided audiences creates a location for common
ideas and issues to be explored in fictional contexts, the struggle to pro-

duce and the various opportunities to learn and apply multiple production strategies affords another form of cultural dialogue. Some techniques will be accepted, some rejected, some modified and applied. Cultural influence has never been free of the display and exercise of power. In the context of that struggle for influence a careful analysis of television's complex cultural role is required for both practice and policy. A fundamental implication of this argument is that cultures that shut out the influence of others are those that are, in the end, impoverished.

These ideas are presented, however, in the face of extraordinary technological changes that may render much of the discussion moot. The next round of technologies may enhance cultural exchange on a far more decentralized and personal level—even though the struggle to control those processes will still engage the central, powerful industries. In this sense technology may outstrip policy. The entire project of film and television production may become something very different from what now exists. It may be far less dominated by industrial infrastructure and marketing combines. Indeed, "Hollywood" itself, as a cultural construction, may become nothing more than one among many producers of expressive media culture. If the cost to create and distribute that culture is dependent on the equivalent of book sales rather than on the creation of mass audiences, we may find, at some moment in the future, that our present quandaries seem as quaint as Melville's diatribe against Shakespeare.

NOTES

1. Herman Melville, "Hawthorne and His Mosses," in *The American Tradition in Literature*, 3d ed., ed. Scully Bradley, Richmond Croom Beatty, and E. Hudson Long (New York: Norton, 1967), 914–915.

2. Jaques Attali, "Hollywood vs. Europe: The Next Round," *Journal of the Writers Guild of America, West* (February 1994): 26.

3. Ibid.

4. Ibid.

5

As the World Turns: Television Soap Operas and Global Media Culture

ROBERT C. ALLEN

IN THE LATE SUMMER OF 1992 viewers of Moscow's Ostankino One television channel were offered a "new" drama: "The Rich Also Weep." Its 249 forty-minute episodes ran throughout the fall, twice a day (morning and evening), three days a week, vying for viewer attention with coverage of the Congress of People's Deputies and news reports of the disintegration of public order, economic collapse, rebellion in the republics, and the rise of organized crime. That "The Rich Also Weep" was a 1974 Mexican *telenovela* rather crudely dubbed into Russian did not seem to deter viewers from watching. Indeed, it was soon garnering the highest ratings ever received by a television program in Russia: an estimated 70% of the viewing population watched regularly. With only slight hyperbole, the *Moscow Times* said that when "The Rich Also Weep" was broadcast, "streets became desolate, crowds gathered in stores selling TV sets, tractors stopped in the fields, and guns fell silent on the Azerbaijani-Armenian front." Another newspaper claimed that the program had done more to increase life expectancy in Russia than any public-health initiative: old people simply refused to die until they discovered how the serial would end.[1]

In January 1987 a serialized adaptation of the great Indian epic "Ramayan" was launched on India's government-run television network. Before they finally ended in July 1988, the Sunday morning broadcasts had become the most popular television event in Indian history. In Jaipur, a crowd of 50,000 gathered at the airport for a glimpse of the show's stars. When news reports were circulated suggesting that the serial would end without representing events in the final books of the epic poem, sanitation workers in several Indian cities went on strike. In Amritsar, where garbage went uncollected for a week, city officials feared an outbreak of cholera and joined the sanitation workers union in a suit against Indian television. A judge ordered that it suspend its plans to terminate the serial.[2]

In January 1991 an American anthropologist traveled to the Chinese city of Hangzhou where, for several years, she had been studying the lives of women working in the silk industry. She found her "subjects" uninterested in talking about anything except "Yearnings," a fifty-part television serial about the lives of two ordinary families in the years between the Cultural Revolution and the late 1980s. Talk about the show dominated dinner discussions among her faculty colleagues as well. "By the time I left China," she wrote, "most people I knew were heatedly debating the qualities of the heroes and villains, as they simultaneously engaged in and critically analyzed the implications of plot and character."[3]

These are but three of any number of instances, spanning the past half century and the world, of television audiences' fascination with serial narratives—both with those serials produced and received within a single culture (as was the case with "Yearnings" and "Ramayan") and with those produced initially for one culture but received within another (as evidenced by the success of "The Rich Also Weep" in Russia—and, coincidentally, in Turkey and South Korea as well). My own fascination with serials—soap operas, if you will—derives in part from my interest in understanding other people's pleasure, as well as my own, in watching them and, by extension, in accounting for their historical and current global success.

From their initial formulation in the early days of American commercial radio, soap operas have been inextricably bound to the economic imperatives of broadcasters and advertisers. And the mode of production of soap operas, in the United States at least, owes more to Henry Ford than to Henry James. At the same time, soap operas (and by extension other forms of television entertainment) play a different role in culture than automobiles or air conditioners or soy beans. Whatever commercial function they serve for broadcasters and advertisers, soap operas are, for their audiences, aesthetic experiences—they "work" by giving pleasure. The challenge for media and cultural studies is, it seems to me, to understand both the nature of those pleasures and the nature of the processes (economic, cultural, political) by which those pleasures are made available. The extraordinary circulation of television serials around the world in the past ten years suggests the need to locate both the economics of soap-opera production and distribution and the aesthetics of their reception within a global context. For more than sixty years, broadcast serial narratives have blurred the boundaries between the fictional worlds they construct and the experiential worlds of their listeners and viewers, as well as between the time of their telling and the time of their reception. As the examples above attest, today soap operas routinely cross cultural, political, and social boundaries as representatives of a new kind of global media culture.

This essay briefly sketches the nature of the serial form and the kinds of pleasures that form operates to produce, linking the structure of the serial text to the form's ability to speak to the culture of its initial reception and, in some cases at least, to quite different cultures. It concludes with some comments on the international flow of serials across national boundaries, particularly into and out of the United States.

▪ ▪ Textual Structure

What all serials share—U.S. daytime soaps, prime-time serials ("Dallas," "NYPD Blue," "Sisters," "L.A. Law"), British serials ("East-Enders," "Coronation Street"), Latin American *telenovelas,* Australian serials ("Neighbours"), and so forth—is, of course, their seriality. That is to say, in the first instance, they share the fact that their narratives are parceled out in installments, continuing story lines linking one installment to the next in a narrative chain. The release of each new installment is to some degree beyond the control of the reader or viewer, so that both the availability of the serial "text" and its reception by the reader/viewer are institutionally regulated. Television is, of course, but the latest vehicle for serial narrative. The rise of the novel in the late eighteenth and early nineteenth centuries depended upon the distribution of novels as a series of installments in weekly magazines. Most of the contemporaneous readers of Dickens knew his works in this serial fashion rather than in the form of their omnibus publication between hard covers.

The serialization of narratives produces a very different mode of engagement and pleasure from that experienced with nonserials. Because narratives unfold in time, we as readers are always poised between shifting temporal boundaries—between the "past" of the text we have already read and the "future" that awaits us in sentences, paragraphs, and chapters (or, in the case of audio-visual texts, shots, scenes, and sequences) to come. To change the metaphor to a spatial one, in reading or viewing we constantly wander between the textual geography we have already crossed and that which lies around the next textual corner.[4]

The curious narrative structure of serials might be responsible, in part at least, for the frequently mentioned loyalty of serial viewers. The regular suspension of the telling of those stories increases the desire to once again join the lives of characters the viewer has come to know over the course of months, years, or even decades of viewing. Because the viewer cannot induce the text to start up again, some of this energy might well be channeled into talk about the text among fellow viewers. Indeed, regardless of the cultural context of their production and reception, regardless of their plot or themes, television serials around the world seem more than any other form of programming to provoke talk about them among their viewers. In her recent book on television serials and women, Christine Geraghty sees this as their defining quality: "Soap operas . . . can now be defined not purely by daytime scheduling or even by a clear appeal to a female audience but by the presence of stories which engage an audience in such a way that they become the subject for public interest and interrogation."[5]

Nonserial popular narratives tend to be organized around a single protagonist or small group of protagonists and to be teleological: there is a single moment of narrative closure (obviously involving the protagonist) toward which their plots move and in relation to which reader satisfaction is presumed to operate. The classic example of this type of narrative is the murder mystery, in which the revelation of the murderer at the end of the story absolutely determines the movement of the plot. By contrast, the serial spreads its narrative energy among a number of plots and a community of characters and, what is even more important, sets these plots and characters in complex, dynamic, and unpredictable relationship with each other. Because serials cut between scenes enacting separate plot lines, the viewer is prompted to ask not only "Where is each of these plot lines going?" but also "What might be the relationship between different plot lines?"

It is at this point that we need to distinguish between two fundamentally different, but frequently conflated, forms of television serial—that is, between what we might call "open" and "closed" serials. U.S. daytime, British, and Australian serials are open narrative forms. That is to say, they are the only forms of narrative (with the possible exception of comic strips) predicated upon the impossibility of ultimate closure. No one sits down to watch an episode of one of these programs with the expectation that this episode might be the one in which all individual and community problems will be solved and everyone will live happily ever after.

In a sense, these serials trade narrative closure for organizational— or what semioticians call paradigmatic—complexity. Just as there is no ultimate moment of resolution, so there is no central, indispensable character in open serials to whose fate viewer interest is indissolubly linked. Instead, there is a changing community of characters who move in and out of viewer attention and interest. Any one of them might die, move to another city, or lapse into an irreversible coma without affecting the overall world of the serial. Indeed, I would argue that it is the very possibility of a central character's demise—something that is not a feature of episodic series television—that helps to fuel viewer interest in the serial.

U.S. daytime soap operas are "open" in another sense as well: Events in a daytime soap are less determinant and irreversible than they are in other forms of narrative, and identity—indeed, ontology itself—is more mutable. In other words, American soap operas routinely transgress or threaten to transgress boundaries of condition, identity, parentage, and family relations. For example, generally, when a character dies in a fictional narrative (assuming we are not reading a gothic horror tale or piece of science fiction), we expect that character to stay dead. In soap operas, it is not unusual to witness the resurrection of a character assumed to be, but not actually, dead, even after the passage of years of intervening story.

Another distinguishing feature of open serials, particularly U.S. daytime serials, is their large community of interrelated characters. It is not uncommon for the cast of a daytime soap to include more than thirty regularly appearing characters—not counting a dozen or more others who have moved away, lapsed into comas, or been incarcerated or otherwise institutionalized, or who are presumed dead. The audience comes to know some of these characters quite literally over the course of decades of viewing. Thus, the community of soap-opera characters shares with the loyal viewer a sense of its collective and individual history, which, in some cases, has unfolded over decades both of storytelling and viewing: the viewer who began watching "The Guiding Light" in 1951 as a young mother caring for infants might now watch with her grandchildren.

The size of the open-serial community, the complexity of its character relationships, and the fact that these characters possess both histories and memories all combine to create an almost infinite set of potential connections among characters and plot events. The revelation of hidden parentage—a plot device common, so far as I can determine, to television serials around the world—is emblematic of this feature of serials, in which to whom someone is or might be related is frequently more important than anything that character might do. Furthermore, complex networks of character relations enable soaps to produce plot developments that threaten to transgress boundaries between socially sanctioned relationships and socially outlawed ones. For example, a romantic plot can be made to collide with one involving mistaken or revealed parentage: two would-be lovers are brought to the point of incest by the revelation that they share the same father.

The absence of a final moment of narrative closure in the open serial also indefinitely postpones any moment of final ideological or moral closure. This probably makes the open serial a poor vehicle for the inculcation of particular values, but it does mean that open-serial writers and producers can raise any number of potentially controversial and contentious social issues without having to make any ideological commitment to them. The viewer is not looking for a moral to the story in the same way that he or she is in a closed narrative, even a closed serial.[6]

Indeed, the open serial frequently provides a more politically acceptable venue for the airing of controversial issues than more determinant forms of television drama. The first successful television serial in the Republic of Ireland was "The Riordans," which ran from 1965 to 1978. This story of family life in a rural community dealt with a wide range of highly charged social issues: the living conditions of farmworkers, sexuality and the use of contraceptives, alcohol and tranquilizer addiction, and the role of the Church in Irish society. That it was able to do so on government-controlled television, in a society of which the majority, as late as 1986, opposed divorce, and under the ever-vigilant gaze of the Catholic Church, was a direct consequence of its open-serial form. It could raise these issues without taking a perceptible stand or proffering solutions.

But it is important to note that by their very nature, the paradigmatic structures of U.S. daytime soap operas themselves carry implicit ideological valences. A recent article in *Soap Opera Digest* listed among the "ten things that you'll never see on a daytime soap opera" cruelty to animals, old people in nursing homes, and homosexual kissing.[7] Although there have been homosexual characters in soap operas, they have in the main been treated like contentious social issues: introduced from outside the boundaries of the community as a part of a specific and limited story line and, after a while, disposed of without having any lasting impact upon the community. The presence of more than a token gay character among the paradigmatically embedded central characters of a soap opera would call into question the very structure of that community.

Where the open serial resists ever closing off its narrative (even when the show goes off the air), the closed serial is designed to end and its narrative to close—although this closure might not be achieved until after several months or more than 200 episodes. The teleological thrust of the *telenovela* privileges the final episodes institutionally, textually, and in terms of audience expectation and satisfaction. The ending of a *telenovela* might be heavily promoted and, in the case of particularly popular *telenovelas,* might become the subject of anticipatory public and private discourse as viewers are encouraged to ask how everything will work out for the various characters whose fates they have been following for the past months.[8] As this suggests, closed serials also offer a definitive boundary between the time of the show's broadcast and reception and a time immediately thereafter, when viewers have an opportunity to look back upon the completed text and discern or impose upon it some kind of moral or ideological order.

It would obviously be a mistake to claim that the only difference between serials has to do with whether they close or not. Every serial is a product of the culture within which it is made and initially broadcast. It reflects particular local conventions of character, storytelling, plot construction, scenic design, editing, and so forth. Producers and writers can assume certain kinds of cultural capital possessed by target audiences; political references, musical allusions, religious mores, social norms, even references to other serials can be woven into the serial "world" and enrich the viewing experience for the *telenovela*'s first audiences.

Serials also differ in the position they occupy in a given country's cultural hierarchy. I have argued elsewhere[9] that since their days on radio in the 1930s, U.S. soap operas have been regarded by the cultural establishment as, to use the words of one commentator in 1940, "serialized drool." Although their cultural status has been elevated somewhat in recent years, actors and writers continue to regard soap operas as one of the lower rungs on the show-business ladder. Indeed, both the narrative structure of daytime soap operas and industry practice work to keep soap actors' status in check. In Latin America, on the other hand, with no dominant film industry setting the show-business status agenda and with *telenovelas* occupying high-profile positions on prime-time television, *telenovela* actors frequently become national icons, and writers do not fear irreparable harm being done to their reputations by involvement in a *telenovela* project. Furthermore, the closed narrative structure of the *telenovela* concentrates greater attention on the show's star or stellar couple, whose fate is determined by the final episode.[10]

▪ ▪ The International Circulation of Television Serials

The large-scale global circulation of television serials is a fairly recent phenomenon. Throughout the history of U.S. radio serials and in the early days of commercial television, daytime soaps were owned primarily by the sponsoring companies themselves (Procter & Gamble, American Home Products, Colgate-Palmolive), for whom the making of radio or television programs was secondary to selling soap. Thus, once a soap episode had been broadcast and, it was hoped, attracted its share of viewers/consumers to its commercials, its economic utility had been exhausted. Indeed, it is telling that the soap opera was the last form of broadcast drama to be recorded on video tape for delayed airing: it was not until the 1970s that soaps ceased to be live, and this occurred in the interests of production economy rather than in anticipation of ancillary markets for soap operas.

Although there had been some international distribution of the prime-time serial "Peyton Place" in the mid-1960s and of miniseries (e.g., "Roots," "Rich Man, Poor Man") in the 1970s, television audiences outside the United States did not associate American television with the soap-opera form until the extraordinary domestic and international success of "Dallas" in the early 1980s. Other American prime-time serials also met with considerable international success in the 1980s—among them, "Dynasty," "Knot's Landing," and "Falcon Crest."

There is good reason why American prime-time serials and not daytime soaps were aggressively marketed internationally. Unlike Procter & Gamble, Lorimar, the production company responsible for "Dallas," was in the business of making television programs, not laundry detergent. As was the case with almost all such producers, it stood actually to lose money on the initial licensing of "Dallas" to CBS for its first network run. Recovering costs and turning a profit would have to wait for sales in the lucrative syndication market. Here, however, a successful program like "Dallas" could be expected to take in, quite literally, hundreds of millions of dollars. As scholars and policymakers have noted for some time, American producers enjoy a considerable advantage over their foreign competitors. Since they are operating in the richest commercial television market in the world, even very high production costs can be recouped domestically. International sales represent clear profit, and the price need bear little relation to the production cost—rather, it is established as whatever the market will bear. "Dynasty," for example, was sold to commercial television in the U.K. for $20,000 an episode, but to state-controlled Norwegian TV for $1,500, and it was dumped in Zambia and Syria for $50.

Although certainly not the first American television program to be widely circulated in other countries, "Dallas" sparked considerable public debate in some countries regarding the role of television in maintaining or destroying national culture. This debate was most vociferous where public funds had been spent by state television services for the right to broadcast "Dallas" or "Dynasty."[11]

Concern over the "Americanization" of other cultures has for decades been a constant refrain in the discourse on the international circulation of cultural production. A 1994 article in the *New York Times* argued that "American popular culture has never been more dominant internationally," citing as evidence the fact that of the one hundred most-attended films in 1993, eighty-eight were American. But the article strongly suggested that what was worrisome about the "dominance" of American popular culture was not primarily its economic consequences or its marginalization of indigenous culture, but the fact that in too many cases the culture being exported was trash culture. Not surprisingly, U.S. soap operas become emblematic of the "inferior" popular culture aggressively marketed by U.S. companies. Instead of our "best" television programs, the writer moans, "foreigners get second-tier shows like *The Bold and the Beautiful* . . . marketed on the cheap." While "Roseanne" is held up as an example of "the best films and television," the effect of exporting "The Bold and the Beautiful" is to "tarnish . . . our national image."[12]

Although I certainly would not want to discount the hegemonic power of the American culture industry, the scenario put forth in this article of the inundation of indigenous media cultures by American products is somewhat misleading. This can be seen even in an area this article cites as evidence for its argument—that of soap operas. Returning for a moment to the early 1980s, the much-vaunted international success of the 1980s American prime-time serials did not mean what some, particularly in Europe, took it to mean—that glamorous American settings and characters, high production values, melodramatic plots, and attendant media hype would irresistibly lure viewers away from domestic drama. Although "Dallas" and "Dynasty" did attract high ratings wherever in Europe they were shown, in those countries with domestic serial offerings, the local soaps consistently outdrew American serials. In Latin America, local *telenovelas* more than held their own against the much more expensively produced American competition. Furthermore, at least one European country that did not have a tradition of serial television drama proved it could outsoap the Americans: in 1986 the German broadcaster ZDF launched its own serial, "Schwarzwaldklinik." While rather blatantly copying some aspects of American prime-time serials, the program also drew upon distinctively German generic conventions. At the height of its popularity in Germany in the early 1980s, "Dallas" was viewed by some 22 million viewers. Within two months of its debut in 1986, viewership for "Schwarzwaldklinik" had reached 28 million and within a year it was estimated that 50 million people had seen at least one episode.[13]

The motor driving the production of prime-time serials in the United States in the 1980s was not, of course, international distribution, which accounted for only a small proportion of revenue for a company such as Lorimar. Despite such desperate devices as consigning one entire season to a character's dream in order to resurrect her dead husband, "Dallas" could not sustain its popular appeal and by the late 1980s was sliding down the network ratings. It also turned out that prime-time serials did not fit well into syndication. Local broadcasters discovered that the cliff-hanger endings of "Dallas" (which had become the show's hallmark) were not well-suited to reruns. By the 1988–1989 season, Lorimar had "de-serialized" it, making it an episodic series of narratively unrelated episodes in order to increase its marketability in syndication. "Dynasty" was canceled in 1989, and the last episode of "Dallas" was broadcast in May 1991.

But what is needed to balance the *New York Times*'s analysis of the success of American serials abroad is recognition of the even more spectacular international success of foreign serials in practically every country in the world except the United States. Ironically, the retreat of prime-time producers from the serial form in the late 1980s occurred at the same time as demand for serials around the world enormously increased. To some degree, this increased demand for serials is a function of the demand for programming of all types occasioned by the development of new program delivery services (especially satellite) and the spread in coverage and channel capacity of cable television. At the same time, and in response to some of the same forces, governments around the world, particularly in Western Europe, began to shift from a public-service model of broadcast policy to a "mixed" or entirely commercial model. The expansion of viewing options through technological innovation and the growth of the commercial-television sector combined to produce the need to build new audiences for television and to find relatively low-cost sources of entertainment programming.

Importing serials from other countries has become an attractive programming option for several reasons. In addition to being internally self-promoting (each episode of a serial is implicitly an advertisement for the next), serials also advertise and promote the medium through which they are delivered to consumers. Serials encourage viewers to consume not only them, but also other types of programs offered through that medium. In other words, in order to enjoy the experience of watching serials, viewers have to "stay tuned" to the channel that provides them. Given the number of hours of programming they represent and the size of audience they can attract, imported serials are relatively inexpensive and, of course, they are always cheaper than producing dramatic programming locally.

But it was not U.S. producers who benefited most from the increased demand for serial programming in the 1980s. Rather, Latin American producers have moved aggressively into the international arena. One of the first and most successful is Brazil's TV Globo, which began exporting *telenovelas* to Europe in 1975. Within a decade, its annual profits on foreign *telenovela* sales to nearly one hundred countries had risen to $20 million, and export revenue increased fivefold between 1982 and 1987. In 1992 TV Globo announced plans to build a new $45 million production facility in Rio, mainly for *telenovelas*. Serials, which account for almost half of the output of Mexico's Televisa, are now exported to fifty-nine countries and have topped the ratings in Korea, Russia, and Turkey. According to a recent *Variety* profile, Venezuela's Radio Caracas TV is now the leading producer of Spanish-language *telenovelas*. Its *telenovelas* have created what one commentator called "novela-mania" in Spain and have been successful in Italy, Greece, Turkey, and Portugal.[14]

Certain factors link these three companies. All are major media conglomerates in their domestic markets and in a position to command a large share of domestic-television advertising revenue. Unlike Lorimar and other American producers of prime-time serials, these companies are both broadcasters and program producers. And unlike the U.S. commercial network broadcasters, there are no restrictions on their financial participation in the marketing of programming they produce.[15] Thus part of the recipe for success for these major exporters of *telenovelas* involves the expectation of recovery of some, if not all, production costs through advertising generated from domestic broadcast—advertising revenue made possible by the extraordinary popularity of *telenovelas* among local viewers. Although *telenovelas* vary in terms of their production budget both among companies and within each company's output, their production costs are tightly controlled. They are tiny compared with those of American prime-time drama and significantly less than the budgets of American daytime serials. Cost estimates range from $25,000 to $60,000 per episode for Radio Caracas serials, although a new "supernovela" is in production that, budgeted at between seventy and eighty thousand dollars per episode, will be its most expensive ever.[16]

The domestic and international popularity of Latin American *telenovelas* raises the question of how these texts speak both to the culture of their production and original reception and to multiple and very different cultures around the world. Ana Lopez notes three strategies.[17] The first, employed most notably by TV Globo, is to adapt *telenovelas* from internationally known works of literature. Second, Televisa in a number of its *telenovelas,* including "The Rich Also Weep," creates non–nationally specific settings for its stories with a minimum of local allusions. Instead, it frequently builds upon urban/rural, traditional/modern dichotomies manifested throughout Latin America and, albeit variably expressed, throughout much of the world. A third recent trend in *telenovelas* has been to build stories around the international mobility of the Latin American middle and upper classes, drawing especially upon resort sites such as Miami. Whereas the second strategy locates the *telenovela* in a geographic and social nowhere, the third presents a kaleidoscope of "real" anywheres.

But there are other strategies for transcultural appeal. For example, in some cases *telenovelas* have been produced in multiple versions, one of which draws directly upon the audience's knowledge of local politics, social issues, and geography, while another version—an "export" version—foregrounds less parochial concerns. In 1993, for example, Radio Caracas produced the enormously popular "Por estas calles" ("In These

Streets"), which referenced week by week the run-up to Venezuela's December presidential election. The 350-episode *telenovela* was trimmed to 250 and some episodes reedited for export to the rest of Latin America and Europe. The converse of this strategy involves a broadcaster in one country purchasing the rights to a serial made in another in order to produce a version more appealing to local tastes and standards. Lopez, for example, mentions the case of the sexy Brazilian serial "Angel Malo" ("Bad Angel"), remade by the Chilean Catholic television channel in the late l980s. In it, not only were settings and characters "Chileanized," racial and class conflicts were toned down and sexual and family issues recast to conform to church doctrine.

The Australian media company Reg Grundy Productions, producer of the hugely successful serial "Neighbours," has taken this cross-cultural serial-adaptation process one step further. In 1992 Grundy entered into co-production arrangments with Dutch and German companies for the production of a daily soap opera entitled "Good Times, Bad Times." The show is actually a recycled version of a now-defunct Australian serial called "The Restless Years." Grundy writers in Los Angeles rewrite the script for each episode, resetting it in the Netherlands and Germany. It is then shot by the co-production partners in the local language with local casts. So far as the audience knows, and so far as local broadcasting regulators are concerned, "Good Times, Bad Times" *is* a domestic production. Both versions debuted in the summer of 1992 and are doing well. In the Netherlands it is regularly among the top ten shows of the week. Grundy executives in Sydney say they hope to enter into more co-production arrangements for this and other serials, particularly in countries where there is little indigenous tradition of serial production.

The inference in the *New York Times* article of a uniformly robust American media sector dumping its products on the uniformly vulnerable and poorly equipped world market is simply not warranted in the case of soap operas. Ironically, the future of U.S. daytime soap operas is perhaps more uncertain than at any time since the genre made its successful transition from radio to television in the early 1950s. Total network viewership, both prime-time and daytime, is steadily falling, as more viewers have access not to three or four channels, but to thirty or forty. For the three major commercial networks, dispersed viewership across an increasingly fragmented market means lower ratings, reduced total advertising revenue, reduced advertising rates, and, with program production and licensing costs not declining, reduced profit margins, especially for daytime programs. Although soap operas have gained in some audience segments over the past ten years—among men and adolescents especially—these are not groups traditionally targeted by the companies whose advertising has sustained the genre for a half century. Total viewership among the most valuable segment of the soap-opera audience—women between the ages of eighteen and thirty-five—has declined since 1980 as more women have entered the paid workforce and as women at home defect to other programming alternatives. The penetration of the VCR into the American market over the same period (currently, over 75% of U.S. homes have a VCR) has had a curious impact on soap-opera viewership. Although soap operas comprise one of the most "time-shifted" genres, soap opera viewing on videotape does not figure into audience ratings data, and even if it did, advertisers would discount such viewership, believing (probably accurately) that most viewers "zip" through the frequent commercial messages.

As they scramble to staunch the flow of audience to cable, satellite, and independent stations, the networks have turned to programming forms that require minimal start-up investment and carry low production budgets—namely, game and talk shows. Both of these genres represent increasingly serious competition for soap operas. Few new network soap operas have been launched in the past ten years, and even fewer are still running. Thus, the international success of "The Bold and the Beautiful" is anomalous. It does not represent a strategy of long standing by which U.S. daytime soaps are successfully exported to other countries. Rather, it is the first U.S. daytime television soap since their advent in the late 1940s to attract a substantial international following.

Ten years ago, as cable systems enlarged their channel capacity and new cable programming services began to target specific audience segments ("narrowcasting," as opposed to the commercial networks' traditional strategy of "broadcasting"), some predicted that cable programmers would turn to the soap opera as a way of attracting and maintaining viewership. This vision of different soap operas for every audience segment has not come to pass. The start-up costs for a new soap opera and the fact that it can take several years for a new soap to find an audience have deterred cablecasters.

Serials have become mainstays of only one segment of the cable programming market—Spanish-language channels, now carried on cable systems throughout the United States. Serials imported from Latin America, especially from Mexico's Televisa, dominate prime-time programming on Spanish-language cable and broadcasting channels. However, because they are not subtitled in English, and since most Americans living north of the southern rim of the country do not speak Spanish, the visible impact of Latin American serials on U.S. broadcast television is as yet fairly low.

However, the success of *telenovelas* on U.S. Spanish-language cable, broadcasting, and satellite services has wider implications and may well have established an interesting precedent. First, Spanish-language services clearly address an audience whose linguistic, ethnic, and cultural interests are not adequately served by commercial network broadcasters. Watching American network television, one would conclude that Spanish is almost never spoken in the United States except by illegal aliens and Latino gang members. Furthermore, one would conclude that all Anglos are incapable of speaking or understanding any language other than English, particularly Spanish. But while the networks continue to be resolutely monolingual and only gesture in the direction of cultural diversity, Spanish-language television services have successfully remapped the boundaries of the American television audience—first, in terms of linguistic competence, and second, in relation not so much to U.S. Anglo culture as to transnational Spanish-language culture. Again, as Ana Lopez points out, on the Spanish-language media map, Miami and Los Angeles are not the southern extremities of Anglo-American culture, but merely northern centers of Latin American culture.

This linguistically based transnational model of Spanish media culture was narratively inscribed in a popular Televisa soap opera, "Dos Mujeres, un camino" ("Two Women, One Road"), in which former U.S. network star Eric Estrada ("CHiPS") played a truck driver who commutes between two lives and two loves in California and Mexico. In the early 1930s American daytime serials were used to attract an audience (adult women) whose interests were underrepresented in "mainstream" (prime-time) programming. Today, *telenovelas* galvanize another American sub-audience similarly ignored by mainstream (network) programmers—only this time, the structuring principle is primarily language rather than gender.

This precedent leads me to wonder if the fate of the serial in the United States is not tied to developments in the global TV market—developments that already have shifted the boundaries of international media culture, and that will continue to do so. From its beginnings in the late 1940s, U.S. commercial network television has been informally closed to foreign programming. With a huge domestic television production infrastructure, the world's richest consumer market to absorb high production costs, and program suppliers able to offer programming to the networks for less than their actual cost of production (because of lucrative syndication, foreign, and other ancillary rights accruing to a series with a successful network run), there was no incentive to seek alternative, offshore sources of programming. Furthermore, using wonderfully circular logic, the networks reasoned that since there was no tradition of watching programs that were dubbed or subtitled, or even programs with different English accents on network television, audiences would not tolerate such programs.

It is possible, however, that the continuing explosion of television viewing options in the United States—occasioned by the expansion of cable and promised by the next generation of computer and telecommunication technology—and the accompanying fragmentation of the viewing audience will work together to create a more favorable climate for foreign programs in general and serials in particular. Foreign programs in general, because programmers may have to go further and further afield to find programming to fill hundreds of hours of weekly schedule; serials in particular, because several countries—Mexico, Brazil, Venezuela, the U.K., and Australia among them—have demonstrated their ability to produce serials that "travel" well beyond their own cultural and linguistic boundaries. The only major market they have not yet penetrated significantly is the American market. Cable may well be their entrée to the American market because cable channels have more need than the networks for inexpensive imported programming and a much smaller and demographically narrower audience to please.

The popularity of television serials around the world suggests something of the complex dynamics of cultural production and reception more generally. The circulation of serials around the world suggests to me not the hegemonic influence of first-world culture industries, on the one hand, or, on the other, the "revenge" of the third world upon the first. Rather, the fascination of Russian viewers for a Mexican *telenovela*, the attraction of French viewers to a soap about teenagers in Australia, and the "novela-mania" prompted by a Venezuelan serial in Spain are all symptomatic of a moment of international media culture in which those in control of new technologies and newly configured media systems are attempting to appeal to new audiences at a time of rapid political, economic, and social change. And we should not be surprised to find the serial narrative of particular currency in this media moment. After all, the serial has been successfully employed to exploit new technologies of cultural production since the eighteenth century.

NOTES

1. Kate Baldwin, "Montezuma's Revenge: Reading *Los Ricos También Lloran* in Russia," in *To Be Continued . . . : Soap Operas Around the World,* ed. Robert C. Allen (London: Routledge, 1995), 285–300.

2. Philip Lutgendorf, "All in the (Raghu) Family: A Video Epic in Cultural Context," in *To Be Continued . . . ,* ed. Allen, 321–353.

3. Lisa Rofel, "The Melodrama of National Identity in Post-Tiananmen China," in *To Be Continued . . . ,* ed. Allen, 301–332.

4. Wolfgang Iser, *The Act of Reading* (Baltimore: Johns Hopkins University Press, 1978), 3.

5. Christine Geraghty, *Women and Soap Opera: A Study of Prime Time Soaps* (London: Polity, 1991), 4.

6. It is interesting in this regard to note the efforts of Western social agencies and third-world governments to use soap operas to instill "pro-social" values— progressive farming practices, family planning, AIDS prevention, and so forth. So far as I am aware, in every case the vehicle employed has been the closed serial. This has been for some obvious, but perhaps also for some not so obvious, reasons. Empiricist-oriented social scientists need to bring their experiments to closure in order to test attitudes, behaviors, ideation, "before and after"—something difficult, if not impossible, to do with an open serial. Also, television programming is expensive, and no government agency is likely to fund a new program indefinitely. But it is also the case that the closed serial can impose an ultimate and determinant message upon the text in a way that the open serial, that always leaves open the possibility of reversal, cannot (though whether or not the audience chooses to take it up in the same way in which the producers and writers intend is another matter). See Larry Kincaid, "The Pro-Social Soap Opera in Changing Behaviors in a Variety of Third World Settings," and Joseph Potter and Emile McAnany, "Popular Culture, Public Policy and Communication Theory: Brazilian Novelas and Family Practice Change," both papers presented at the 1993 Conference of the International Communication Association.

7. Quoted in Joy Fuqua, "There's A Queer in My Soap!: The AIDS/ Homophobia Storyline of One Life to Live," in *To Be Continued . . . ,* ed. Allen, 199–212.

8. Nico Vink, *The Telenovela and Emancipation: A Study on Television and Social Change in Brazil* (Amsterdam: Royal Tropical Institute, 1988), 179.

9. In Robert C. Allen, *Speaking of Soap Operas* (Chapel Hill: University of North Carolina Press, 1985).

10. See Ana Lopez, "Our Welcome Guests: Telenovelas in Latin America," in *To Be Continued . . . ,* ed. Allen, 256–275.

11. Jostein Gripsrud, "Toward a Flexible Methodology in Studying Media

Meaning: Dynasty in Norway," *Critical Studies in Mass Communication* 7 (1990): 117–128.

12. John Rockwell, "The New Colossus: American Culture as Power Export," *New York Times,* Jan. 30, 1994, pp. 1, 30.

13. Alessandro Silj, *East of "Dallas": The European Response to American Television* (London: BFI, 1988), 76–79.

14. *Variety,* October 11, 1993, pp. 181, 188.

15. FCC policies governing the financial participation of the networks in program syndication have, of course, recently been changed to allow greater network control.

16. *Variety,* October 11, 1993, p. 181.

17. See Lopez, "Our Welcome Guests," 265–268.

Part Three

Cultural Trade and Identity: Mexico

6

Will Nationalism be Bilingual?

CARLOS MONSIVÁIS

ON AUGUST 22, 1992, IN A RITUAL intervention, the secretary of industry and commerce, Jaime Serra Puche, met with a group of writers and artists. He insisted that the North American Free Trade Agreement (NAFTA) leave Mexicans "untouched" in matters of culture, because "art is not subject [to] negotiation, and they do not have to tell us how to do it." In addition, the secretary praised the Mexican film industry for its quality, refused to prophesy about national identity, and guaranteed that "there will not be transculturation because the agreement's terms will be translated into three languages, so that each country will use the correct translations . . . We will not become North Americans: McDonalds and Domino's Pizza are here and for that we will not stop being Mexicans, and what is to be done is to strengthen our culture, cling to it so that it will survive." This, as quoted in *La Jornada* (August 22, 1992), is what he said: "Cling to our culture so that it will survive" . . .

What is important about NAFTA and culture is always put aside, dispersing debate with banalities and commonplaces, like the ones administered by Minister Serra Puche. But what—if something so difficult to handle can be predicted—is nationalism's future? To begin with, the organic integration with the North American economy, certainly not a new aspect in Mexican life, affects culture and underlines Americanization's extreme importance—Americanization, understood not as the disappearance of Mexican national culture, but as a psychological adaptation of a people to rules of the game imposed from outside. To the process, already well advanced, of economic integration the integrationist technique almost becomes a Mexican's duty because, as the politicians say, "we have to build, but now seriously with capitalism, the only successful way on a world scale, and we have to do it without the populist's concessions, without imitating the Welfare State, and without 'nationalist distractions.'" Mexico's "singularity" was retired a long time ago, but now the government's ideological strategy is transparent—namely, that the words, and what in them remains of critical attitudes, will not get in events' way. Keep silent, Nationalism. You came out of the past.

▪ ▪ Modernization vs. Nationalism

But what is modernization and what are its contexts? The project of "modernization at all costs" only admits Mexico's availability, with no past that can provide weight to it. Of course, no one from the government will publicly adopt slogans like the one issued during Pinochet's regime—"let the inefficient perish"—but the modernizers demand that individuals accept the "natural destiny" imposed by the free market and give up any democratic aspiration. After all, President Salinas de Gortari stated several times that "in poverty there is no democracy."

Without the need for a deliberate strategy, what is wanted in neoliberal terms is the disappearance of the meaning of critical nationalism. Instead, what neoliberals propose as a replacement is a new social Darwinism, another thesis of the most capable surviving. "Modernization" is placed where the "Mexican Revolution" used to be (this is literal—try it with any speech), and then the attempt is made to replace nationalism with productivity. The dangerous dreams are not needed, and the "ideological aspect" (who needs ideas nowadays?) are seen as leading to stubborn illusions: existence and use of rights, the community's participation in decisions, etc. When I try to describe all this process, I am not making a plea on behalf of nationalism, a very complex notion or set of notions in need of being defined. I am only pointing out the technocrat's wish to diminish the sense of history, and to teach the young that they have no history worth studying, only a future whose common name in practical terms is NAFTA.

▪ ▪ Nationalism is the Fervor that Makes Us Mexicans Recognize the Image of the Virgin of Guadalupe at First Sight

For a long time, selective modernity's supporters have been attributing to nationalism the "psychology of the disadvantaged" that "isolates us from the world." What they are saying, if you trust me with the translation, is this, more or less: that if the viable nature of the nation is what matters, let romantic objectives be destroyed. Let us understand each other: modernity is a Noah's ark with first and tourist class; those who do not arrive on time will be arrested and shot; and it is better to get rid of ethical judgments, which only dull our comprehension of reality.

President Echeverría was determined, through his "Third World" sermon, to revitalize and increase nationalism; but he only succeeded, when nationalism's limitations became visible, in enhancing its ridiculous aspects. And technocrats establish the (dramatized) opposition between *underdevelopment* and *modernity:* the former is the attachment to tradition, the latter is the tradition of lack of attachment. José López Portillo and Miguel de la Madrid never, really, worried about nationalism; they verbally worshipped it if necessary, but the term itself looked to them like some relic. Even when nationalizing our own gestures ("They already sacked us! They won't sack us again!"), López Portillo did not call on popular support. And de la Madrid really considered nationalism a voluntarist act, a cultural and political exercise that only showed a plebeian spirit. And in NAFTA's times, in Salinas de Gortari's regime, nationalism was not considered a social force, only a psychological attribute.

▪ ▪ The Latecomers to Civilization

Before I go on with nationalism, let me try to respond to a vital aspect of Mexican culture at the time of NAFTA. Certainly, culturally speaking, Mexico is a modern country, in the Western tradition. In the thirties, our great writer Alfonso Reyes wrote: "We come late to the banquet of Western civilization," and poet Octavio Paz tried to explain on several occasions our modernity's weakness, noting the absence of the Enlightenment, and the century—the nineteenth century—that Mexico spent trying to form the nation-state. Anyhow, in the arts and humanities Mexico possesses an extraordinary legacy and a most dynamic present, from prehispanic art to muralism, from the poet Netzahualcóyotl to Octavio Paz and Jaime Sabines, from Mariano Azuela to Juan Rulfo, from Agustín Yáñez to Carlos Fuentes, from Rufino Tamayo to Francisco Toledo, from Juan Soriano to Julio Galán, from Sor Juana Inés de la Cruz to Elena Garro, Rosario Castellanos, and Elena Poniatowska, from Martín Luis Guzmán to Fernando del Paso, from Silvestre Revueltas to Agustín Lara and José Alfredo Jiménez.

Of course, we lacked a good many things: we have a national university with more than three hundred thousand students and a lot of cultural offerings in Mexico City, but a poor library system and almost no offerings in the rest of the country. As everywhere, the educational system is in bad shape, and the newly qualified professional, despite trying hard to get a job, any kind of job, usually meets without success, unless his or her family owns an industry or belongs to the supreme elite of thirteen Mexican billionaires (as *Newsweek* informs us, only the United States, Germany, and Japan have more). The print industry is in bad shape and bookstores are closing all over the country. But we have museums (some of them very good), and very important, far more important than the number of readers, is the role of intellectuals.

▪ ▪ Cultural Nationalism: *Como México No Hay Dos*

Now the exhaustion of cultural nationalism is obvious. And almost nobody is trying to use the term. But for some time, let's say between 1910 and 1950, cultural nationalism was an extraordinary force. This kind of nationalism creates the great mythology still prevailing and produces an invention that, while remaining itself, leads to psychological certainties and cultural creations: the *Mexicanidad,* the peculiar character created by the marriage of national roots and advertising. When citizens' rights and duties dim, the idea of *Mexicanidad* spreads. The clergy for its part proposes an equivalent idea: the Guadalupana condition, never the same as the believer's condition, but, better yet, the exercise of national identity through faith.

In the sixties the cultural vanguard thinks it urgent to jettison numerous nationalist traditions. To a significant sector of intellectuals, nationalism is chauvinism, demagoguery, show business, bureaucratization of what perhaps, at some point, was a legitimate feeling. A nationalist speech bores or irritates, *la provincia* (the countryside) is observed with acquiescence and sarcasm, and the nationalist's manifestations are worn-out rituals. And replacing official nationalism is another kind of sentimental heritage of the migrants and of those who would like to migrate. In sentimental nationalism you may count:

1. The religions (not as before *the* religion, since at least 21% of the population is not Catholic anymore, even though the majority professes loyalty to past generations and a deep belief in a few images and a few dogmas—"The Mexican is a religious illiterate," the Catholic bishops say);
2. The nostalgia, the utopian look back in happiness and sorrow;
3. The speech that is complicity's net and the "obscene" pleasures of those who lack a public voice;
4. The civic conviction that arises from the knowledge glimpsed (more than acquired) in elementary school;
5. The popular culture understood as a catalog of shared pleasures and obligatory practices (for lack of alternatives).

Nationalism is the technique of emotional stability in deprivation, the Exodus, the transfer of a desired future to sons or grandchildren.

▪ ▪ "If You Take Away Nationalism, You Only Leave Me the Nation"

The government supports national history and the worship of all kinds of symbols, and the cultural industries take care of the emotional contents of nationalism, that goes from civic duty to sentimental orgy. To be *Mexican* is, indeed, an experience progressively untied from politics and social compromise. (We are only beginning to evaluate the meaning of Chiapas.) A person is *Mexican* (with deliberation) only in determined moments of spare time, especially when faced with movies, radio and television programs, or the infrequent reading of the newspaper, in reactions to transcendent events (decisions that affect daily life like presidential elections, etc.). For the rest, you are employed or unemployed, without possible national name.

The nationalism that prevails is friendly, noisy, belligerent, corny, rough, devoted, uncivilized, hard-pressed, too damned sentimental. As everywhere, I may say. It is the nationalism of the excluded, of the Visible Nation, or of only the included, or of political trips of the PRI, the unwilling *acarreos* or transportations. It is the nationalism of soccer, of popular music, of regional memories, of anti-imperialism in after-dinner talk, of reflections on dawn, of the empty and circular dissertations on Mexican character, of the conditioned reflexes of a patriotism not too clear on its historic registry. At least, this was all believed before the great explosions of 1985 and 1988 that still wait for a detailed study, and, most certainly, before the Chiapas upheaval. What happened in the days and weeks after September 15, 1985, the day of the great earthquake in Mexico City? Was it only an outbreak of solidarity and civic protest, or was there a nationalist and Christian spirit of "support for our less fortunate brothers"? And what happened on July 6, 1988? Was it, like members of the PRI say, a mere vote of resentment against economic policy, or was it just about a revival of nationalism in the spirits of the masses?

▪ ▪ Let Me Delay on One Point: Culture and Politics

Nowadays, we have a new commonplace, enforced by neoliberalism. According to this, politics (dissident politics, of course) is an evil force, alien to literature and the humanities. I am not talking about the ancient quarrel between art for art's sake and literature engagé. I am talking about the neoliberalist assumptions—namely, that politics is dead, that society's will is dead, and that we are witnessing the end of history, the end of class struggle, the end of social criticism, the end of cultural creativity. This is the opposite of demands for freedom to write and publish and the rejection of the overpoliticized tradition of social realism and its consequences all over the world, some of them dreadful (Oh, the romance with the Soviet tractors!). In Latin America, the over-politicization of literature gave way, even in recent years, to propagandistic novels, sorrowful poems, devastating plays with *guerrilleros* in the place of Christian symbols and bleeding hearts in the place of people, and so on and so forth. But we are talking about something different. The great transformations in Eastern Europe and the sacralization of the free market, the new religion of private enterprise, tried to sweep away not the agonic revolutionary rhetoric and its influence on a lot of novels, poems, plays, and attitudes. They tried to sweep away two ideas: equality and social justice.

Nevertheless, this is only a fashion from governments. In Latin America's cultural history, politics is a constant presence, in a way described with great poignancy by the late Michel Foucault. Debating with Noam Chomsky, Foucault replied to another panelist, who was amazed by his interest in politics:

> What blindness, what deafness, what awful weight of ideology have to prey on me to forbid my concern on what's probably the most

important issue in our existence, that is, the society in which we live, its economic structure and the power system that defines norms, attitudes and prohibitions in our culture? After all, the essence of our life has to do primarily with the political function of society.

In these days of neoliberalism we need to examine the attempts to destroy political consciousness in the name of freedom. To identify interest in politics and social repression is part of the advertising campaign that, at the moment, identifies social causes (from democracy and defense of human rights to ecology issues) with Stalinism, and pretends to implant a social vacuum in the arts. In this context I will try to examine briefly the history of the relationship between intellectuals and the State in contemporary Mexico.

Even in the 1950s I went to university knowing that ours was a wonderful culture, but just for ourselves. We belonged to the peripheral countries, and Mexico then did not even belong to the third world. That was to come. For the time being, we were inhabitants of the sleepy and singing South, full of dreamy peasants with the burrito, and populated by hideous killers, dressed à la Pancho Villa. We knew, as students, that we belonged to the Western world, but that we played the role of a marginal culture. The idea of arriving late to the banquet of Western civilization became a sentence on the wall. Because we were not present at the beginning, we could never be fully integrated. End of the delay.

Above all, and again, what is nationalism today? Is it, as is said from managerial and government positions, a stance that is merely defensive? Is it, as could also be sustained, an invention that has exhausted its usefulness? Is it useful as a development project platform, of cultural construction, etc.? According to the criteria strengthened by NAFTA, the Americanization is, after all, only the skill to make a deal with global reality. The *gringo* each time is less the other, even though many *gringos* are really the other, in their versions of employers and racist police, of promoters of cynical interventions in the name of freedom. At a certain level, Mexico is Chicano-ized and the choice of intermediations or compromises results, essential to whoever transports their notion about the future to North America.

It does not make sense anymore to discuss the abstract notions around cultural identity, debates that have not advanced since *The Profile of Man and Culture in Mexico* by Samuel Ramos and *The Labyrinth of Solitude* by Octavio Paz. There is no answer to the basic questions:

Does an "essence about the Mexican" exist? Will this "essence" survive technology's offensive? In any case, more useful than speculating about the irreducible "identity" of something that changes every day are, to me, the specific studies about the migrant's values, women's development, the conditions of minorities, spoken and written Spanish in Mexico, and so forth. And it is convenient also to remember one fact: the main translator of the Mexican experience in Mexico is, of course, television. Without ideologically labeling it (its function is obvious), what is true, by force of accumulating images and commonplaces, is television's translation of reality. And above all, thanks to the nonexistence of alternatives, Televisa is the most favored interpreter of reality. Religion, too, as the transmissions from the Basilica of Guadalupe prove, continues to be extremely important, but certainly needs TV in case the Catholic Church needs more power of seduction over so many multitudes at a time.

Let me note, by the way, an important fact: When you have an alternative, even a small one, people tend to believe in it, despite TV's powers. In the first two months of 1994 in Mexico, the realm of credibility was granted to the critical press and the oral culture, not to Televisa, a professed enemy of the rebels in Chiapas.

▪ ▪ I Want to Live in America. No Place for You in America

Where are the cultural strategies of *la gente,* the people, in the age of NAFTA? Certainly not in any kind of fundamentalism, nor in the total oblivion of tradition or the worship of newness, of inevitable progress. As far as I can see, some of the cultural strategies depend on adaptability, some on imitation, some on assimilation. I will try to give you some examples. Six or seven years ago, in a small town near Veracruz, a group of people came to see the mayor and the local priest. "Mr. Mayor, Señor Cura," they said, "in a few months from now we'll have Holy Week, and in the enactments on Good Friday, we don't want the Roman legionaries any more. We don't relate to them, they are meaningless to us. Instead, we prefer the new symbols of evil surrounding Our Lord and flogging him and spitting on him, symbols like Darth Vader of *Star Wars,* Freddy Krueger of *Nightmare on Elm Street,* the goonies," and so on and so forth. The mayor and the priest tried to persuade them of their error and the evils of cultural colonialism—that it would be a historical mistake, a blasphemy, a theological monstrosity. "We don't care," they answered. "We want symbols we can relate to, and also we need some kind of contemporary excitement . . ." Finally they found a solution, a truce: after the usual staging of the Passion, they would dramatize Christ's death with the characters from the movies surrounding the cross.

Another example: Each Sunday, in the Basilica of Guadalupe, the greatest of Mexican shrines, the center of popular religion, groups of folk dancers known as *concheros* dance for hours in honor of the Virgin and her son. The Indian sector of the *concheros* (there is a yuppie faction, but that is not the point) wear masks, a product of ancient handicrafts. But the masks are now collectors' items, so the Indian people sold them in order to survive, to get the money from gringos or wealthy Mexicans. And they substitute for the carved masks of their home towns the masks of wrestling figures, or the outfits of Batman and Spider Man. We almost can hear the prayer: "Sorry *patroncita.* Sorry Holy Virgin. I know you're now thinking I'm a traitor. Please, Mother, don't condemn me. We love you and we take for granted your pardon. See, our faces are not the masks."

In the popular milieu, every day we observe the same landscape: traditions are vanishing, and traditions refuse to die. Take the Day of the Dead, the first two days of November. By now they blend in with Halloween, so we can perfectly declare that Halloween (the carnival of witches and pumpkins) belongs by now to Mexican traditions. Or take, for instance, the new attitudes of Indian women. Of course, in the great festivities they still wear their dresses and proudly exhibit themselves for cameras and videorecorders. But the rest of the year they act in new ways: in their fashion many of them are pro-choice, and they refuse to see themselves as typical Indian women. In Oaxaca, for instance, some of them declare: "We prefer jeans. It's a practical outfit and we need it. Sure, we've got traditions, but once a year." On the whole, migrations are the changing force. People travel, work in California, Texas, Illinois, try to understand technology and simply adore the gadgets. The youngsters like rock or reggae or rap. And back in their towns they try to be modern.

Modernity appears and transforms the context of national identity. Four or five years ago the elders of an Otomí tribe, near the Valle del Mesquital, went to see the authorities of the *Instituto Nacional Indigenista* (National Indigenous Institute). They were angry with a band, formed by some youngsters who, in the States, had adopted the punk style, and who, back again in their town, played the Ramones or the Sex Pistols or Nina Hagen the whole day long, and played it with loudspeakers. "Expel them," the elders shouted. "We can't stand the noise." The Otomí punks defended themselves: "Wait a minute. We bring money to the community. If they accepted our dollars, they can also hear our music."

I am going to give an excellent proof of my thesis, or so I think. On January 1, 1994, a group declared itself the *Ejército Zapatista de Liberación Nacional* (the Zapatista National Liberation Army) and took over four places in Chiapas: San Cristóbal, Ocosingo, Altamirano, and Las Margaritas. Its members wore ski masks and bandannas, and made it plain that their presence and their demands represented the concerns of the Indians in Mexico, the people they said NAFTA was going to wipe out. After a week of battles, chaos, and at least five hundred deaths, there came a truce, and the biggest national debate I have witnessed. Everybody intervened, and to begin with a new instant commonplace was established: Mexico still has great poverty, misery indeed, and without social and political reform, instability may yet wreck all the work of economic reforms. On the one hand, you have the boast of global competitiveness; on the other, you have what anthropologist Guillermo Bonfil, in a controversial book that has now become an instant classic, called the Deep Mexico, *el México Profundo*. According to Bonfil, the Deep Mexico is a hotbed of Indian resistance, of genuine popular culture, of the behavior of the majority of the people. Well, but as we have seen, this *México Profundo,* as almost everybody in the press is calling Chiapas, needs modernity, uses it, and even, as writer Carlos Fuentes and the *New York Times* boldly put it, contains a display of postmodernity. The rebels have used the mass media, they became pop celebrities, they sent faxes from the Selva Lacandona, they almost declared in a filmic manner, "With God as our witness, we swear we will never be humiliated again."

Technology, in Mexico and everywhere, is transforming the countries and the mentalities, in a leap from reality to virtual reality and back again. I do not know, nobody knows, the extent of the metamorphosis, but at the end of a century of Americanization it is possible to affirm that we are still Mexicans, and proudly so, as they used to say in the forties, but a different kind of Mexicans. If it is a mirage, the very notion of *Mexicanidad,* something so concrete even the government used to say that it is impossible to define, what is real is the national culture, with international, national, and local traditions. Mexico is a Western country with strong Indian elements, Mexico is an Americanized country with a nationalistic perspective. Then can we talk about a specific difference? There is one, every country on earth has it, and in this case it takes root in the strength of certain traditions, the richness of some aspects of its culture, and, like every Latin American country, the weight of inequality, the emphasis of poverty, ignorance, machismo, social injustice, and naked authoritarianism.

I am not saying that poverty is the essence of a neo-Dickensian reality. I am talking, as the author D. Smith has pointed out, about the role of ethnohistory, its myths, values, memories, and symbols, in assuring collective dignity (and through that, some measure of dignity for the individual) for populations that have come to feel excluded, neglected, or repressed in the distribution of values and opportunities. Also, according to many, the only guarantee of preservation of some form of identity is in the appeal to "posterity," to the future generations that are ours, because they think and feel as "we" do.

I offer you no conclusions. At the beginning of NAFTA Mexican culture is alive and well, even if society is not exactly in as good shape as it is everywhere else, I suppose. The liberal economic reforms are going to prevail for the time being, simply because there is no alternative in sight. But neoliberalism is not having an effect on creativity and learning, and I am certain that these are going to be some of our most effective assets. NAFTA is certainly more than a trade agreement, but national cultures, American, Canadian, Mexican, are also much more than NAFTA.

North Americans or Latin Americans?
The Redefinition of Mexican Identity
and the Free Trade Agreements

NÉSTOR GARCÍA CANCLINI

ON JANUARY 1, 1994 THE North American Free Trade Agreement
(NAFTA) between Mexico, the United States, and Canada became law.
On the same day an indigenous uprising broke out in Chiapas. The in-
stigators, in addition to challenging the exploitation and injustice suffered by the region's indigenous ethnic groups and campesinos, demanded that NAFTA be annulled. As the Mexican writer José Emilio
Pacheco wrote, "The day we expected to celebrate our entrance into the
first world, we actually stepped backward a century . . . We hoped and
believed that we would become North Americans but along the way we
encountered our destiny as Central Americans."

These two incidents seem to be extreme examples of a long-term
contradiction, synthesized in debates on specific aspects of Mexican culture. Prior to the negotiations of NAFTA, economic and social multi-
nationalization had created new challenges for Mexico's traditional
nationalism. The expansion of cultural industries and the effects of international migration and tourism are just some of the factors that during the second half of the twentieth century have partially blurred
boundaries in this country, as they have in many other countries that
have evolved images distinct from those of their neighbors.

NAFTA is accelerating Mexico's process of reorientation in relation
to both North America and Latin America. How can the traditional Mexican characteristics, both "real" and imaginary, be reclassified within the
multicultural and hybrid flux of contemporary identities? Will depen-

dency on Anglo–North American culture be increased with NAFTA? How will distinct regions of the country and different social sectors be involved in the processes of multinational integration?

In this text I will describe some crucial elements of the debate from the Mexican point of view. But it should be stated that such a national perspective is in itself questionable: One of the changes generated by NAFTA concerns the need to broaden national viewpoints in order to incorporate multicultural issues. Therefore, my first hypothesis is that a Mexican perspective should include interactions with other North American countries and with Latin America, as well as with other processes of regional integration, especially those taking place in Europe and the Pacific.

▪ ▪ Theoretical Constructivism versus Political Fundamentalism

In its initial stages, discussion in Mexico about NAFTA lapsed into either fears or elation. Traditionalists said that Mexico's NAFTA-inspired opening to foreign influences would have catastrophic effects on national identity and way of life. Modernizers, on the other hand, maintained that NAFTA would only bring about commercial reorganization, and that this would be indispensable in order to improve the competitiveness of the Mexican economy and to reorient it in an interdependent world. Politicians, particularly the economists involved in the negotiation process, tend to underestimate the cultural impact of the agreement. This is not because they underestimate culture itself. Quite the contrary: their speeches customarily praise the country's ancient traditions. It is precisely because they believe that these are so rich and substantial that they assume we have no reason to worry. When a Canadian journalist asked Mexico's chief NAFTA negotiator, Jaime Serra Puche, secretary of industry and commerce, whether the inclusion of cultural industries in NAFTA would affect national identity, he replied: "This has little relevance for Mexico. If you have time, you should see the exhibition 'Mexico, Thirty Centuries of Splendor' [which was being exhibited at the time at the New York Metropolitan Museum of Art] and you will realize there is no cause for concern."

I find at least three reasons to be apprehensive when the sociocultural implications of the free trade agreements are stated in this way. The first is that the debate presents a Manichaean vision, a kind of Western opposition between the traditional and the modern that is unacceptable within the current development of social sciences. Second, I am concerned by the divorce of academic theory from political doctrines and movements. And third, I am disturbed by how slowly we reconceptualize the cultural aspects of identity in the context of rapid technological, economic, and social changes that have created a trend toward hegemonic internationalization and globalization. I shall begin by examining these issues in terms of the division between social sciences and political practice.

1. Identity has traditionally been a theme for historical, anthropological, and folklore studies. Its analysis has related to ethnic or national groups, rooted in territories with a certain internal homogeneity due to the reproduction of customs, rituals, and forms of thought that defined a space. The classic anthropological and folklore studies gave "scientific" justification to ethnic recovery and the constitution of modern autonomous nations, but have dealt very little, or badly, with issues of multiculturalism and interculturalism.[1] Their greatest contribution to the coexistence of peoples and ethnic groups within a world order was to inspire an abstract recognition of the universality of human rights and the relative autonomy of each culture, as was proclaimed by the United Nations in 1948.

During the last fifteen or twenty years the social sciences have reformulated the notion of identity in terms of at least four conceptual changes: (a) The historically constituted (thus not substantialist) nature of these identities; (b) the role of imaginary components in the formation of ethnic and national identities, such as in the characterization of differences from other ethnic groups and nations; from this perspective, identity would not be a "natural" or "normal" expression of relationships with a territory, but rather a reflection of the way in which it is imagined that these relationships are experienced and in which group members believe they share these experiences of community; (c) the multicultural and hybrid composition of the specific identities of each nation or ethnic group; and (d) the growing role of transnational conditioning in the formation of new identities (as youths, migrants, business people, artists, and intellectuals) and the shrinking of territorial and racial conditioning even in the development of ethnic and national identities.

2. In contrast, many political movements are becoming active. On the increase are fundamentalist movements that make absolutist analyses of biological and regional characteristics, stating these dogmatically as if they were naturally or even divinely established and unrelated to

the vicissitudes of history and contemporary change. In interethnic and international conflicts from Bosnia to Peru there is evidence of the tendency to insist on obstinately conceiving of each identity as a hard and compact nucleus of resistance demanding total loyalty from group members and anathematizing those who criticize or dissent. A defense of purity is imposed in many countries to counter modern tendencies to put specific elements of each ethnic group or nation into a relative context in order to construct democratic means of coexistence, complementarity, and multicultural forms of governing.

▪ ▪ What Will Change under NAFTA?

In addition to these varied conceptions of identity, numerous debates on the meaning and the sociocultural scope of NAFTA arose during the negotiation process. Would it affect Mexico's education, traditions, and cultural industries? Once the agreement was signed, what would change in terms of commercial relations was evident: In 1994 the United States was already beginning to drop tariffs on 84% of Mexican exports to the United States, compared with Mexico's dropping tariffs on 40% of U.S. exports to Mexico. In five years the United States will eliminate tariffs on 1,200 products and Mexico will eliminate tariffs on 2,500 products (20% of Mexico's total imports from the United States). In 2004 the United States will drop tariffs on 7% of Mexican exports, while Mexico will do the same for 30% of its imports from the United States. In 2009 the remaining 1% will be freed of tariffs in both countries.

Public sector educational services were not negotiated within NAFTA; the three countries remain free to determine their own policies on public and private education. Nevertheless, the validation of international studies was considered in the agreements and a procedure was included for its future coordination among educational institutions of the three countries. The governments' role will be limited to encouraging the educational institutions corresponding to various professions to meet and make recommendations on how to carry out reciprocal validation of studies.

In the debates prior to the signing of the agreement there was great concern over the electronic media. However, it was decided under NAFTA not to change the current situation: in Mexico radio and television broadcasting companies should still be owned solely by Mexicans. The only opening created was in cable television. From the day NAFTA became law, up to 49% of foreign investment was allowed in this kind of business. Newspapers still require a Mexican majority holding, except in those cases where material is published simultaneously in Mexico and abroad (as in the case of the European and Asian editions of the *Wall Street Journal*).

Radio and television programming maintain their current open status in Mexico. As a result of NAFTA, the United States will eliminate a restriction that has discriminated against Mexican radio and television stations on the border. As a result, these companies are increasing their capacity to reach the Spanish-speaking population on the U.S. side of the border.

The three countries reaffirmed the illegality of nonauthorized copying of videos, discs, and software, at the same time consolidating commercial free trade that already existed among them.[2]

▪ ▪ A New Multicultural Scenario

There seemed to have been an imbalance between the changes agreed to within NAFTA in the cultural and educational sectors and the importance given in the press and in political and academic debates to possible effects in these sectors. This can be understood as resulting from the fact that NAFTA provoked a debate on the negotiation process that lasted longer than the current debate—in terms of productive and commercial opening, privatization, and commercialization—on restructuring broad areas of Mexican society and culture.

NAFTA is not a simple commercial rearrangement of ties between the United States, Mexico, and Canada. It is both a deepening and completion of a process of opening that began in 1982 to deal with the serious financial crisis Mexico was facing at that time. These changes were sharpened with the country's entrance into GATT in 1986 and with the privatization and deregulation of many areas of production and marketing in the 1980s.

Similarly, current changes in education and culture are not generated primarily by NAFTA, though in part such changes are related to the agreement. These changes are part of a longer process of the national and international reconstitution of cultural markets and the modernization or adjustment of the educational systems in relation to the new requirements of production and international commerce. NAFTA has an economic and cultural prehistory that began with the technological innovations and demands for economic viability imposed by neoliberal policies on educational, scientific, and cultural activities. Three trends in these changes were evident prior to NAFTA—first, the predominance of cultural industries over traditional means of production and dissemination of culture, whether "high" or popular; second, the increase of culture in private homes (in the form of radio, TV, and video) and a reduction of attendance at the movies, theater, concerts, and shows that have involved the collective use of urban space; and third, the transfer of responsibility from the State to the private business sector, both national and international, in the production, financing, and distribution of culture.

If this is the context in which NAFTA made its appearance, it is possible to predict that its major effect will not emerge within traditional forms of cultural development, which, apart from the economic opening, are losing significance all over the world. Rather, its major impact will occur in the communication industries that are responsible for mass production of culture, and whose products are consumed in the privacy of the home.

In the mass audiovisual media, where state intervention has declined in the last few years and independent initiatives such as independent noncommercial radio stations[3] are still scarce in comparison with their prominence in other countries (including the United States), both voice and image are virtually the exclusive property of the corporations. It is not easy to imagine how public interests could find a balance with commercial concerns, or how to avoid increased technological, economic, and cultural dependence on foreign production as long as there is no policy on video production and other advanced cultural technologies. During NAFTA negotiations it was believed that providing better conditions for investment by foreign businesses could reduce Televisa's monopoly and stimulate competition, which would improve quality. However, the expansion of television programming due to the appearance of Multivision (a subscription service based on reception via coded antennae) made it clear that as long as the opening occurs only for U.S. programming with a completely commercial orientation, it will bring no real diversification or cultural enrichment to Mexican television.[4]

▪ ▪ Challenges for the Social Sciences

Can research in the social sciences be effective toward integrating the current multicultural issues into cultural policies? First of all, we can help with the task of rethinking national identities as multideterminant scenarios where diverse symbolic systems intersect and interact. This restating of issues is the basis for renewing the social sciences' contribution to the design of policies on culture and communications. Only those studies that explore the heterogeneous nature of society and the coexistence of various symbolic codes within the same group, and that, even for a single subject, promote intercultural borrowing and exchanges, will be able to say anything meaningful on the processes of identity formation in this age of globalization. More than the affirmation and "rescue" of traditional identities, we need policies that work with the polyglot, multiethnic, migrant character of modern identity, including within the popular sectors.

My second suggestion concerns a theoretical question: How can one construct a contemporary definition of identity? When it is constituted not only in relation to territory but also in connection with international networks of electronic information and goods, the definition of identity should be not only *socio-spatial* but also *socio-communicational*. Thus, any definition will have to articulate the local, national, and postnational cultural referents that are restructuring the local or regional brand names established as a result of distinguishing territorial experiences. Identity will be formed by roots in a territory as well as through participation in nonlocal networks of communication.

In the third place this debate on sociocultural change and free trade agreements situates the interaction between the symbolic and economic meanings of cultural process. Industrialization and the mass production of culture require high levels of investment. It is therefore logical that private businesses take their place in this context and that they demand good performance. But it is worth asking whether the sociocultural significance of a society can be produced like merchandise and accumulated like capital. Isn't it also a triumph of modern development to maintain that certain areas of culture and of social life such as human rights, artistic experimentation, scientific research, and the collective construction of historical meaning, being of public interest, cannot be privatized or subjected to rules of pragmatism and economic yields?

▪ ▪ Cultural Policies: Is the Market the Same as Civil Society?

In order to respond to these questions we must rethink the meaning of what is public in communications and culture, as well as the responsibility of the State within this framework. Neoliberal criticism has served to put an end to the idealization of the State as the focus of land-based nationalism, as an efficient administrator, and as an agent of charity. But doesn't the State continue to be indispensable as an expression of public interest or as arbitrator or guarantor that collective needs for information, recreation, and innovation not be subordinated to economic profitability? In this case, we need public education, publications, libraries, museums, centers for scientific research, and artistic experimentation to continue to be subsidized by society through the State or through mixed systems in which the cooperation of government, private foundations, and independent associations makes it possible for public interests not to be overwhelmed by competition from merchandisers and speculators.

With regard to this last point I would like to say that I personally find the debate that has developed around NAFTA to be rather feeble. A few articles written by Mexicans and Canadians do state the issues, but almost all the actors get swept up in the neoliberal discounting of the State, and in their belief that letting culture, communications, health, and everything else be subject to market forces would be the same as transferring initiative to civil society.

For this reason it is of the greatest interest to enrich North American discussion on commercial liberalization with analyses made in recent years on European economic integration. To show the contrast between these two perspectives, I will examine the confrontation between the United States and some European countries in the recent GATT agreements on the subject of communications.

I find it interesting that in the Brussels meeting of December 1993, at which 117 countries approved the greatest commercial liberalization in history, cultural and media considerations became for the first time a topic of primary importance in international economic policy. The GATT was on the verge of collapsing because of disagreements in three areas—agriculture, textiles, and audiovisual communications. Differences in the first two topics were resolved thanks to mutual concessions made by the U.S. and European governments. But what were the discrepancies in cultural matters that impeded agreement on movies and television and obliged them to leave these media outside the agreement?

The United States demanded the free circulation of its audiovisual products, while the Europeans sought to protect their communications media, especially the cinema. The divergences derive from two different conceptions of culture. For the United States, entertainment ought to be handled as a business, not only because that is what it is, but also because it constitutes, after the aerospace industry, the United States' second most important source of export income. In 1992 the North American producers sent entertainment programs and films to Europe worth $4,600 million.[5] In the same period, the Europeans exported programs and films worth $250 million to the United States.[6]

At the time of writing, global statistics were not available for 1994, but it is clear that U.S. earnings have grown, as has U.S. control over European cinemas and television stations. In 1993 North American distributors managed 80% of the French and 91% of the Spanish film industry. The consequent loss of screen time for films produced by these countries generated outbursts from local artists and producers. The most irritated reactions occurred when *Jurassic Park* opened simultaneously in 100 cinemas in Spain and in another 400 in France.

Cinema workers' associations defend their jobs but also argue that movies are not just a commercial product—they constitute a powerful instrument that records and affirms its own language and culture and its dissemination across borders. But will the play of the international market allow equitable multicultural opportunities? The Europeans ask why the United States demands the unrestricted circulation of its message abroad while in the United States itself Act 301 of the Trade Law allows restrictions to be placed on foreign cultural products. The North American radio and television stations not only dedicate nearly their entire space to U.S. programming, they also undercut imported products by advertisements such as: "Why buy music that you don't understand?"

▪ ▪ The Crisis of the Film Industry is not Just an Internal Problem for Each Country

Until a few years ago it was believed that to strengthen national cinema it was necessary to assign quotas for screen time (in Mexico this was 50% for the Mexican films). In this way an attempt was made to limit North American expansion in the field. We know that cinema attendance is dropping all over the world for more complex reasons. In 1957, 411 million tickets were sold in France; in 1990, only 121.1 million were sold.[7] In the 1980s large numbers of Latin American cinemas closed their doors when attendance dropped by 50%. Mexican cinemas, which in 1984 had some 410 million visitors, had only 170 million by 1991.[8] Strictly speaking, what this drop in attendance implied was not that the cinema would disappear, but that television and video were changing the place of access to films to the home.[9] If North American companies took advantage of these changes in technology and cultural habits, it is because they adapted to them more rapidly than other countries did. They promoted them enthusiastically and gained control of distribution outlets of TV and video as well as cinema in almost the entire world.

What can non-American producers, filmmakers, and distributors do? The reaction has not been the same in every country, or in every sector. The British and Germans, according to the GATT negotiations, claim not to understand "what is happening with the image industry; they gave up having their own culture in this area years ago." [10] France, Spain, and Italy try to maintain quotas for national and European cinema; they are trying to improve production and to establish new subsidies to support their own film production—which the United States criticizes as "dumping."

Even among the Latin European countries that defend the "cultural exception" in free trade, there are those that conceive of cinema and television as simple markets where open competition should let the viewers decide what is worth showing and what is not. Nevertheless, others are trying to review the relation between what is public and what is private in the current transnational reorganization of the markets of symbolic goods. The European states—which have carried out a neoliberal slimming down of their cultural apparatus similar to that of Latin America—are now recognizing that it is not only identity that is at play exclusively, or even principally, in the fine arts, literature, and the historically traditional heritage. They continue giving public funding to these classic areas of culture, especially in the Latin countries, but they identify the audiovisual media as the decisive areas in which mass tastes are shaped and through which the masses learn to think and feel.

As in Latin America, the wave of privatization in Europe led to turning over radio stations, television channels, and a large portion of information and cable imaging circuitry to private corporations. The governments reduced their cultural activities to the protection of their historical patrimony (museums, archaeological sites, and so forth) and the promotion of the traditional arts (painting and sculpture, music, theater, literature); given that these areas of public culture are losing their audience, they will have serious difficulties if governments do not give them artificial respiration. The communication and information media linked to new technologies, those requiring the largest investment but which also reach the widest sectors, were given up to private corporations, in many cases North American and Japanese.

But today it is clear that the redefinition of national identities has taken place not only in film, television, and video but also in the networks of the "information highways." Satellite transmission and new fiber-optic cable networks are currently transforming scientific communication (electronic mail, video medical services), electronic offices, banking and interbusiness services, and, of course, the distribution of entertainment. In the United States the Turner Organization manages the distribution of movies, cartoons, and news programs to many Latin American countries and is now starting distribution to some European countries, including France. In a few years films from the United States will be broadcast by satellite to cinemas in hundreds of cities on every continent without the complications of having to pass cans of film and videos through customs. In addition, access by means of television and home computers to video games, shopping channels, and national and international information is becoming more widespread in many societies. Europeans are asking who will manage these networks. Spain and Italy are, for practical purposes, not yet connected to cable networks, and France is only connected to a small extent. But it has been predicted that this market will grow by 50% in the next four years.

In Europe the recent discussions of GATT mobilized leading filmmakers (Almodóvar, Wim Wenders, Bertolucci), actors' associations, and cinema and TV directors, as well as entrepreneurs and politicians. Some of the film directors, writers, sociologists, and anthropologists participating in the debate have shown through their work that they are aware of regional and even local traditions: they create films and novels that are undoubtedly Spanish or French or even Catalan, Breton, or Roman. But they also understand that the possibility of their continuing to make films and to distribute them, as well as their ability to distribute videos and books relating to local culture, depend on the degree of control maintained over the most advanced international communications networks. In Latin American terms we could say that although a good part of our identity continues to be rooted in indigenous and campesino cultures, handicrafts, and traditional music, it is necessary to take into account that 70% of the population lives in cities and a growing proportion has access to the cultural industries. These industries contribute to a world folklore whose main examples are U.S. television series and the films of Spielberg and Lucas—a set of spectacular story lines created from myths intelligible to the viewers of any country, religion, or ideology.[11] Will our cultural policies remain consigned to dirt roads or will they move onto the cultural pavements, the international communications highways?

▪ ▪ From Film to Multimedia Culture

In European countries before the GATT negotiations there was more flexibility on agricultural and industrial concessions than on concessions for audiovisual areas. "France could stop producing potatoes and still be France but if we stopped speaking French, having French films, theater and our own literature, we would become just another suburb of Chicago," commented one television executive.[12]

Five days before GATT was signed, the Spanish government approved a legal decree that established minimum quotas for European films, whereby cities with a population larger than 125,000 had to show one film from an EU country for every two from other continents. Other measures established higher fees to be charged for showing a film on television. There was also discussion of the idea that video companies and dealers contribute part of their profits to financing the film industry: it is becoming increasingly evident that the survival of cinema no longer depends only on screenings in movie houses, but must turn to its new role in the field of electronic audiovisuals. Films today are multimedia products that must be financed by support from their various outlets of distribution.

However, some participants in the debate believe that the survival of cinema, though important, is a minor issue compared with the pressure exerted by the United States to have total freedom within the entire realm of the media. The combination of fiber-optic networks, digitalization, and image compression will ensure that 500 channels will cover Europe before the end of the century. Juan Cueto, director of Spanish Television's Channel +, says that the cinema is a "mcguffin" (a scene from a Hitchcock film that contributes nothing to the suspense, but draws it out). "Film is the locomotor, the Hitchcockian mcguffin, but the important thing about these networks is everything that follows."

A similar future can be predicted for Latin America. Traditional movie houses have closed in Buenos Aires, São Paulo, Caracas, Bogotá, and Mexico City, while in some of these cities more than 50% of homes have VCRs. Between 70% and 90% (depending on the country) of the stock of video clubs, the main source of films, consists of films from the U.S.–European cultures, with which Latin Americans have longstanding ties, and other cultures of our region barely constitute 10% of the available titles in television and video. But the hegemony of the United States is even greater in terms of control of information and cable imaging. In no Latin American country except Brazil are there any consistent state policies of investment for research, production of equipment, or the training of high-level personnel in order to take part in the generation of these cultural innovations linked to advanced technologies.

▪ ▪ Nationalism Again?

The United States has been overtaken in many aspects of industrial development by Germany and Japan. Still, it has overwhelming control of the postindustrial world—that is, of electronic information and communications. After the fall of the Soviet bloc and the disintegration of Soviet ideological and cultural production, the "American way" expanded its spectacular productions "Jurassically," throughout the entire universe. The energetic European position in the GATT negotiations and the internal measures some countries adopted to protect their audiovisual production are among the few consistent forces that make it possible to imagine a symbolic world where everything is not in the hands of Hollywood and CNN. At least, as Regis Debray wrote, it helps to consider whether what is good for Columbia and Warner Brothers—which we already know is good for the United States—is also good for humanity.[13]

Some intellectuals become alarmed at what they consider a revival of nationalism, "anti-North Americanism, based on ideological myths," and the statist interventions that foster authoritarianism. Mario Vargas Llosa says: "when operated freely, the market allows, for example, films produced in 'the periphery' to suddenly find a way to be projected in millions of cinemas throughout the world, as happened with *Like Water for Chocolate* and *The Mariachi*."[14] These exceptions reveal themselves to be extremely rare cases when we consider the modest place that Latin American and European (and Asian and African) films have in the movie, television, and video club advertisements in any North American city, or in all countries where programming is subject to U.S. distributors. In the United States only 1% of all the tickets sold in cinemas are for films in languages other than English.[15] There is no available data to make us believe what Vargas Llosa says—that "the disappearance of borders, the integration of the peoples of the world within an exchange system for the benefit of all, and above all, for the countries that urgently need to escape underdevelopment and poverty . . . those ideals of our youth" which socialism did not achieve, have been achieved by "capitalism and the marketplace."[16] A novelist's story?

The recent European debate is not so much a confrontation between nationalism and international free trade. It is based on the recognition of globalization and interculturalism, but it questions whether the free play of the market will solve the asymmetries and inequalities among countries and among sectors within each country. Economists and politicians are beginning to recognize that culture is too important to be relinquished exclusively to the competition among international markets. And they ask how the search for profits that require high investment in technological innovation can be made compatible with each society's own memory and the promotion of creative freedom.

After the euphoria following the fall of the Berlin Wall and the complications this brought to all of Europe, thinkers such as Alain Touraine wrote that the market is useful for tearing down "the centralized State, clientelism or totalitarianism" but "it does not constitute a basis for construction or for the generation of social life." New questions then emerged, concerning "how to permit State intervention without falling into the trap of defending national traditions" and how to combine aid "for the creation and survival of businesses able to compete in the market" with "a policy of patronage and indirect subsidies by means of support to cultural institutions, schools, museums, universities and associations." [17]

These are the questions that are also important in Mexico's integration with other Latin American countries and in the Latin American countries' integration with the United States. It is necessary to pay attention to them if free trade is not to drown multiculturalism or subordinate diverse identities to a single identity that only one of these imagines the others should be. If identity is to be risked and transformed principally into communications, governments should agree on rules and conditions in order to continue producing and distributing their own films, television, and other expressions of their own culture. If this does not happen—according to public interest and multiculturalism—the destiny of societies on the periphery will be reduced to one of paying their money as consumers, with the occasional possibility of providing the location or dubbing a few films.

NOTES

1. For a criticism of anthropology and folklore on this point, see J. Clifford and G. Marcus, eds., *Writing Culture: The Poetics and Politics of Ethnography* (Berkeley: University of California Press, 1986); and Renato Rosaldo, *Culture and Truth: The Remaking of Social Analysis* (Boston: Beacon Press, 1989).

2. These facts were taken from the text of NAFTA as it was signed, and from an article by Fernando Mateo, Mexican chief negotiator for the service sector: "The Pull of the NAFTA," *Nexos* 189 (September 1993): 66–67.

3. We refer here to what is called "radio libre" in Latin America and Europe.

4. A more extensive analysis of these perspectives can be found in *La educación y la cultura ante el Tratado de Libre Comercio*, ed. Gilberto Guevara Niebla and Néstor García Canclini (Mexico: Nexos-Nueva Imagen, 1993).

5. "A business worth more than 500,000 million pesetas," *El País*, December 11, 1993, p. 3.

6. Interview with Edouard Balladur, the French prime minister. "What does the U.S. want . . . the disappearance of the European film industry?" *El Nacional*, October 23, 1993, p. 27.

7. Joelle Farchy, *Le cinéma dechainé: Mutation d'une industrie* (Paris: Presses du CNRS, 1992), 37–38.

8. Information provided by the Instituto Mexicano de Cinematografía.

9. See the following study carried out on these changes: *Los nuevos espectadores: Cine, televisión y video en México*, ed. Néstor García Canclini (Mexico: Instituto Mexicano de Cinematografía, 1994).

10. *El País*, December 11, 1993, p. 35.

11. See an excellent analysis of this process in Charles Albert Michelet's article, "Reflexions sur le drole de drame du cinéma mondial," *CinémAction* (1988): 156–161.

12. *El País*, December 11, 1993, p. 35.

13. Regis Debray, "Respuesta a Mario Vargas Llosa," *El País*, November 4, 1993.

14. Mario Vargas Llosa, "La tribu y el mercado," *El País*, November 21, 1993. For a broader view of the discussion, see Pierre Musso, "Audiovisuel et télécommunications en Europe: quelles recompositions?" *Quaderne, La revie de la communication* (Winter 1993).

15. Marco Vinicio González, "Cine mexicano en Nueva York," *La Jornada Semanal*, November 7, 1993 (no. 230), p. 46.

16. Vargas Llosa, "La tribu."

17. Alain Touraine, "La excepción cultural," *El País*, December 11, 1993.

8

Media Reception on the Mexican Border with the United States

JOSÉ CARLOS LOZANO

MEXICANS LIVING ALONG THE BORDER with the United States have been experiencing for years what their compatriots in the interior are only beginning to realize with the recent opening of the country's economy and NAFTA: an intense coexistence and exposure, on a daily basis, to U.S. culture and mass media. During the last few years, the economic policies of the Mexican government and the rapid introduction and diffusion throughout Mexico of new communication technologies (cable systems, VCRs, videocassette rentals, satellite dishes, compact discs, and so forth) have dramatically increased the contact with, and the consumption of, U.S. media products.

Ironically enough, given the widespread fear of many Mexican scholars, journalists, and politicians concerning negative impact on the cultural identity of Mexican audience members from U.S. movies, television programs, music, news, magazines, and other media products, relatively little systematic research has investigated the basis of those concerns. Very few studies have measured the exposure of Mexican audiences to U.S. media products, and even fewer have confronted the issue of the mass media's impact on their cultural identity.

This chapter reports the findings of a reception study carried out in late 1991 with adolescents living on the Mexican side of the Mexico–U.S. border. No other place seems more appropriate to study the reception of American media products and their interaction with, influence on, or redefinition of Mexican audience members' cultural identity. While in the interior of the country U.S. media products are usually identifiable as imported because they are dubbed or subtitled, on the Mexican border residents receive U.S. television and radio signals directly from the transmitter. Mexico's border states also have the country's greatest concentration of national and local mass media, providing a great diversity of choices for audiences.

▪ ▪ Fears of Erosion of National Identity

For years, Latin American scholars have expressed concern about the devastating impact of transnational communication on the national identity of their countries' audience members. After a comprehensive review of Latin American research on this topic, Beltrán (1978, p. 75) concluded that the vast quantities of imported programming on Latin American television presented a composite of images consisting of, among others, the following elements: individualism, elitism, racism, materialism, conservatism, aggressiveness, and authoritarianism. These "pictures," he claimed, were characteristic of U.S. media messages and were generally regarded by the scholars he reviewed as contrary to the aspirations for autonomous, humanistic, and truly democratic national development in the region (p. 62).

In Mexico historical fears of U.S. cultural influence on Mexican identity dating from the nineteenth century have been revitalized by the massive presence of American cultural products on Mexican media. Cremoux (1988) began examining this problem in the 1960s. He found that 80% of the television programs preferred by junior high school students in Mexico City originated in the United States (among them were "The Fugitive," "Batman," "Gilligan's Island," "Daniel Boone," and "The Patty Duke Show"). He concluded that the majority of these programs were detrimental to Mexican youngsters because of the stereotyped depiction of characters and situations (p. 59). Montoya and Rebeil (1986), looking again at the exposure of junior high school students to Mexican television in 1982, argued that: "commercial television has become in Mexico a vehicle for the transmission of North American culture, constantly eroding national identity and local cultures" (p. 147). They explained that the loss of national values and culture, a longstanding problem in Mexican society, had accelerated with the introduction of television (p. 155).

In a study of cable television in Mexico City, García-Calderón (1987, p. 56) argued that the large volume of U.S. programs made cable TV a principal vehicle through which foreign values were displacing Mexican national culture: "Cable TV promotes a cultural colonization which affects the middle and upper socio-economic sectors who have access to it. That is the reason why, in addition to being a commercial enterprise, Cable TV has become a cultural dependency factor" (p. 57).

This view has persisted. Esteinou (1990) argued that Mexican television promotes a consumerist culture and the veneration of the American way of life (p. 106). He accused Mexican electronic media of fostering the mental "denationalization" of the Republic, by fostering psychological and cognitive perceptions among the population that are in opposition to the nation's own cultural roots, ethnic background, and Constitution. Through its exposure to television, Esteinou explains, the Mexican middle class has abandoned its Catholic cultural background,

> adopting the transnational culture of Superman, Wonder Woman, Star Wars, Batman and Robin, Walt Disney, and so on. Thus, in less than a generation the roots of the transnational, the North American, have been planted in our conscience. Today, we can say that in Mexican territory the first generation of "norteamericanos" [Americans] has been born. (p. 116)

▪ ▪ Cultural Erosion in the Border Region

If Mexican concern over the widespread loss of cultural identity is great, the fears are most concentrated in the border region. The consequences of direct exposure to U.S. culture and media systems for Mexican border residents was considered so critical in the early 1980s that the de la Madrid administration established the Programa Cultural de las Fronteras, a federal program to promote nationalistic cultural manifestations and to support research on the impact of U.S. culture on border residents' national identity. The Salinas de Gortari administration continued funding for the program.

Mexican scholars concerned with the dangers of U.S. cultural infiltration in the border region assume that national values and traditions have been or are being replaced by the all-powerful American culture. A typical example appeared in a national magazine:

> Far away from God—and from Mexico—and very close to the United States, Tamaulipas' border residents are victims—although they consider themselves to be beneficiaries—of a "denationaliza-

tion" phenomenon so deep that it represents . . . not only a threat, but a feint against Mexico's sovereignty in that borderline.

Every day, the border resident receives the brutal impact of American culture: films, radio, and TV; books, magazines, newspapers; customs and attitudes about life itself; food to eat, clothes to wear. (Candelaria 1987, p. 16)

Despite the many alarms, serious research about the actual loss of cultural identity has been scarce. Very few studies have attempted to measure the exposure of Mexican northerners to U.S. mass media, and fewer yet have faced the issue of the actual impact of mass media on attitudes and values (see, e.g., Iglesias 1988; Malagamba 1986).

I would suggest that in order to account for any impact of transnational media on the cultural identity of Mexicans, whether border residents or not, the following four conditions must be met: 1. Foreign media content must be available, whether delivered by the local communication systems or transmitted directly from the foreign country; 2. audience members must have significant exposure to that foreign content; 3. assimilation of the ideological values contained in the foreign media content must result from exposure to them; and 4. the audience members' cultural identity must show signs of erosion due to the assimilation of the foreign media content. Each of these conditions will now be discussed in turn.

▪ ▪ Availability of Foreign Media and Foreign Media Content

This first condition is fulfilled not only in the Mexican border region but in an increasing area of the country, due to the expansion of cable systems carrying American channels, video rental stores, and satellite dishes. Mexico's economic opening in anticipation of NAFTA and the general lack of governmental policy and regulation related to new technologies have permitted the spread of U.S. media television channels, films, video games, news, and so on throughout the country (cf. Gómez Mont 1992, p. 40). Now that NAFTA is a reality, this trend is bound to intensify.

In contrast with the lack of reception studies, the flow of cultural products from the United States to Mexico and the availability of American contents in Mexican media systems are well documented. Sánchez-Ruiz (1993, p. 19) found that 30% of the total number of Mexican television programs received over the air were imported (75% of the imports being from the United States), and the percentage was higher in prime time—almost half the total (47.6%). In early 1994 two national television networks (Televisa's Channel 5 and Televisión Azteca's Channel 7) devoted almost 100% of their prime time to American imports such as "Alf," "Beverly Hills 90210," "Saved by the Bell," "The Simpsons," "Emergency 911," "Melrose Place," "The Wonder Years," "Heroes in Blue," "Eyewitness Video," and U.S. films. The figures for cable were higher; most local systems carried U.S. channels such as CNN, TNT, USA, HBO, ABC, CBS, NBC, A&E, the Cartoon Network, and MTV Latino. American titles in video rental stores accounted for as much as 80% of all the available films, and half the new film releases in Mexican theaters during the last ten years have been American (Sánchez-Ruiz 1993, p. 20).

American media content, however, is not the only content available for Mexican audiences either in the border region or in the rest of the country. Boyd-Barrett (1982) has pointed out that countervailing local influences have to be taken into account when evaluating the totality of relevant exogenous media influences. This is indeed necessary in the case of Mexico, which has very strong media production industries. The other two national networks (Televisa's Channel 2 and Televisión Azteca's Channel 13) enjoy much higher ratings than their counterparts dominated by U.S. programs; they devote all of their prime time to Mexican television productions—*telenovelas*, game shows, sitcoms, and news. Cable systems all over the country carry the four national networks, and in most cities the two Mexican public stations, Channel 11 and Channel 22, as well. There are also Mexican versions of MTV that transmit videos of Mexican groups and vocalists, and channels that transmit Mexican movies twenty-four hours a day. Many systems include the U.S.-based Spanish-language networks Univisión, Telemundo, and Galavisión, which transmit mostly Latin American television productions. The Mexican cinema has been revitalized recently with such movies as *Like Water for Chocolate* and *Cronos*, which have recaptured the interest of Mexican middle- and upper-class filmgoers. The Mexican music industry is the strongest of all Latin American countries, and few radio stations air U.S. music.

In sum, while U.S. media content is widely available in Mexico, there are plenty of local options to choose from. Thus, the first condition—that is, for there to be American influence via the mass media—is met, but its impacts are not proven.

▪▪ Exposure to Foreign Media Content

Availability of foreign media content is a necessary condition for, but not proof of, cultural imperialism. If local media content is also available—as it is in Mexico—reception studies must determine whether local audiences are significantly exposed to media imports, as well as whether they prefer their own media or a combination of both.

Unfortunately, the numerous studies of foreign media supply have not been matched by research on the consumption side. As Sepstrup (in de la Garde 1993, p. 45) has argued, "the lack of interest in the consumption of the observed flows has remained a serious shortcoming of the research on international television flows."

The findings of the few available studies, however, point out that supply of foreign media content should not be equated with its consumption. In his analysis of media consumption in Québec, de la Garde (1993, pp. 37–43) found that despite a significant availability of American media and media content, Québec's audiences preferred their national supply "in all programme categories and in all entertainment subcategories." For example, Québecois devoted 88 percent of their viewing time to watching national television. Caron and Bélanger (1993, p. 136) argue along the same lines that locally produced television series, in Québec, "are often winners in the ratings, attracting as many as half the total population on some nights. Very few American programmes even come close to such ratings."

In Mexico ratings are not available for most media, making it difficult to replicate de la Garde's comparison between supply and consumption patterns. However, some related reception studies (which do not directly address the question of media exposure and cultural identity) suggest that a situation similar to Québec's is in place. By far the highest rated television channel in Mexico City, Guadalajara, and Monterrey, the three largest Mexican cities, is Televisa's national Channel 2 (see Aceves 1991; *El Norte* 1993; García Canclini and Piccini 1993). This channel devotes almost all of its air time to Mexican productions such as *telenovelas,* sitcoms, musical programs, and news. The other national network operated by Televisa, Channel 5, offers imported programs from the United States, mostly cartoons and series such as "Beverly Hills 90210," "Bucker," and "The Equalizer." In Mexico City, in 1989, 45% of the population preferred Channel 2, while 28% preferred Channel 5 (García Canclini and Piccini 1993, p. 68). In Guadalajara, in the same year, 52% preferred Channel 2 and 19% preferred Channel 5 (Aceves 1991, p. 153). In Monterrey, a large city close to the Mexican border with the United States, in March 1993, the ten highest-rated television programs were all Mexican productions, except for "Sábado Gigante" (second place), a variety show, and "Cristina" (eighth place), a talk show (similar to "Geraldo"), both of which are produced by the U.S.-based Spanish-language network Univisión, which is owned in part by Televisa (*El Norte,* March 11, 1993). None of these ten most-watched programs was transmitted on Channel 5; none was a standard American dubbed-to-Spanish program.

Consequently, the strong U.S. media content of Mexican television was not mirrored by high levels of audience exposure to it. As in the case of Québec, local media productions commanded the higher ratings, and the national networks transmitting American programming were not the most popular.

▪ ▪ Assimilation of Foreign Media Content

In their review of the salient research conducted in Canada and the United States, Caron and Bélanger (1993) affirmed that we possess limited knowledge "on the 'cultural effects' of imported cultural products."

In the early 1980s Boyd-Barrett and Fejes had pointed out the same problem. It is easier, Boyd-Barrett (1982) argued, to determine the number of hours of imported television programming or the percentage of international news originated by transnational agencies than it is to assess cultural changes in audience members due to their exposure to imported media messages,

> yet the weight of evidence for theses of media imperialism often relies heavily on the latter. . . . Too much weight may sometimes be given to Western influences on one particular medium without reference to the general character of all media output or to evidence concerning respective media impacts. (p. 180)

Similarly, Fejes (1981, p. 287) argued that the cultural impact often went unaddressed in detailed studies of transnational media:

> While a great deal of the concern over media imperialism is motivated by fear of the cultural consequences of the transnational media—of the threat that such media pose to the integrity and the

development of viable national cultures in Third World societies—
it is the one area where, aside from anecdotal accounts, little progress has been achieved in understanding specifically the cultural
impact of transnational media on Third World societies.

In addition to Boyd-Barrett and Fejes, other critical scholars have
pointed out cultural imperialism's neglect of issues of media reception
and the cultural imports' actual impact on cultural identity. De la Garde
(1987, p. 191) explains that many dependency theorists assume that if
transnationalization of the production process occurs, the transnationalization of the reception process follows logically. He considers this an
unwarranted conceptual shortcut that reflects a central weakness in
critical research:

> Although it is mandatory to understand the undeniable commer-
> cial and industrial nature of many of the products which make up
> our cultural environment, it is equally important not to forget that
> people are not mirror reflections of their environment; rather they
> are prisms. Culture as a dynamic process of sense-making does not
> end, but rather starts, with the reading of a book, the listening to a
> pop record or the thrill of a movie. (p. 191)

García Canclini (1988a), a leading Latin American scholar, explains
that another major problem with cultural imperialism is its conceptualization of audience members as passive recipients of all-powerful communication messages. In this approach, he claims,

> audiences and consumers are seen as passive executants of practices
> imposed by the dominant, incapable of distinguishing between
> those messages which benefit and those which harm, between the
> use value in given goods (which is assumed to be "authentic") and
> their exchange or symbolic value (which is considered "artificial").
> The methodological consequence is the belief that purely by study-
> ing the mass media's economic aims and the ideological structure
> of their messages, one might deduce the needs they create in the
> audience. No autonomy on the part of popular cultures is recog-
> nized, nor is the complex relation between consumers, objects and
> social space. (p. 472)

Smith (1990) shares this view, pointing out that "images and cultural traditions do not derive from, or descend upon, mute and passive

populations on whose tabula rasa they inscribe themselves" (p. 179). Instead, he says, the meaning embedded in transnational media messages
derives not only from the intentions of the producers, but also from the
historical experiences and social status of audiences.

Fejes (1984) equated the perception of media as all-powerful and
audience members as passive recipients of dominant ideology with the
old hypodermic-needle (or "powerful effects") model used in propaganda research conducted by behaviorist scholars before and after World
War II. He argued that the audience had become almost invisible in the
theory and research of critical scholars as a result of their focusing on
issues of media content and production. More recently, Caron and Bélanger (1993, p. 136) argued that studies of foreign-media availability in
national systems, "although very useful from the point of view of cultural merchandising, . . . procure little additional understanding of the
ways in which people appropriate the meaning(s) of the images/sounds
they consume."

The foregoing discussion is relevant to analyses of the third condition for an impact of foreign-media content on national identity. Even
if local audiences are exposed to media imports—and this is questionable in the case of Mexico, as we have already seen—that does not mean
that they will automatically accept and assimilate the ideological values
and world views that the products reflect.

Unfortunately, if media consumption studies in Mexico are scarce,
the situation is even worse for empirical studies on the processes of appropriation, assimilation, or redesigning of meanings embedded in foreign media content. While García Canclini (1988b) and Barbero (1988)
have made valuable conceptual contributions to the development of
Latin American cultural studies, few researchers have tested their theories empirically.

One of the first tasks of researchers interested in analyzing the appropriation of foreign media content is to identify and describe the
ideological values embedded in it through semiological analysis or content analysis. In the process, they should determine whether those values
are in opposition to those that could be defined as "national" or "local."
Again, studies in this area are almost nonexistent. Some analyses were
carried out during the 1970s and early 1980s by theorists utilizing the
cultural imperialism approach (see Beltrán 1978; Dorfman and Mattelart
1978; Dorfman 1980; Santa Cruz and Erazo 1981). However, these studies
were few and focused on specific media messages (Walt Disney comic

books, *The Lone Ranger, Reader's Digest, Cosmopolitan*); moreover, they are somewhat outdated and do not reflect the content of media imports today.

A major challenge in this kind of research is in identifying a general ideological content across all U.S. media imports. Could anybody assume that the same U.S. ideological values are in place in cultural products as different from each other as "Daktari," *Rambo*, Calvin and Hobbes, Oliver Stone's *JFK*, CNN news, and "Beverly Hills 90210"? Although all respond to an industrial capitalist logic of production and tend to reproduce their system's ideology, culturalists and semioticians have shown that media messages are polysemous, offering a wide variety of meanings, both preferred and alternative (cf. Hall 1989; Fiske 1992). This, in turn, facilitates "negotiated" readings by audience members. Consequently, it is difficult to argue that all kinds of U.S. media reflect the same world vision, values, and meanings monolithically and without internal contradictions. We need semiotic content analyses that assess the particular ideological meanings in order to have a clearer picture of what Mexican audiences may really be assimilating.

Of course, these content analyses would not be enough. It is not possible by simply looking at the message to make conclusions about the particular readings audience members make. Thus, reception analyses are needed. Even if content analyses conclude that U.S. media messages do indeed carry clear hegemonic U.S. values and ideological meanings, reception studies might discover that audience members reject, negotiate, or redesign them, thereby mediating their impact.

The next section presents the findings of a reception study I carried out in November and December 1991 among junior high school students living in a Mexican border town. In my analysis, I discuss each of the three conditions outlined above. While limited in its generalizability to one particular segment of the population and to one particular border city, this study may provide some useful data with which to start tackling the question of the impact of foreign cultural products on the national identity of Mexican audiences.

The Setting

The U.S.–Mexico border consists of 2,234 miles. Texas, New Mexico, Arizona, and California are the U.S. border states, and Tamaulipas, Nuevo Leon, Coahuila, Chihuahua, Sonora, and Baja California are the states on the Mexican side. One of the most important Mexican border cities is Nuevo Laredo (Tamaulipas), with a population of 217,912, according to the 1990 Mexican census.

Nuevo Laredo is the main terrestrial port for Mexican imports from and exports to the United States. Most of the economic activity gravitates around international trade between these two countries. Many jobs are in service industries such as forwarding agencies, custom brokers and government agencies, transportation, and so on. The *maquiladora* (assembly plant) industry is also very strong: there are seventy-two plants in Nuevo Laredo, employing around 20,000 workers.

Nuevo Laredo is also characterized by an overwhelming presence of mass media, both Mexican and American. At the beginning of 1991 there were two local television stations, one of which was affiliated to the most powerful national television channel in the country (XEW, Channel 2). Signals from three stations in Laredo, Texas could also be received— affiliates of CBS, NBC, and Telemundo, a U.S. Spanish-language network. The local channel (XEFE 2) based its programming on *telenovelas,* U.S. movies and action series dubbed to Spanish, U.S. and Mexican sports (NFL games, major league baseball, soccer, boxing, Mexican wrestling), and the news magazine of a national commercial network. The other station, XHBR Channel 11, was affiliated to the most-watched national network, and based its morning programming on ECO (a CNN-style news show), a block of local programs in the afternoon (a one-hour news program, a thirty-minute sports program, and a thirty-minute interview program), two blocks of *telenovelas* (one from 5:00 P.M. to 8:00 P.M., another from 9:00 P.M. to 10:00 P.M.), and Mexican comedy shows in the style of "The Golden Girls," "Doctor, Doctor," and stand-up comedy.

There were twelve local radio stations, and the signals of five stations from the U.S. side could also be received over the air. Of the twelve local radio stations, none transmitted English-language programming; most based their programming on Mexican traditional and popular music, and three offered Spanish-language modern pop music. Of the five Laredo, Texas stations, two had Spanish-language programming (Mexican "country" music [ranchera] or Tex-Mex and Mexican modern music), one was a Catholic station, and two transmitted U.S. pop music.

Residents could rent either Mexican or U.S. movies from more than fifty video stores in Nuevo Laredo or watch them in one of the nine theaters located in different parts of the city. There were five daily newspapers, all locally owned, with a combined circulation of around 18,000, and the only English-language newspaper, printed in Laredo, Texas, had a daily circulation of around 1,000 on the Mexican side. All these facts support the selection of this border town as the place in which to carry out research on media and national identity.

Method

The survey was based on interviews with a representative sample of students attending both private and public *secundarias* (junior high schools) in Nuevo Laredo. Schools were stratified to assure representation of upper-, middle-, and lower-class students. In November 1991 there were 8,486 junior high school students in Nuevo Laredo. Of those, 8,078 attended public schools and 403 attended private schools. An adequate sample size for this total population of students was 400, but since upper-class students represent a very small percentage of the total population, the original number of upper-class cases to be included in the total sample size of 400 was too small. I therefore decided to oversample the upper-class students to allow comparisons to be made between them and middle- and lower-class students. The final sample size, then, was 575. In the tables reporting the data, $N = 400$ is used when referring to the *secundaria* students in general and $N = 575$ is used when comparisons are made between the three social-class groups. The fieldwork was done in 1991, during the last two weeks of November and the first week of December.

Results

TELEVISION STATIONS PREFERRED

Table 1 shows that despite the availability of two U.S. English-language television channels (CBS and NBC) operating from Laredo, Texas, *secundaria* students strongly preferred the stations with Mexican or Spanish-language programming. XHBR Channel 11 (affiliated to the national Televisa channel XEW) was the most frequently watched station, with a mean of 4.41 on a scale of 1–5 (1 = never, 5 = every day). The second-most-watched station was KLDO Channel 27 (mean = 4.00), which, although located on the U.S. side of the border, was affiliated to the Spanish-language network Telemundo, which airs many Mexican movies, soap operas, and sports. In third place was the local

TABLE 1   Means (*M*) and Standard Deviations (*SD*) of Frequency with which Students Watch Different Television Stations

Station	*M*[a]	*SD*
Air reception		
XHBR (Televisa)	4.41	0.88
KLDO (Telemundo)	4.00	1.06
XEFE (Local)	2.86	0.99
KVTV (CBS)	2.44	3.78
KGNS (NBC)	2.07	0.95
On cable		
Mexican channels (*n* = 61)[b]	3.44	1.31
U.S. channels (*n* = 62)[b]	3.11	1.26

[a] Mean on the scale 1 = "Never," 2 = "Rarely," 3 = "Sometimes," 4 = "Frequently," 5 = "Every day."
[b] *n* = number of students answering the question.

television station XEFE 2, with a mean of 2.86 ("rarely" watched), and in the last two places were the two U.S. stations, one affiliated to CBS (mean = 2.44) and the other to NBC (mean = 2.07).

Those with access to cable television—which offers many more U.S. English-language channel options—still preferred to watch Mexican television stations.

MOST-WATCHED TELEVISION PROGRAMS

While U.S. programs were available in English on the two Laredo, Texas stations and dubbed to Spanish on XEFE 2, *secundaria* students were clearly more interested in watching Mexican programs (see Table 2). Out of the thirty-three most-mentioned television programs, the first sixteen were either produced in Mexico or the United States, but by the Telemundo network (in Spanish, with Latino actors or artists). All but one of the eight most-mentioned programs were produced by Televisa; "Papá Soltero," "Anabel," "Chespirito," and soap operas such as "Muchachitas" are examples. In seventeenth place was the most-mentioned U.S. program type—cartoons. In twenty-second place appeared U.S. films shown on CBS or NBC, while locally dubbed versions of "Magnum" and "Dukes of Hazzard" occupied twenty-fifth and twenty-eighth place, respectively. "CHiPS" and "Teenage Mutant Ninja Turtles" ranked last.

TABLE 2 Rank of Favorite Television Programs
(U.S. programs are in **boldface**)

Rank	Programs	Number of Times Mentioned[a]
1	Mexican soap operas (Televisa or XEFE)	226
2	"Papá Soltero" (Televisa)	153
3	"Anabel" (Televisa)	153
4	"Chespirito" (Televisa)	144
5	"Cine Millonario" (Telemundo)	135
6	"Cándido Pérez" (Televisa)	131
7	"Muchachitas" (Televisa — Mexican soap opera)	109
8	"Andale" (Televisa)	79
9	"Cara a Cara" (Telemundo)	64
10	"Lucha Libre Mexicana" (Televisa)	51
11	"Todo de Todo" (Televisa)	45
12	"Mujer, Casos de la Vida" (Televisa)	40
13	TVO (Televisa)	35
14	Mexican movies (Televisa)	34
15	"Ocurrió Así" (Telemundo)	33
16	"La Movida" (Televisa)	31
17	**Cartoons in English** (NBC or CBS)	31
18	"A la Cama con Porcel" (Telemundo)	26
19	**Dubbed-to-Spanish cartoons** (XEFE)	17
20	MTV International (Telemundo)	16
21	"Siempre en Domingo" (Televisa)	16
22	**U.S. movies in English** (NBC or CBS)	15
23	"Primera Tanda" (Telemundo)	13
24	"Un millón de Amigos" (Telemundo)	13
25	**"Magnum"** (XEFE, dubbed)	12
26	"Cine en Su Casa" (Telemundo)	12
27	"Contacto" (Telemundo)	11
28	**"Dukes of Hazzard"** (XEFE, dubbed)	11
29	"La Telaraña" (Televisa)	10
30	"Eco" (Televisa)	10
31	"Primera Tanda" (Telemundo)	10
32	**"CHiPS"** (XEFE, dubbed)	10

TABLE 2   *Continued*

Rank	Programs	Number of Times Mentioned[a]
33	**"Teenage Mutant Ninja Turtles"** (CBS)	10
	Others (mentioned less than 10 times each)	
	On Telemundo	62
	On Televisa or XEFE	59
	In English	53
	U.S. programs dubbed to Spanish	44
	Mexican or Latin American programs	19
Total		1,943

[a] Every student mentioned five of his or her favorite programs; data refer to the total number of times each program was mentioned.

Exposure to U.S. television programs was thus not significant among the students, despite their availability in both English and Spanish.

DIFFERENCES IN EXPOSURE TO U.S. TELEVISION BY SOCIAL CLASS

Table 3 shows that social class accounts for differences between upper-class and middle-class students in terms of exposure to U.S. television, the middle-class students being the heavier consumers of U.S. dubbed-to-Spanish series such as "Magnum," "CHiPS," and "Daktari." Exposure to U.S. television among the three social groups (mean = 2.17 on a scale of 1–5), however, was considerably lower than that to Mexican television (mean = 3.59).

RADIO STATIONS PREFERRED

Exposure to radio stations and music in general was very similar to that of television. Table 4 shows that the students overwhelmingly chose Mexican Spanish-language stations when listening to the radio. The twelve most-listened-to radio stations were local stations, ranging between means of 3.19 and 1.29. The four radio stations located in Laredo, Texas were in the last five places. Consequently, Nuevo Laredo *secundaria* students, despite their geographical proximity to the United States, showed patterns of exposure that favored national over foreign media.

TABLE 3   Means (M), Standard Deviations (SD), and Analysis
of Variance (ANOVA) of Frequency with which Students Watch
Mexican and U.S. Television Programs, by Social Class

				ANOVA	
Social Class	n	M[a]	SD	F	Significance
Mexican television programs[b]					
Upper	150	3.51	0.71	1.35	.2612
Middle	268	3.63	0.79		
Lower	93	3.62	0.87		
Total	511	3.59	0.79		
U.S. television programs[c]					
Upper	144	2.05*	0.54	3.03	.0494
Middle	261	2.22[†]	0.79		
Lower	90	2.23	0.72		
Total	495	2.17	0.79		

*[†] Significantly different means (Tukey's b)
[a] Mean on the scale 1 = "Never," 2 = "Rarely," 3 = "Sometimes," 4 = "Frequently,"
   5 = "Every week."
[b] Combined mean for the following six Mexican television programs: "Papá Soltero," "Anabel," "Cándido Pérez," "Chespirito," Mexican films, and Mexican
   wrestling.
[c] Combined mean for the following six U.S. television programs: "CHiPS," "Magnum," "Daktari," "Dukes of Hazzard," "Teenage Mutant Ninja Turtles," and
   U.S. films.

PREFERRED RADIO MUSIC AND GROUPS

Table 5 shows that the music most frequently listened to on the radio was modern Spanish-language music, with a mean of 3.87. In second
place was Mexican ranchera or traditional music, with a mean of 3.14,
closely followed by U.S. pop music, with a mean of 3.13.

The list of most popular groups or singers shows that Mexican artists were much more popular than American ones. Table 6 shows that
50.9% of group and singer identification went to artists playing Spanish-
language modern music, 36.9% to Mexican popular music, and just
12.2% to English-language music. This result confirms that of Table 5,
which showed English-language music to be in third place.

Again, as in the case of television, border youngsters were much

TABLE 4   Means (*M*) and Standard Deviations (*SD*) of Frequency with which Students Listen to Local Radio Stations (U.S. stations transmitting from Laredo, Texas are in **boldface**)

Rank	Station	Type of Music	*M*[a]	*SD*
1	XHTLN	Ranchera music	3.19	1.36
2	XHNOE	Modern in Spanish	3.17	1.53
3	XHMW	Modern in Spanish	2.96	1.29
4	XHNK	Modern in Spanish	2.76	1.44
5	XEFE	Modern in Spanish	2.39	1.23
6	XEWL	Ranchera music	2.11	1.31
7	XENLT	Modern in Spanish	2.06	0.97
8	XEGNK	Ranchera music	1.75	1.06
9	XEAS	Ranchera, salsa	1.69	1.03
10	XEBK	Ranchera, tejano	1.56	0.87
11	XENU	Ranchera	1.52	0.86
12	XEK	Varied	1.39	0.73
13	**KVOZ**	Contemporary (English)	1.37	0.88
14	XEMU	Varied	1.29	0.75
15	**KOYE**	Contemporary (English)	1.23	0.69
16	**KLAR**	Varied (Spanish and English)	1.22	0.66
17	**KRRG**	Varied (English)	1.21	0.66

[a] Mean on the scale 1 = "Never," 2 = "Rarely," 3 = "Sometimes," 4 = "Frequently," 5 = "Every day."

TABLE 5   Means (*M*) and Standard Deviations (*SD*) of Frequency with which Students Listen to U.S., Mexican Modern, and "Ranchera" Music

Type of Music	*M*[a]	*SD*
Mexican modern music	3.87	1.25
Mexican ranchera music[b]	3.14	1.33
U.S. music	3.13	1.27

[a] Mean on the scale 1 = "Never," 2 = "Rarely," 3 = "Sometimes," 4 = "Frequently," 5 = "Every day."
[b] A wide term embracing different types of music liked by the lower classes in Mexico, and including *corridos* (ballads), salsa, cumbia, and tejano music.

TABLE 6   Favorite Music Groups or Singers

Type of Group or Singer (in terms of music performed)	Times Mentioned[a]	(%)
Mexican modern music	417	50.9
Mexican ranchera music	302	36.9
U.S. music	100	12.2
Total	819	100

[a] Every student mentioned two of his or her favorite groups or singers; data refer to the total number of times mentioned.

TABLE 7   Means (*M*), Standard Deviations (*SD*), and Analysis of Variance (ANOVA) of Frequency with which Students Listen to U.S., Mexican Modern, and Mexican Ranchera Music, by Social Class

Social Class	*n*	*M*[a]	*SD*	*F* (ANOVA)	Significance (ANOVA)
U.S. music					
Upper	159	3.98*	1.04	31.23	.0000
Middle	290	3.13†	1.24		
Lower	101	2.98†	1.35		
Mexican modern music					
Upper	161	4.12*	1.13	3.88	.0213
Middle	297	3.86†	1.20		
Lower	103	3.72†	1.38		
Mexican ranchera music					
Upper	159	2.17*	1.23	40.18	.0000
Middle	297	3.06†	1.30		
Lower	102	3.53**	1.32		

*†** Significantly different means (Tukey's b).
[a] Mean on the scale 1 = "Never," 2 = "Rarely," 3 = "Sometimes," 4 = "Frequently," 5 = "Every day."

more likely to listen to, and prefer, Mexican artists than U.S. artists. Geographical proximity to the United States seems not to be a factor in increasing the likelihood of Mexican youngsters choosing U.S. television or radio content.

DIFFERENCES IN EXPOSURE TO U.S. MUSIC BY SOCIAL CLASS

Table 7 shows that there were significant differences between upper-, middle-, and lower-class youngsters with respect to the frequency with which they listen to U.S. and Mexican music. Upper-class students listened to U.S. music significantly more (mean = 3.98) than those in the middle class (mean = 3.13) and those in the lower class (mean = 2.98). However, upper-class students also listened to Mexican modern music more than their middle- and lower-class peers. In fact, they listened more frequently to Mexican modern music (mean = 4.12) than to U.S. music (mean = 3.98), rejecting the possibility of any simple correlation between social class and preference for U.S. media contents. Looking at the frequency with which students listen to each type of music, it is easy to see that in all cases, regardless of social class, exposure to Mexican music (either modern or traditional) is more intense than exposure to U.S. music. While upper-class students are more likely to listen to American singers or groups, they tend to devote even more attention to their national music.

MOST-WATCHED FILMS

If *secundaria* youngsters clearly prefer Mexican television and radio messages over U.S. contents, the reverse is true for films. Table 8 shows that 84.8% of the films most recently viewed by the students on VCR and 77% of the films seen at cinemas were U.S. films. Most of these American movies were seen dubbed or with Spanish subtitles. The fact that U.S. movies were rented on the Mexican side of the border in national video rental chains or seen in local cinemas affiliated to national distribution chains reflects the widespread availability of U.S. films all over Mexico and not just in the border region.

Whether or not exposure to American movies is common throughout the country, the fact is that Nuevo Laredo's *secundaria* students do watch them, opening the possibility for some kind of ideological influence or impact on their cultural identity. I will return to this possibility below in the discussion of youngsters' responses to the cultural-identity questions.

TABLE 8   Films Watched Recently on VCR or at the Cinema, by Origin

	Times Mentioned[a]	
Origin of Films	n[a]	%
VCR		
Mexican	73	15.2
U.S.	408	84.8
Total	481	100
Cinema		
Mexican	147	23.0
U.S.	484	77.0
Total	639	100

[a] Every student mentioned the name of the last two films he or she had played on the VCR or watched at the cinema. Films were classified according to their origin, as "Mexican films" or "U.S. films." Totals refer to the number of titles mentioned, not to the number of students contacted.

DIFFERENCES IN EXPOSURE TO U.S. FILMS BY SOCIAL CLASS

In the case of movies seen on the VCR, Table 9 shows that upper-class students were significantly more likely to watch American movies (mean = 4.09) than were their middle- (mean = 3.64) and lower-class (mean = 3.43) counterparts. In contrast with their music preferences, they were less likely to watch Mexican movies (mean = 2.72) than U.S. movies. Middle- and lower-class youngsters also tended to watch U.S. films more frequently than Mexican movies, which underscores the tendency for U.S. media influence to be more concentrated in film than in television and radio messages.

While the preference for viewing U.S. films in cinemas held for upper- and middle-class students, lower-class students were more likely to prefer Mexican films over U.S. ones (see Table 9). These findings point out the complexity of media reception and the coexistence of different patterns of exposure, in the case of films, among *secundaria* students.

CULTURAL IDENTITY AND MEDIA EXPOSURE

Table 10 shows that there were no significant differences in frequency of exposure to U.S. television programs between those students who said they would want to be Mexican citizens if they were to be born again and those (a minority) who said they would rather be U.S. citizens.

TABLE 9   Means (*M*), Standard Deviations (*SD*), and Analysis of Variance (ANOVA) of Frequency with which Students Play Mexican and U.S. Films on the VCR or Watch Them at the Cinema, by Social Class

Social Class	n	M[a]	SD	F	Significance
				ANOVA	
VCR					
Mexican films					
Upper	154	2.72*	0.95	12.00	.0000
Middle	206	3.15†	1.04		
Lower	50	3.38†	0.99		
U.S. films					
Upper	154	4.09*	0.90	11.48	.0000
Middle	207	3.64†	1.10		
Lower	49	3.43†	1.17		
Cinema					
Mexican films					
Upper	161	2.21*	1.08	20.30	.0000
Middle	293	2.85†	1.19		
Lower	100	3.02†	1.22		
U.S. films					
Upper	161	3.85*	1.24	44.26	.0000
Middle	291	3.00†	1.27		
Lower	100	2.40**	1.29		

*†** Significantly different means (Tukey's b)
[a] Mean on the scale of 1 = "Never," 2 = "Rarely," 3 = "Sometimes," 4 = "Frequently," 5 = "Always."

On a scale of 1 ("never") to 5 ("every week"), both groups rated their exposure to American television programs at 2 ("rarely"), with no significant difference between their mean scores. There were significant differences, however, in their responses concerning the frequency with which they watched U.S. movies on the VCR or at the cinema. This suggests that preference for U.S. citizenship was moderately associated with higher degrees of exposure to U.S. film contents.

The same was true in the case of exposure to U.S. music (see Table 11): those who said they would rather become U.S. citizens listened

TABLE 10   Means (M), Standard Deviations (SD), and t Tests of Frequency with which Students are exposed to U.S. and Mexican Television and Film Contents, and Nationality Preference

Nationality Preference	n	M[a]	SD	t	Significance
U.S. television programs[b]					
Mexican	238	2.16	.75	−1.40	.163
U.S.	73	2.30	.79		
Mexican television programs[c]					
Mexican	247	3.66	.77	−.46	.644
U.S.	73	3.71	.84		
Mexican films at the cinema					
Mexican	268	2.97	1.15	3.11	.002
U.S.	75	2.49	1.23		
U.S. films at the cinema					
Mexican	267	2.77	1.30	−2.60	.010
U.S.	74	3.22	1.36		
Mexican films played on the VCR					
Mexican	180	3.26	1.00	2.09	.038
U.S.	54	2.93	1.06		
U.S. films played on the VCR					
Mexican	179	3.52	1.11	−2.05	.041
U.S.	55	3.87	1.14		

[a] Mean on the scale of 1 = "Never," 2 = "Rarely," 3 = "Sometimes," 4 = "Frequently," 5 = "Always."
[b] Combined mean for responses to the following U.S. television programs: "Dukes of Hazzard," "CHiPS," "Daktari," "Magnum," U.S. films on television, and "Teenage Mutant Ninja Turtles."
[c] Combined mean for responses to the following Mexican television programs: "Cándido Pérez," "Chespirito," Mexican wrestling, "Papá Soltero," "Anabel," and Mexican films on television.

to U.S. music significantly more often (mean = 3.62) than those who said they would rather remain Mexican (mean = 2.97). This dissatisfaction among students with their actual nationality seemed to coincide with a higher degree of exposure to U.S. music and lower exposure to Mexican traditional music.

Table 12 demonstrates no associations between exposure to U.S. television programs and films exhibited at theaters and how proud

TABLE 11   Means (*M*), Standard Deviations (*SD*), and *t* Tests of Frequency with which Students are Exposed to U.S. and Mexican Music, and Nationality Preference

Nationality Preference	n	*M*[a]	SD	t	Significance
U.S. music					
Mexican	267	2.97	1.23	−4.08	.000
U.S.	74	3.62	1.19		
Mexican modern music					
Mexican	272	3.95	1.17	.52	.606
U.S.	76	3.87	1.30		
Mexican ranchera music					
Mexican	272	3.29	1.32	3.41	.001
U.S.	74	2.70	1.30		

[a] Mean on the scale of 1 = "Never," 2 = "Rarely," 3 = "Sometimes," 4 = "Frequently," 5 = "Every day."

TABLE 12   Pride in Being Mexican, by Exposure to U.S. and Mexican Media Contents (Pearson *r*)

Media Contents[a]	Pride in being Mexican[b] (N = 228)
Mexican television programs	.0203
Mexican films at the cinema	.1281
Mexican films played on VCR	.1090
Mexican modern music	.1165
Mexican ranchera music	.0809
U.S. television programs	.0532
U.S. films at the cinema	−.1222
U.S. films played on VCR	−.2153**
U.S. music	−.1784*

*p = .01; **p = .001.
[a] Measured on a scale of 1 = "Never," 2 = "Rarely," 3 = "Sometimes," 4 = "Frequently," 5 = "Always."
[b] Measured on a scale of 1 = "Not proud at all," 2 = "A little," 3 = "Neutral," 4 = "Proud," 5 = "Very proud."

TABLE 13   Knowledge of English, by Social Class

	Class			
Knowledge of English	Upper (%) (n = 161)	Middle (%) (n = 298)	Lower (%) (n = 106)	Total (all classes) (n = 565)
Nothing, a little	31.7	73.1	91.5	64.8
More or less	44.7	23.2	7.5	26.4
Good to very good	23.6	3.7	1.0	8.8
Total	100	100	100	100

χ^2 = 134.16, d.f. = 4, p = .0000

TABLE 14   Means (*M*), Standard Deviations (*SD*), and One-Way Analysis of Variance (ANOVA) of the Frequency with which Students are Exposed to U.S. Media Contents, and by Knowledge of English

				ANOVA	
Knowledge of English	n	M[a]	SD	F	Significance
By frequency with which students watch U.S. television programs					
Nothing, a little	273	2.17	0.75	2.1485	.1181
More or less	83	2.36	0.86		
Good, very good	13	2.08	0.28		
By frequency with which students watch U.S. films at the cinema					
Nothing, a little	308	2.70*	1.26	18.339	.0000
More or less	87	3.44[†]	1.33		
Good, very good	15	4.13[†]	1.30		
By frequency with which students play U.S. films on the VCR					
Nothing, a little	189	3.49*	1.15	5.336	.0053
More or less	73	3.94[†]	1.00		
Good, very good	13	4.00[†]	0.82		
By frequency with which students listen to U.S. music					
Nothing, a little	306	2.98*	1.23	9.841	.0001
More or less	88	3.61[†]	1.24		
Good, very good	14	3.57[†]	1.28		

*[†] Significantly different means (Tukey's b)
[a] Mean on the scale of 1 = "Never," 2 = "Rarely," 3 = "Sometimes," 4 = "Frequently," 5 = "Every week/always/every day."

Nuevo Laredo's *secundaria* students were of being Mexicans. Exposure to U.S. films played on the VCR and exposure to U.S. music, however, showed significant, although low, correlations ($-.2153$ and $-.1784$). Consequently, exposure to U.S. media was either not related or moderately related to lower degrees of satisfaction of the students with their nationality. Again, U.S. films and music, more so than U.S. television programs, seem to play a part, however moderate, in lower levels of cultural identity.

KNOWLEDGE OF ENGLISH

Table 13 shows that close to 65% of *secundaria* students did not know any English, while 26.4% had some knowledge of it, and only 8.8% knew it well or very well. This explains in part their low exposure to U.S. television and radio stations and their preference for dubbed programs and films. By not knowing the language, most students were "protected" from receiving foreign values and ideologies directly over the air from U.S. media across the border, at least in terms of the verbal content of those media. As might be expected, upper-class students were the most likely to know English, although even among them, the vast majority— over 75%—did not know it well.

Table 14 shows that except for television, exposure to U.S. media contents was related to knowledge of English. The more English the students know, the more they choose U.S. films and U.S. music. Exposure to television, however, was not correlated with knowledge of English. Students who knew the language very well watched U.S. television contents as rarely as the ones who did not. Again, this calls for a more sophisticated interpretation of the processes of exposure to media contents. Variables such as knowledge of English may be related to higher degrees of exposure to some U.S. media contents than to others. In fact, it may well be that the knowledge of English is dependent upon the student's social class, upper-class students being more likely than lower-class youngsters to know English. Thus even a straightforward variable such as knowledge of English may not have a direct and decisive impact on degree of exposure to U.S. media.

■ ■ **Discussion**

The findings of the survey show that *secundaria* students consistently select a wide spectrum of mass media, and that they do so in a differentiated way, especially along class lines.

That the students are significantly exposed to a wide variety of media content, and that they clearly prefer Mexican over American television programs and music, supports Boyd-Barrett's (1982) suggestion that "countervailing local influences" be taken into account in analyses of foreign media influences.

Secundaria students, in fact, select more local media products than American ones, despite the widespread availability of the latter. This evidence conflicts with cultural imperialism's assumptions about automatic exposure to foreign media content in developing countries, and supports culturalist assertions about the active role of subordinate groups in their selection of, and exposure to, mass-media products.

The findings also support culturalists' emphasis on the importance of variables such as social class in mediating and differentiating exposure to the media. Upper-class students tended to be exposed significantly more to U.S. films, television programs, and music than middle- and lower-class youngsters. They were also more likely to say they would rather be U.S. citizens if they were to be born again.

The findings, however, do not support a simplistic relationship between social class and exposure to U.S. media or erosion of cultural identity. While upper-class students were more likely than middle- or lower-class students to be exposed to U.S. media content, they still overwhelmingly preferred Mexican over American television programs and music. While they were more likely than middle- and lower-class youngsters to say they would rather be U.S. citizens, there were no significant differences between them and their middle- and lower-class counterparts in terms of how proud they felt of being Mexican. Consequently, it is important to emphasize and follow the recent tendency of cultural studies to include social mediations and variables other than just social class when conducting this kind of cultural analysis.

Exposure to U.S. films and its relationship to students' pride in being Mexican—or the nationality they would like to have if they were born again—merits particular attention. More than 75% of the movies recently seen by the students were American films. The small group who said they would rather become U.S. citizens (74 out of 341) watched U.S. films significantly more often than their counterparts.

These findings indicate the need for more research on the particular impact that U.S. movies may have on different indicators of national identity. In this particular case, availability of U.S. cultural products results in their significant consumption by audience members, and this consumption seems to be associated with lower scores in at least two indicators of national identity. Further research should explore more fully the relationship between exposure to American films and the assimilation of ideological values (as opposed to those related to national identity). While a great deal of attention has traditionally been paid to television flows, this study suggests that it may be necessary to start focusing more on the availability and consumption of U.S. films. In fact, some studies show that in the interior of Mexico and throughout Latin America, consumption of American films is high (see González 1992, pp. 257–258; Muñoz 1992), suggesting that the findings reported here may be relevant not only for the Mexican border area but for the region in general.

In addition, the findings of this study show that the processes of consumption and assimilation of foreign cultural products are much more complex than contributors to the cultural imperialism thesis suggested. Audience members seem to prefer their national media in some instances and foreign media in others. Social class appears to be the most important variable to consider when analyzing exposure to U.S. music and films. Availability of foreign media contents, especially in the case of television, does not necessarily lead to their consumption.

We are left with the question of which conclusions are more valid—those of cultural imperialism concerning the erosion of the national identity due to the availability and consumption of foreign media content, or those that argue that "getting to know more about the ways of life, values and norms of others through imported cultural artifacts does not correlate with an increased, unconditional admiration of these artifacts in detriment of one's own culture" (Caron and Bélanger 1993)? In light of the manifold difficulties involved in defining cultural identity and measuring the degree to which audience members experience it, perhaps a more sensible approach is to change the focus of the problem to that of "cultural development" and "cultural diversity." Hamelink (1989, p. 424) has argued that "the focal point of analytical inquiry should not be cultural identity but the conditions for cultural development and the interest-guided forces that resist these conditions." For Hamelink, mass-media content should satisfy the three conditions essential for cultural development to exist: dynamism, diversity, and dispute. It needs to reflect the changing processes of human interaction with the environment, the diversity of cultural manifestations within and between nations, and the open discussion of cultural choices "in order to exclude certain interests from deciding on behalf of all others what choices to make" (p. 422). A similar position is espoused by Schroder (1993, p. 131), who argues that we should restrain our interest in educating the masses, respecting the diverse tastes and making sure that "cultural production caters to cultural diversity and not some petrified notion of cultural quality."

In the end, we can agree that cultural identities thrive when diversity and plurality are allowed in a society. Exposure to local media content in Mexico or any other country will not ensure the well-being of national identity if the commercial, "modeled" structure of the local media is responsible for the homogenization of formats and contents "to the lowest possible denominator for the largest possible audience" (Hoffmann-Riem 1987, p. 64). The government and all institutions and organizations interested in the preservation of cultural identity should promote and adopt policies geared toward strengthening the four dimensions of diversity distinguished by Hoffmann-Riem: diversity of formats and issues, diversity and plurality of contents, diversity of persons and groups, and diversity of geographical regions (p. 61).

While research on the availability and consumption of foreign cultural products may still be relevant, it is important not to neglect cultural diversity and cultural development as real issues when discussing the impact of mass communication on audiences' national identity.

BIBLIOGRAPHY

Aceves, Francisco. 1991. "La televisión y los tapatíos" (Television and the people of Guadalajara). *Comunicación y Sociedad* 13 (September–December): 131–161.

Barbero, Jesús-Martín. 1988. "Communication from culture: The crisis of the national and the emergence of the popular." *Media Culture and Society* 10(4): 447–465.

Beltrán, Luis-Ramiro. 1978. "TV etchings in the minds of Latin Americans: Conservatism, materialism, and conformism." *Gazette* 24(1): 61–85.

Boyd-Barrett, J. Oliver. 1982. "Cultural dependency and the mass media." In M. Gurevitch, T. Bennet, J. Curran, and J. Woollacott, eds., *Culture, society and the media*. London: Methuen.

Candelaria, José Isabel. 1987. "La americanización de la frontera tamaulipeca" (The Americanization of the Tamaulipas border). *Momento* 3(2): 5–9.

Caron, André, and Pierre Bélanger. 1993. "A reception study of American television in Québec." In *Small nations, big neighbour: Denmark and Québec/Canada compare notes on American popular culture*, ed. Roger de la Garde, William Gilsdorf, and Ilja Wechselmann. Acamedia Research Monograph, no. 10. London: John Libbey.

Cremoux, Raúl. 1968. *La televisión y el alumno de secundaria del Distrito Federal* (TV and the Junior High School student of the Federal District). México: Centro de Estudios Educativos.

de la Garde, Roger. 1987. "Is there a market for foreign cultures?" *Media, Culture, and Society* 9(2): 189–209.

———. 1993. "Dare we compare?" In *Small nations, big neighbour: Denmark and Québec/Canada compare notes on American popular culture,* ed. Roger de la Garde, William Gilsdorf, and Ilja Wechselmann. Acamedia Research Monograph, no. 10. London: John Libbey.

Dorfman, Ariel. 1980. *Patos, elefantes y héroes* (Ducks, elephants and heroes). Buenos Aires: Ediciones de la Flor.

Dorfman, Ariel, and Armand Mattelart. 1978. *Para leer al Pato Donald* (How to read Donald Duck). Mexico City: Siglo XXI Editores.

Esteinou, Javier. 1990. "Crisis cultural y desnacionalización: La televisión mexicana y el debilitamiento de la identidad nacional" (Cultural crisis and denationalization: Mexican television and the weakening of national identity). *Comunicación y Sociedad* 9(May–August): 97–121.

Fejes, Fred. 1981. "Media imperialism: An assessment." *Media, Culture, and Society* 3:281–289.

———. 1984. "Critical mass communication research and media effects: The problem of the disappearing audience." *Media, Culture and Society* 6(3): 219–232.

Fiske, John. 1992. "British cultural studies and television." In *Channels of discourse, reassembled,* ed. Robert C. Allen. Chapel Hill and London: University of North Carolina Press.

García-Calderón, C. 1987. *Para conectarse a Cablevision* (Connecting with Cable TV). México: Ediciones El Caballito.

García Canclini, Néstor. 1988a. "Culture and power: The state of research." *Media, Culture and Society* 10: 467–497.

———. 1988b. "Cultura transnacional y culturas populares" (Transnational culture and popular cultures). In *Cultura transnacional y culturas populares* (Transnational Culture and Popular Cultures), ed. N. García Canclini and R. Rocangliolo. Lima: Instituto para América Latina (IPAL).

García Canclini, Néstor, and Mabel Piccini. 1993. "Culturas de la ciudad de México: Símbolos colectivos y usos del espacio urbano" (Mexico City's cultures: Collective symbols and uses of the urban space). In *El consumo cultural en México* (Cultural Consumption in Mexico), coord. Néstor García Canclini. Mexico City: Consejo Nacional para la Cultura y las Artes.

Gómez-Mont, Carmen. 1992. "El desarrollo de las nuevas tecnologías de información en México, proscrito a las reglas del mercado" (The development of new technologies in Mexico left to the rules of the market). *Revista Mexicana de Comunicación* 5(25): 34–40.

González, Jorge. 1992. "Videotecnología y modernidad: Por los dominios de Pedro Páramo" (Videotechnology and modernity: Around Pedro Páramo's domains). In *Comunicación y democracia: VI Encuentro Nacional Coneicc)* (Communication and democracy: VIth National Conference of Coneicc), ed. Javier Esteinou. Mexico City: Coneicc.

Hall, Stuart. 1989. "Cultural studies: Two paradigms." In *Media, culture and society: A critical reader,* ed. R. Collins, J. Curran, N. Garnham, P. Scannell, P. Schlesinger, and C. Sparks. London: Sage.

Hoffmann-Riem, Wolfgang. 1987. "National identity and cultural values: Broadcasting safeguards." *Journal of Broadcasting & Electronic Media* 11(1): 60–65.

Iglesias, Norma. 1989. *Medios de comunicación en la frontera norte* (Mass Media along the Mexican Border with the United States). Mexico City: Fundación Manuel Buendía.

Malagamba, Amelia. 1986. *La televisión y su impacto en la población infantil de Tijuana* (Impact of television on the juvenile population of Tijuana). Tijuana: Cuadernos Cefnomex.

Montoya, Alberto, and María-Antonieta Rebeil. 1986. Commercial television as an educational and political institution: A case study of its impact on the students of Telesecundaria. In *Communication and Latin American Society: Trends in Critical Research, 1960–1985,* ed. R. Atwood and E. McAnany. Madison: University of Wisconsin Press.

Muñoz, Sonia. 1992. "Mundos de vida y modos de ver." In *Televisión y melodrama,* coord. Jesús-Martín Barbero and Sonia Muñoz. Bogota: Tercer Mundo Editores.

"Regios prefieren el 'Canal de las Estrellas'" (Monterrey's people like Televisa's "Channel of the Stars"). 1993. *El Norte.* March 11, p. 8E.

Sánchez-Ruiz, Enrique. 1993. "Notas sobre la globalización, el TLC y el espacio audiovisual mexicano" (Notes on globalization, NAFTA and the Mexican audiovisual space). Paper presented at conference, La comunicación hoy: Escenarios y contraescenarios, November 23–25, at Universidad de las Américas–Puebla, Mexico.

Santa Cruz, Adriana, and Viviana Erazo. 1981. *Compropolitan.* Mexico City: ILET-Nueva Imagen.

Schroder, Kim Christian. 1993. "Can Denmark be Canadianized? On the cultural role of American TV-Serials in Denmark." In *Small nations, big neighbour: Denmark and Québec/Canada compare notes on American popular culture,* ed. Roger de la Garde, William Gilsdorf, and Ilja Wechselmann. Acamedia Research Monograph, no. 10. London: John Libbey.

Smith, Anthony D. 1990. "Towards a global culture?" In *Global Culture: Nationalism, Globalization and Modernity,* ed. Mike Featherstone pp. 171–191. London: Sage.

The U.S. – Mexico Border as Post-NAFTA Mexico

EDUARDO BARRERA

THE CULTURAL INDUSTRIES ARE excluded from NAFTA, a *de facto* situation in the case of Canada and a *de jure* situation in the case of Mexico. Annex 1001.1B-2 of NAFTA Canada is consistent with Article 2005 of the bilateral agreement that excluded cultural industries from the negotiations. Mexico opens to foreign investment in entertainment services such as MMDS (multichannel multipoint distribution system) and videotext, and opens to imports with few restrictions in the rest of the now aseptically called "entertainment services"—a euphemism that fetishizes the production and consumption of cultural texts.[1] This opening on the part of the Salinas de Gortari administration could not have been possible without a discourse that relied on the border as a paradigm of post-NAFTA Mexico.

The U.S. – Mexico border has shifted from a marginalized and stigmatized geographic area and academic subject to an export zone of global importance and a fashionable trope to illustrate global and national changes. The U.S. side of the border has been appropriated by poststructuralist theorists and artists who replace the use of the border as the synecdoche of the nations it divides with a metaphor of the co-existence of symbolic systems.[2] On the Mexican side, the border was seldom an aesthetic or academic subject until the boom of "border cinema" dealing with drug traffic and migrant dramas and the boom of immigration and *maquiladora* studies. Both booms occurred in the early 1980s.

The objectives of this exercise are to analyze the uses of the border as a paradigm of post-NAFTA Mexico in the emerging official and academic discourses and to problematize some of the assumptions regarding border audiences by examining the television industry in this geographic area.

▪ ▪ Traditional Views of the Border

In an exhaustive review about the Mexican literature dealing with culture on the border in the the last few decades, Víctor Zúñiga (1992) found that these analyses could be collapsed into the following three broad visions: (1) the border as a cultural desert, (2) the border as a cultural edge, and (3) the border as a cultural trench.

The first depiction implies a hierarchy of cultures, combining simultaneously the elitist distinction of high culture/popular culture and the more anthropological distinction between culture of exotic societies and psychology of Western societies.[3] The former distinction was a result of the contrast between the artistic and cultural infrastructure of Mexico City, with its museums of history, anthropology, and modern art—among others, the Palace of Fine Arts—and other concert halls and theaters, conservatories and art schools, and the almost nonexistent facilities in the border region, which leaves, on the other side of this distinction, a popular culture that is, by implication, second class. The other distinction—between culture of exotic societies and psychology of Western societies—is not stated explicitly, but refers to the contrast between the pre-Columbian ceremonial centers, with their simplicity, and the grandiosity of Colonial architecture, and takes these studies to the logical conclusion that the border lacks the cultural heritage and exotic element that make a society worth being studied.

This vision depicts the border as the site of cultural penetration on the part of the frivolous and alienating American mass culture. This is largely based on the telluric position of the second view, which assumes that the essence of Mexico will radiate from its political center, and that the border population consists either of traitors or passive victims of the song of the Boreal Siren.

▪ ▪ Emerging Views of the Border

These three visions found by Zúñiga may be giving way to three emerging visions that not only move away from the national zealotry and fatalism that characterize the preceding ones and make the everyday interaction of the border unproblematic, but that become the radiating center of the new essence of Mexicanness. These three new visions are: (1) the border as the site of reaffirmation of national identity, (2) the border as the laboratory of postmodernity par excellence, and (3) the border as the paradigm of modernization.

▪ ▪ Post-Imperialist Mexico

The Border as the Site of Reaffirmation of National Identity

The first of these new visions developed in the same axis of the border as cultural trench, as a reaction to the depiction of border inhabitants as passive consumers of American mass media.[4] In contrast to those critics who fear that NAFTA will open the border to the American Way of Life, that the trick-or-treat of Halloween will replace the altars of the Day of the Dead, and that Emmitt Smith will replace Jorge Campos as the national hero, are those scholars who are quick to reassure us that this nightmare is far from happening. There is a fresh body of literature that affirms that national identity on the border is even stronger than in the interior because we live side by side with the "other." Jorge Bustamante argues that

> the goal of reducing or eliminating the inequality with the neighbor implies a strong motivation . . . an historical conscience . . . Vis-à-vis the otherness of *the neighbor,* the border inhabitant relies on the reaffirmation of traditional values learned from the elders and which is reproduced in family relations, relying, perhaps intuitively, on the values of his/her own definition of mexicanness, stimulated by the contrast with the cultural otherness with which he/she is interacting.[5]

He substantiates this with the measurement of "national cultural identity" in the border region, that is compared with that in nonborder cities, and shows that it is stronger in the former.

This position is a step ahead of the earlier visions of the border in that it eliminates the telluric character of Mexicanness, but it still has some limitations to overcome—namely, (1) its reification of "otherness," (2) its negative conception of identity, and (3) its emphasis on the "residual" elements of cultural activities.

The "other" is reified through a process of singularization that erases the possibility of differences. This leaves the true and only "other" as the WASP U.S. citizen. Minorities, including Mexican-Americans, do not constitute Others. This is a severe limitation in theory as in practice, as is demonstrated by Pablo Vila (1994), who shows the tensions and differences between Mexican-Americans, undocumented and intra-Mexican migrants, and the rest of the border population. He found many cases in Ciudad Juárez, where

> Mexican-Americans are regarded as the principal other, while for poorer Juarenses sometimes the dividing line lies between their poverty with dignity and the poverty without dignity of Mexican Americans. . . . some Mexican Americans . . . tried to distinguish themselves from Mexican nationals by constituting them as the stigmatized "other." . . . They revindicate their Mexican heritage, but stressing that they are proud of the Mexico of the past, not the "corrupt, poor, violent, and machista" Mexico of the present. On the other hand, they separate themselves from the contemporary Mexicans, who are not recognized as their own people. . . . And this Mexico of the present from which these interviewees want to separate themselves . . . , to preserve their identities of "Mexicans" of the past, is felt as so strange that it is characterized as being "a completely different world" . . . from which there is no bridge that can close the gap they feel separates them now from what was united before.[6]

The second limitation is the negative conception of identity—that is, the idea that cultural identity is what is left after we isolate the other. José Manuel Valenzuela Arce points out that collective identities are constructed through a process of differentiation from the "other."[7] This view implies an intrinsic subordination of the identity that is constructed negatively. As Eagleton points out,

> [The "Other"] is always anterior to us and will always escape us, that which brought us into being as subjects in the first place . . . We desire what others . . . unconsciously desire for us; and desire can only happen because we are caught up in . . . the whole field of the "Other" which generates it.[8]

Stam, Burgoyne, and Flitterman-Lewis summarize the construction of the identity in the Lacanian mirror phase as the "'other' perceived as a whole, it mistakes this unified, coherent shape for a superior self."[9] Bustamante ameliorates the negative nature of this process but only by essentializing a historical conscience, which is only triggered by the "other."[10]

The third limitation is the definition of Mexicanness by equating it with "traditional values," operationalized by Rogelio Díaz Guerrero as the alignment with a gender division of labor or the subordination to figures of authority. This means that there cannot be a Mexican Feminist or a Mexican Revolutionary. This position, particularly as espoused by Bustamante, privileges the reliance on residual elements and considers subcultures such as *cholismo* as "a nationalism expressed in manifestations of popular culture."[11] Valenzuela Arce does give more space to emergent elements but anchors them in class rather than nationalism.

The media-centered logical extension of this approach that also rejects the Americanization of the border stresses the appropriation of American holidays, festivities, and rituals, giving new "uses" to these signifying practices by emphasizing the "negotiation" of meaning that takes place when receivers are exposed to mass-media messages.[12] This view points out that no matter how many messages the border population is exposed to, it will negotiate their meaning by decoding them with its own Mexican codes. This position also tends to analyze isolated messages and signifying practices without taking into account that the globalization of cultural industries involves not only vertical but horizontal integration, and that a single marketing campaign is present in a myriad of cultural fronts at once—film, television, video games, print, music, store window displays, billboards, stickers, clothing, bedding, toys, board games, food products, fast-food chains, and so on. There is a point at which the presence of a cultural influence in the environment ceases to be quantitatively significant and instead its critical mass becomes significant qualitatively.[13]

The Border as the Laboratory of Postmodernity

The second of the emerging visions presents the border as—to use García Canclini's term—the "laboratory of Post-modernity."[14] Here we find not just a fascination with a new conceptual toy—the postmodern— but a view that tends to fall into a form of symbolic determinism. The application of postmodern theory to the border not only has the limitations of catachresis and aporia that are inherent to the construct, but privileges the cultural sphere, transforming the economic, political, and social spheres into epiphenomena—that is, into phenomena that are not basically symbolic in nature, but that can be fully explained by what happens in this (cultural) sphere. This view is complementary to that of the border as the site of reaffirmation of national identity, in that it posits that the juxtaposition of symbolic systems—namely, of those migrants from the South, including those from traditional peasant communities and those from such metropoles as Mexico City and Guadalajara—is processed by the different codes coexisting in the border population. However, the emphasis on this coexistence does not acknowledge the asymmetries between these systems in the struggle for hegemony. The view of the border as an ungrounded communal base was borrowed from the work of performance artist Guillermo Gómez-Peña, in which there seems to be an essence of a syncretic culture that irradiates from the border and reaches the cultural centers:

> All major metropoli have been fully borderized. In fact, there are no longer visible cultural differences between Manhattan, Montreal, Washington, Los Angeles or Mexico City. They all look like downtown Tijuana on a Saturday night.[15]

In this new cartography where the East–West Coast cultural axis is being replaced by a North–South one[16] and where the North is third-worldized, the border becomes an omnipresent nomad center. Although Gómez-Peña rejects the label *postmodern* in favor of *intercultural,* he does so as a strategic move to focalize the border without subordinating it as an appendix to the established discourse of power centers in the art circles. By reclaiming the autonomy of the voice of the border, Gómez-Peña appropriates it. This type of ventriloquism is criticized by Haraway because the appropriated others are

> carved out of one collective entity and relocated in another, where they are reconstituted as objects of a particular kind—as the ground of a representational practice that forever authorizes the ventriloquist. Tutelage will be eternal. The represented is reduced to the permanent status of the recipient of action, never to be a co-actor in an articulated practice among unlike, but joined, social partners.[17]

The tutelage-by-appropriation strategy is not exclusive to this artist but is also present in academe, where publication titles interpellate "other" academics from the border, claiming exclusivity of the object of study.[18]

A general problem in the literature is the essentialization of The Modern. When a music video or a building is classified as postmodern, the assertion is made based on the hybridization of formal codes, the decontextualization or the rejection of a modern exemplar.[19] However, hybridization is also a modern strategy as seen in dadaist collages, Picasso's masks, and Duchamp's ready-mades. The problem is twofold, involving the labeling of art works by their formal characteristics and not by their circulation and uses, and the singularization of the modern. The postmodern label should be applied, if applied at all, not to the intertextuality but to the inter-textuality of signifying practices. The former refers to "a set of signifying relations that is alleged to be manifest within a text, the product of the permutation of texts it deploys," while the hyphenated version refers to "the ways in which the relations between texts are socially organised within the objective disposition of a reading formation."[20] Not only is there also a need to distinguish between modernism, modernity, and modernization,[21] there is a need, too, to pluralize them. Aníbal Quijano points out the contradictions between two historical traditions concerning the "modern"[22]—that is, between the "Franco-Continental Enlightenment" of Voltaire and Rousseau that equated it to rationality and tried to "free society from all inequality, arbitrariness, despotism and obscurantism; in short, it was in opposition to the ruling power," and the "Anglo-Scottish Enlightenment" of Locke, Hume, and Smith that, by focusing on the individual, vindicated the "privileged position of some groups in respect of others within society."[23] In the case of theoretical frameworks, the mere rejection of a grand or totalizing modern theory is not necessarily postmodern; as Margaret Rose points out, "simply 'deconstructing the modern' should only be seen as being 'late modern'."[24]

The border has a small high-income sector that constitutes what Mitsubishi calls "Technologically Advanced Families" (TAFs) that use their leisure time to cultivate a competence that is more "productivist" than "culturalist," and whereby informatic codes largely replace artistic ones that require a renewed "aesthetic disposition"[25] due to the fragmentary and decontextualizing intertextual nature of postmodernisms. Postmodernisms are the first artistic movement that is produced and consumed simultaneously in the first and third worlds. Latin American postmodernisms would be characterized by the organic syncretism of cultures that coexist, while those of the North are basically a formalistic hybridization. The best-known writers on postmodernism, such as Jean Baudrillard, Jean-François Lyotard, and Marshall Berman—whose uncritical positions vary in terms of degree—not only do give a total autonomy, but privilege the cultural sphere over the economic one. A more recent trend has taken an opposite position critically and epistemologically, but has the danger of falling into reductionist and deterministic schemas. Frederic Jameson, working within the theoretical framework of Mandel, argues that postmodernism is the cultural logic of late capitalism. Antonio Negri draws the parallel between postmodernism and romanticism because

> [they identify] a period of crisis and the subjection of society and work to capitalist domination. Bearing in mind the Marxian distinction between formal subsumption and real subsumption, what the romantics had documented in formal terms, postmodernism registers in real terms.[26]

Harvey problematizes the relation between the cultural and economic spheres by pointing out that

> since crises of overaccumulation typically spark the search for spatial and temporal resolutions, which in turn create an overwhelming sense of time-space compression, we can also expect crises of overaccumulation to be followed by strong aesthetic movements . . . [and in turn] the development of cultural production and marketing on a global scale has itself been a primary agent in time-space compression.[27]

The difference between working time and leisure time seems more diffuse than ever before in capitalism, which is not the case for the unequal access to that capital, whose description as "symbolic" must be revised. García Canclini points out the new structuring of leisure time by turning it into an extension of work and profit.[28] To the asymmetry in production and use between individuals and societies that García Canclini discusses we should add the differences related to the bias in the sensorium and control in the user-technology interface. While the youth of low-income sectors have access to video games that develop and fine-tune skills that require visual and motor coordination that can later be capitalized by flexible producers, their high-income counterparts from TAFs are being trained in technologies whose software requires decision-makers who can also interact with data banks and strategic networks that can generate information of a very high marginal value. The competence developed by these youths in private higher-education institutions, such as the Monterrey Tech, that link to e-mail systems, academic networks, and international data banks is radically different from that developed by trade schools largely attended by *maquiladora* workers. These class asymmetries cross with an asymmetry between nations that is going to be reinforced with the information-highway initiative, which would be an institutionalization of the "chosen instrument" policy, through which the U.S. government has given formal and substantive support to the private sector. The current high-tech industry in the United States would be unthinkable without subsidized consortia such as MCC and Sematech, and that in HDTV.[29]

We find that, subsumed under the postmodern border, the border region is a precursor of a postideological two-party Mexico where the political issues are not ideological, but a matter of honesty and efficiency. The political clientele of the border can choose only between two parties, the PRI and the PAN, both of which are on the same point of the political spectrum.[30]

The Border as a Paradigm of Post-NAFTA Mexico

The third emerging border has been presented in the official discourse and the media as the paradigm of what the whole country will be once NAFTA takes its course as the culmination of neoliberal policies, incorporating synthetically the previous two. The biased handling—not necessarily conspiratorial—of rates of open unemployment, wages in qualified positions, cultural resistance, availability of a larger variety of consumer goods, and so forth, has a key role in legitimating official policies and decisions.[31]

The *maquiladora* industry is seen as the model of industrialization and job creation for the rest of the country in the near future. In a recent meeting between border scholars and Mexican senators the benefits brought by the *maquiladora* cited above were mentioned over and over again, with some economic indicators being taken at face value without being read critically.

- Open unemployment in Tijuana and Juárez are often cited, and the point stressed that their respective unemployment rates of 0.8% and 1.1% are the lowest in the country, without the fact being mentioned that this low rate is also true of such cities as León, Mérida, and Orizaba. Nor is it mentioned that border cities such as Matamoros have a higher index than Mexico City, Guadalajara, and Monterrey. The validity of this very economic indicator is not questioned, and it is not taken into account that according to this International Labor Organization indicator, if a person works just sixty minutes in a week, she or he is not considered to be unemployed.

- The *maquiladora* labor force is said to earn more than its counterpart from further south. While it is true that overall the wages tend to be higher, a worker at one of the Big Three auto manufacturers will earn much less in the *maquiladora* plants than in the domestic plants in the Mexico City valley. Even if the argument of higher average wages in the border is accepted, this does not translate into a higher standard of living, as indicated by the lower access to public services and housing. Compared with cities in the interior, Ciudad Juárez has around 8.3% less access to water, sewage, electrical power, and gas, while in terms of housing, its deficit is more than 18% in comparison with those cities. This is compounded by the attitude of the government, which perceives the lack of infrastructure to be a natural compensation for the higher income.

- The *maquiladora* industry is seen as a trigger for the local economy and its various sectors. The economy of *maquiladora*-centered cities becomes dependent on the economic cycles of the U.S. economy, a problem that will only become deeper, as NAFTA's "rules of origin" discourage Japanese and European investment. This industry can cause not only the health problems associated with pollution, but also economic illnesses, as in the case of the so-called Dutch Disease, where the accelerated growth of an industry cripples the growth of other sectors.[32]

The Salinas de Gortari administration uses the terms modernization and modernity indiscriminately. The modernization attempt is evident, but this is not the case with the increasingly incomplete modernity. The current regime of accumulation echoes the deepening global asymmetries and couples with the "electoral fatigue" that results from an obscene authoritarianism in the "democratic exercises" of a political system where political mobilization is highly dysfunctional.[33]

The rhetoric of modernization constitutes an attempt to replace the "modern" logic of the Mexican revolution, which has remained the source of legitimation of postrevolutionary administrations. The rupture occurs when elements are maintained as axes of continuity. Operating simultaneously are the empty hypernominalist reminiscence of "social liberalism" and the hyper-essentialism pointed out by Roger Bartra:

> The idea that there is a unique subject of National history—"the Mexican"—is a powerful cohesive illusion . . . a specific texture— "the Mexican"—which is also part of the cultural processes of political legitimation of the modern State. The definition of "the

Mexican" is more than anything a description of the form [by which] it is dominated and, above all, the way in which exploitation is legitimated.[34]

The new rhetoric attempts to overcome the contradictions it collides against by ameliorating them with visions of the future that, to reach, Mexicans must concert in an antirevolutionary climate that allows the project to run its due course so that everybody enjoys its fruits. The ascent of neoconservatism in countries such as the U.K. and the United States included the "self-adscription of a progressive vocabulary and the appropriation of a liberal or leftist lexicon . . . the term 'revolutionary' [was] frequently used to describe the politics of Reagan, [as well as] a 'macho' rhetoric in the international arena."[35] This lesson in "discursive reconversion" was learned and put into practice by Salinas in his attacks on the "new reactionaries" at his party's 1992 annual meeting. The international component of this discourse interpellates the Mexican people not only as national citizens, but as citizens of the world, who must commerce in the global market of capitals and commodities, but without trespassing across the borders of national labor markets. New technologies are a key feature of the "rhetoric of the sublime future as an alternative to political revolution and a stimulus to acquiescence."[36] The official discourse is permanently recycling the future, a future that is always around the corner, a corner that is always as far as the carrot on a stick.

▪ ▪ The Border Cultural Industries: The Case of Television in Ciudad Juárez–El Paso

As discussed in the first emerging view, not only does the border constitute the new site for the reaffirmation of national culture, it fits in perfectly with the new approaches of the active audience. Besides the degree to which they emphasize voluntarism, "mediationism,"[37] and alternative and oppositional readings of mass-produced texts, most studies assume that the Mexican and U.S. media are distinctly different. Lozano (1991a, 1991b) and Valenzuela Arce (1993) contradict the traditional assumptions of how the Mexican border audiences were exposed to U.S. programs and manipulated by U.S. media, pointing out how these audiences prefer Mexican media outlets. Contrary to most of the media analyses in the Anglo tradition of cultural studies, this border research has not neglected the political economy of the cultural industries. This is in part because the latter is incipient and can develop without paradigmatic breaks, revisions, or clashes. However, it does privilege the reception over the production of cultural texts. In some cases we find that institutional analyses are severed from audience studies, while others use them as mere backdrop. This results in research that reduces the political economy of media to issues of ownership and programming. However, cultural studies as an invisible college or interpretive community is reaching a phase in which, even when cultural texts are analyzed as "floating signifiers" where discourse is the only reality,[38] some of the leading figures are conducting political economy analyses. While Larry Grossberg places the rise of popular conservatism against the background of regimes of accumulation as developed by French regulation theory, Tony Bennett admits that "[those with] the capacity to do sophisticated statistical and economic work have a major contribution to make to work at the cultural studies/policy interface—perhaps more than those who engage solely in cultural critique."[39] While the former is a theoretical operation, the latter is part of a strategy to arrive at provisional closures of Gramscian cultural studies to engage in "a politics of articulation, to organize those (oppositional) subjects—however loosely, precariously, and provisionally—into a collective political force which acts in opposition to a power bloc."[40] This strategy has resulted in the creation of

> the *Culture: Policies and Politics* series [which] is intended to help bring about a significant transformation in the political ambit and orientation of cultural studies . . . through more detailed and scrupulous attention to the various policy structures and processes— from government inquiries through the activities of the statutory bodies which regulate the legal environment of the cultural industries to *specific industry practices and procedures*—which influence the ways in which the relations between culture and politics are practically mediated.[41]

NAFTA is another mechanism in the globalization and concentration of media firms that leads to "two apparently antithetical processes occurring simultaneously: a proliferation of micro-markets for individualized ('designer') products and the internationalization of major markets for mass consumer products."[42] The cultural texts available to the border population are determined by the structure of the local television industry and the role it plays in the local and national economy.

Between 97%[43] and 87%[44] of households on the U.S.–Mexico border have at least one TV set. If U.S. advertisers are willing to pay up to US$10,000 for a 30-second spot on a border station (Table 1), it is not

TABLE 1   Selected High Rates for 30-Second Spots

Channel	City	High Rate (in U.S. dollars)
2	Juárez	71,000
10	San Diego	7,500
12	Tijuana	7,000
4	Harlingen	3,000
4	El Paso	500
44	Juárez	350
26	El Paso	300
13	Laredo	250

Source: TV & Cable Factbook (1988), Medios Publicitarios Mexicanos (1992)

only for the U.S. audience, but also for its counterpart on the other side. The latter has not only a high-income segment which is important to retailers, but sectors such as the *maquiladora* industry labor force, consisting of 393,415 people in the border states.[45] These workers spend between 10% and 40%[46] of their income in the United States. Of the total amount spent by these workers in El Paso, 51 percent is spent on clothes and 45 percent is spent on basic goods. Electronic goods account for 25 percent of the expenditures, food for 9 percent, canned goods for 6 percent, footwear for 5 percent, and perfume for the remaining 2 percent.[47] This high expenditure in these areas is reflected in the high share of jobs generated by the retail sector in nonagricultural activities in such cities as El Paso (44.7%) in comparison with the national average (28.3%).[48]

Advertising expenditure in Mexico for 1980 was 1,558 million pesos (0.36% of the gross domestic product [GDP]), while the 111 TV stations, along with the 856 radio stations, generated 1,095 million pesos (0.25% of the GDP).[49] Most of those stations belong to Televisa or other powerful media firms (e.g., Grupo Cañón or the Meneses family). A recent trend involves the use of programming services from U.S. networks, such as Telemundo and Univisión.[50] Usually they will use the services of large firms as sales representatives in the United States (e.g., Univisión uses Blair Television).

The U.S. border has 24 TV stations, most of them linked to large corporations such as Knight-Ridder or McGraw-Hill. Three out of four stations are affiliated to one of the three networks. Large advertising agencies such as Katz Television and Seltel have several accounts in the border television industry. It should be pointed out that TV stations outside the top twenty markets usually have a higher profit margin.[51] However, except for the San Diego and Tucson SMSAs (standard metropolitan statistical areas), the border population has a per capita income below the national average.[52]

Ciudad Juárez is the site with the highest number of TV households on the Mexican border, with 124,000, while the El Paso–Las Cruces market ranks 105th in the United States, with 212,000 TV households (Table 2). Juárez has 21 radio and television stations and 131 advertising agencies that generate 0.19% and 1.17% of the municipal tertiary sector.[53] El Paso has 36 advertising outlets that generate 288 jobs.[54]

Viewing the advertising of four television stations for twenty-four hours reveals the striking parallels and differences between the Juárez and El Paso stations, the local and retransmitted stations, and the

TABLE 2   TV Households on the U.S.–Mexico Border

Mexican city (Pop. 10³) [a]	TV Households (10³) [b]	U.S. city	TV Households (10³)	Market (US ranking)
Tijuana (742.6)	116	San Diego	787	25
Mexicali (602.3)	94	El Centro/ Yuma	58.9	182
Nogales (107.1)	15.8	Nogales/ Tucson	301	81
Cd. Juárez (797.6)	124.6	El Paso/ Las Cruces	212	105
Nuevo Laredo (217.9)	32.7	Laredo	34.2	199
Reynosa-Matamoros [c] (730.2)	116.1	McAllen-Brownsville	179.2	116

[a] Population of Mexican border cities from *Resultados preliminares: XI Censo general de población y vivienda* (1990).

[b] Estimates based on city population and TV penetration (.87), divided by the following averages of inhabitants per household: Tijuana and Mexicali, 5.57; Nogales, 5.9; Juárez, 5.57; Nuevo Laredo and Matamoros-Reynosa, 5.47; derived from raw data from Coplamar (1989).

[c] Includes population from the municipalities of Reynosa, Río Bravo, Valle Hermoso, and Matamoros.

TABLE 3   TV Stations in Ciudad Juárez–El Paso

Channel	Call Letters	City	Programming	Owner
2	XEPM	Juárez	Televisa (XEWTV-2)	Televisa
4	KDBC	El Paso	CBS	United Broadcasting
5	XEJ	Juárez	Televisa	Grupo Meneses
7	KVIA	El Paso	ABC	Marsh Media
9	KTSM	El Paso	NBC	Tri-State Broadcasting
11	XHCH	Juárez	Canal 13	Canal 13
13	KCOS	El Paso	PBS	PBS
14	KCIK	El Paso	FOX	Santa Fe Comm.
22	KRWG	Las Cruces	PBS	PBS
26	KINT	El Paso	Univisión	Paso del Norte Broadcasting
38	XEPM	El Paso	Independent	NA
44	XHIJ	Juárez	Telemundo	Cabada Family
48	KZIA	Las Cruces	Independent	Bayport Comm.
56	XHBJ	Juárez	Televisa	Televisa
65	KJLF	El Paso	Independent	NA

English- and Spanish-language stations. Even when this binational market does not rank the highest along the border, it is a unique case in the world, with 15 stations transmitting (Table 3).

Of the 15 stations, 13 are commercial, and of these there are four important categories: Mexican network retransmitters, Juárez stations with predominantly nonlocal programming, English-language El Paso stations, and Spanish-language El Paso stations. Channels 2, 44, 4, and 26 are representative of these categories.[55]

There is great similarity between the products and services advertised by the two regional Spanish-language stations ($rp = .80$), moderate similarity between them and the regional English-language station ($rp = .58$ and $rp = .51$), and low similarity between the national network and the rest (Tables 4a and 4b).

There is also great similarity between the two El Paso stations ($rp = .91$) and moderate similarity between the regional Spanish-language stations ($rp = .68$). The correlation between the Mexican network and the other three is negative because of the number of national accounts (86%). Most of the accounts (43 percent) for the Juárez station are local,

TABLE 4A Spots by Product

Sector	2		4		26		44		Total	
	No.	%	No.	%	No.	%	No.	%	No.	%
Promos	151	32.9	201	46	259	58	210	51	821	34.6
Services	19	4.1	73	16.7	73	16.4	28	6.8	193	8.1
Food	41	8.9	100	22.9	21	4.7	15	3.6	177	7.5
Cosmetics/personal care	39	8.5	57	13.1	30	6.8	14	3.4	140	5.9
Furniture	14	3.1	19	4.4	23	5.2	37	9	93	3.9
Department stores	2	0.4	12	2.8	31	7	46	11.2	91	3.8
Restaurants	4	0.9	40	9.2	16	3.6	25	6.1	85	3.6
Films/Videos	30	6.5	23	5.3	5	1.1	18	4.4	76	3.2
Public service	25	5.4	8	1.8	23	5.2	16	3.9	72	3
Pharmaceutical	5	1.1	53	12.2	3	0.7	8	1.9	69	2.9
Apparel	2	0.4	26	6	25	5.6	16	3.9	69	2.9
Electronic/appliances	13	2.8	30	6.9	14	3.2	11	2.7	68	2.9

Automotive	6	1.3	30	6.9	11	2.5	20	4.9	67	2.8
Soap/detergent	16	3.5	31	7.1	11	2.5	4	1	62	2.6
Recordings	5	1.1	3	0.7	28	6.3	25	6.1	61	2.6
Publications	37	8.1	1	0.2	3	0.7	10	2.4	51	8.1
Soft drinks/juice	8	1.7	15	3.4	8	1.8	5	1.2	36	1.5
Supermarkets	0	0	2	0.5	17	3.8	13	3.2	32	1.3
Beer/liquor/cigarettes	20	4.4	2	0.5	2	0.5	6	1.5	30	1.3
Nightclubs/entertainment	5	1.1	3	0.7	6	1.4	15	3.6	29	1.2
Real estate	0	0	12	2.8	7	1.6	3	0.7	22	0.9
Cultural/art centers	11	2.4	0	0	0	0	0	0	11	0.5
Toys	0	0	8	1.8	0	0	0	0	8	0.3
Banks	1	0.2	1	0.2	4	0.9	1	0.2	7	0.3
Political	6	1.3	0	0	0	0	0	0	6	0.3
Total	460		750		620		546		2,376	

NOTE: Percentage totals may not add up to 100 due to rounding.

TABLE 4B　Nonparametric Correlation among Channels for Spots by Sector

Channels	r	p
26–44	.80	.00
4–26	.58	.002
4–44	.51	.008
2–4	.37	.063
2–44	.25	.21
2–26	.21	.295

TABLE 5A　Advertising by Type of Account

	Television Channel							
	2—Juárez		4—El Paso		26—El Paso		44—Juárez	
Type of Account	%	(No. of spots)	%	(No. of spots)	%	(No. of spots)	%	(No. of spots)
Transnational	14	(44)						
U.S.A.			83	(452)	48	(166)	25	(86)
Mexico	86	(266)					7	(24)
El Paso			17	(93)	39	(136)	24	(85)
Juárez					14	(48)	43	(145)

Note: Number of spots is approximate.

TABLE 5B　Nonparametric Correlation by Type of Account

Channels	r	p
4–26	.91	.03
26–44	.68	.202
4–44	.34	.572
2–4	.62	.259
2–44	.86	.06
2–26	.86	.06

close to the total amount of U.S. accounts, including local and national (Tables 5a and 5b).

The genres in which the advertising is inserted are very similar for Televisa, the Juárez station, and the English-language station (rp 2–44 =.79, rp 2–4 =.74 and rp 4–44 =.70), moderately similar between the Univisión station and the Juárez and English-language stations (rp =.74 and rp =.70), and of low similarity between the two regional Spanish-language stations (Tables 6a and 6b).

TABLE 6A   Advertising by Genre

			Television Channel				
	2—Juárez		4—El Paso		26—El Paso		44—Juárez
Program genre	%	(No. of spots)	%	(No. of spots)	%	(No. of spots)	%	(No. of spots)
Children's shows	8	(38)					4	(22)
Game shows			9	(67)	5	(33)		
Variety shows			6	(45)	19	(122)	3	(16)
Series	4	(18)	8	(60)	6	(39)		
Films	8	(38)	12	(90)			31	(169)
News	34	(157)	28	(210)	23	(144)	33	(180)
Telenovelas	27	(125)	19	(143)	35	(219)	21	(115)
Advertising spots	18	(83)	18	(135)	9	(62)	8	(44)
Total	100	(459)	100	(750)	100	(619)	100	(546)

Note: Number of spots is approximate.

TABLE 6B   Nonparametric Correlation by Genre

Channels	r	p
2–44	.79	.018
2–4	.74	.032
4–44	.70	.048
4–26	.59	.115
2–26	.48	.222
26–44	.28	.492

The Juárez station (Channel 44) is the only one with an important volume of local production, while for the El Paso stations it constitutes less than 6% (Table 7). Local production of Channel 44 is aimed at low-income segments and includes public service programming that won a national journalism award in 1992.[56]

Fifteen- to twenty-second spots are much more pervasive than longer ones in all stations, while minute-long commercials are almost nonexistent (Table 8). This follows Sut Jhally's (1987) further elaboration of Dallas Smythe's theory of audience-as-labor, where shorter commercials constitute a form of relative surplus value.

The cost of TV advertising depends on the time, but especially on the ratings (Tables 9 and 10). Mexican markets are usually measured by INRA, using research methods of questionable reliability based on recall. Ratings are not systematically used and when a station hires the agency, it may do so secretly and broadcast blockbuster movies to increase the ratings.

There is a great parity between Channels 44 and 2 in AAA Time Slots, with .46 and .44 shares, respectively. Contrary to the assumptions

TABLE 7   Advertising Spots by Source and Language

| | Television Channels | | | | | | | |
| | 2—Juárez | | 4—El Paso | | 26—El Paso | | 44—Juárez | |
Source/ Language	%	(No. of spots)	%	(No. of spots)	%	(No. of spots)	%	(No. of spots)
Local/ English			5.7	(43)				
Network/ English			94.3	(707)				
Local/ Spanish					5.8	(36)	41.1	(226)
Network/ Spanish	100	(459)			94.2	(537)	58.6	(320)
Total	100	(459)		(750)		(619)		(546)

Note: Number of spots is approximate.

TABLE 8   Length of Advertising Spots

	Television Channels						
	2—Juárez		4—El Paso		26—El Paso		44—Juárez	
Length (in secs)	%	(No. of spots)	%	(No. of spots)	%	(No. of spots)	%	(No. of spots)
60	4	(19)	2	(15)	4	(25)	3	(16)
30	29	(133)	26	(195)	33	(204)	32	(173)
15	67	(307)	72	(540)	63	(390)	65	(351)
Total	100	(459)	100	(750)	100	(619)	100	(546)

Note: Number of spots is approximate.

of a vast literature, English-language television gets only a five percent share of the Mexican border audience (Table 10).

■ ■ Final Considerations

The selling of NAFTA in Mexico required a substantive change in the collective imaginary of Mexico, to one where the border became a key trope, serving as the paradigm of what Mexico was going to be like once the trilateral agreement was in place. This caused the emergence of new organic intellectuals and institutions whose role was to replace the old views that stigmatized the border population. The future displaced the past, or rather, the past was reconstructed as a teleological scenario that contained the seeds of a strong Mexico immersed in global free trade and inserted in a global culture while resisting total assimilation. These emerging views privileged communication studies that focused on the moment of reception, subordinating, if not neglecting, the material practices of the cultural industries. The celebration of appropriation of foreign signifying practices, as well as the alternative and oppositional readings of mass-produced texts and the preference of Mexican pro-gramming, assumed that Mexican texts were significantly different from U.S. texts. An examination of the material practices of the border tele-vision industries shows how the differences in television programming can be explained more in terms of class characteristics than in terms of

TABLE 9   Advertising Costs (in pesos)

Channel 2

"AAA" Class:

5:00 P.M.–12:00 A.M.	Break[a]	Program[b]
20 seconds	$107,000	$124,000
30 seconds	$160,500	$186,000
40 seconds	$214,000	$248,000
60 seconds	$321,000	$371,000

"A" Class:

12:00 A.M.–5:00 P.M.		
20 seconds	$54,000	$61,000
30 seconds	$81,000	$93,000
40 seconds	$108,000	$124,000
60 seconds	$162,000	$186,000

Rates: 24 hours

20 seconds		$147,000
30 seconds		$220,500
40 seconds		$294,000
60 seconds		$441,000

Channel 44

"AAA" Class:

5:00 P.M.–12:00 A.M.	
20 seconds	$724
30 seconds	$1,086
40 seconds	$1,448
60 seconds	$2,172

"A" Class:

12:00 A.M.–5:00 P.M.	
20 seconds	$506
30 seconds	$759
40 seconds	$1,012
60 seconds	$1,518

Source: *Medios Publicitarios Mexicanos* (1992)
[a] Spots between programs.
[b] Spots during programs.

TABLE 10   Ratings by Time Slot

TV Channel	12 noon–2:00 p.m. %	(Size)	8:00–10:00 p.m. %	(Size)	10:00–10:30 p.m. %	(Size)	10:30–11:00 p.m. %	(Size)
2—Juárez	9	(4)	44	(20.75)	42	(14.2)	49	(13.8)
5—Juárez	4	(1.1)	4	(2)	7	(2.2)	6	(1.8)
26—El Paso	20	(6.4)	1	(0.5)	4	(1.4)	3	(0.8)
44—Juárez	64	(20.5)	46	(21.75)	39	(13.2)	33	(9.4)
English-lang. TV	3	(1)	5	(2.35)	8	(2.8)	9	(2.6)
Total	100	33	100	47.35	100	33.8	100	28.4

Note: Size represents total share.

national origin of the audiences. The focus on the content of the broadcast industries as well as its reception loses sight of the reason for the existence of these industries—namely, the production of audiences. In his discussion of the 1988 Free Trade Agreement, Mosco (1990) stated that the agreement was not about culture but that it was culture. The discussion about free trade and the cultural industries so far has focused on the production and reception of cultural texts, while neglecting the culture of producing audiences. Future discussions should view signifying practices as being determined by material conditions, and material practices and their narration as cultural practices.

NOTES

1. It fetishizes production in the classical Marxist sense by hiding the creation and distribution of exchange value. It fetishizes consumption by describing the process as plain entertainment, without acknowledging the way in which cultural capital, in Bourdieu's (1984) sense, is produced and distributed. The audience-commodity and audience-labor approaches developed originally by Smythe (1981) and elaborated further by Jahlly would go beyond these views by claiming that commodities (audiences) and work forces (audiences) are being traded.

2. For an analysis of these uses of the U.S.–Mexico border, see Fox (1993), who cites the following as examples: D. Emily Hicks, *Border Writing: The Multidimensional Text, Theory and History of Literature* (Minneapolis: University of Minnesota Press, 1991); Iain Chambers, *Border Dialogues: Journeys in Postmodernity* (London: Routledge, 1990); Henry Giroux, *Border Crossings: Cultural Workers and the Politics of Education* (New York: Routledge, 1992); Trinh T. Minh-ha, *When the Moon Waxes Red: Representation, Gender and Cultural Politics* (New York: Routledge, 1991); Maggie Humm, *Border Traffic: Strategies of Contemporary Women Writers*

(New York: St. Martin's Press, 1991); and Renato Rosaldo, *Culture and Truth: The Remaking of Social Analysis* (Boston: Beacon Press, 1989). Predecessors include: Jacques Derrida, "Living On: Border Lines," trans. James Hulbert, in *Deconstruction and Criticism*, ed. Harold Bloom, pp. 75–176 (New York: Seabury, 1979); Jacques Derrida, "The Parergon," *October* 9 (Summer 1979): 3–41.

3. See Rosaldo (1989).

4. This strong influence of the Frankfurt School was seen particularly in such approaches as cultural imperialism and electronic colonialism. In Latin America the works of Armand Mattelart and Ariel Dorfman are representative of this perspective. In Mexico the writings of Javier Esteinou are examples of the same position.

5. Bustamante (1992), 99–100. Italics added.

6. Vila (1994), 160, 213–215.

7. Valenzuela Arce (1992a, 1992b, 1992c). Although Bustamante and Valenzuela share the centrality of the "other," Bustamante's analysis is founded in the Weberian notion of social interaction and in Mario Ojeda's thesis of power asymmetry, while Valenzuela bases his in the theories of new social movements of Touraine, Melucci, and Smelser.

8. Eagleton (1983), p. 174.

9. Stam, Burgoyne, and Flitterman-Lewis (1992), p. 129.

10. The development of a cultural identity through a process of paradigmatic differentiation evolves genealogically from Saussurian linguistics to Lacanian psychoanalysis to contemporary scholars, such as Homi Bhabha (1994), who work within a framework that includes the axes of ethnicity, gender, and class. However, there is not only the possibility of "positive" identities through differentiation, but an important distinction should be made between these accounts of "horizontal-secular" processes of differentiation and the "vertical-natural" processes. The former are based on the differences between the material and signifying practices of the everyday lives of social actors. The latter are more noticeable in precapitalist/premodern societies, where eschatological founding myths narrate the process of differentiation from divine elements and ground the social actors in relation to their habitat, and where ethnicity, gender, and class are secondary effects. Telluric accounts can be found in Mexican border cities such as Nuevo Laredo (Ceballos 1992) and Tijuana (Díaz Castro 1992). The creation of the Free Trade Zone regime for the border (with renewed variants through several decades) can be regarded as the founding myth for the whole region that constituted the new border subject who is so important in this emerging view.

11. Bustamante (1992), p. 103.

12. See Lozano (1991a) and Valenzuela Arce (1993), both of whom celebrate appropriation and resistance along the border, relying on the work of Jesús Martín-Barbero and Néstor García Canclini that was built upon Gramscian cultural studies and informed by Cirese, Foucault, and de Certeau.

13. See Schiller (1991).

14. García Canclini (1990).

15. Gómez-Peña (1992), p. 60.

16. Gómez-Peña (1993), p. 60.
17. Haraway (1992), p. 312.
18. Jorge Bustamante is a scholar who uses this strategy frequently.
19. Néstor García Canclini reproduces Frederic Jameson's position.
20. Bennett and Woollacott (1987), p. 86.
21. Anderson (1984).
22. Gilly (1988) points out that the "first modernity, that of the Italian Renaissance, the Protestant Reform and the discovery of the world, was just starting in Europe. It came to America under feudalist forms, but in its heart there already was the exchange value" (p. iv).
23. Quijano (1988), p. 109.
24. Rose (1991), p. 17.
25. "Competence" is used in Bourdieu's (1984) sense. Cultural competence is the capacity to decode symbolic goods textually and intertextually. In this new phase the convertibility of cultural capital into economic capital would be transforming it into a more direct transaction. The rejection of use value of cultural goods would vanish, giving priority to exchange value. "Popular taste applies the schemes of the ethos, which pertains, in the ordinary circumstances of life, to legitimate works of art, and so performs a systematic reduction of the things of art to the things of life" (Bourdieu, p. 5). He adds that "submission to necessity . . . inclines working-class people to a pragmatic, functionalistic 'aesthetic,' refusing the gratuity and futility of formal exercises" (p. 376). "Aesthetic disposition" refers to the distanced relation with the world and "objective" needs, which is cultivated by the bourgeoisie and which is determined by schooling and by the history of social position.
26. Negri (1989), p. 207.
27. Harvey (1989), pp. 327, 348.
28. García Canclini (1990).
29. Mosco (1989).
30. Although there are some PARM enclaves in the border state of Tamaulipas, they fall within the same scheme.
31. In 1930 Antonio Gramsci (1987) defined what an organic intellectual was: "Every social group, when born on the ground that originates an essential function in the world of economic production, also creates, organically, one or more classes of intellectuals that give it homogeneity and consciousness of its function not only in the economic arena, but in the social and political . . . as a constructor, organizer, 'permanent persuader' and not pure speaker . . . superior to the abstract mathematic spirit; from work technique arrives to science technique and to historic-humanistic conception" (pp. 50–55).

These functions currently materialize, more than in individuals, in institutions whose formal pluralism gives them a stronger legitimation, institutions from periodicals to research centers. The ruling class and organic institutions maintain a noninstrumental relation that constitutes a very asymmetric negotiating process between nonmonolithic parties. Even when the political agenda of the individual or institution differs from the official agenda, the benefits obtained will be greater and will strengthen the party with more power. Co-optation mechanisms that have characterized the Mexican political system may allocate more bargaining power to the former critical intellectual, who, in one and the same movement, loses the capacity for structural change.

32. Jesús Amozurrutia (1990) shows that the correlation between U.S. industrial production and employment in the *maquiladora* industry in a time series analysis is 0.85.

33. Meyer (1991).

34. Bartra (1987), p. 22.

35. Franco (1987), pp. 66–67.

36. Carey (1989), p. 180.

37. Mediationism would refer to the process described by Martín-Barbero (1987), involving the circulation of popular culture elements in mass-produced texts.

38. Harris (1992).

39. Bennett (1992), p. 35.

40. Ibid, p. 25.

41. Bennett, Craik, Hunter, Mercer, and Williamson (1993), pp. x–xi. Italics added.

42. Mattelart (1991), p. 55.

43. Average TV penetration for the 24 stations in California, Arizona, New Mexico, and Texas. *TV & Cable Factbook* (1988).

44. Electricity is used as a proxy measure for the Mexican side of the border. *Chihuahua cuaderno de información para la planeación* (1986), *Coahuila cuaderno de información para la planeación* (1986), *Nuevo León cuaderno de información para la planeación* (1986), and *Tamaulipas cuaderno de información para la planeación* (1986). The *UNESCO Statistical Yearbook* (1988) reports 11.7 TV sets for 100 people, which would translate into 58.7% of the households. Jorge González (1993) estimates that 85% of Mexican households have TV sets.

45. CIEMEX-WEFA (1994).

46. 10%—Grupo Bermúdez; 40%—Estimate traditionally used by the Texas Department of Commerce. Francisco Lara Valencia (1990) specifies transborder expenditures by this labor force as follows: direct labor, 39.4%; technicians, 28.6%; and administrative, 42.7%.

47. Gonzalez-Aréchiga et al. (1990). Data reported in original were not clear. One possible explanation is that categories are not mutually exclusive; for instance, "basic goods" might include other reported categories.

48. U.S. Bureau of the Census (1988).

49. Elaborated from raw data from *Sistema de cuentas nacionales de México* (1985).

50. Univisión was bought by a group in which Televisa figures prominently. Puig and Cabildo (1992) point out that Televisa is planning English broadcasts from the Mexican-side outlets. There is already a station in Tijuana owned by Emilio Azcárraga that uses FOX programming.

51. Arriaga (1980).

52. Niles Hansen (1981).

53. Desarrollo Económico (1991).

54. U.S. Bureau of the Census (1991).

55. Programming and advertising data correspond to March 25, 26, 27, and 30, 1992, for Channels 44, 4, 26, and 2, respectively.

56. Even when this programming is classified as informative, it is closer to soap operas because of its similarities to melodrama, which "operates in Latin America a primordial sociality . . . [and] by melodramatizing everything, people get a self-fashioned revenge for the abstraction imposed by the commodification of life and cultural dispossession" (Martín-Barbero 1991, p. 5).

BIBLIOGRAPHY

Amozurrutia, Jesús. 1990. "El empleo en la industria maquiladora mexicana y los ciclos económicos de los Estados Unidos." In *Subcontratación y empresas transnacionales*, ed. Bernardo González-Aréchiga and José Carlos Ramírez, pp. 287–308. Mexico City: COLEF-Friedrich Ebert.

Anderson, Perry. 1984. "Modernity and Revolution." *New Left Review*, 144(March-April): 96–113.

Arriaga, Patricia. 1980. *Publicidad, economía y comunicación masiva (México-Estados Unidos)*. Mexico City: Nueva Imagen.

Avance de información económica. 1991. Mexico City: INEGI.

Barrera Herrera, Eduardo. 1992. "De carreteras electrónicas a ciudades cableadas." *Ciudades* 13(January–March): 21–26.

Bartra, Roger. 1987. *La jaula de la melancolía.* Mexico City: Grijalbo.

Bennett, Tony. 1992. "Putting Policy into Cultural Studies." In *Cultural Studies*, ed. Lawrence Grossberg, Cary Nelson, and Paula Treichler, pp. 23–37. London and New York: Routledge.

Bennett, Tony, Jennifer Craik, Ian Hunter, Colin Mercer, and Dugald Williamson. 1993. "Series Editor's Preface." In *Rock and Popular Music: Politics, Policies, Institutions*, ed. Tony Bennett, Simon Frith, Lawrence Grossberg, John Shepherd, and Graeme Turner, pp. x–xi. London and New York: Routledge.

Bennett, Tony, Simon Frith, Lawrence Grossberg, John Shepherd, and Graeme Turner, eds. 1993. *Rock and Popular Music: Politics, Policies, Institutions.* London and New York: Routledge.

Bennett, Tony, and Jane Woollacott. 1987. *Bond and Beyond: The Political Career of a Popular Hero.* London: Macmillan.

Bhabha, Homi K. 1994. *The Location of Culture.* London and New York: Routledge.

Bourdieu, Pierre. 1984. *Distinction. A Social Critique of the Judgement of Taste.* Cambridge, Mass.: Harvard University Press.

Bustamante, Jorge. 1992. "Identidad y cultura nacional desde la perspectiva de la frontera norte." In *Decadencia y auge de las identidades: Cultura nacional, identidad cultural y modernización*, ed. José Manuel Valenzuela Arce. Tijuana: COLEF.

Carey, James. 1989. *Communication as Culture: Essays on Media and Society.* Boston: Unwin Hyman.

Castellanos Guerrero, Alicia, and Gilberto López y Rivas. 1981. "La influencia norteamericana en la cultura de la frontera norte de México." In *La frontera del norte: Integración y desarrollo*, ed. Roque González Salazar, pp. 68–84. Mexico City: El Colegio de México.

Ceballos Ramírez, Manuel. 1992. "La epopeya de la fundación de Nuevo Laredo: El nexo entre la tradición y la historia." In *Entre la magia y la historia*, ed. José Manuel Valenzuela Arce, pp. 99–107. Tijuana: COLEF.

Chihuahua cuaderno de información para la planeación. 1986. Mexico City: INEGI.

CIEMEX-WEFA. 1994. *Maquiladora Industry Analysis* 7, no. 1 (January).

Coahuila cuaderno de información para la planeación. 1986. Mexico City: INEGI.

Coplamar. 1989. *Geografía de la marginación*, 4th ed. Mexico City: Siglo XXI.

Deetz, Stanley. 1991. Transnational Corporations and Inner Colonization: From National to Corporate Culture in the USA. Paper presented at the 1991 International Communication Association, Chicago, May 23–27.

Desarrollo Económico de Cd. Juárez, A.C. 1991. *Cd. Juárez en cifras—1991: Estadísticas socioeconómicas básicas*. Ciudad Juárez: Desarrollo Económico de Cd. Juárez.

Díaz Castro, Olga Vicenta (Sor Abeja). (1992). "La tía Juana." In *Entre la magia y la historia*, ed. José Manuel Valenzuela Arce, pp. 109–133. Tijuana: COLEF.

Eagleton, Terry. 1983. *Literary Theory: An Introduction*. Minneapolis: University of Minnesota Press.

Fox, Claire F. 1993. Mass Media, Site-Specificity, and Representations of the US-Mexico Border. Paper delivered at conference, The Border, organized by the Whitney Museum, New York, April.

Franco, Jean. 1987. "La política cultural en la época de Reagan." In *Políticas Culturales en América Latina*, ed. Néstor García Canclini. Mexico City: Grijalbo.

Frederick, Howard. 1993. *Global Communication & International Relations*. Belmont, Calif.: Wadsworth.

García Canclini, Néstor, ed. 1987. *Políticas Culturales en América Latina*. Mexico City: Grijalbo.

———. 1990. *Culturas híbridas: Estrategias para entrar y salir de la modernidad*. Mexico City: Grijalbo.

Gertner, Richard, ed. 1984. *International Television Almanac*, 31st ed. New York: Quigley.

Gilly, Adolfo. 1988. *Nuestra caída en la modernidad*. Mexico City: Joan Boldó i Climent, Editores.

Gómez-Peña, Guillermo. 1992. "The New World (B)order." *High Performance* 15(Summer/Fall): 58–59.

———. 1993. *Warrior for Gringostroika*. St. Paul, Minn.: Graywolf Press.

González, Jorge A. 1990. *(El regreso de . . .) La cofradía de las emociones in/terminables (II): Telenovela, memoria, familia*. Comala, Colima: Universidad de Colima. Mimeo.

———. 1992. Problemas y oportunidades del comercio en la zona fronteriza. Paper presented at Oportunidades de Inversión en la Frontera Norte, Monterrey, Nuevo León.

———. 1993. "Video-Tecnología y Modernidad." *Dia · Logos de la Comunicación* 36 (August).

González-Aréchiga, Bernardo, and José Carlos Ramírez, eds. 1990. *Subcontratación y empresas transnacionales.* Mexico City: COLEF-Friedrich Ebert.

Gramsci, Antonio. 1987. *La alternativa pedagógica.* Mexico City: Fontamara.

Grossberg, Lawrence, Cary Nelson, and Paula Treichler, eds. 1992. *Cultural Studies.* London and New York: Routledge.

Grupo Bermúdez. n.d. *The Maquiladora Industry: Creating Jobs in the United States.* Ciudad Juárez, Mexico: Pamphlet.

Hansen, Niles. 1981. *The Border Economy: Regional Development in the Southwest.* Austin: University of Texas Press.

Haraway, Donna. 1992. "The Promises of Monsters: A Regenerative Politics for Inappropriate/d Others." In *Cultural Studies,* ed. Lawrence Grossberg, Cary Nelson, and Paula Treichler, pp. 295–337. London and New York: Routledge.

Harris, David. 1992. *From Class Struggle to the Politics of Pleasure: The Effects of Gramscianism on Cultural Studies.* London and New York: Routledge.

Harvey, David. 1989. *The Condition of Postmodernity.* Cambridge, Mass.: Basil Blackwell.

Hepworth, Mark. 1990. *Geography of the Information Economy.* New York: Guilford.

Huber, Peter. 1989. "The New Competitive Environment." *Society* 26(5): 27–31.

Iglesias, Norma. 1990. *Panorama de los medios de comunicación en la frontera norte de México.* Mexico City: Fundación Manuel Buendía–Programa Cultural de las Fronteras.

INRA. 1992. Untitled. Mimeo.

Jhally, Sut. 1987. *The Codes of Advertising: Fetishism and the Political Economy of Meaning in the Consumer Society.* New York: St. Martin's Press.

Lara Valencia, Francisco. 1990. El gasto transfronterizo de los empleados de la industria maquiladora: Patrones e implicaciones para Sonora y Arizona. Paper presented at COLEF I. Tijuana, October 27–28.

Leiss, William, Stephen Kline, and Sut Jhally. 1986. *Social Communication in Advertising: Persons, Products & Images of Well-Being.* New York: Methuen.

Lipietz, Alain. 1987. *Mirages and Miracles: The Crises of Global Fordism.* London: Verso.

Lozano, José Carlos. 1991a. "Enfoques teóricos para el estudio de la cultura en la frontera México con Estados Unidos." *Río Bravo* 1(1): 27–46.

———. 1991b. *Prensa, radiodifusión e identidad cultural en la frontera norte.* Tijuana: COLEF.

Malagamba Ansótegui, Amelia. 1986. *La televisión y su impacto en la población infantil de Tijuana.* Tijuana: CEFNOMEX.

Malone, Thomas, and John Rockart. 1991. "Computers, Networks and the Corporation." *Scientific American* 1991(September): 128–136.

Martín Barbero, Jesús. 1987. *De los medios a las mediaciones: Comunicación, cultura y hegemonía.* Mexico City: Gustavo Gili.

————. 1991. "Telenovela: Melodrama e identidad." *Circuito* 15(April): 5.

Mattelart, Armand. 1991. *Advertising International: The Privatisation of Public Space.* New York: Routledge.

Medios Publicitarios Mexicanos, S.A. de C.V. 1992. *Medios audio-visuales: Tarifas y datos* 92, no. 2.

Meyer, Lorenzo. 1991. "El límite neoliberal." *Nexos* 163(July): 25–34.

Monsiváis, Carlos. 1987. "La cultura popular en el ámbito urbano: El caso de México." In *Communicación y culturas populares en Latinoamérica,* ed. Seminario del Consejo Latinoamericano de Ciencias Sociales, pp. 113–133. Mexico City: Ediciones G. Gili.

Mosco, Vincent. 1989. *The Pay-per Society.* Norwood, N.J.: Ablex.

————. 1990. "Toward a Transnational World Information Order: The Canada-U.S. Free Trade Agreement." *Canadian Journal of Communication* 15(2): 46–63.

Murdock, Graham. 1982. "Large corporations and the control of the communications industries." In *Culture, Society and the Media,* ed. Michael Gurevitch, Tony Bennett, James Curran, and Janet Woollacott, pp. 118–150. London: Methuen.

Negri, Antonio. 1989. *Politics of Subversion.* Cambridge, Mass.: Polity Press.

Nuevo León cuaderno de información para la planeación. 1986. Mexico City: INEGI.

Pitelis, Christos. 1991. "Beyond the Nation-State?: The Transnational Firm and the Nation-State." *Capital and Class* 43 (September).

Puig, Carlos, and Miguel Cabildo. 1992. "Televisa sin fronteras: Estados Unidos, Venezuela, Perú, Chile, Argentina, España . . . ." *Proceso* 823(August 10): 21.

Quad, Ward L., and James A. Brown. 1976. *Broadcast Management: Radio Television,* 2nd ed. New York: Hastings House.

Quijano, Aníbal. 1988. "A different concept of the private sector, a different concept of the public sector (Notes for a Latin American debate)." *Cepal Review* 35.

Resultados preliminares: XI Censo general de población y vivienda. 1990. Mexico City: INEGI.

Rosaldo, Renato. 1989. *Culture as Truth: The Remaking of Social Analysis.* Boston: Beacon Press.

Rose, Margaret. 1991. *The Post-modern & the Post-industrial.* Cambridge: Cambridge University Press.

Schiller, Herb. 1991. "Not Yet the Post-Imperialist Era." *Critical Studies in Mass Communication* 8(March): 13–28.

Seiter, Ellen, Hans Borchers, Gabriele Kreutzner, and Eva-Maria Warth, eds. 1989. *Remote Control: Television, Audiences & Cultural Power.* London: Routledge.

Sistema de cuentas nacionales de México. 1985. Mexico City: INEGI.

Smith, Anthony. 1991. *The Age of Behemoths: The Globalization of Mass Media Firms.* New York: Priority Press.

Smythe, Dallas. 1981. *Dependency Road: Communications, Capitalism, Consciousness, and Canada.* Norwood, N.J.: Ablex.

Stam, Robert, Robert Burgoyne, and Sandy Flitterman-Lewis. 1992. *New Vocabularies in Film Semiotics.* London and New York: Routledge.

Tamaulipas cuaderno de información para la planeación. 1986. Mexico City: INEGI.

TV & Cable Factbook. 1988. Vol. 1, no. 56.

UNESCO Statistical Yearbook. 1988. Paris: UNESCO.

U.S. Bureau of the Census. 1988. *County Business Patterns 1986,* United States (no. 1) and Texas (no. 45). Washington, D.C.: Government Printing Office.

———. 1991. *County Business Patterns 1989,* Texas (no. 45). Washington, D.C.: Government Printing Office.

Valenzuela Arce, José Manuel, ed. 1992a. *Decadencia y auge de las identidades: Cultura nacional, identidad cultural y modernización.* Tijuana: COLEF.

———, ed. 1992b. *Entre la magia y la historia.* Tijuana: COLEF.

———. 1992c. "Identidades culturales: Comunidades imaginarias y contingentes." In *Decadencia y auge de las identidades: Cultura nacional, identidad cultural y modernización,* ed. José Manuel Valenzuela Arce. Tijuana: COLEF.

———. 1993. "Las identidades culturales frente al TLC." *Sociológica* 8(12): 103–129.

Vila, Pablo Sergio. 1994. "Everyday Life, Culture and Identity on the Mexican-American Border: The Ciudad Juárez–El Paso Case." Ph.D. diss., University of Texas, Austin.

Williams, Frederick. 1990. *The New Telecommunication: Infrastructure for the Information Age.* New York: Free Press.

Zúñiga, Víctor. 1992. Visiones de la frontera. Paper presented at COLEF II, Tijuana, October 22–24, 1992.

Part Four

Cultural Trade and Identity: Quebec

10

Walking on a Tightrope: The Markets of Cultural Products in Québec

CLAUDE MARTIN

THE QUÉBEC ECONOMY IS HEAVILY influenced by the proximity and strength of the United States. Three-quarters of Québec's exports find their way to the American market, from which nearly half of Québec's imports originate. In comparison, Mexico's trade situation in Québec is negligible, amounting to only 1.4% of Québec's exports and 1% of its imports.[1] A number of major corporations in Québec are controlled by American interests.[2] Public institutions and private companies in Québec regularly borrow capital[3] and sell shares in American markets.[4] On another level, Québec is very much a part of America's sphere of technological activity. Industrial production, from the manufacture of nuts and bolts to lumber and office supplies, electricity, and television, conforms to American technical standards. And the Canadian telephone system is thoroughly integrated into the American system (even though majority control remains in Canadian hands).

In line with the preoccupations of this study, it can also be said that Québecois and American culture have much in common. When they are viewed in anthropological terms, a number of common threads can be seen. In fact, it becomes quite clear that to be American is not necessarily to be from the United States. In terms of intellectual production, it is clear that American cultural products have been rapidly and mas-

Translated by Reynolds Kanary (Department of Languages, Collège Edouard– Montpetit, Longueuil, Québec)

sively spread throughout Québec by cultural industries and artistic circuits (conversely, a small number of Québecois products have found their way to the United States). Generally speaking, life in Québec greatly resembles life in the New England states. Despite several distinctive and important traits, it can be argued that Québec's economy and even its society have developed according to a model very much like that of the United States.

It is a question not of a model imposed by the United States, but rather of a model that is to a great extent the result of a similar development. Some of the contributing factors are proximity, European colonization, access to natural wealth, available land, and analogous political systems. Nevertheless, although the model has not been imposed, it remains subject to the influence and, at times, the goodwill of the United States. As an example, construction of the Saint Lawrence Seaway became a reality only when the United States recognized that its existence would be in the United States' interest. However, the seaway has had an enormous impact on the economies of cities and towns bordering the Saint Lawrence River, as well as on the development of mineral wealth in Québec. Finally, it should not be forgotten that Canada is party to a bilateral military pact with the United States (NORAD) and that its defense is part and parcel of the American system of defense. Québec holds a strategic position with regard to American military and economic security, which, as a result, has influenced Québec's economic and social development in a number of ways.

There are important differences between the two countries (besides the direction of flow of Arctic air during the winter months). Unlike the United States, Canada was not created following a violent rupture with England. On the contrary, it came into being partly as a result of a British imperial effort to curb northward expansion by the United States. One slogan popular during the 1930s, "The State or the States,"[5] highlights the importance of this basis for state intervention by Canadian governments. This distinction between the United States and Canada became more pronounced following World War II, when Canada began adopting social policies that were wider ranging than those in the United States. Canada's health and education systems are two of the most obvious examples of these differences.

The years following the war have also set the stage for a confrontation between the polarized visions of Canadian economic development held by continentalists and nationalists in Canada. The boom in the development of natural resources and domestic consumption has led to a major increase in American control of the Canadian economy, including Québec's share. Many Canadian companies have prospered and thousands of workers benefited from stable, well-paying jobs. Elsewhere in the world, this same period has been one of decolonialization and struggles for independence. In Québec a movement that has gained greatly in importance has been arguing that French Canadians should take control of the levers of their own economy. The main instrument of this operation would be the Québec government, which would create a number of public institutions favoring the emergence and development of Québec-style capitalism. In the rest of Canada a comparable movement has succeeded in establishing limits over foreign investment. During the 1960s and 1970s Canadian and Québecois control over the economy clearly increased.

Although these movements are both political and economic, there is also an important cultural component. In this instance, the case of Québec is akin to that of Mexico. Economic and social development has led to cultural development; however, the road has been a long one. Following the British conquest that separated French Canada from France, Catholicism and the French language acted to isolate French Canadians from the other populations of North America. Even though this cultural isolation has exacted a price in terms of development, it has otherwise allowed for the establishment of a stronger social bond. Cultural industries have contributed greatly to the creation of this bond and have at the same time assisted in destroying the isolation. In Québec cultural industries have played a paradoxical role, and continue to do so. On the one hand, they have been the best means for producing a world view unique to Québec; yet on the other, they have provided the main point of entry for a variety of different world views, particularly those coming from the United States. These, then, are the main components of the fragile equilibrium found in the system of cultural industries in Québec. Seen from Hollywood, they may appear as a futile if not wasted effort, or simply as protectionism. Seen from Québec, they represent the possibility of continued existence.

The following section analyzes several aspects of cultural industries in Québec according to one version of the classic paradigm of industrial organization.[6] From this perspective, the performance of companies and industries can be explained by market structures—that is, by the influences on the supply and demand for products. Industrial performance can be evaluated in terms of society's expectations. Society requires that industries be profitable and that they contribute to the creation of jobs, to an equitable distribution of wealth, to technical progress, and so on. In the area of cultural industries it might be worthwhile to add to the list of expected performance a contribution to the cultural "reproduction" of society.

Thus, the purpose of this paper is to analyze the performance of cultural industries in Québec. To this essentially economic discussion will be added a historical dimension, since an analysis made only in relation to market characteristics will not be able to deal adequately with certain aspects of the problem, in particular those concerning power struggles among cultural industries.

▪ ▪ The Origin of Cultural Industries in Québec

In Québec, as elsewhere, the first manifestation of the industrialization of cultural production can be seen in the field of print and in the production of magazines and books. The first newspaper in Québec was printed in 1764 and the first book in 1765. However, the press of the eighteenth and nineteenth centuries was essentially an opinion-based press and directed primarily toward the elites. Literacy did not reach the majority of citizens until close to the middle of the nineteenth century.[7] The publication of French-Canadian books and literature began to expand during the final quarter of the nineteenth century.[8] In 1876 the provincial government began to distribute French-Canadian books as prizes in schools. This policy was in response to the appeal by a group of writers for the establishment of a national literature. By the beginning of the twentieth century, opinion-based newspapers had been quickly left behind by the proliferation of information-based newspapers, themselves a product of the advance in literacy, demand for advertising, and improvements in print technology and telecommunications. At the same time, it should be noted that in a society where economic activity had been generally controlled by the English, the publication of newspapers and books was in the hands of French capital. The contribution of the State was considerable in both instances. It bought a share in book publication through the school system and assisted the newspaper industry through lucrative printing contracts (in return for unquestioned loyalty, it should be added). Nevertheless, each industry could be clearly distinguished by its impact on the population. The press was able to reach all levels of society, whereas books reached only a small, well-educated minority.

The first movie theater opened in Montréal in 1906, only a few years later than in New York.[9] Many others followed and were generally owned by French Canadians. Films were bought in New York and subtitles were translated into French in Montréal. A theater owner produced local newsreel footage that was screened the same day it was filmed. However, the situation changed in the 1920s, when control of the theaters wound up in American hands, in particular those of Famous Players (which continues today as part of the Paramount empire). The films that were screened were for the most part American, although some had a peculiar look—namely, those dealing with supposedly Canadian subjects although products of American studios. French Canadians were relegated to the role of the "bad guys," much as the Indians were in westerns.[10]

This turn of events provoked harsh criticism of the moral content of the films being screened and their disrespect for French-Canadian values. It resulted in laws establishing a minimum age for admission to theaters as well as the creation of a censorship bureau. In addition, several priests, inspired by the opportunities for religious and nationalist propaganda, produced several documentaries on French-Canadian life. In 1931 a company under the name of France-Film was founded that distributed films and operated theaters devoted solely to French movies. By 1940 films in French represented 10% of all screenings. As for France-Film, it was later responsible for the production of the first fictional Québecois films and set up the first private television station in Québec.

The beginnings of the recording industry were also marked by the predominance of foreign products, although to a lesser extent than in film. As early as 1901, Emile Berliner, an American, was producing recordings in Montréal with French-Canadian singers.[11] Several hundred recordings, often inspired by folklore, were made at the beginning of the century. In the 1920s, radio and electric recording techniques made possible the broadcast of new kinds of popular American and French music. Québecois imitators inspired by American and French crooners succeeded in carving out an important niche on the airwaves and in the aisles of record stores.

Radio was born in Québec at the same moment as in the United States.[12] Even though the first station was English, the second (CKAC) followed only a few months later and was French, established by *La Presse*, the largest French daily in Montréal. The first radio stations were in the hands of private interests but required a government license. Public debate on the control of radio led to the creation of a federal commission of inquiry in 1928. It was feared that Canadian radio would fall under the grip of the American networks. In the end, the Canadian government opted for a mixed system that gave birth to a public radio corporation (Canadian Broadcasting Corporation [CBC]) with two networks (English and French) that would coexist with private radio stations. In 1938 the French network became independent (Radio-Canada).[13]

Television had its beginning in Québec several years later than it did in the United States. In 1952 Radio-Canada opened a bilingual television station in Montréal. It soon became unilingual French when an English station joined the English network of CBC. In quick order, regional stations were established in many Québec cities, and with them, the public French television network began to take shape. And so public television became a focal point for Québec society. It presented a new outlook on the world and on Québec in particular, and took part fully in the political and cultural renewal of the time. In 1960 the federal government granted licenses to private television stations, thus ending the monopoly of public television. This opened the door to intense competition for audience attention, which grew when the introduction of cable greatly increased reception of American networks.

Thus, the emergence of Québec's cultural industries can be explained by several important factors:

- a French majority in close proximity to a large English minority (i.e., in Québec; of course, the opposite was the case in the rest of North America);
- an economic development similar to that of the United States and sufficient to generate advertising expenditures able to finance newspapers, radio, and television;
- the strategies of private local business people who saw profit in cultural industries;
- the massive import of American and French cultural products and the widespread adoption of American standards for Canadian and Québecois cultural products;
- nationalist, Canadian, and French-Canadian ideologies that led in particular to the production of French cultural works and information media;
- government strategies for intervention to stimulate or even create institutions in the field of cultural industries.

■ ■ The Québec Model

Today, Québec has a population of almost seven million, with an average family income of about U.S.$37,000 (1990). This level of revenue allows for an overall expenditure on cultural industries equivalent to about U.S.$1,200 per family, or three billion U.S. dollars in total.[14] The per capita sum is considerable, but the number of consumers is not large enough, in many cases, to absorb the costs of production, especially in the case of large-scale audiovisual productions.

But the restrictedness of the Québec market constitutes a major structural element because cultural products are often characterized by a production structure in which fixed costs (independent of audience size) are high. If the audience is small, this normally entails a higher price for the product, which in turn decreases demand and finally limits distribution or even halts production. The expected result is that there would be little or no production with products imported from countries that would be able to meet the costs. However, this has not been the case for Québec, which has in large part been able to escape this vicious cycle.

Table 1 gives the number of jobs in Québec's main cultural industries and provides a measure of the economic clout of different industries. They can be put into different categories, the first category comprising those supported by advertising (newspapers, magazines, radio, and television). This is the most important category and the wealthiest. Cable companies also do well, but they represent an unusual kind of cultural industry, in that their list of products is mostly created by other industries. The book, recording, and film industries resemble one another, since they receive their greatest share of revenue directly from the consumer, with no help from advertising. As a result, their situation is more difficult than that of the first two categories.[15] The performing arts constitute a special case, since they do not use any mechanical means of reproduction or broadcasting. Their situation, too, is relatively difficult. Museums also constitute a special case, as much because of the nature of their media as because of their funding.

Local production is usually in the hands of private capital or Canadian or Québecois public organizations. Table 2 summarizes the main characteristics of control of cultural industries in Québec. Control by Québec interests takes a variety of forms: diversified conglomerates or conglomerates operating solely in the field of communications; small and medium-sized companies; and state enterprises. American capital

TABLE 1   Number of Jobs in Specific Sectors of Québec's
Cultural Industries (1990)

Industry	No. of Jobs
Museums (1988–1989)	1,500
Performing arts	5,800
Book publishing	1,200
Bookstores and distributors (1986)	3,100
Newspapers (1989)	4,200
Magazines and periodicals (1989)	1,400
Sound recording production	1,000
Film (production and distribution)	3,600
Cinema	1,600
Radio	2,100
Television	2,300
Public radio and TV (1986)	3,500
Cable TV (1989)	2,500
Total	**33,800**

NOTE: Not included are the following: many freelance artists, actors, and writers;
  magazine distributors and retailers; record distributors and retailers.
SOURCES: Bureau de la statistique du Québec, *Statistiques culturelles, édition 1993,*
  Québec, Government House, 1993; C. Martin, *Le poids économique des industries
  culturelles non publicitaires,* research for Québec's Ministère des Affaires culturelles, 1986.

is most visible in film distribution and ownership of movie theaters.
French capital is found in book distribution. Private Canadian capital is
important in newspapers and magazines. The Canadian presence in radio and television is Radio-Canada, the state corporation.

Table 3 shows annual revenue (or budget), main areas of business,
and financial control for several of the main players alluded to in Table 2.
The largest organizations under Québecois control can be found in media supported by advertising (newspapers, magazines, television, and
radio). The most important, in terms of revenue, is Québecor, a diversified company with interests in every aspect of printing. Québecor has
developed around tabloid-style newspapers. Other important companies
under Québecois control are involved in cable (Vidéotron, CFCF, and
Cogeco). Among these large companies, the presence of Radio-Canada
and its television and radio networks should also be highlighted. Radio-

TABLE 2 Control of Cultural Industries in Québec

Industry	Main Origins of Control	Main Form of Capital
Museums	Québec	State (Québec, Canada, local) nonprofit organizations
Performing arts	Québec	small or medium-sized firms State (Québec)
Book publishing	Québec	small or medium-sized firms State (Québec)
Book distribution	Québec France	small firms
Newspaper and periodical publishing	Québec Canada	communication or financial conglomerates
Periodical distribution	Québec	communication conglomerates small firms
Record production	Québec International "majors"	small firms international conglomerates
Record distribution	Québec Canada	small firms
Film and video production	Québec Canada	small or medium-sized firms State (Canada)
Film and video distribution	USA Canada Québec	communication conglomerates small firms
Radio stations	Québec Canada	communication conglomerates State (Canada)
Television stations	Québec Canada	communication conglomerates State (Canada, Québec)
Cable	Québec	communication conglomerates

Canada is an important program producer, especially of fictional series, often in collaboration with private producers. CBC/Radio-Canada brings to radio and television a type of programming that has affected the private sector. For instance, when Radio-Canada shows fictional series, TVA, the main private French network, is induced to do so as well, in order to keep attracting audiences. Radio-Canada is a source of quality programming and this helps in setting standards for every broadcaster. Radio-Canada is also the main source of expertise on broadcasting in Québec. Its economic clout helps to compensate for the small internal

TABLE 3   Annual Revenue/Budget, Main Areas of Business, and Financial
Control for Some of Québec's Main Cultural Organizations

Organization	Revenue/Budget		Industries	Control (residence)
	C$million	Year		
Quebecor	2,433.7	1990	dailies, magazines, printing	Péladeau (Québec)
Canadian Broadcasting Corp./Radio-Canada	1,391.2	1991	TV, radio	gov't of Canada
Vidéotron	421.9	1990	cable TV, TV	Chagnon (Québec) + gov't of Québec
Transcontinental GTC	415.6	1990	magazines, printing	Marcoux/Dubois/ Kingsley (Québec)
Astral	286.2	1990	film/video, production and distribution	Greenberg/Bronfman (Québec)
Télémédia	223.0	1990	radio, magazines	De Gaspé Beaubien (Québec)
Gesca	196.5	1990	dailies, TV guides	Power (Desmarais) (Québec)
CFCF	162.6	1990	TV, cable TV	Pouliot (Québec)
Unimedia	148.0	1989	daily, weeklies	Hollinger (Black) (Ontario, Canada)
Télé-Métropole	138.7	1990	TV, film dubbing	Vidéotron (Chagnon) (Québec)
Cogeco	116.0	1990	cable TV, radio	Audet (Québec)
National Film Board	88.6	1992	film	gov't of Canada
Radio-Québec	80.0	1992	TV	gov't of Québec
Radiomutuel	33.0	1990	radio, music TV	Beauchamp/Beaulne (Québec)
Musée de la civilisation	24.5	1991	museum	gov't of Québec
Montréal Museum of Fine Arts	15.5	1991	museum	nonprofit organization
Montréal Symphony Orchestra	13.6	1989	live shows and records	nonprofit organization
Place des Arts	12.2	1989	live shows	gov't of Québec
Cirque du Soleil	11.5	1989	performing arts	private

TABLE 3   **Continued**

Organization	Revenue/Budget		Industries	Control (residence)
	C$million	Year		
Musée du Québec	8.9	1991	museum	gov't of Québec
Les Publications du Québec	8.3	1991	book publishing, distribution and retail	gov't of Québec
Montréal Jazz Festival	5.2	1989	performing arts	private
Musée des arts contemporains de Montréal	3.5	1989	museum	gov't of Québec

SOURCES: *Les Affaires,* June 15, 1991, Montréal; André Coupet, *Étude sur le finance-ment des arts et de la culture au Québec,* Québec, Ministère des Affaires culturel-les, 1990; *Le Bulletin des communications,* December 1991, Québec, Ministère des Communications; and the organizations themselves.

market. But Radio-Canada is probably more important for Québec than for the rest of Canada. Its audience share is much stronger in Québec than in the rest of Canada. In comparison, Radio-Québec, a public sta-tion run by the Québec government, has a small budget and only a single network, for educational and cultural programming. Several organiza-tions (museums, orchestras, and festivals) of lesser financial importance have been included in this table because of their renown in the prov-ince's cultural scene and even worldwide.

Thus, the state is quite visible in the area of cultural industries thanks to its institutions. State intervention includes regulation and a variety of cultural industry subsidies. Table 4 gives the main aspects of government policy covering cultural industries. They are the result of shared jurisdiction between the federal and Québec governments. The federal government has exclusive jurisdiction over broadcasting, includ-ing cable, while other industries are subject to interventions at both levels of government. Often Canadian and Québec policies have been inspired by American, British, and French policies. But just as often, they represent an original contribution that has been emulated in other countries.

The central objectives of Canadian and Québecois policies target: the quality of media content; the promotion of Canadian and Québecois

TABLE 4 Main Policies by Industry

Museums	• public museums • subsidies
Performing arts	• lower provincial value added tax rate • ad hoc subsidies to companies or shows
Books	• government-operated publishing houses • subsidies for printing and marketing • public schools and libraries as buyers of books • policy on Canadian control of publishing • policy on Québecois control of bookstores
Newspapers and periodicals	• advertising in foreign publications taxed as profit • policy on Canadian or Québecois control of publishing
Records	• subsidies for production and marketing • Canadian and French minimum content in radio
Films and videos	• public organization in production (NFB) • subsidies for production and distribution • minimum number of French copies in theater • age classification
Radio	• supply controlled by licensing • must be controlled by Canadians • strong public radio and private stations and networks • advertising on foreign stations taxed as profit • content rules (Canadian, French, formats)
Television	• supply controlled by licensing • must be controlled by Canadians • strong public television and private stations and network • limits on advertising time • ban on advertising for children (Québec only) • advertising in foreign stations taxed as profit • content rules (Canadian, formats) • cable program substitution if same as distant station
Cable and satellites	• supply controlled by licensing • must be controlled by Canadians • rules on channel content (stations carried) • Pay-TV and specialized services on cable • price regulation (cable) • satellites policy not yet clear

cultural products; the profitability of the industries; the protection of jobs in cultural industries; the control of Canadian or Québecois industries; and the promotion of cultural-product export. It is clear that many of these objectives involve the position of Canadian and Québecois cultural products in relation to foreign products.

▪ ▪ Markets Open to the Outside

Another important structural dimension concerns the degree to which Québec markets are open to foreign products and capital. Despite their formal exclusion from the free trade treaties with Mexico and the United States, cultural products move about easily in a market that is quite open. This free movement relies on a number of factors—geographic proximity to the United States, former colonial ties with France and the U.K., wide use of both French and English in Québec, democratic traditions of freedom and human rights, and, finally, worldwide movement of ideas, products, and methods.

The Québec book market can be divided into three different types of players who hold shares that are relatively equal in proportion to one another—namely, Québecois, the French, and the Americans. Books enter Québec without barriers, other than the costs of transportation. Transportation costs are significant in the case of important best-sellers. As a result, certain French publishers print some of their best-sellers in Québec. About 85% of Québec's population speaks French at home. Thus, books published in English can count on only 15% of the population (i.e., the English-speaking proportion of the population).[16] A percentage of the French population also reads in English (although often only to obtain a cheaper version than that sold in translation). In addition, rights to American and British books are usually sold to French publishers, who translate them for their markets, including Québec. Best-seller lists clearly demonstrate the strength of these two import sources. Thus, in one respect, France has paradoxically become the exporter of Anglo-Saxon culture to Québec!

At another level, foreign capital is available in the Québec book market, but its free circulation suffers from more obstacles than does the free movement of products. Theoretically, nothing in Québec prevents foreign ownership of publishing houses, distributors, and bookstores. In practice, however, two barriers have been erected. The first involves bookstores. A formal policy stipulates that public purchases of books may be made only at bookstores that meet certain criteria (i.e., that possess a stock of Québec books). This policy has encouraged a decline in foreign ownership of bookstores in Québec. With regard to publishers, the federal government as a matter of policy uses regulation of foreign investment to limit control of Canadian publishers by foreign capital. This has still left a number of publishers in foreign hands, particularly in the field of textbooks, but the extent of foreign control has been limited.

The Québec newspaper market is completely dominated by Canadian and Québecois capital. The major dailies are controlled in Montréal. Local content and the language barrier explain the situation in part. Tax law favors Canadian control of newspapers, since advertisers are unable to deduct the cost of space in a newspaper that is not Canadian owned. Foreign newspapers are nevertheless available without restriction, other than the cost of transportation, but they are not an interesting media for advertisers.

The case of magazines is different. In the monthly category, more or less one quarter of magazines sold in Québec is from outside the province.[17] A look at a magazine vendor shows that a large proportion of titles are foreign.[18] Although foreign magazines move about freely, Québecois magazines are clearly dominant in terms of numbers sold. Here again, local and national content is the primary interest of readers.

Nevertheless, the audience of certain American magazines is sufficient to interest advertisers despite tax laws concerning expenses. In particular, *Time* is able to sell almost 400,000 copies in Canada, with about 15% in Québec. The major Québec magazines sell from 300,000 to 400,000 copies. However, even when they are produced in Québec, the financial control of important magazines may reside elsewhere, as, for example, in the cases of *L'Actualité* and *Châtelaine*, published by Maclean-Hunter (a communication conglomerate with its head office in Ontario), and *Elle Québec*, published by Télémédia (see Table 3) but with an agreement with Hachette, from France.

The field of recording is quite different. The impact of worldwide trends in music has been actively experienced in Québec. Foreign recordings in the past have been subject to a duty of 15%, but direct importation of recordings has never been an important segment of the market. When the volume justifies it, foreign recordings are reproduced in Québec or Ontario, thus eliminating import duties and transportation costs. In retail outlets, it can be seen that the great majority of recordings are of Anglo origin. French recordings are divided more or less equally between those from France and those from Québec. With regard to the production of new recordings, foreign multinationals hold only a portion of the market, having for the most part withdrawn during the difficult years of the 1980s. This has left the market to local enterprise. Distribution is also under Québecois control, contrary to the situation in other provinces. State intervention in Québec takes the form of subsidies for production and promotion and minimum levels (not without controversy) of Canadian and French content on radio stations and television music channels. The recording business is almost completely free, although product promotion is not.

The situation in the film industry is more complex, since it targets a number of markets, mainly theater, television, and advertising. In movie theaters, there are no restrictions on foreign films. However, one rule requires that versions dubbed in French must be quickly made available for films with wide distribution. The distribution of American films has been encouraged as a result, because they are now available to a much wider audience. Theater networks and the distribution of films are dominated or controlled by American capital, which is also used to promote the films.

Québec film producers find better outlets for their products among television networks and advertising agencies. Television networks are required to broadcast a percentage of Canadian-content programming. They produce a good part themselves, but they contract out the rest to independent producers. Government subsidies targeting audiovisual production help. Thus, government regulations have had an important effect on the development of the industry.

There are no significant restrictions on the importation of advertising material and commercials. Nonetheless, Québec advertising agencies have amply demonstrated their effectiveness. Their most important clients are Québecois companies and the Québec government. More than half of the commercials appearing on French television are produced in Québec.[19]

Radio, television, and cable are regulated by a government agency (the Canadian Radio-Television and Telecommunication Commission [CRTC]), which controls licensing and, therefore, supply. Control is exercised in the name of objectives that are democratic (diversity of sources), cultural (promotion of Canadian culture), and economic (profitability, jobs). At the heart of the system can be found a rule that forbids foreign control of businesses in these areas. Those with licenses must conform to a minimum level of Canadian content. Once the content rules have been met, the license-holder is free to broadcast imported material, although remaining subject to other programming commitments that were made when the license was granted.

Pop music programming on radio must adhere to a rule requiring 30% Canadian content. French stations are generally required to broadcast 65% French music (from Québec, France, or elsewhere). Conventional television stations must broadcast 50% or more Canadian content. Cable companies must give priority to local stations (i.e., Canadian or Québecois) in their channel selection. They are also required to substitute local commercials for those supplied by distant stations (usually American) when the local Canadian station is broadcasting a program taken directly from the distant station.

Nevertheless, all these rules leave a great deal of room for foreign content. The first reason for this is that direct access to American radio and television stations is simple—they can be received using an ordinary antenna when one is close to the border, which is the case for millions of Canadians. Satellite dishes are available, even though they remain expensive. Cable offers a choice of the major U.S. networks (NBC, CBS, ABC, PBS, CNN, and, at times, Fox). Moreover, Canadian stations regularly broadcast American programs or music recordings. American television can be viewed in English or, several months later, in French after dubbing. Voices may have Québec accents when dubbed locally or viewers may enjoy cowboys with Parisian accents when the programs are dubbed in Paris.

From a certain perspective, what has been described above might be seen as a bureaucratic nightmare and quite contrary to the spirit of free trade. However, it must be realized that American products are readily available in Québec. American books sell for less than Québecois books and for less than translations of the same American book. American music holds first place in the hearts of many disc jockeys and is heard on the airwaves of almost every radio station, even dominating the programming of some. American films are by far the majority of those available in theaters and represent the largest share of films available on videocassette. American miniseries, game shows, and sporting events receive preferential scheduling on both English and French television stations. Cable services include American stations as part of their basic subscription rate. This kind of access to foreign cultural products certainly constitutes an important characteristic of the markets for Québec cultural products. Everything is up for comparison—the price of books, the beat of the music, the rhythm of a televised production . . . Young viewers identify quality with the way that Americans do things. Intellectuals buy American for the lower prices and to keep up to date.

Geographic proximity and the cultural and economic power of the United States explain the relative force of American products when compared with those of France and the U.K., the former centers of cultural strength. The French presence, nevertheless, remains very evident in the areas of books and recordings. In theaters and on television, certain productions have met with great success. The British are also visible in the areas of books and pop music, but much less so on television and in the theaters.

The free trade agreements concluded with the United States and entered into between Mexico, the United States, and Canada have left intact the essence of what has been described above. American cultural products enter Canada as freely as before and restrictions on their presence remain. Cultural industries have been formally excluded from the agreement. One might speculate that this situation is the model for the "cultural exclusion" clause introduced into the negotiations of the recent GATT agreement. Certain aspects of these agreements, however, affect or can affect cultural industries. Perhaps the most important of these are copyright rules that require a Canadian cable station to pay for the right to retransmit the signal from a distant American or Canadian station. In the medium term, a commercial conflict could directly affect cultural industries, since the free trade agreement allows for reprisals in sectors that are different from those in which the wrong has occurred.

▪ ▪ A Measure of Cultural Performance

To measure the performance of cultural industries in the production of Québec's cultural identity, a simple factor, the share of various cultural markets held by local products (Table 5), will be used. Unfortunately, there is no solid data on this crucial subject, other than that dealing with the electronic media. Thus, data based on trade literature, word of mouth, and, when available, lists of best-selling products, especially books and records, will have to suffice.

The strongholds of Québecois cultural industries are clearly newspapers and magazines. They are protected by the language barrier and benefit from the fact that an important component of their content is information on Québec and its regions. Books are not protected in the

TABLE 5   Origins of Cultural Products in Québec

Product	Main Sources	Québec's Share of Market (approximate %)
Best-sellers	Québec, France, U.S.	40
Daily newspapers	Québec	95
Consumer magazines	Québec, U.S., France, Canada	75
Records	U.S., Québec, France, U.K.	25
Films/videos	U.S., France	5
Music on radio	Québec, U.S., France	50
Television	Québec, Canada, U.S.	60

same way—first, because publishers in France are able to work within the language barrier, and second, because book selection is often related to stories remote from daily life. As a result, Québec's book publishers are quite active in nonfiction but less so in fiction. This may be the result of a tendency among Québecois novelists to write for elite French-speaking audiences, a strategy better adapted to Parisian writers. Of course, this is not the case with all writers of fiction.

Television is also a sector with a high percentage of content of local origin, but to a varying degree. The hand of the government remains clearly visible. Networks are forced by regulation to develop Canadian content and audiences seem to be satisfied with this situation for the most part. In Montréal, English-language radio stations can (and must, by regulation) broadcast songs mostly in English, which allows them to rely on content originating in the United States. This puts pressure on some French-language stations that are trying to appeal to a younger audience. These stations tend to play music in French at the lowest level that Canadian and French content rules permit.

The record industry is softer. Records and cassettes are made at low cost in Canada with imported masters. Producing a local artist is a serious risk, even with subsidies and Canadian content rules applying to radio. Finally, the performance of the film industry has been very weak in terms of market share, stemming from a clear imbalance between production costs and internal market size. State subsidies have filled the gap for a few productions, but the industry survives mainly by producing commercials and a few programs for television stations.

▪ ▪ Conclusion

History has left a small but thriving French-speaking population in North America. Culture, politics, geography, and other factors have made possible its participation in the economic prosperity of the continent. These factors, combined with economics and technology, have contributed to the development of a system of cultural industries. Politics has been particularly important, since Québec and Canada's cultural industries have benefited from government policy. Nevertheless, it remains a small system living next to the American giant, as well as in the shadow of France and the U.K., its former colonial masters. To a certain extent, it can be argued that Québec's cultural industries reflect the influence of these three traditions.

Québec's small market makes it difficult to achieve low unit costs in cultural products. This disadvantage is partially offset by the role played by strong private and government organizations in cultural industries. The hand of the government is often visible, either through its institutions or as a result of the protection its policies provide private corporations. These corporations and institutions behave in an industrial fashion and endeavor to give their audiences what they seek—again, sometimes under the supervision of the State.

The result is the existence of a solid network of strong cultural institutions and corporations with an interesting share of Québec's cultural markets. Unfortunately, this share is not sufficient to give its creators the prosperity they hope for, and so the small market hinders profitability and stability. Government protection is in constant jeopardy as trade barriers are being questioned all over the world. Cultural products from elsewhere in the world are available to fill the gap created by any weakness in local production.

Thanks largely to government policy and the ever-present language barrier, the system appears to have enough internal resilience to compete. This became obvious during the 1980s, when the market share for many Québecois cultural products decreased, especially in the case of recordings and best-sellers. It was also felt in television, as the share of listening hours going to American programs increased, and in radio, when the government agreed to lower quotas on French songs. But this was not the last round. By the end of the 1980s, the trend had reversed in each of these markets. How? In the same way that the system was constructed, with a mixture of cultural creativity, marketing, nationalism, and government intervention. Success was not complete, however. In television the process has led to a (temporary) financial crisis among private stations. Yet many players remain in the field because they think there is money to be made. Others are staying in cultural industries for cultural or political reasons.

The building of this system over a long period of time is also a proof of its capacity to survive. It demonstrates that Québec's cultural industries are the result of both a social and a nationalistic imperative whose "invisible hand" has been steering individuals and organizations just as strongly as it has markets. It also demonstrates that although state intervention is needed to compensate for a small market, it can also coexist easily with freedom of expression and free markets on the economic side of cultural industries.

NOTES

1. Data for 1987. Bureau de la statistique du Québec, *Le Québec statistique,* 59th ed. (Québec: Government House, 1989), 965, 976.

2. The following American-controlled companies are among the largest in Québec in terms of number of employees: Pratt & Whitney (aircraft engines), Sears (retail), Stone Consolidated (pulp and paper), McDonald's restaurants, General Motors, General Electric, Price Club (retail), IBM, and Kraft General Foods.

3. The Government of Québec and Hydro-Québec in particular.

4. For example, Québecor (printing, newspapers, etc.).

5. This was the slogan of the supporters of public, as opposed to private, radio in Canada. The Canadian Broadcasting Corporation (CBC) was the fruit of their efforts.

6. See F. M. Sherer, *Industrial Market Structure and Economic Performance,* 2d ed. (Boston: Houghton Mifflin, 1980), 4; or R. Arene, L. Benzoni, J. De Brant, and P.-M. Romani, *Traité d'économie industrielle* (Paris: Economica, 1988), 139.

7. Allan Greer, "L'alphabétisation et son histoire au Québec," in *L'imprimé au Québec: Aspects historiques (18ᵉ–20ᵉ siècle),* Yvan Lamonde, director (Québec: Institut québecois de recherche sur la culture, 1983), 37.

8. Maurice Lemire, "Les relations entre écrivains et éditeurs au Québec," in Lamonde, dir., *L'imprimé au Québec,* 216.

9. Yves Lever, *Histoire générale du cinéma au Québec* (Montréal: Boréal, 1988), 54–55.

10. Lever, *Histoire générale,* 55–56.

11. Jacques Schira, "Les éditions sonores au Québec," in *Les aires de la chanson québecoise,* Robert Giroux, director (Montréal: Les Éd. Triptyques, 1984), 84.

12. Station XWA, owned by the corporation Canadian Marconi, began broadcasting in September 1919, before Station KDKA, the first American station; see Robert E. Babe, *Telecommunications in Canada* (Toronto: University of Toronto Press, 1990), 202.

13. See Marc Raboy, *Missed Opportunities: The Story of Canada's Broadcasting Policy* (Montréal and Kingston: McGill-Queen's University Press, 1990), 62.

14. This figure takes into account advertising costs in the mass media, the purchase of cultural products, and government expenditures. The amount was calculated on the basis of a variety of sources, including *Statistiques culturelles* (an annual publication) from the Bureau de la statistique du Québec and data supplied by the Maclean-Hunter Research Bureau in *Canadian Advertising Rates and Data* (a monthly publication).

15. This does not include international shows touring Québec.

16. It should be noted that English is not the mother tongue of all anglophones included here. The mother tongue of about 7% of those living in Québec is a language other than English or French.

17. Data for 1985 in C. Martin and R. De La Garde, "Si Gutenberg m'était compté. De la presse d'entreprise aux entreprises de pre$$e," in *Les pratiques culturelles des Québecois: Une autre image de nous-mêmes*, J.-P. Baillargeon, director (Québec: Institut québecois de recherche sur la culture, 1986), 49.

18. According to data that is not very recent (1978), 85% of publications are foreign, and of these, a quarter are from France.

19. To be exact, 60% of different commercials on CBC's French station between 8 A.M. and midnight during one week in March 1992 were produced in Québec. Data from David Giguère, "Les stratégies persuasives dans la publicité télévisée québecoise" (master's thesis, University of Montréal, 1993).

11

There Goes the Neighborhood: Montréal's Television Market and Free Trade

ROGER DE LA GARDE

OUR OVERALL INTENT IS TO present an objective description—or at least one containing as little subjectivity as possible—of the television market in Montréal, the largest metropolitan area of the Canadian province of Québec, and home to a little less than half of its total population of nearly seven million. French is the official language in Québec, which means that it is the language of politics—Québec, like every other Canadian province, has a legislative body, the *Assemblée Nationale,* that deals with matters falling under provincial jurisdiction—and it is also the language of the job markets in situations where employers, in both the private and the public sector, have a payroll of more than fifty workers. A little over 85% of Québec's population declares French as its mother tongue and speaks French at home. The balance is made up of 12% anglophones and 3% allophones (the latter speaking neither French nor English). Nearly 60% of Québec's French-speaking population, 85% of its English-speaking population, and almost 90% of the allophone populations live in the large Montréal metropolitan area.

This particular television market serves two major linguistic communities, French and English, since there are no multilingual channels, nor is there a unilingual channel serving a minority linguistic community. As in many North American metropolitan areas, the cable industry services nearly 75% of the homes and offers Montréal television viewers a basic service of some 30 channels, including Canadian, Québecois, and U.S. networks, pay-TV, and a host of specialized channels (e.g., those showing music videos, weather, news, and so forth) and community channels. This alone does not justify any particular scientific inquiry. What does justify such an effort is the fact that this particular situation provides a good example for a case study of transborder flow of mass-produced cultural products and the related debate on cultural imperialism.

It is no secret that English-language, U.S.-dominated television programs inundate the screens of this largely francophone market. In absolute terms it is a very small market[1] within the global North American economy. In relative terms, however, it is the largest of its kind in North America. In other words, what goes down in Montréal has a direct bearing on the cultural production and cultural identity of a quarter of the Canadian population. Thus the question of the economic vitality of the French-language television industry in Montréal is of importance to any discussion related to the cultural and national identity of any small "nation" (de la Garde, Gilsdorf, and Wechselmann 1992) living under the shadow of the U.S. giant—be it a genial giant or otherwise. Of course, exactly the same statement, as nuanced as need be, can be made in regard to the other main cultural industries: music, print (books, magazines, newspapers), cinema, and computer software.

Within the borders of this present-day French-language North American society—Québec—one can raise the question of trade and culture, of free trade and free culture, and gauge the relationship between the two in terms of the following question: to what extent will the liberation of trade, the free flow of goods and services, pave the way for the liberation of cultures? The media history of Québec makes it clear that a free flow of cultural products did not wait for any free trade agreement. English-language U.S.-made media and cultural products have been flowing upward and inward into Canada and Québec for many, many decades before NAFTA—in fact, for well over a century.

In the 1920s Canada's political and intellectual elites laid the foundation for an alliance to regulate (i.e., to better resist) this northbound, one-way flow. It was not the survival of the "national" language that was at stake but the burgeoning notion of a Canadian nation. The same flow was resisted in Québec for mainly moral reasons, and met with limited success. Some Québecois intellectual circles, following in a small nineteenth-century "liberal" tradition (Bernard 1971), felt that a "window" to the South would help push the idea of creating a new French-speaking, pluralist, North American society. As in Canada, language was not openly threatened by the American "invasion." The free flow of U.S.

entertainment and news products was looked upon as a cultural issue, not a linguistic one. In Canadian circles the fear was that American values would soon overcome Canadian values, partly because it was felt that the close ties to the U.K. would not suffice to defend this "new" North American culture whose roots were not as deep as those of the isolated Québecois culture. Within some Québecois circles, this overture to American cultural products was seen as beneficial because it offered a model of modernity to be viewed as an alternative to both the traditional, conservative, rural, catholic model and the British imperial model, both of which they rejected. Here was an example of a modern culture which, correctly appropriated, would liberate an enclaved culture.

We use the term "enclaved," in the sense of a ghetto culture, and not "enslaved." The term "culture" refers to a coherent, but not necessarily cohesive, universe of meanings, a universe that temporally, and continually, strives to make sense out of persistent ambiguities and contradictions without pretense to a final solution. It is used here in a singular, noncapitalized fashion because in any and every modern society there coexist, co-conspire, many cultures. The particular culture to which we refer in this study is "public culture"—in other words, that culture, or universe of meanings, made public. It is those words, images, and symbols that permeate, but do not transcend, all social classes, positions, and groups. As we understand it, our view is quite closely akin to Curran's model of a democratic media system based on a conception

> of the public sphere as a core surrounded by satellite networks and organized groupings. The core public sphere is the public space where all interests interact with one another in seeking to establish agreement or compromise about the direction of society. Feeding this core are a number of umbilical cords that connect it to the life force of civil society—different interpretative communities with a shared normative conception of society . . . different organized groupings . . . different sub-culture . . . , and different social strata with distinctive interests and social experiences. (As quoted in Raboy 1993, pp. 30–31)

This culture-made-public, this ongoing public process of sense-making can, in certain cases, be national in scope. It is the case in both Canada and Québec where, since the turn of the century, a systematic effort has been made to publicly engage in "nation building." Among the main playing fields for such concerted efforts have been the Canadian Broadcasting Corporation (CBC—radio and television) and the National Film Board. In Canada, debate as to whether there exists such a public culture is still going on. In Québec, however, there is little doubt that such a public culture exists.

It is our hypothesis that this public questioning and groping for answers began long before the 1960s. What has changed is that the site for discussion and its main discussants have been displaced from the relatively closed intellectual and moral/religious circles to a more open arena created by modern media—particularly television—with their "pop star" politicians, "common man" philosopher journalists, and cultural entrepreneurs. Further, we argue that this displacement, this transformation of an existing enclaved (ghetto) culture into an industrially based, mass-distributed public culture was helped by free-flowing U.S.-produced cultural products, upward and inward into Québec.

In other words, our working premise is that there now exists in Québec a public arena, or sphere, where a particular culture is being constantly defined and refined, and that this particular culture exists in its own right and is not enclaved by other cultures (political, religious, or otherwise). This particular culture, moreover, lays claim to participate in a quest for nationhood, for a collective identity to which individuals may one day freely opt to belong—in other words, to actively participate in the constitution of a nation. This particular culture evolved and continues to evolve within the confines of a market for cultural products, one that was set up to compete with the centuries-old, gigantic, easily accessible U.S. market. If one wishes to speak of free trade between Québec and the United States in the area of cultural industries, it is between two unequal, but vibrant, cultural markets, and not within an expanded, monopolized North American cultural market.

It is within this view that we root our study of Québecois television. We can therefore look at Montréal as a delineated television market where products (i.e., ideas and symbols) circulate within recognizable forms and formats (such as program genres and commercials). These products originate in different locations, a few are co-produced, and while some are publicly funded, the vast majority rely on advertising revenues. Some 60% of the television programs are broadcast in the English language and are carried over national networks—American, Canadian, and Québecois. We can therefore take stock of this market, in terms of what enters it, at what point, what the trajectory of different products is, what the rate of success of each is, what its "consumer" profile is, and so on. In a word, we can chart this particular television market in terms of supply and consumption.

It is our view that the television market, like any other cultural market (books, films, music), is basically a location where individuals come to browse, to select, and to consume products that are offered by competitive suppliers who vie for the attention of the many different categories of potential consumers. Both consumers and suppliers, however, share an implicit faith that this so-called market, with its industries, its channels of distribution, its market strategies, and so on, is somehow deeply interconnected with the private daily routines of everyday living. As long as they continue to share the belief that what is "happening out there" in the public arena of mass media is of some deep significance and is relevant to their sense of longing and of belonging, we are justified in reading into television research and television market analyses considerations other than those concerning structured distribution of goods and services, and in offering interpretations about popular success that go beyond the traditional reference to market strategies.

In the case of a long-standing internationalized cultural market such as Montréal, where visual images and sounds constitute a language of communication as meaningful as the written language, the consumption charts should match the supply charts. But in this cultural market where images (video) and sounds (music) are as compelling as words, where English-language films and records are quite user-friendly even for unilingual French audiences, French-language Québecois products are among the top best-sellers, a showing that is in proportion neither to their financial nor their creative capital. In other words, with considerably less capital and know-how they manage, year after year, to place themselves among the "very best." Historical evidence suggests that the success of Québec's cultural industries is not due to chance, to indiscriminate audiences, or to the philanthropic attitudes of the U.S. conglomerates, but, rather, that it is due to historical cultural production practices, discriminate audiences, and the presence of a strong imperial competitor.

If, in an open, transnationalized and internationalized, structured, historical, U.S.-dominated cultural market located within a small, linguistic, and nationalistic community that is geographically bounded to a larger, powerful, linguistically different society, consumption of popular cultural products does not match the supply, questions other than those concerned with market research, promotion, and capital investment are warranted. At the very least, questions concerned with meaning appropriation, reality construction, and active audiences are needed.

Here again, the intent of this chapter is to justify the raising of such questions, not to answer them. If evidence can be brought to show that in an historically structured, U.S.-dominated, English-language television market (i.e., Montréal)[2] the consumption not only does not match the supply but, in fact, inverts it,[3] we can at the very least claim legitimacy for the concept of audience as an agent of reality construction and for a cultural approach to the study of mass-mediated consumption.

Presently, Québec houses a number of ethnic and linguistic communities, of which three are of considerable historical importance (namely, aboriginal, francophone, and anglophone), though only two are at the forefront of the current social agendas: the francophone because of its size, political power, and accumulative financial wealth, and the anglophone because of its historical status and socioeconomic power base. It is within this context that the cross-circulation of the supply and consumption of television programs in North America's largest French-language cultural market will be analyzed.

▪ ▪ Television: A Field Study

Limits of Interpretation

To study the television market of greater Montréal we rely on the published reports of the Bureau of Broadcast Measurement (BBM),[4] a cooperative-style ratings agency to which radio and television broadcasters and various provincial and federal regulation bodies subscribe. It is generally recognized that the BBM's methodology validates the results of its survey polls. It offers a panoply of data-collecting services to both radio and television industries. Among these are quarterly reports on two bilingual television markets, Montréal and Ottawa (the federal capital of Canada). These reports give not only the overall rating of each broadcast television program but also the rating given to each by both major linguistic communities, according to select age groups.

As with census reports, we will analyze data produced by researchers using a methodological protocol over which we have no control. The debate centering on the validity of ratings data is perpetual and all-encompassing, ranging from the statistically technical to the ideological (to wit, can we really trust an agency of the broadcasting industry to produce *factual* evidence on program consumption?).

While we do recognize the fixed constraints under which a rating agency must work and the efforts, both technological and statistical, that are developed to reduce biases, we are also sensitive to Ien Ang's argument (1991) as to the "discursive" and constructionist nature of such data. To someone who wishes to study a particular television market, the options are few; either she/he conducts a more thorough and expensive survey, thus ensuring more strongly validated data, or she/he uses available data whose validity is recognized as being limited. For obvious reasons (i.e., financial) we chose the second option, taking comfort in the rather self-serving statistical principle that an avowed bias systematically replicated over a long series of identical surveys tends to produce reliable, quantitative information of an ordinal nature. For example, while one cannot take too seriously the numbers that indicate the ratings of popular sitcoms, the "fact" that sitcoms regularly reach ratings that are twice as high as those of game shows, over a considerable span of time, can be interpreted or construed as a "reality."

Admittedly, we are not analyzing hard empirical "facts" but rather an empirically constructed representation of a probable reality. There are sufficient guarantees in the BBM's procedure of collecting and of aggregating viewing data that one can be reasonably certain of not erring too far from the "truth" if one stays within its published narrow methodological boundaries. What we find is a fabricated reality, a television market in which we have a relatively accurate knowledge of the supply side—one can always verify, at a very low cost, whether the publicized television program (in *TV Guide*, for example) was in fact broadcast— and a relatively consensual knowledge of the consumption side.

But, fundamentally, what we have is the end product of a process of which we have less than intuitive knowledge. What we are studying, the object of analysis, is programming and how different age groups presumably reacted to it. What we do not know is how this object, this programming, was produced.

In the case of Québecois television, the policymakers of individual networks must take into account not only the Canadian Broadcasting Act (revised in 1991) but also the economics of the television market, the social climate of the Québecois society, and the political agendas of both federal and provincial governments. As a small indication of the complexity of mediating the situation facing television's top-level policy management, we will quote at some length from an article by Gaëtan Tremblay (1992, pp. 237–238).

In Canada, broadcasting is considered an instrument of production and diffusion that must contribute to the maintenance and development of Canadian culture and its various components. The 1968 Broadcasting Act was quite explicit on this matter. The recent Broadcasting Act, adopted by Parliament in February 1991, is even more explicit. Article 3,[5] which defines Canadian broadcasting policy, has several paragraphs pertaining to this subject. It begins by defining the maintenance and the enhancement of national identity and cultural sovereignty as fundamental objectives . . . Further along the Act addresses the necessity to encourage Canadian cultural creation and expression . . . Finally, the Act obliges broadcasters to draw upon, as much as possible, Canadian talent and resources in the make-up of their programming.

To this federal mandate the Québec government, which "has always argued for the control of communications within its territory with respect to its responsibilities for the defense of Québecois culture" (ibid., p. 238), adds its own particular requirements. Tremblay (ibid.) cites a 1971 Québec policy paper whose basic tenet still holds sway some twenty years later.

It devolves first and foremost upon Québec to elaborate a global communication policy. This policy is indissociable from the development of its education system, its culture and all that belongs to Québec. While this policy must be coordinated with those of other governments and be coherent with the North American setting, it must first be congruent with Québec's priorities and as such guarantee the maintenance and the unhindered evolution of our society as a dynamic element within the Canadian and North American totality. For Québec, a communications policy is not useful, it is necessary, all the more so with each passing day. (L'Allier 1971, p. 2)

In the Montréal market three television industries compete under three different sets of rules: the major U.S. private and public networks, under a most liberal set of guidelines which favor commercial activities; the major Canadian private and public networks, under a double mandate of being commercially viable and of offering a truly Canadian national public service; and the French-language public, private, and educational networks located in Montréal, under a triple mandate of being commercially viable, of offering a truly Canadian national public service, and of developing Québec's culture and of enhancing its educational system. At this level alone, one can only imagine the complexities of establishing programming policy in the case of the Québec networks. When one adds other elements such as economic stability and the perceived social issues that fuel public opinion, a managerial migraine sets in.

While we acknowledge the importance of studying the production side of programming, our aim is to analyze program and station performance in terms of matching supply and consumption in a particular television market.

Methodology

Our study is based on the 1987 and 1993 autumn reports published by the BBM.

> Ratings provided in this report are given separately for the francophone and the anglophone populations estimated on the basis of home language distribution as determined by Statistics Canada. . . .
>
> Because of the importance of other language groups in the Montréal population and the desirability of reporting the total population, those respondents with a home language other than French or English have been assigned to a principal language group on the basis of additional information. . . .
>
> The universes for this special report are the francophone and the anglophone populations estimated as of January 1st, 1994. (BBM 1993, p. 1)

For our purposes we extracted from the BBM report data pertaining to the television consumption by four different francophone and anglophone audiences: children (age 2–11), teenagers (12–17), women (25–54), and men (25–54). These age/sex strata are designed by BBM to satisfy the information needs of their clients, who are mainly advertising agencies, program directors, and departments of market media research. We believe these groups to be the main targets for ratings/marketing strategies by television broadcasters and, quite likely, the main consumers of television fare.

The BBM's report details the list of all cabled television shows that attracted at least 0.5% of the viewing population over a three-week "sweep period" during November. Not included in the BBM survey are about two dozen specialty channels, such as distance education channels, community channels, public service channels without advertising (such as the one that broadcasts parliamentary debates in both Québec

City and Ottawa), a weather channel, music video channels, pay-TV, and the multilateral[6] transatlantic francophone channel, TV5. It is estimated that the total ratings of all these unsurveyed channels represent less than 10% of the overall ratings of the channels selected for our analysis. Because of either extremely low ratings or not being a member of the BBM, none of these channels was included in the published BBM autumn reports and they are, therefore, not included in our survey. Our study for 1993[7] includes data for twelve cable television channels, which comprise about a third of the available channels, but represent over 90% of all viewing time of the cabled francophone and anglophone households in the greater Montréal television market.

The anchor stations of Québec's four French-language television networks are located in Montréal. They consist of two nonprofit public service broadcasters with advertising income (CBFT, the flag station of the Société Radio-Canada, which is the French-language Canadian public television network, and CIVM, the flag station of Radio-Québec, which is Québec's public education or "cultural" television network) and two private commercial broadcasters (CFTM and CFJP, the flag stations of TVA and Quatre Saisons, Québec's two private television networks). Also located in Montréal are the major affiliates of two Canadian television networks—a nonprofit public service broadcaster with advertising income (CBMT, a major affiliate of the English-language Canadian public television network CBC) and a private commercial broadcaster (CFCF, a major affiliate of the English-language Canadian private television network CTV). In addition to these stations Montréal households have access to CJOH, an affiliate of CTV, which is located in Cornwall, Ontario, some 150 kilometers from Montréal, and to five American channels—the three major commercial networks through their respective affiliates, WVNY (ABC) and WCAX (CBS), located in Burlington, Vermont, and WPTZ (NBC), located in Plattsburg, New York; and the public television network PBS through two of its affiliates, WETK in Burlington and WCFE in Plattsburg.[8]

To use Sepstrup's terminology (1990, pp. 11–12), these channels can be classified as "national" (CBFT, CFTM, CIVM, CFJP) and "bilateral" (CBMT, CFCF, CJOH, WETK, WCFE, WVNY, WCAX, and WPTZ). National is defined as supply and consumption of television programs distributed by a domestic media covering the entire national territory. The reference to "national" television needs to be clarified. While most state policies fall under the exclusive jurisdiction of the federal government of Canada, a select few domains (for example, education, property rights, and civil law) fall under Québec's provincial jurisdiction. To the extent that Québec's historic claim to nationhood, though challenged, remains unshaken, and to the extent that Québec's right to promote and protect the francophone culture within its borders still commands a widespread public recognition, one may describe Québec's intervention in matters of education, language, and culture as "national" policies. This claim is strengthened by the suggestion made by a federal task force on Canadian broadcasting (Task Force on Broadcasting Policy 1986) that the Canadian broadcasting system (radio and television), with its English- and French-language public and private sectors, is not only bilingual but, to a certain extent, binational. Since the production and consumption sides of both the private and public French-language sectors of the Canadian broadcasting system are overwhelmingly concentrated within the Québec borders,[9] and since Québec still maintains its self-perception as a nation, there is increasing acknowledgment that there exists a *national* (Québecois) broadcasting unit within a national (Canadian) broadcasting system. As Marc Raboy reminds us (1990, p. 17),

> The task force consequently recommend[ed] that "Canadian broadcasting policy should recognize the special character of Québec broadcasting, both in itself and as the nucleus of French-language broadcasting throughout Canada" (Task Force 1986, p. 156). It recommended that the autonomy of French-language radio and television services within the CBC be recognized and that French-language CBC [Société Radio-Canada] be allowed to develop distinctly from English-language CBC.

Admittedly, when we refer to the French-language television of Canada as national television (almost exclusively located within Québec's borders), we use the term in a cultural (even political) sense, but in a way that is not to be equated with the concept of state/nation.

Bilateral is here defined as supply and consumption of television programs originating in specific foreign media and reaching the national territory under study (Québec) simultaneously and unedited over the air or by some other technical medium. In all cases the content of the television programs may be either domestically produced or imported.

In what follows we will attempt to show that between 1987 and 1993, (1) the internationalization of supply varied between the U.S. television networks and those of Canada and Québec, (2) the internationalization of supply varied little between the public and private broadcasting sectors in Québec, (3) the internationalization of consumption did not follow that of supply, and (4) the variation of consumption patterns was less determined by age than by linguistic affiliation.

Program Categories

When we first undertook our study (de la Garde and Paré 1991), we found the traditional program categories to be unsatisfying because they were not mutually exclusive—for example, genre categories such as drama and news are regularly compared with age categories such as children's programs. We therefore elaborated what we believe to be a rather simple typology with four mutually exclusive categories.[10] These are defined in a commonsensical fashion and refer to Charles R. Wright's classical distinction between the "major communication activities" of surveillance, correlation, transmission of culture, and entertainment (Wright 1962).

Our *information* category refers to Wright's categories of surveillance and correlation,

> the collection and distribution of information concerning events in the environment, both outside and within any particular society. To some extent it corresponds to what is popularly conceived as the handling of *news* [and also includes] interpretation of information about the environment and prescription for conduct in reaction to these events. In part this activity is popularly identified as *editorial* or *propaganda* [our emphasis]. (Wright 1962, p. 16)

Combining journalistic styles and formats, we chose to define four subcategories ranging from hard to soft journalism: newscasts, public affairs, specialized news magazines, and news magazines of general interest.

The newscast category is rather straightforward; it refers to those programs featuring an anchorperson and journalists revealing, in words and pictures, the most recent occurrences of some significance to the general public. Most, if not all, of these programs are graphically identified with the "news."

Public affairs programs are those that feature a moderator, journalist, or otherwise public figure who, with one or many invited guests, and with or without the presence of a public in the studio, discusses one topic (or many), which is in some way related to a news event of the day. It is the format rather than the journalistic significance of the topic that is our guiding criterion. For this empirical reason we will classify in the same category of "public affairs" such a range of programs as *This Week with David Brinkley, The MacLaughlin Group, Oprah Winfrey,* and local versions of *Meet the Press* (such as *Forum 22*).

The magazine formats, specialized and general, are designed to present within a specific time frame a series (usually three or four programs) of reportages, or investigative journalism, whose aim is to "go beyond, or behind, the news headlines." The stories investigated may or may not be directly related to the news of the day, but they are linked to the issues of the day: corruption, environmentalism, health, sports, arts, armed conflicts, violence, politics, education, and so on. The main difference between specialized magazines, such as *Wall Street This Week* or *Entertainment Today,* and magazines of general interest, such as *60 Minutes, 20/20, Now,* and *48 Hours,* is the focus—that is, whether it is a recurring, fixed perspective (e.g., economics, entertainment, sciences) or a more eclectic, multi-faceted one (such as one finds inside the covers of *Time* and *Newsweek*).

These subcategories are relatively easy to handle in the abstract and their operationalization does not present many difficulties. There are, however, three exceptions, and we shall indicate here how we dealt with them. The first exception consists of those programs that involve children and adolescents. Programs that deliver news to the younger generation, with or without young reporters, are classified as newscasts. Programs in which the invited guests are young people discussing issues, usually with an adult moderator but sometimes not, and which target that particular audience are classified as public affairs. The second exception consists of those programs labeled "infotainment," such as *Top Cops, Rescue 9-1-1, Unsolved Mysteries,* and *Emergency Call.* Without making a judgment call, they appear to meet the criterion of "going beyond the headlines," of engaging in some form of investigation or background research associated with journalistic practices. For this reason we classified them as specialized magazines. In other words, infotainment is a hybrid child (to be politically correct) of journalism standards.

Our last group of exceptions concerns those shows that cover topics, either in a specialized or a general fashion, much as the newsmagazines do, but whose intent is to advise. For example, the program *Driver's Seat* is about testing different models of the car industry and pointing out their strong and weak points. *Sneak Previews* does the same with movies. The Québec program *Téléservice* covers a wide area of concerns (culinary, electrical equipment, building materials, educational toys, financial services, and so on). While these programs do deliver up-to-date and background information, they address themselves to the viewer as a consumer of goods and services rather than as a consumer of information or knowledge. In a rather broad sense they appear to be more concerned with "knowledge of" than with "knowledge about," to use Park's terminology. For this reason we have classified these programs in the subcategory of "popular education" (see below).

The *entertainment* category "refers to communicative acts primarily intended for amusement irrespective of any instrumental effects they might have" (Wright 1962, p. 16). Here again, relying on general genres and formats, we defined six subcategories: drama series, sitcoms, varieties, game shows, performances, and cinema. While these subcategories are self-explanatory, it should be clarified that the subcategory "performances" refers to once-only non-news events, broadcast either live or in a delayed fashion. Such events may be, for example, athletic (sports), musical (concerts), religious (services), or theatrical (plays, dances). Thus sports is not a program category; surveillance of the "world of sports" is classified in one of the four information subcategories, as would information about any other type of social occurrence. The event itself (i.e., the sport event) is classified as a performance. The same can be said about other non-news events (musical, religious, or theatrical; national or political ceremonies, and so forth). The purpose of such a classificatory design is to build into program analysis some valid bases for comparison. By classifying under the generic heading of "information" all programs involving surveillance of events, whatever their particular status (political, musical, religious, and so on), we believe that television's function of constructing the "outside" worlds will be more adequately calibrated. It thus becomes more instructive to measure the share of information pertaining to these various "worlds" (of politics, of music, of sports, and so on). The events themselves (i.e., performances) then become a matter for distinct analysis and measurement. For example, information about the world of sports as distinct from the sport events themselves offers a more fruitful classificatory design than the catch-all category of "sports programs," which tends to set sports apart by confusing their information and entertainment components. In other words, it tends to depoliticize sports in the sense that sports reporting and presentation are believed to be exempt from those biases found in information programs, or from those commercial interests found in entertainment. The same argument can be made for musical, religious, and children's programs.

Fictional series, whether with animated or real-life actors, are classified according to their dramatic or comic overtone. Children's programming, as a category, disappears within the set of our entertainment, information, and education subcategories. A newscast for children is classified as a newscast; an animated cartoon show is classified either as drama or sitcom; a Walt Disney movie "for kids" is classified as cinema. The same can be said for the nonspecific category of "family shows." In classifying programs as children's, or sports, or family, it is the point of view of supply (the classificatory choice of the broadcaster or of the researcher) that prevails. The problem, to take the category "children's programs" as an example, is that many programs that children *do* watch are not sufficiently taken into account.[11] In other words, what are called children's programs may be watched by a relatively significant audience of nonchildren, while what are called nonchildren programs may be watched by a significant audience of children. The blind spot in the "children's program" category is the unfounded assumption that these programs constitute the main diet of children's consumption. This may very well be the case, but too frequently not enough attention is paid to their consumption of other program categories.

Our third category, *education,* refers to what Wright (p. 16) calls "[the] transmission of culture [that] focuses on the communicating of information, values, and social norms from one generation to another or from members of a group to newcomers. Commonly it is identified as educational activity."

Three subcategories were selected: academic, popular, and moral. "Academic" refers to programs that are recognized by the education system (for example, a ministry), under the supervision of an educational institution, and that are broadcast to those seeking accreditation. "Popular" refers to the transmission, in a didactic fashion, of social knowledge (or "knowledge of") by persons or group representatives who are identified as being knowledgeable in such matters as norms, values, and behavior of whatever nature (political, social, economic, cultural). "Moral" refers specifically to the transmission, in a didactic or rhetorical fashion, of norms, values, and behavior of a spiritual or ethical nature (e.g., tele-evangelical teachings).

Our fourth and last category is *advertising,* whether of commercial design or intended as a public service. Within this category, the first subcategory is that of "paid publicity," and covers all those short audiovisual productions regrouped in 1-to-3-minute time slots inserted at regular intervals within a scheduled program. Canada's federal regulations commission, the CRTC (Canadian Radio-television and Telecommunications Commission) has ruled that advertising material shall not exceed twelve minutes per hour of transmission. Thus, as a general rule of thumb, one can say that 20% of Canadian/Québecois television supply is made up of advertising.[12] Since these are not classified or recorded by the ratings agencies, we can neither refine our general category nor determine their consumption rate by any audience. In what follows, we have bracketed the category of paid publicity as a fixed appendage. By so doing, we hope to correct a constant bias in many studies of television programming whereby, in ignoring a very important television content (20%), the commodification function of television is made to appear trite, to the point of banal acceptance, while at the same time, the content/functions of information, entertainment, and education are overstated.

The BBM's 1993 report introduces a second category, the "paid program." This, essentially, is a thirty-minute program in which, under the guise of "infoducation," some product or service is described, explained, and validated either through actual demonstration (e.g., some cooking apparatus may be operated) or with the help of bona fide testimonies (e.g., people may tell how a get-rich scheme or a hair-growing formula actually works). These thirty-minute "shows" are really showcases for a full range of products and services. Such paid programs are to be found in regularly scheduled time slots, within a network's programming. They can, therefore, be tabulated both on the supply and the consumption sides. Included in this subcategory is the single fifteen-minute paid political program that we found.

▪ ▪ The Supply Side

Before we present an overview of our empirical results, we repeat that our data cannot be generalized to either the Québec or the Canadian television market. The data applies only to the greater Montréal metropolitan area. Because more than half of Québec's French-speaking population and 85% of its English-speaking population are to be found in this area, the data undoubtedly reflects the general situation. But it cannot be construed that it reflects the television markets in either the French- or the English-speaking populations of Canada.

The 1993 Market

What, then, would a typical viewer have found on his or her screen if he or she were to have videotaped the entire programming of the selected twelve television stations for one full week during autumn of 1993? This viewer would have ended up with some 1,898 hours of viewing (or 316 six-hour videocassettes), which would require 11.3 weeks of continual, 24-hours-a-day viewing in order to watch one week's supply. Barring repeats, it might be possible to save one or two days of viewing. To calibrate what was being offered, a dedicated researcher, working a 40-hour week, would be occupied for 47.5 weeks. Little wonder that researchers rely on sampling analysis, and those who pretend to know exactly what contents are being broadcast should not be taken too seriously.

What we profess to measure is the supply of television programs in terms of general categories of genres, and in addition, we give some indications concerning the general consumption patterns. We do not profess to know the specific contents of what is being offered or watched.

Our data base covers a total of 1,295 programs, of which we were able to fully document 1,188. On average, the French-language population of the province of Québec watches television 24.6 hours per week, while the English-speaking population watches 23.2 hours of television per week (Statistics Canada 1992). This works out to little more than 1% consumption of what is being offered (1.3% for the francophone population and 1.2% for the anglophone). Stated in these terms, it would appear that there is tremendous waste, or overkill. To eliminate waste would simply require some 1,295 "blocks" of 77 francophones or 82 anglophones to each watch a different program during their television vigil. This would result in all 1,898 hours of broadcast programs being "consumed" and there would be no loss. All the available stock would have been "sold out." Of course, reality (i.e., the actual pattern of viewing) lies somewhere in the large in-between.

The waste is relative and the overkill necessary because as long as network television does not operate in the pay-per-view mode, it remains less costly to fill unwatched television hours. The "cost" of this relative waste can be established as follows: in the English-language television market, a small fraction (9%) of the total program supply accounts for 60% of the total viewing time, while in the French-language market, the fraction is even less (7%), thus leaving a large scattering of programming (between 91% and 93%) to account for the remaining 40%.

This core programming that attracts such a large following is made up, so far as the anglophone population is concerned, of 23% information, 54% entertainment, 3% education, and 20% advertising. This same core is also composed of 17% Québecois production, 65% American production, and 18% Canadian production. In terms of the francophone population, the core programming that attracts 60% of the viewing time is made up of 34% information, 46% entertainment, 0% education, and 20% advertising. The share among television producers of this core supply is as follows: Québecois, 87%; Canadian, 1%; and American, 12%.

Logic would suggest that broadcasters should eliminate "unproductive" programming. Two reasons for not doing this are that no one can safely predict what will guarantee high ratings, and that by doing so, one would be eliminating real advertising revenues. Although the return on investment in less popular shows is significantly lower, the costs of production are also lower. In other words, broadcasters/producers hope to make large profits on a few high-cost productions and to make a marginal profit on a bountiful supply of low-cost productions. It is what Bernard Miège (1986) calls the "editorial logic" of cost-profit sharing. One can only guess, but the numbers seem to indicate that this arrangement is prevalent in the Montréal television market, regardless of whether the broadcasters are English or French, public or private, Québecois, Canadian, or American.

How can we characterize what the twelve selected network channels offered during one week in November 1993?[13] There are different ways to answer this question. It could be phrased in terms of the fact that both the English- and the French-speaking Montréal viewer had access to an overall supply that was almost 61% English and almost 39% French, with programs from other countries or cultures (European, Australian, and Aboriginal) comprising the tiniest fraction of one percent. Another way of restating the facts is to say that 63% of the total supply is American produced, 12% Canadian, and 25% Québecois, or that 41% of the content is broadcast over public stations and 59% through private channels. These figures can be broken down further by content: 23% of the programming hours are filled with information, 41% with entertainment, 14% with educational programs, and 22% with advertising.

In sum, the general picture of the Montréal market is one of American-filled, English-language entertainment programming, mostly distributed through private channels. Beyond these figures, however, it is possible to locate two major markets within this general picture.

Even though the Canadian and Québecois television networks only produce 37% of the total supply of programming in the Montréal market, they produce a greater share of the information supply (57%) than do the American networks. They produce their fair share of education programming (37%), while they substantially lag behind in the field of entertainment (24%). This translates into a supply profile that highlights the importance of the different components within each "national" television network (Tables 1 and 2).

The Québecois (or French-language) television stations present a profile that is as entertainment-oriented as that of their American counterpart, but much less so than the Canadian profile. If a distinction is made between the public and private sectors of television (Table 3), it is clear that all sectors are entertainment oriented (except the education network and PBS). The Québecois public sector is the least "entertaining," which, in turn, makes it the most "informative." The outline of two markets begins to become evident: a French-language market that offers greater diversity because of a relatively high information-content network (public) and a relatively high entertainment-content network (private), and that also has a relatively high education content; and an English-language market that is less diversified and that offers a supply of television that is relatively high in entertainment content (in both the Canadian public and private sectors and the American private networks) as well as in education content (in the American public sector).

As stated above, 63% of the total market supply, excluding supply from outside North America, is American in content (Table 4). It comes as no surprise that the content of the American private networks is 100% American and that of the American public sectors, 94.5% is American. It may be surprising, if not cause for Canadian cultural nationalists to worry, that the supply of the Canadian private sector is 56% American in content. The Canadian public sector and the Québecois private sector are comparatively similar with, respectively, 32% and 36% of their content being American. And, at the opposite end of the continuum, the Québecois public and educational networks have programming that is, respectively, 11% and 12% American in content. To some extent the Québecois and American networks are the most "national" in terms of content, with the former being more "open" or transnational than the latter.

We may tentatively conclude that in the Montréal metropolitan area there exist two language-based major television markets. The French-language market offers a relative choice between public (information-oriented), educational, and private (entertainment-oriented) Québecois networks. The English-language market offers a relative choice between, on the one hand Canadian and American (entertainment-oriented) networks and, on the other, American public (education-oriented)

TABLE 1 Distribution of Program Categories According to National
Television Networks[a]

Networks	Total (%)	Information (%)	Entertain- ment (%)	Education (%)	Advertising (%)
Québec	25	38	14	27	23
Canada	12	19	10	10	12
United States	63	43	76	62	64
Total[b]	100	100	100	100	100

[a] Excluding contribution from other (European) sources
[b] In some instances the sum of the individual percentages does not equal 100 because of rounding.

TABLE 2 Share of Program Categories within the Supply of National
Television Networks

Networks	Information (%)	Entertain- ment (%)	Education (%)	Publicity (%)	Total (%)
Québec	27	39	14	20	100
Canada	25	47	8	20	100
United States	19	38	19	24	100

TABLE 3 Programming of the Private and Public Sectors of National
Television Networks

Networks	Information (%)	Entertain- ment (%)	Education (%)	Publicity (%)	Total[a] (%)
Québec	27	39	14	20	100
public	33	43	4	20	100
educational	21	14	45	20	100
private	26	50	5	20	100
Canada	25	47	8	20	100
public	21	49	10	20	100
private	26	47	7	20	100
United States	19	38	19	24	100
public	13	20	47	20	100
private	23	49	2	26	100

[a] In some instances the sum of the individual percentages does not equal 100 because of rounding.

TABLE 4   Origin of Programming in the Private and Public Sectors
of National Television Networks

Networks	Québec (%)	Canada (%)	United States (%)	Other (%)	Total[a] (%)
Québec	72	1	24	3	100
public	82	2	12	4	100
educational	84	4	11	1	100
private	61	0	36	3	100
Canada	8	42	49	1	100
public	8	57	32	3	100
private	9	35	56	0	100
United States	0	0	98	2	100
public	0.2	0.2	94.5	5	100
private	0	0	100	0	100
Total	24	12	61	2	100

[a] In some instances the sum of the individual percentages does not equal 100 because of rounding.

networks. Again relatively speaking, both sectors of Canadian television appear to be associated with entertainment and thus with the American model of television. (This is also the case for the Québecois private sector.) In other words, in comparison with both Canadian and American television networks, the French-language television offers greater diversity, thus highlighting greater similarity between Canadian and American television.

If the 1993 data are compared with our 1987 findings, we find a few major changes and a reaffirmation of our view of the two distinct television markets in the Montréal area.

The 1987 and 1993 Markets Compared

First, the recorded supply is on the increase, due mainly to the added access to two stations. In 1987 the ten television channels in our survey broadcast an average of 128 hours per channel per week. In 1993 the twelve channels supplied the market with an average of 158 hours per channel per week (an increase of 23%).

The second, and perhaps the greatest, shift occurred in the sources of the supply. In 1987 the United States accounted for 47% of the supply, while Canadian television produced 13.5% and Québecois television 33%. The remaining 6% was supplied by other, mostly European, television companies. In 1993 the American share rose to 61%, while that of Canada remained stable at 12% and the Québecois share dropped to 25%, as did the share of other television networks, decreasing from 6% to 2%.

Third, the shift toward a greater American / English-language supply continues to manifest itself. Between 1987 and 1993 English-language programs' share of the total supply rose from 54% to 61%. This translates into a decrease in national content, particularly in Canadian television and in the Québecois private sector (Table 5).

While the shift in supply has been toward a greater amount of English and American content, Table 6 shows that there has been a corresponding decrease in the share occupied by entertainment.

The increase in education-oriented programming is due to the added access to two PBS stations and to the expanding "popular education" category, while the increase in television advertising publicity is due to the unprecedented scheduling of "paid programs." The above shifts explain why, within Québec's supply of TV programming, the public sector's share remained the same, at 51%, between 1987 and 1993, while the public sector's share in the Canadian supply fell sharply from 50% to 30%. (This pattern is also due to the access to a second private station, CJOH, which was not available to the Montréal viewer in 1987.) While the share of the Québecois public sector remained the same, of greater significance is the increase not of domestic production but of French-dubbed versions of American programs. In 1987 Québecois programs represented 85% of the public sector's supply, while American programs represented 3%. In 1993 the percentages were, respectively, 83% and 12%. The same trend is evident in the private sector, where, in 1987, Québecois programs represented 76% of the supply and American programs represented 21%, while in 1993 the Québecois share dropped to 61% and American programming rose to 36%.

In the Canadian public sector the share of American programs rose from 28% in 1987 to 32% in 1993, while the share of English-dubbed Québecois programs rose from less than 0.5% to 8%. The Canadian supply did witness a drop in its share, from 68% to 57%. It is interesting to note that French-dubbed Canadian programs were not shown on Québec's networks, either private or public, in 1987, and in 1993 they represented a modest 1% of supply. This seems to be a question of economics. Dubbed American programs have a better market pull than

TABLE 5   Percentage of National Content within the Supply of the Major
National Television Networks

	Québecois	
Networks	1987	1993
Québec	(%)	(%)
public	79	82
education	79	82
private	71–79	61
	Canadian	
	1987	1993
Canada	(%)	(%)
public	66	57
private	47	35
	American	
	1987	1993
United States	(%)	(%)
public	not available	94.5
private	91–99	100%

TABLE 6   Distribution of Québec's Television Supply by Genres, 1987–1993

	1987[a]	1993
Genres	(%)	(%)
Information	25	23
Entertainment	50	41
Education	8	14
Publicity	20	22

[a] The sum of the individual percentages does not equal 100 because of rounding.

dubbed Canadian programs, while dubbed Québecois programs seem to be worth the financial risk in that particular audience market.

In the private Canadian sector the American and Québecois programs' shares both rose, though not to the same extent, while that of the Canadian programs dropped. Between 1987 and 1993 the shares shifted as follows: American rose—from 49% to 56%; Québecois rose—from less than 0.5% to 9%; Canadian dropped—from 47% to 35%.

With very little room for improvement, the American content in the American private networks rose from 96% in 1987 to total closure (i.e., 100%) in 1993.

One could argue that the production capacity of the American television networks is such that they can fully satisfy their home market, and then some. The American television industry being self-sufficient, it needs to import very little. Between 1987 and 1993 a trend seems evident in the supply side of Canadian and Québecois networks. In 1987 Québec's television, which has a smaller market and less industrial capability than Canada's, imported half as much as Canada. In relative terms, American programs represented 12% of Québec's supply side and 39% of the Canadians'. In 1992 we concluded our study of the 1987 television market by stating: "The import figures for Canadian television, because of the overwhelming presence of US products, can be interpreted in terms of dependence, while the lower Québec figures and wider internationalization would indicate a 'policy' of check and balance." The 1993 figures indicate a dramatic shift in the composition of the supply side, with American programs representing 24% of the Québec supply and 49% of the Canadian.

We have, we believe, shown that between 1987 and 1993, (1) the internationalization of supply between the U.S. television networks and those of Canada and Québec not only varied but spanned both ends of a spectrum of relatively low import (Québecois), half import (Canadian), and total closure (American); and (2) the internationalization of supply varied relatively less between the public and private broadcasting sectors in Québec than between the equivalent Canadian sectors. Since the question of imports is indicative not only of industrial strength and market size but also of cultural preferences, we must now look to the consumption side to see whether similar shifts have occurred there.

▪ ▪ The Consumption Side

There are some marked differences between the viewing patterns of Québec's French- and English-speaking populations (Statistics Canada 1992). Francophones consume 1.4 hours per week more television than their anglophone counterparts (24.6 hours compared with 23.2). The average number of hours of television viewing per week for Québec is the second highest total among Canada's ten provinces. In both linguistic communities, women 18 years and older are the heaviest consumers (28.8 hours per week for francophones and 26.7 hours for anglophones). Adolescents are the lightest consumers (17.9 hours in the francophone community and 15.7 in the anglophone community). Francophone men 18 years and older consume more than their anglophone counterparts (23.6 hours compared with 21.7 hours), while francophone children consume less (18.9 hours compared with 20.1 in the anglophone community).

In our study of the 1987 data we only looked at the viewing patterns of the francophone community. Our diachronic comparison will only touch this linguistic community, while our synchronic comparison, for 1993, will touch both communities.

1987–1993: The French-Speaking Audience

Since we do not have any data on the viewing patterns of advertising, we will exclude this category in the following comparison of both the supply and the consumption sides of the television market.

The 1987 figures revealed an almost perfect match between overall supply and consumption by the francophone viewers in terms of our general categories. Information consumption (i.e., the share of viewing time spent on information content) was slightly higher (33%) than information supply—information's share in the total supply of television content (30%); entertainment consumption (56%) was slightly lower than the supply (59%); and education consumption (10.5%) and supply (10.6%) were equal.

In 1993 these results were skewed in favor of entertainment: information consumption (27%) was almost on a par with the information supply (30%); entertainment consumption (68%) was considerably higher than the supply (52%); and education consumption (5%) was considerably lower than the supply (18%). This shift toward more entertainment consumption and more French-language programs, including American dubbed, occurred among all age groups of the francophone audience.

While there was a shift toward greater consumption of entertainment, the consumption ratings of the Québecois television networks, which were already high in 1987, rose in 1993 in all age groups (Figure 1). This increase is all the more significant when we consider that in 1987 French-language programs represented 46% of total supply and 88% of

FIGURE 1   Consumption of national and bilateral television networks, Montréal's francophone audience, 1987–1993

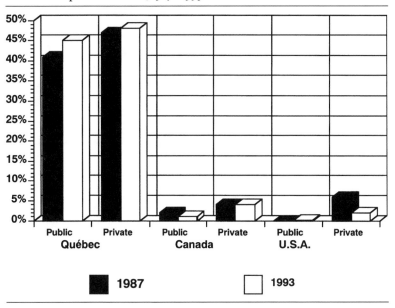

TABLE 7   Consumption of French-Language Television Programming, Montréal's Francophone Audience, 1987–1993

Supply	1987 (%)	1993[a] (%)
Québecois	66	75
Other (French)	0	1
French-dubbed American	10	14
French-dubbed Canadian	0	1
French-dubbed "others"	11	0
Canadian	2	1
American	9	7
Other (English)	2	2

[a] The sum of the individual percentages does not equal 100 because of rounding.

total consumption, while in 1993 they represented 39% of total supply and 92% of total consumption.

It would seem that this shift in content preference by the francophone audience has benefited both the Québecois public and private sectors, to the detriment of the American private networks.

The 1993 consumption pattern of the francophone community shows a slight increase in French-language programs in both Québecois-produced and dubbed American programs (Table 7). The source of dubbed programs from "other" television (mainly Japanese and European) dried up.

The shift in viewing patterns toward greater consumption of entertainment and of American content parallels a similar shift toward greater viewing of French-language, Québecois-broadcast content. The apparent paradox dissolves when one considers language to be the discriminating factor, since the increase in French-language content is, in part, due to an increase in American dubbed programs.

This, however, raises a question of cultural policy: should Québecois television cater to French-language programs or to Québecois production? The dilemma can be stated in the following terms: if language is synonymous with culture, one should encourage the consumption of French-language television programs, even of dubbed American programs because of their low cost and high viewing appeal. If, on the other hand, culture is more than language, the question is raised of whether the consumption of dubbed American programs, while reinforcing the vitality and public awareness of the French language, also introduces American values into the cultural fabric of the Québecois identity, or whether language blocks or filters out such values. While market analysis raises questions it cannot answer, it does render a valuable service in pointing out the cultural and political impact of a television industry that operates under North American market conditions.

1993: Montréal's Francophone and Anglophone Audiences

Besides differences in terms of hours per week of television viewing and whether same-language programs are preferred or not, are there any concurring or divergent patterns in the consumption patterns of the two linguistic communities? One discerning difference stems from the strong competition that exists between the public and private sectors of Québecois television in attracting the francophone viewing audience, resulting in consumption being almost evenly split between the two categories of broadcasters; on the anglophone side, in contrast, the private stations (Canadian and American) are clearly more popular than their public counterparts, by almost three to one.

Another discerning characteristic is that the francophone audience is slightly more information oriented, while the anglophone audience is slightly more entertainment and education orientated. These tendencies are relative, since both audiences display a similar overall pattern of consumption—that is, consumption of entertainment is greater than supply, while supply of information and education programs is greater than consumption.

While differences are slight, consumption patterns do cut across linguistic lines when it comes to age groups. As might be expected, in both communities viewing preferences of adults differ from those of the younger generation. But while viewing habits of the francophone adults do differ somewhat from those of their anglophone counterparts, there are very few differences between the young across linguistic communities.

The basic differences are to be found in the choice of national broadcasters, television programs, and specific entertainment sub-genres. All age groups in the francophone community show a deep loyalty to Québecois broadcasters, while Canadian and American broadcasters compete for the anglophones' viewing time. The Canadian broadcasters seem to do well in all age groups except among the very young. It is clear that language is the determining factor in both cases—that is, Canadian broadcasters have to compete with their American counterparts within a same-language market, while the Québecois broadcasters do not.

Because Canadian and Québecois broadcasters serve, more and more, as carriers for American programs, it is worthwhile to compare the consumption patterns in terms of programming. It is here that we find the most vivid evidence of what we perceived to be two distinct markets on the supply side (Figures 2 and 3).

While each linguistic community chooses same-language programs, the francophones overwhelmingly consume national (i.e., Québecois) productions, while the anglophones overwhelmingly consume bilateral (i.e., American) productions. In other words, francophone audiences seem to find in the Québecois broadcasters (public, private, and educational) both diversity value and linguistic familiarity. These broadcasters supply them with French-language programs, both nationally produced and American dubbed, in all major categories of programming (entertainment, information, education). The anglophone audiences also seem to seek diversity value and linguistic familiarity, but they find these

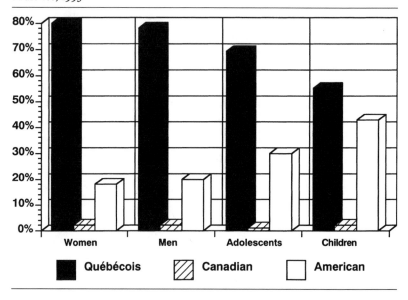

FIGURE 2   Consumption patterns of programming, Montréal's francophone audience, 1993

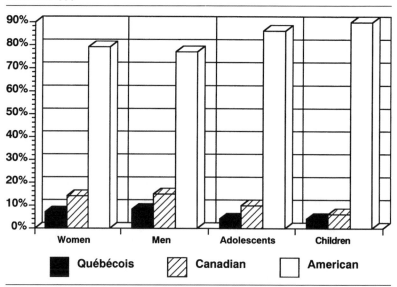

FIGURE 3   Consumption patterns of programming, Montréal's anglophone audience, 1993

things, rather paradoxically, in American programs supplied mostly by Canadian broadcasters.

Therein lie the two markets. They are both anchored in programs. The basic difference is that whereas the francophone consumption of programs (the market) coincides with French-language Québecois broadcasters (carriers) and national production (supply), the anglophone market of English-language programs is characterized by American production and Canadian carriers (broadcasters).

If we consider that Québecois broadcasters are competing with Canadian and American broadcasters within a general market, we may conclude that the francophone consumption patterns do not reflect the supply side, which is predominantly English in terms of language and American in terms of content. But if we locate, within this general area, two distinct markets we may conclude that supply and consumption, in both markets, do seem to fall into step. Broadcasters and consumers, in both markets, seem to have reached some "agreement" as to what the market should contain, even if most of the "goods" produced are "wasted" (i.e., not consumed).

A further indication of the validity of the two-market hypothesis is provided by the top popular entertainment genres found in both linguistic communities. Among the francophones, Québecois-produced drama series, varieties, and performing arts top the list. Topping the list among the anglophones, in contrast, are American sitcoms and drama series.

As indicated above, the viewing patterns of the younger francophone viewers differ significantly from those of their elders insofar as the former view a greater share of American content. Again, such data raises the open-ended question of whether we should take comfort in the fact that they watch French-language (dubbed) programs or whether we should be concerned with the process of acculturation of American values. Is this the perfect case for cultural imperialism, where people are adopting alien values unknowingly, in what they perceive to be the security of their own language?

A short-term answer is that comparative data between 1987 and 1993 seem to suggest that as the younger francophone viewers grow older, their television viewing patterns change to resemble more and more closely those of the adult generation. In other words, Québecois producers and broadcasters have the ability to rejuvenate their audiences. For example, the most popular entertainment genre, the *téléroman* (literally, a tele-novel), has remained at the top of the television "pop charts" for over thirty years. Much as the American soap opera and prime-time teleseries have done, it creates a loyal following with each new generation of television viewers. So, it would seem, while young francophone viewers do consume American dubbed programs in a relatively large proportion, they tend to consume, as they grow older, more and more Québecois production. But does this change in viewing patterns suffice to eradicate the assimilation of alien values at a young age? And what happens to the anglophone community, in which not only the younger generations, but also the older ones, consume a high proportion of American products? Is this also a perfect case for cultural imperialism, where people, again, are adopting alien values unknowingly in what they perceive to be the security of their own language? The question then becomes one of whether cultural imperialism transcends the languages of the viewers.

As stated at the outset, we are not in a position to answer such questions; rather, we are able to offer some empirical data to sharpen the questions regarding transborder flow, media consumption, and the thesis of cultural imperialism.

We could conclude, as we did in 1992, that the thesis of cultural imperialism falters when confronted with empirical analyses such as ours. If one examines the consumption patterns of the predominantly French-language television audience in the predominantly English-language television market of Montréal, one must admit that American cultural imperialism does not seem to have much effect. It is not only the consumption of French-language programs that is high—the consumption of Québecois production is high also. In fact, there exists within this predominantly English/American television market a diversified, productive, popular Québecois television industry and market. By the same token, when one examines the consumption patterns of the minority anglophone audience one is very tempted to conclude that American cultural imperialism is ravaging.

There are many in both linguistic communities who will reject such a conclusion: English-speaking Montréalers who watch American programs consider themselves 100% Canadian, while French-speaking Montréalers who hardly watch American programs will argue that television itself is a tool of American imperialism. In a word, empirical data does not, by itself, prove anything; at best, it can point to possible interpretations of a socially constructed reality such as imperialism.

What our data suggest is that perhaps the question of transborder flow of user-friendly American cultural products should focus on the role of language both as a discriminating factor in selecting television programs and as a carrier/filter of the program's symbolic contents.[14] When the question is put in these terms, there are three possible interpretations. The first is that language is a "natural" carrier of cultural values. Thus the American use of the English language in American programs will naturally carry American values. This interpretation applies in the case of the anglophone viewing community of Montréal and gives credence to the thesis of cultural imperialism.

The second interpretation, an inversion of the first, states that the cultural values embedded at the production phase of a program will become, at the very least, clouded if the program is broadcast in a "nonnatural" or non-congenial language—that is, in a dubbed language. Not only will the French-speaking audience be able to resist cultural imperialism because they will negotiate, at reception, these cultural meanings in a foreign tongue, but the meanings themselves will have already been negotiated by the very dubbing process itself. This interpretation gives credence to the thesis of cultural resistance.

The third interpretation is that language does not "carry," in the sense of Carey's transport model, particular cultural values or insights, but, rather, guides the consumer toward those meanings that the artist/producer wants to convey. Thus, a dubbed American program in Québecois or Parisian French will not necessarily undercarry Québecois or French cultural references because the language, be it French or whatever, can guide the consumer toward the original—that is, American—values. This is usually the case. People who choose to watch, in the language of their choice, an American program expect to recognize American content even though the New York cop speaks with a Parisian accent. This interpretation would, in fact, place the Montréal francophone viewer on the same footing as the anglophone viewer—that is, both would fall within the first interpretation. In other words, the French language does not necessarily offer more room in which to resist or negotiate cultural imperialism or a better position from which to do so. The real test comes when the viewers, in whatever language, discuss or pass comments on the American program, whether it is dubbed or not. The only way English-speaking Canadians can resist or negotiate the cultural meanings thus delivered through their television set lies in the use they make of the English language in the reception of such programs—that is, in the way in which they discuss or comment on these programs.

If this is a valid interpretation, some may conclude that we are back at square one—that is, that American cultural imperialism is a no-lose situation and that the diverse popular cultures in media-saturated societies are nothing but multilingual American popular culture. For lack of empirical data, this can be qualified at best as a pessimistic hypothesis. Again in the absence of empirical data, one can formulate an optimistic hypothesis, one that builds onto a program analysis or market analysis a study of the conditions of reception. It is our belief that the language used by the viewer to frame the reception of a television program, whatever the language of broadcasting, will have a definite impact on whether there is identification (accepted or negotiated) or not or whether there is rejection (passive or active) of the cultural references contained within such a program.

It goes without saying that a vital function of the French-language television market in Montréal is to broadcast local productions in which there can be inserted cultural references to values upon which a "national" or collective identity could be structured. But more important, perhaps, is the fact that the very presence of such a market favors a continual, ongoing circulation and relaying of French-language programs whether they are original Québecois or dubbed American. By doing so, it helps to maintain a French-language public culture, one that resonates within the privacy of the home and in daily, mundane conversations. It thus sustains the general use of a French vernacular that is then used to frame the reception of those same French-language television programs, whether they are Québecois or American.

Pushed to caricatural extremes, French-language television, whatever its programming, could be described as contributing to making French congenial to the social construction and expression of a particular cultural identity, of a particular cultural entity.

French-language Québecois television does not create a Québecois public culture, but it does help to create and to maintain the conditions in which such a culture can take shape and develop. The outcome—that is, the public culture—is dependent on its conditions of production but is not determined by them. In fact, French-language Québecois television could quite possibly contribute to the emergence of a francophone public culture that is American in essence, as well as to the emergence of a public culture that is Québecois in essence.

A most probable outcome of the viewing patterns of the English-speaking community in Montréal is the production of an American-based Canadian public culture. A more optimistic, but just as realistic, hypothesis would be to admit the possibility of a truly Canadian public culture as an outcome of heavy consumption of American television.

Admittedly the television markets in both linguistic communities are quite distinct. But in the final analysis, any two of the following scenarios are possible: a French-language public culture that is American in essence; a French-language public culture that is distinctly Québecois; an English-language public culture that is American in essence; an English-language public culture that is distinctly Canadian.

There is of course a much broader hypothesis, one that cannot be addressed within the narrow confines of this study because it is fundamentally political in nature—namely, the possibility that both French- and English-language communities, through their distinctive use of television supply, and particularly through their use and interpretation of American television content, contribute to the making of one public culture, predominantly francophone, in the Québec society.

Whatever the outcome, television, like any other major mass-media industry, is central in any discussion of the thesis of cultural imperialism and transborder flow of cultural products in a free-trade market economy because it is central to the social construction of a public culture. It is within this public culture, and not within television per se, that the battle for cultural imperialism or cultural sovereignty is waged.

Television, like all other cultural industries, sets the stage and the mood for the enactment of public culture but it does not, it cannot, write the play—that is, what is played out.

Will American cultural imperialism triumph in Québec's public cultures, francophone and anglophone? We can look to television programming, supply and consumption, to measure the forces at play within the products that are broadcast and consumed, but we must look to reception, to the framing of the consumption of these products, to see how these forces will play out.

NOTES

This research is funded by the Social Sciences and Humanities Research Council of Canada. I wish to thank Charles-Édouard Boivin, my research assistant who provided much of the valuable data on television programming. I would also like to thank Michel Gagné, documentalist at the Ministry of Communication in Québec, for access to the BBM Reports.

1. Québec's French-speaking population represents about 20% of the Canadian population and less than 2% of the combined English-speaking population of Canada and the United States. In other words, in Québec there is one anglophone for every four francophones; in Canada there are approximately four anglophones for

every one French-speaking Québecois; and in Canada and the United States there are approximately sixty anglophones for every one French-speaking Québecois. The demographic weight of both linguistic communities is indicative of Québec's position of vulnerability in an era of increasing transborder flow and free trade.

2. By far the most U.S.-dominated media market is the record industry. We chose to focus on television, however, because data on consumption is more abundant and available.

3. In other words, whereas the supply side is made up of 70% English-language and 30% French-language TV programs, the consumption side is 70% French and 30% English.

4. The BBM is a Toronto-based, private, nonprofit cooperative whose members are mainly broadcasters and which specializes in producing the ratings of television and radio programs.

5. "3(1). It is hereby declared as the broadcasting policy for Canada that the Canadian broadcasting system operating mainly in the English and French languages and comprising public and private elements, makes use of radio frequencies that are public property and provides, through its programming, a public service essential to the maintenance and enhancement of national identity and cultural sovereignty" (Bill C-40, 1991 [quoted in Tremblay 1992]).

6. Multilateral is defined by Sepstrup (1990, 12) as television supply and consumption originating outside the national territory under study and whose flow has no single intended direction.

7. Our 1987 data are for ten cable television channels: four French-language Québecois stations, two English-language Canadian channels, and four American channels.

8. In 1987 Montréal's viewers were offered access not to CJOH but to CHLT, an affiliate of the French-language private network TVA, and to only one PBS affiliate.

9. Produced in Québec, by Québecois, they reach 98% of the total households, and over 95% of their audience is Québecois.

10. This typology was designed by Denise Paré.

11. A recent Québec study has started to address this concern (Caron et al. 1990).

12. Imperialistically, we "decreed" that this rule of thumb should also apply to the American television supply.

13. We have removed all programs whose genre it was not possible to identify, and those imported from other television networks, such as European and Australian. This left us with a total of 1,701 hours of programming.

14. We do realize, of course, that the investigation does not end at this point and that the role of language in the actual reception of the program must also be addressed and researched.

BIBLIOGRAPHY

Allard, Jean-Marie. 1989. *La pub: 30 ans de publicité au Québec.* Montréal: Libre expression.

Ang, Ien. 1991. *Desperately Seeking the Audience.* New York: Routledge.

Bernard, Harry. 1924. "Théâtre et cinéma." *L'Action nationale* 12: 69–80.

Bernard, Jean-Paul. 1971. *Les Rouges: Libéralisme, nationalisme et anticléricalisme au milieu du XIXe siècle.* Montréal: Presses de l'Université du Québec.

Bertrand, Claude-Jean, and Franci Bordat, directors. 1989. *Les médias américains en France. Influence et pénétration.* Paris: Belin.

Boyd-Barrett, Oliver. 1977. "Media imperialism: Towards an international framework for the analysis of media systems." In *Mass Communication and Society,* ed. James Curran, Michael Gurevitch, and Janet Woolacott. Beverly Hills, Calif.: Sage.

Brym, Robert J., and Bonnie J. Fox. 1989. *From Culture to Power. The Sociology of English Canada.* New York: Oxford University Press.

Bureau of Broadcast Measurement (BBM). 1987. *Special Report. Montréal, Fall/Automne.* Toronto: Bureau of Measurement.

———. 1993. *Special Report. Montréal, Fall/Automne.* Toronto: Bureau of Measurement.

Caron, André H., et al. 1990. *Télévision et vidéocassettes pour les jeunes. Analyse de l'offre et de l'écoute.* Montréal: Université de Montréal.

de Bonville, Jean. 1988. *La presse Québecoise de 1884 à 1914. Genèse d'un média de masse.* Québec: Presses de l'Université Laval.

de la Garde, Roger. 1987. "Is there a market for foreign cultures?" *Media, Culture and Society* 9: 189–207.

———. 1990. "To speak one's culture." *The London Journal of Canadian Studies* 7: 28–51.

de la Garde, Roger, W. Gilsdorf, and I. Wechselmann, eds. 1992. *Small Nations, Big Neighbour. Denmark and Québec/Canada Compare Notes on American Popular Culture.* Acamedia Research Monograph, no. 10. London: John Libbey.

de la Garde, Roger, and Denise Paré. 1991. "La télévision: L'offre d'une programmation ou la programmation d'une demande?" *Communication* 12(1): 101–148.

Filion, Michel. 1993. "L'américanisation de la radio Québecoise et l'émergence du service national de radiodiffusion au Canada." *Communication* 14(2): 197–221.

Goto, Kazuhiko. 1969. "Programming, one of the fields of broadcasting studies." *Studies of Broadcasting,* pp. 5–29.

Hébert, Chantal. 1989. *Le burlesque Québecois et américain: Textes inédits.* Québec: Presses de l'Université Laval.

L'Allier, Jean Paul. 1971. *Pour une politique Québecoise des communications.* Québec: Ministère des Communications.

Lealand, G. 1984. *American Television Programmes on British Screens.* London: Broadcasting Research Unit.

Lee, C.-C. 1980. *Media Imperialism Reconsidered. The Homogenizing of Television Culture.* Beverly Hills, Calif.: Sage.

Lemieux, Jacques, and Denis Saint-Jacques. 1990. "Un scénario motif dans le champ des best-sellers." *Voix & Images* 44: 260–268.

L'Herbier, Benoit. 1974. *La chanson Québecoise.* Montréal: Éditions de l'Homme.

Litman, Barry R. 1992. "Economic aspects of program quality: The case of diversity."

Studies of Broadcasting. Special Issue on Quality Assessment of Broadcasting Programming 2: 121–156.

Magnan, Odile. 1980. "La musique à Québec 1908–1918: À travers l'action sociale et l'action catholique." Master's thesis, Conservatoire de musique de Québec.

Mattelart, Armand, Michele Mattelart, and Xavier Delcourt. 1984. *International Image Markets: In Search of an Alternative Perspective.* London: Comedia Publishing Group.

Miège, Bernard. 1986. "Les logiques à l'oeuvre dans les nouvelles industries culturelles." *Cahiers de recherches sociologiques,* pp. 93–110.

Mondoux, André. 1984. "Médias et société : Le cinéma à Montréal 1896–1929." Master's thesis, Université Laval, Québec.

Mowlana, H. 1986. *Global Information and World Communication.* London: Longman.

Nordenstreng, Karl, and Tapio Varis. 1974. *Television Traffic—A One-Way Street? A Survey and Analysis of the International Flow of Television Programme Material.* Reports and Papers on Mass Communication, no. 70. Paris: UNESCO.

Raboy, Marc. 1990. "From cultural diversity to social equality: The democratic trials of Canadian Broadcasting." *Studies of Broadcasting* 26: 7–41.

————. 1993. "Towards a new ethical environment of public service broadcasting." *Studies of Broadcasting* 29: 7–35.

Read, William. 1976. *America's Mass Media Merchants.* Baltimore: John Hopkins University Press.

Resnick, Philip. 1990. *Letters to a Québecois Friend.* Montréal & Kingston: McGill-Queen's University Press.

Roy, Bruno. 1977. *Panorama de la chanson au Québec.* Montréal: Leméac.

Schiller, Herbert I. 1976. *Communication and Cultural Dominance.* White Plains, N.Y.: International Arts and Sciences Press.

Sepstrup, Preben. 1990. *Transnationalization of Television in Western Europe.* Acamedia Research Monograph, no. 5. London: John Libbey.

Smythe, Dallas. 1981. *Dependency Road: Communications, Capitalism, Consciousness.* Norwood, N.J.: Ablex.

Sonnenberg, Urte. 1993. "Channel multiplicity and programme diversity in television." *Studies of Broadcasting* 29: 71–92.

Statistics Canada. 1992. *Television Viewing 1992.* Catalogue No. 87–208. Ottawa: Minister of Supply and Services.

Task Force on Broadcasting Policy. 1986. *Report.* Task force co-chaired by Gerald Caplan and Florian Sauvageau. Ottawa: Minister of Supply and Services.

Tremblay, Gaëtan. 1992. "Is Quebec culture doomed to become American?" *Canadian Journal of Communication* 17: 237–245.

Tunstall, Jeremy. 1977. *The Media Are American.* New York: Columbia University Press.

Wright, Charles R. 1962. *Mass Communication. A Sociological Perspective.* New York: Random House.

12

U.S. Best-Sellers in French Québec and English Canada

JACQUES LEMIEUX AND DENIS SAINT-JACQUES

SINCE THEIR MASSIVE APPEARANCE at the beginning of the 1970s,[1] best-selling books, both fiction and nonfiction, have been largely a cultural import in French-speaking Québec. It must be said that the Canadian book industry is not as state-regulated as, for example, the television and radio industries. Of course, the federal and provincial governments subsidize, to a certain extent, local authors and publishers. Nevertheless, the Canadian book market is a free market, open to authors and publishers from all over the world. French publishers are, however, the only ones to have seized this opportunity, and that creates what could be called a "two-layered cultural imperialism" wherein publishers from France, dominating the book market in Québec, massively feed the readership not only with their own products but also, and perhaps increasingly, with French translations of English (mainly U.S.) best-sellers, particularly fiction.

Until the early 1980s this phenomenon was largely neglected in Québec—not only by the book industry, but also by scholars of literature as well as of communication. In fact, best-sellers were left in a kind of theoretical and methodological no-man's-land between these two disciplinary fields. For mass-communications specialists, books were not true "mass media," while scholars of highbrow literature considered best-sellers too aesthetically poor to be worthy of interest; meanwhile, popular-literature specialists preferred typified genres such as science fiction, crime novels, and romance.

However, the increasing popularity in Québec's universities of the concept of cultural industries and of the cultural studies approach has proved best-sellers to be a strategic field of interest for multidisciplinary research. Industrially produced and distributed, best-sellers imply transnational marketing, advertising, public relations, and audience measurement. Moreover, top-selling novels and biographies usually become multimedia products, being adapted for the film or the television industry, or for both. The best-seller may then be recognized as a true "public communication" phenomenon and as a legitimate field for communication research. Moreover, it appears to literature specialists that as middle-range products, best-sellers are aesthetically and ideologically more complex than formerly presumed. Best-sellers also become a particularly interesting field of inquiry for a renewed interest in literary reception studies (concerning reader response and reception aesthetics), as well as in the sociology of culture or of knowledge: as a "common denominator of a literary culture" (Long 1985), best-sellers can be studied as the embodiment of some of the dominant ideological and aesthetic structures in a specific historical context. Then relations between text and reader should show the main trends in the hegemonic worldview of a given collectivity.

In this context, an interdisciplinary research team of communication sociologists and economists, literary semioticians, and narratologists from Université Laval (Québec City) and Université de Montréal was formed in the mid-1980s. The present chapter seeks to illustrate this team's main findings relating to the situation of national and foreign best-sellers in French-speaking Québec's book market. It develops in three parts, the first of which deals with a few methodological considerations; this is followed by results focusing on quantitative analysis of best-seller lists in Québec dailies, with comparisons with similar (but more summarily analyzed) lists in English Canada and in the United States; finally, qualitative aesthetic and thematic observations are made of top-ranking best-sellers in those three book markets.

▪ ▪ Which Books are Truly Best-Sellers?

Our theoretical and methodological approach to best-sellers can to some extent be related to cultural studies, since it considers that culture must be understood "both as a way of life . . . and a whole range of cultural practices" (Grossberg, Nelson, and Treichler 1992, p. 5); we also think that cultural practices must be "examined from the point of view of their intrication with and within relations of power" (ibid., p. 3) and that cultural consumption is a dynamic process in which "consumers choose both the tools and materials available to them in order to make sense of what is at hand" (Krieling 1978). Nonetheless, our model in fact evolved gradually from a series of field operations, loosely related at the outset, but increasingly integrated thereafter, which considered best-sellers as the "meeting place" of publishers' strategies, books' aesthetic and ideological structures, and readers' tastes and expectations.

More than most other kinds of cultural products, best-sellers cannot be adequately analyzed without an integrated "production-product-reception" approach. First, those books do not constitute a literary genre; rather, they comprise a "people's choice"—a book becomes a best-seller when it is bought (and usually, but not necessarily, read) by a large audience, whatever its utilitarian or symbolic content. Second, one can ask whether the reader's choice is a free one, or whether it is managed (at least partially) by industrial marketing processes. Finally, as a consequence of their popularity, best-sellers attract a socially and culturally heterogeneous audience whose members are likely to negotiate different meanings for these messages.

At the outset, the problem is to elaborate a valid operational definition of a best-seller. Indeed, it would be easy to identify the books that "sell best" if it were possible to obtain reliable statistics from publishers or distributors; but in Québec, these data are well-kept industrial secrets. On the other hand, key informants from the book industry would likely be subjective. The same could be said about best-seller lists in the print media, since their compilation usually relies on a few informants from a small number of bookstores. However, it can be assumed that pinpoint biases, clearly visible in a single weekly list, will cancel each other out in a very large number of such lists. In other words, even if such a list does not include all possible best-sellers, all books mentioned can nevertheless be considered as true best-sellers, particularly those appearing at the top of the list.

On the basis of this assumption, we compiled in the mid-1980s a first sample of over 100 top-ranking novels and biographies for the period 1970–1982,[2] from weekly best-seller lists appearing in Montréal's *La Presse* (Québec's top daily newspaper). This first sample was then validated by ten professionals in the book industry (publishers, distributors, and booksellers); these people were astonished to observe that in spite of all bias in the making of best-seller lists, the selection thus obtained truly gave a representative sample of top-sellers. This sample was then used as a corpus for narrative and ideological content analysis (Martin 1986; Saint-Jacques 1987; Lemieux and Saint-Jacques 1990). But it soon appeared that such data could also be used for statistical analysis.

Thus, from this initial experiment, we constructed a more elaborate data bank, which records the twenty-five top-ranking books (fiction and nonfiction) from French Canada (*La Presse*), English Canada (the *Montreal Gazette*), France (*L'Express* magazine), and the United States (*Publishers Weekly*) for each year from 1970 to 1992.[3] This data bank makes it possible to perform, on either a national or a transnational basis, a number of different statistical analyses—concerning the national origin of a book's author or publisher, whether it is fictional or nonfictional, and whether it has narrative or nonnarrative status—and also allows the conceptualization of some rough thematic content categories (Bonnassieux, Lemieux, Martin, and L'Italien 1991; Martin 1994). However, due to methodological problems and limited funding, detailed analysis applies presently only to the Québec list. Much is still to be done with its Canadian, French, and U.S. equivalents.[4] For this reason, our demonstration here relies mainly on the Québec data base; comparisons with U.S. and Canadian best-seller lists can be made only on a general and exploratory basis.

▪ ▪ General Overview of Québec's Best-Sellers: Twin Cultural Imperialism

From this data bank, an analysis of 451 top-ranking best-sellers in the Québec market, written in (or translated into) French between 1970 and 1990,[5] and from now on called "Québecois top-sellers," reveals a number of findings, of which the main ones are now described.

Over the whole period, as Figure 1 shows, Québecois authors and publishers averaged about 40% of all top-sellers; this proportion may seem small, but it compares quite well with a 5% Québecois share in top-ranking films and a 25% share in popular music, both of which, unlike books, are strongly subsidized and protected against foreign competition. Figure 1 also shows that the publishers' share is generally 6% greater than that of the authors—simply because Québec's publishers print foreign authors in a greater proportion than French publishers edit Québecois writers.

Yet diachronic analysis shows a curvilinear evolution in the proportion of top-selling books written or published in French in Québec. At the beginning of the 1970s, Québecois authors and publishers were re-

FIGURE 1   Weekly lists in Montréal's *La Presse* through August 1990.

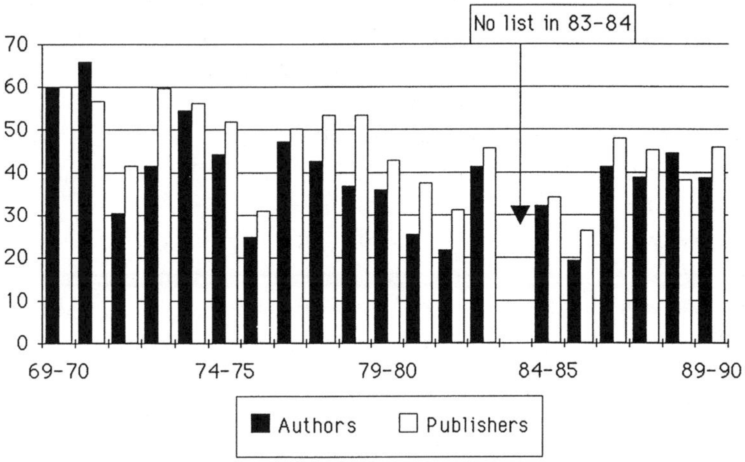

SOURCE: Weekly lists in Montréal's *La Presse* through August 1990. Market share is calculated from scores obtained according to rank in the list and month of the year, for 25 leading titles of each year (total = 451 titles). There was no list in 1983–1984, owing to a long union strike.

sponsible for more than 50% of all top-sellers. This may at least partly be explained by a strong nationalist movement in Québec during this period.

However, from the mid-1970s to the mid-1980s, this proportion of Québecois top-sellers fell under 30%. The main reasons for this situation are probably the lower prices of books imported from France, owing to the conjunctural weakness of the franc relative to the Canadian dollar, combined with a more aggressive strategy from French publishers and distributors. But it may also be another sign of a collective depression that struck Québec intellectuals after the lost referendum on Québec's independence in 1980, because a similar unrest appeared during the same time in Québec's television and popular music industries.

From the mid-1980s to the 1990s, however, Québecois authors and publishers succeeded in turning the tide, so that their share of top-selling books increased again to some 40% (the average for the whole period 1970–1990). A similar recovery was also observed in other cultural industries, particularly television and music (Dassas 1992; Grenier 1992).

This recovery may to a certain extent be explained by new public policies supporting Canadian and Québecois cultural industries, but it was mostly the result of a kind of general mobilization of artists and decision makers that succeeded in winning public support for national culture. For example, in the book industry, the Québec government established in 1984 a new policy favoring reading, and the Canadian federal government undertook in 1985 to help the print industry financially and to favor its control by Canadian corporations.

Nevertheless, for the period 1970–1990, more than 60% of top-sellers in Québec are of foreign origin, and the situation appears quite different depending on whether authors or publishers are considered. For the whole period, while Québec authors led with 38% of all titles (*n* 451), U.S. authors accounted for 31% and French writers followed with 24%; other English-language writers (mostly British) represented a meager 2.6%, yet ranked better than English-Canadians (who accounted for less than 2%). Writers from the rest of the world shared the remaining 4.6% of all titles.

Figure 2 shows that these general trends did change—though not dramatically—over time. As has been said before, Québecois authors showed a strong start, lost 10% in the middle period, and made a comeback at the end. The same trend, but less important, may be observed with French authors, while U.S. and other foreign writers showed a growing presence from 1970 to 1975, then attained a relative stability.

If the distribution of top-selling authors according to national origin shows signs of a "tricultural struggle" (between Québec, the United

FIGURE 2   The 451 leading titles in Montréal's *La Presse* weekly lists (1970–1990)

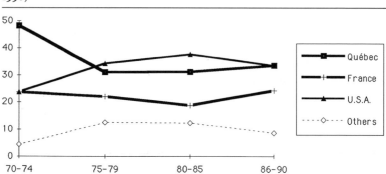

States, and France), the situation appears quite different with publishers. Here the battle involves only two opponents: Québec publishers controlled about 47% of top-selling books from 1970 to 1990, while French publishers led with more than 52% of all titles (the remaining 1%—four titles—comprised three France-Québec co-productions and a single book from a U.S. publisher). Whereas Québec publishers are responsible for almost all top-sellers of Québecois or Canadian origin, French publishers control most of their own national production as well as imports from the United States. True, most U.S. best-sellers in Québec are translated and published in France before they appear on the Québec market: from 1970 to 1990, of the 125 top-sellers of U.S. origin, 96 (i.e., 77%) came through France. Moreover, this domination by French publishers increased over time: from 1976 to 1990, their share of U.S. titles climbed from 63% to 94%.

To sum up, even though at the beginning of the 1970s Québecois authors and publishers showed a small lead over their French and U.S. competitors, their share of the market dramatically dropped thereafter, until the mid-1980s, and their following recovery was not big enough to get back to the former situation. The main reason for this evolution lies in the increasing presence among Québec top-sellers of French-published translations of U.S. and other English-written best-sellers, creating a very unusual situation in Québec's cultural industries. Logically, France might be expected to help Québec maintain its French culture, or at least, as in the television, film, and popular music industries, France may be too far away to offset the massive invasion of U.S. cultural products. In the book industry, however, France not only dominates the French-speaking international community (including Québec), it also acts as "the relay of U.S. cultural imperialism" (Saint-Jacques 1987).

This multicultural configuration of Québec best-seller lists contrasts radically with the overwhelming presence of local authors in *Publishers' Weekly* yearly lists of best-sellers in the United States (1968–1992). Table 1 shows that during this period, U.S. authors accounted for 87% of all 619 titles;[6] other English-language writers (essentially from the U.K. and Commonwealth countries) accounted for 11%, and the rest of the world shared the remaining 2%. If one considers only the 100 top-ranking books, it appears that U.S. authors are responsible for about 90% of all titles. The U.S. domination seems to increase slightly over time, but variations between U.S. and foreign top-sellers stay within a 3% range around the average.

By comparison, an English-Canadian list of 200 top-sellers from

TABLE 1   Top-Ranking Best-Sellers in the United States According to Authors'
National Origins (%)

Origins	1968–1972 (n = 125)	1973–1977 (n = 125)	1978–1982 (n = 124)	1983–1987 (n = 122)	1988–1992 (n = 123)	Total (n = 619)
USA	83.2	84.8	85.5	90.2	86.2	85.9
English-language	12.8	12.0	12.9	7.4	13.0	11.6
Others	4.0	3.2	1.6	2.5	0.8	2.4
Total	100	100	100	100	100	100
Missing[a]			1	3	2	6

SOURCE: *Publishers Weekly*'s annual lists of 25 top-ranking titles, 1968–1992.
[a] Six titles in the *Publishers Weekly* list could not be located (see note 6).

the Montréal's daily *Gazette* (1969–1987) shows that titles of Canadian
origin (including a single book by a French-Canadian author)[7] accounted for only 20%, British and Commonwealth titles for 11%, and
other foreign titles for less than 3%; the remaining 66% were U.S. best-
sellers. If one considers only the 100 leading books, Canadian titles numbered only 14; there were 11 British and Commonwealth best-sellers, and
2 other foreign books; U.S. best-sellers numbered 73—a proportion that
is only 14% smaller than U.S. authors' share in their own national market! This Canadian top 100 list also indicates that U.S. domination
is increasing, from 73% of the 52 top-sellers of the 1970s to 81% of the
48 leading titles of the 1980s; during the same period, Canadian books
dropped from 17% to 8% (the proportion of other imports remained the
same—around 10%).

The English-Canadian best-seller market thus appears much more
dominated by U.S. competition than the Québec and French-Canadian
market. Despite the French publishers' strategy of offering to Québecois
readers hundreds of translated U.S. successes, the barrier of language
gives Québec an effective cultural defense, whereas in English Canada,
British and Commonwealth cultural traditions offer at the most a very
small degree of protection against U.S. invasion.

▪ ▪ U.S. Fiction: The Main Cultural Invader?

The persistent if not growing presence of U.S. best-sellers in the
Québecois and Canadian lists must, however, be examined by distin-

guishing between genres. In Québec it coincides with the increasing popularity of the novel (a best-seller field in which imports dominate) and the diminishing importance of essays and practical or "how-to-do" books (in which Québecois authors and publishers previously enjoyed their greatest successes).

The Québec top-seller sample makes the usual distinction in media best-seller lists between fiction and nonfiction, with further categorizations between nonfiction works, these distinctions being dictated by the needs of thematic and aesthetic analysis.[8] Five categories of best-sellers are thus obtained: (1) fiction (mainly novels, a few collected short stories, and comic books) represents the leading category, with 224 of the 451 titles (49.7%); (2) biographies (narrative nonfiction) represent 85 books, or 18.8%; (3) essays (nonnarrative and nonfunctional nonfiction) make up 18.4% of the top-sellers (83 titles); (4) practical books (nonnarrative and functional nonfiction) account for 11.5%, or 52 titles; and (5) others (nonnarrative fiction—poetry, dramatic works, song lyrics), comprising the residual category, represent only 1.6% (7 titles) for the whole period.

From 1970 to 1990 these global proportions changed significantly, as shown in Figure 3. The main evolution relates to the increasing presence of fiction (novels), whose proportion went up from a modest 32% at the beginning of the 1970s to an overwhelming 72% at the end of the 1980s. Other categories of best-sellers conversely dropped: biographies

FIGURE 3   The 451 leading titles in Montréal's La Presse weekly lists (1970–1990)

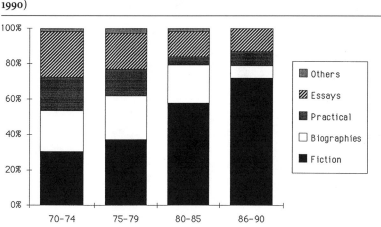

showed the greatest decrease (from 22% to 7%), but essays and practical books also fell significantly (from 26% to 13% and from 19% to 8%, respectively). This increasing popularity of best-selling fiction is indeed corroborated by surveys of readership made for Québec's department of culture: in 1989, out of a total population of about 7 million Québecers (6 million of whom were French-speaking), 4 million read books (all kinds) "at least from time to time"; of these, 2.7 million read books "regularly"; moreover, there were 2.7 million "at least occasional" best-seller readers, including 1.8 million "regular" readers. These data also indicate that novels are the favorite books of 53% of all readers, and of more than 60% of best-seller fans (Lemieux and Martin 1993, pp. 12–14).

However, the growing importance of best-selling novels may also be seen as a menace for Québecois writers, because it is precisely in novels that foreign competition is stronger. Figure 4 clearly indicates that while fiction represents around 60% of U.S. and French best-sellers, it constitutes only 32% of titles written by Québecois authors. Since Québecois writers account for 40% of all kinds of best-sellers, this means that they are responsible for only 25% of novels. On the other hand, local authors have written 57% of essays and 75% of practical books. This is quite normal, since essays and how-to-do books are often related to the socio-political context and the lifestyles (health, education, consuming, and so forth) of a given collectivity.[9] Yet essays and practical books, as previously shown in Figure 3, are proportionately losing importance in Québec's top-seller lists. So the main challenge to Québecois authors pres-

FIGURE 4   The 451 leading titles in Montréal's La Presse weekly lists (1970–1990)

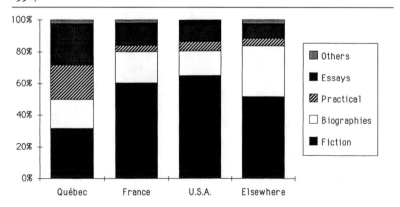

ently relates to their ability to write novels that are as popular as foreign imports.

A similar but surely more problematic situation is also observed in English Canada: if Canadian authors are responsible for only 14 of the leading 100 best-sellers (14%) for the period 1970–1987, these Canadian titles include only 4 works of fiction out of 51 (8%), against 10 nonfiction titles out of 49 (20%). If one considers the 200 most popular best-sellers, the Canadian presence increases to 20% globally, or to 11% for fiction and 27% for nonfiction.[10] As observed with Québecois writers, Canadian authors succeed better with essays and practical books of local concern than with novels. But contrarily to the situation in Québec, the U.S. appeal in Canada is also predominant in nonfiction: more than 25% of nonfiction best-sellers appearing on the U.S. top 100 list also figure on the equivalent Canadian list. A common language between neighbors thus seems to facilitate also sharing the same popular culture. However, the opposite is not necessarily true: the small number of translated U.S. nonfiction books that figure on Québec best-seller lists, compared with the strong presence of U.S. novels, might be a result of a lack of interest in U.S. nonfiction not so much among Québecois readers as among French publishers (who view the content of such works as often appearing irrelevant for European readers).

Being part of North America, Québec obviously shares with its Canadian and U.S. neighbors (and particularly with New England and Eastern Canada) many common geographical and historical experiences, as well as economic, political, and cultural values. This similarity is clearly evident in most popular culture products (television, cinema, music, but also in sports, hobbies, clothing, food, and so forth).

This, however, does not mean that there are no differences. In the case of best-sellers, Bonnassieux (1990, p. 123; Bonnassieux et al., 1991, pp. 84–85) emphasizes that 64% of 383 top-ranking best-sellers listed in *La Presse* (1970–1987) are "super-sellers" only in Québec; they appear neither in U.S. nor in French or English-Canadian top-seller lists. This 64%, of course, includes nearly all (98%) of the best-sellers written by Québecois writers, but also 41% of all super-sellers of foreign origin: 95 titles (43 of them U.S., 49 French, and 3 English Canadian) that either enjoyed moderate success on their national best-sellers lists or never figured on them at all were nevertheless acclaimed in Québec. Bonnassieux further adds that even if U.S. titles are generally sold in Québec by French publishers, only 20 of the 100 most popular U.S. best-sellers in Québec are present on French best-seller lists.

From these data it appears that Québec's readership does not accept indiscriminately any kind of cultural import. However, this collective selectivity cannot be explained simply by international marketing processes, much less by local ones, since for all its specificity, the choice does not favor Québecois authors and publishers. What, then, does explain Québecois readers' activity in the reception of best-sellers? Does Québecois culture favor specific aesthetic, narrative, factual, or ideological values in best-seller content? Clues to the answers to these questions might be found first in general thematic analysis of the *La Presse* sample, then in comparative analysis of a few top-ranking books in Québec, Canada, and the United States.

▪ ▪ How to Summarize a Book in Two Words

Studying best-selling novels in the United States from 1969 to 1979, Long (1985) points out the following recurrent themes: sex, love, ethnic or racial conflict, success or failure, and lack of deep interpersonal relationships. Our analysis of the 451 titles from the Québec top-seller sample (*La Presse*, 1970–1990) offers quite similar findings; moreover, differences can be partially explained by methodological specifications.

Each title in the Québecois top-sellers sample is summarily coded [11] along two classical dimensions in sociological analysis—namely, the dominant themes in both the "private" and "public" spheres of social relations.

In the private sphere (see Table 2), analysis focuses on the personal goals suggested to readers by either characters (fiction and biographies) or topics (all kinds of books); the leading categories are "social or economic success/failure" (wealth, fame, and power), which accounts for 25% of all best-sellers, followed by "affective success" (love and friendship: 18%), "psychological success" (personal self-esteem, self-control, and balance: 15%), and "cultural success" (arts, science, and sports: 9%); there are, however, 27% "unclassifiable" books, as well as more than 5% with "no leading private theme." It must be said that titles appearing in these last two categories are mostly essays and practical books.

If one considers works of fiction separately from biographies, clear differences appear; indeed, 69% of biographies are in the combined social and cultural success categories, compared with 39% of fiction titles, while the affective and psychological success stories are novels (44%) much more often than they are biographies (19%). There are no significative diachronic differences in these general trends; indeed, as shown

TABLE 2   Private-Life Themes in Québec Top-Ranking Best-Sellers According
to Genres, 1970–1990 (%)[a]

Themes	Fiction (n = 223)	Biographies (n = 86)	All books (n = 451)
Social success	29.9	45.9	25.3
Cultural success	9.4	23.3	9.3
Love/affection	27.8	5.8	18.0
Internal struggle	16.6	12.8	15.1
None	7.6	10.6	26.8
Unclassifiable	8.6	2.3	5.5
Total	100	100	100

SOURCE: 451 leading titles in Montréal's *La Presse* weekly best-seller lists (1979–
1990).
[a] There is no list for 1984.

later by qualitative content analysis of typical titles, these characteristics
of fiction titles and biographies are easily explained.

Yet much more interesting differences become visible by cross-
tabulating private themes and authors' national origins, which shows
that 50% of all stories (fictional and biographic) written by U.S. authors are social-success stories, compared with 36% of those created by
Québecois writers, and only 19% of those written by French authors. On
the other hand, affective success seems to be a French specialty, forming
28% of their narratives (35% of works of fiction), compared with 22% of
Québecois, and 17% of U.S. stories. Best-seller readers in Québec appear,
then, to keep alive a very old stereotype, since they prefer U.S. tales
about money and power, but French stories about love, while top-selling
Québecois fiction titles and biographies borrow from both traditions.

Differences are less clear-cut in the public sphere, the main reason
being the greater number of categories, for which we were generally
inspired by the Marxist distinction between infrastructure and super-
structure, but mostly by empirical observation of various kinds of social conflicts mentioned in the corpus, including class, race, gender, and
generation.

Table 3 indicates that macrosocial problems (politics, social classes,
science, religion, and so on) account for 48% of all titles, while microsocial problems (gender, generation, or unspecified interpersonal relationships, meaning relations inside small groups and peer groups)

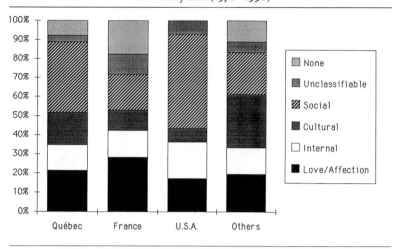

FIGURE 5   The 309 fiction and biographical titles included in the 451 leading titles in Montréal's *La Presse* weekly lists (1970–1990)

TABLE 3   Public-life Themes in Québec Top-Ranking Best-sellers according to Genres (%)

Themes	Fiction (n = 223)	Biographies (n = 86)	All Books (n = 451)
Macrosocial			
Politics	4.9	28.9	14.9
Race/Ethnicity	11.7	7.0	7.3
Freedom	9.4	9.3	6.4
Class	8.1	7.0	6.0
Environment	1.8	–	3.5
Science	0.9	2.3	5.6
Religion	3.6	3.5	4.4
Crime	14.3	12.8	9.8
Microsocial			
Interpersonal	12.6	23.3	11.3
Gender	12.6	2.3	8.6
Generation	7.6	2.3	5.3
None	4.5	2.3	12.0
Unclassifiable	8.1	–	4.9
Total	100	100	100

SOURCE: 451 top-ranking best-sellers in Montréal's *La Presse* weekly lists (1970–1990).

represent 25%; crime (a category including both micro and macro dimensions) represents 10%. There are 54 books (12%) with no visible or leading public theme; most of these (33) are practical books.

In macrosocial categories, fiction distinguishes itself by the importance attributed to class and ethnic/race relations, while (party) politics dominate in biographies; essays also show a strong interest for politics (the theme of 31 out of 83 essays), but also for science (11) and religion (8).

Crime is more a concern for fiction or biographic tales than for essays. In microsocial categories, relations between genders and generations appear more often in fiction and essays; biographies rather characterize themselves by general interpersonal relations.

Thematic differences according to authors' origins are not as easily observed in the public as in the private sphere; still, crime is a distinct U.S. specialty (18 of 33 crime stories were written by U.S. authors, accounting for 23% of all U.S. novels and biographies). U.S. authors also lead slightly in stories dealing with classes and generations. Freedom (as opposed to oppression) is a French favorite (44% of all stories in this category were written by French authors). The single Québec distinction appears in the small "environment" category (all 4 stories in this category were written by Québecois writers).

Crime—the typical U.S. specialty—is also the principal category whose presence increased from 1970 to 1990, but particularly in the late 1980s; politics and generations also increased (but less significantly) during the same period. On the other hand, freedom, genders, and interpersonal relations lost popularity. It should be pointed out, however, that these differences are observed on very small numbers of titles (10 or less) for each category and period.

Is there a winning combination between private and public themes? It appears that social success is mainly combined with societal problems or struggles such as crime (18 books), race/ethnicity (14), and class (11), while affective success is combined, predictably, with gender (15) and interpersonal relations (11). Freedom often appears without any significant private theme (10 titles): collective liberation makes individual goals irrelevant.

To sum up, our analysis of 451 top-ranking best-sellers (including 309 fictional and biographic stories) suggests that in Québec, from 1970 to 1990, French-speaking readers preferred books of foreign origin in a proportion of 62%; of those cultural imports, essentially from French publishers, U.S. authors (translated into French) represented the major part (31%, compared with 23% for French authors and 8% for other foreign writers). With a share of only 38% of their national best-seller market, Québecois writers were in a far more precarious position than U.S. authors, who shared more than 85% of their market; nevertheless, Québecois writers compared well with their English-Canadian colleagues, whose presence in their own market, from 1969 to 1987, showed a weak 20%.

The persistent if not growing presence in Québec of foreign best-sellers can also be related to changes in the tastes of the best-selling readership, with nonfiction (more often local) increasingly losing ground from the 1970s to the 1990s against (mostly imported) fiction. That does not mean, however, that Québecois best-seller readers indiscriminately accept any imported book, since more than 40% of foreign top-sellers in Québec do not appear in Canadian, French, or U.S. lists of top-ranking titles. The Québecois readership also distinguishes itself by thematic selection according to national origin: it prefers French stories whose private and public leading themes deal with love and freedom, but most of all enjoys U.S. stories telling about wealth and crime.

Finally, this statistical analysis indicates that Québecois writers and publishers fared better in the late 1980s than during previous periods. This seems to suggest that the local book industry's actors finally understood the changing trends in readers' tastes. It could be expected, then, that recent local productions in Québec would either show growing thematic similarities with foreign competition or better develop specific fields of interest for their readership.

These hypotheses rely, of course, on concise statistical classifications that may certainly be considered superficial. The next part of this paper, then, will aim to document our demonstration, with broad narratological and ideological analysis of a smaller sample of typical U.S., Canadian, and Québecois super-sellers.

▪ ▪ A Closer Look at Selected Samples

We shall try now to get a closer look at the texts at issue. For this, we have selected the ten most successful best-sellers in terms of amount of time spent on the lists for the last two decades from each of the three markets—Québec in the French language, Canada in English, and the United States. Though so limited as not to be totally reliable in relation to the general statistics of distribution according to national origin, genre, or main themes, these samples do give us a more concrete idea of the differences between the three markets. The books they isolate make a small enough number that they can actually be analyzed for content and compared according to a number of different criteria. And it is easy enough to add a few more items to try and recover meaningful categories missing from these very restricted assortments.

Shortlists from Three North American Super-Seller Charts

QUÉBEC IN FRENCH

1. Toffler, Alvin. 1971. *Le choc du futur* (*Future Shock*), United States.
2. Peck, M. Scott. 1987. *Le chemin le moins fréquenté* (*The Road Less Traveled*), United States.
3. Norwood, Robin. 1986. *Ces femmes qui aiment trop: La radioscopie des amours excessives* (*Women Who Love Too Much*), United States.
4. Hebert, Anne. 1970. *Kamouraska*, French ed. Québec.
5. Cousture, Arlette. 1986. *Les Filles de Caleb. Tome II: Le Cri de l'oie blanche. 1918–1946* (*Caleb's Daughters: The Snow goose's shriek*),* Québec.
6. Mahmoody, Betty, and Marilyn Hoffer. 1988. *Jamais sans ma fille* (*Not Without my Daughter*), United States.
7. Bach, Richard. 1973. *Jonathan Livingston le goéland* (*Jonathan Livingston Seagull*), United States.
8. Bergeron, Léandre. 1970. *Petit manuel d'histoire du Québec* (*Little textbook of Québec's history*),* Québec.
9. Lambert-Lagacé, Louise. 1988. *Le défi alimentaire de la femme: Préserver son capital santé en retrouvant le plaisir de manger* (*The Feminine Dietary Challenge: To Protect One's Health Capital while Rediscovering the Fun of Eating*),* Québec.
10. *Le nouveau Bescherelle: L'art de conjuguer. Dictionnaire des 8,000 verbes* (*The art of verb conjugation*).* 1972 and regular new editions. Belgium.
11. Bourin, Jeanne. 1989. *Les pérégrines* (*The women pilgrims*),* France.
12. Jardin, Alexandre. 1988. *Le zèbre* (*The Zebra*),* France.

CANADIAN ENGLISH

1. Fonda, Jane. 1981. *Jane Fonda's Workout book*, United States.
2. Iacocca, Lee. 1984. *Iacocca, an Autobiography*, United States.
3. Puzo, Mario. 1968. *The Godfather*, United States.

* These titles are not, to our knowledge, available in English translation.

4. Peters, Thomas, and Robert Waterman. 1982. *In Search of Excellence*, United States.
5. Shulman, Morton. 1979. *How to Invest your Money and Profit from Inflation*, Canada.
6. Michener, James. 1978. *Chesapeake*, United States.
7. Bach, Richard. 1970. *Jonathan Livingston Seagull*, United States.
8. Clavell, James. 1981. *Noble House: A Novel of Contemporary Hong Kong*, published in the United States; the author, however, has at different times been based in Australia, U.K., Canada, and the United States.
9. Stewart, Mary. 1979. *The Last Enchantment*, U.K.
10. Herriot, James. 1981. *The Lord God Made Them All*, U.K.
11. Atwood, Margaret. 1981. *Bodily Harm*, Canada.

UNITED STATES
Note: All titles on this last list are from the United States.

1. Givens, C. 1988. *Wealth Without Risk.*
2. Allen, Robert. 1980. *Nothing Down.*
3. Fonda, Jane. 1981. *Jane Fonda's Workout Book.*
4. Uris, Leon. 1976. *Trinity.*
5. Diamond, Harvey and Marilyn. 1985. *Fit for Life.*
6. Fulghum, Robert. 1989. *All I Really Needed to Know I Learned in Kindergarten: Uncommon Thoughts on Common Things.*
7. Iacocca, Lee. 1984. *Iacocca, an Autobiography.*
8. Kowalski, R. W. 1987. *The 8 Week Cholesterol Cure.*
9. Bach, Richard. 1977. *The Adventures of a Reluctant Messiah.*
10. Dyer, W. W. 1976. *Your Erroneous Zones.*
11. King, Stephen. 1976. *The Dead Zone.*
12. Ludlum, Robert. 1982. *The Parsifal Mosaïc.*
13. Michener, James. 1978. *Chesapeake.*

For instance, works of fiction normally tend to turn over in the market-place more quickly than works of nonfiction and so offer more variety, as readers of the latter tend to acquire fewer of their chosen genre than do readers of the former (how many recipe books have you ever read, and how many novels?). Thus the super-sellers do not give as prominent a position to narrative fiction as one might expect: only three such titles are to be found on the Québecois shortlist, a less unsatisfactory five on the Canadian one, but only a meager two on the American one. To give another perspective on this, consider the fact that the five best-placed authors in terms of overall showing on the American lists are all novelists (Stephen King, Robert Ludlum, James Michener, Tom Clancy, and Sidney Sheldon). It is, then, particularly appropriate to consider the frequency not only of titles but of authors on the lists and to modify the samples accordingly.

This modification leads to the addition to the American selection of a Stephen King title (*The Dead Zone*), a Robert Ludlum title (*The Parsifal Mosaïc*), and a James Michener title (*Chesapeake*—already on the Canadian list); to the Canadian list of Margaret Atwood's *Bodily Harm*; and to the Québecois list of Jeanne Bourin's *Les pérégrines* and Alexandre Jardin's *Le zèbre*. It also allows for the appearance in the Canadian group of a Canadian novelist, when there was none in the list of ten; and in the Québecois group, it corrects another imbalance according to national origin, as the Québecois list of ten includes only American, Québecois, and Belgian authors. Both Bourin and Jardin are French, and French writers account for at least one quarter of all best-sellers in the Québecois market. Even though such additions lead to an unequal number, the samples thus provide an adequate enough ensemble of qualitative data for comparison.

Before going on to any content analysis, a predictable difference in mobility from market to market for the super-sellers originally written in English should be pointed out. While seven of the top Canadian super-sellers are also part of the top 100 American best-sellers (Fonda, Iaccoca, Peters and Waterman, Michener, Clavell, Herriot, and Le Carré, and not counting Bach, on it for a different title), none of Québec's translated super-sellers are from this restricted ensemble. The distance here is not only linguistic but geographical as well, as we observed at the beginning: books translated from English mostly come to Québec from France.

Even so, the strength of U.S. editors on this continent appears quite overwhelming, especially when one considers the cultural lack of interest of the American public for its close neighbors. Mexico, being somewhat more exotic than Canada, has had the privilege of being the subject of a specific Michener saga and was of course dealt with in *Texas;* nonetheless, these works have not as yet proven to be among the most successful of his novels on the market. As for Canada and Québec, we are obviously talking here of a no-man's-land, of a virtual nowhere. Typically, in *Chesapeake,* a novel that ranges as far as Africa and the West Indies, Canada is twice alluded to, once as a place where snow geese hatch and once as a haven for runaway slaves; nothing more. As one can easily see, in this sense, the already very free market of mass-circulation books on this continent is essentially a U.S. one, the only effective barriers to its actual monopoly being linguistic—Spanish or French.

It still remains for us to look at what it is that these authors say with which their public so strongly agrees. The main topics that seem to bring success in nonfiction are how to make money (Givens, Allen, Iaccoca, Peters and Waterman, and Shulman), how to maintain good physical health (Lambert-Lagacé, Fonda, Diamond, and Kowalski), how to maintain good mental health (Peck, Norwood, and Dyer), and how to achieve wisdom (Bach, Herriot, and Fulghum). Sex is strangely left out of the limelight; Penney's *How to Make Love to a Man* ranks 37th in the American super-seller list, and one has to go as far down as the 75th position to find the counterpart, *How to Satisfy a Woman Every Time.* In this respect, the other two markets do not show appreciable differences.

Otherwise, the Québecois list is somewhat atypical. Wealth does not seem to matter as much, while a sound mind is more of a fascination—one finds no money books on it, but two out of the three psychology ones. Foretelling the future (Toffler), resisting kidnapping (Mahmoody), understanding one's national history (Bergeron), and writing correctly (Bescherelle) only appear on that list. What is telling in this instance is that Norwood, Peck, Toffler, and Mahmoody, all of whom show strongly on the list, were first published by American editors. With the change of market, these books were promoted in the scale of relative success. Their impact, and therefore their cultural value, changed.

▪ ▪ Reading the Novels

There remain the novels whose themes are in most cases more equivocal. We have studied elsewhere the existence of a very basic form of plot valid for a majority of the narrative best-sellers—in a nutshell, that of a character of exceptional strength enduring hardship until he forces destiny to his side (Saint-Jacques et al. 1994, chapter 3). It is sufficient here to say that it is a typical American form of plot, as *Trinity, The Dead Zone, The Parsifal Mosaïc, The Godfather, Chesapeake, Jonathan Livingston Seagull,* and *The Reluctant Messiah* easily reveal to any attentive reader, though the last one does so in a roundabout kind of way. It carries over national boundaries, as *Bodily Harm, The Last Enchantment,* and *Les filles de Caleb* also show. Only *Kamouraska, Les pérégrines,* and *Le zèbre,* all in French in the Québecois market, deviate from this model, all of them dealing mainly with sentimental passion while escaping from the sentimental romance mold.

This leads us to a wider type of variance. While in all developed countries women tend to read more novels than men, the top of our charts contain more books "for men." We shall consider here works written by male authors, with male heroes and an emphasis on action rather than sentiment, as books for men. Eight such novels are among the samples (*Trinity, Chesapeake, The Dead Zone, The Parsifal Mosaïc, The Godfather, Noble House, Jonathan Livingston Seagull,* and *The Reluctant Messiah*), and all are American; to this group one can add *The Last Enchantment*—of the same type, though from a British female author. The five others (*Les pérégrines, Les filles de Caleb, Le Zèbre, Kamouraska,* and *Bodily Harm*) are all of other origins, three from Québec and two from France in the Québecois market, and one from Canada in the related market. On the other hand, Danielle Steel, Judith Krantz, and Colleen McCullough, the most successful writers for women, do not fare as well, ranking, in terms of the United States' most widely read authors of best-sellers, 7th, 12th, and 25th, respectively. As for the feminists, no matter what you hear about *Fire with Fire* or *Backlash,* they rate even lower, though even that might still appear to be a considerable event from time to time. *Bodily Harm* appears as the strongest title in our English-language samples, at only the 54th position on the Canadian list, and the equivalent on the American list is Nancy Friday's *My Mother, Myself,* which is no higher than 55th. Women have obviously not yet overcome.

How should this curious imbalance be interpreted? A possible hypothesis could be that as women read more, so they also consume a more varied fare, while men stick to well-known and tried authors whom they trust. Another explanation might be that women tend to partake more as consumers of "men's" novels than men do of "women's" novels. And, of course, the sentimental romance that accounts for such a strong part of the feminine market does not show in this context of best-sellers. Is anybody more widely read today than Barbara Cartland? Whatever the reasons, with the King, Ludlum, Clancy, Sheldon, L'Amour group, joined recently by John Grisham, crowding the top of the American best-seller lists, the United States manages to reign supreme on the English-language popular market of male violence and bloodshed in book form as well as on television and film.

The Québec situation is different again; though King has the strongest American individual showing on the charts, the most widely read

American writers are not mainly from the group into which King falls. Bach's *Jonathan Livingston Seagull,* a kind of fable and the highest-ranking American work of fiction on the list, is anything but a violent suspense. Of the nonfiction works, those by Norwood and Mahmoody are obviously meant for a female public, while those by Toffler and Peck are rather more unisex in appeal. The four French-language novels in the sample are typical feminine fare, mostly about love. One should notice, though, that Jardin is a male author with a hero of the same sex in his novel—but is it ever completely about love, and even marriage! One should also note that Germaine Greer's *The Female Eunuch* maintains the 20th position overall, for a much stronger feminist showing on the Québec list than on the other two lists. We can offer no easy explanation for the better visibility of women's readership in Québec but it is difficult not to notice. Actually this is exactly what should be expected in relation to the larger proportion of women readers, and it is the English-language market that offers the unexpected.

There are yet other differences. One is clearly linked to a commonly held prejudice about the American people's lack of interest for its own high culture. Of the 100 top super-sellers from the United States, very few call to mind the literary canon of critically established great works—at best, Herman Wouk's *War and Remembrance* and an indisputable foreign occurrence, Gabriel Garcia Marquez' *Love in the Time of Cholera,* amounting to 2 titles in all. One would have expected maybe Philip Roth, William Styron, Saul Bellow, John Irving, or Paul Auster. The Canadians make a place at the top for their own Northrop Fry, Margaret Atwood, Farley Mowat, and Robertson Davies, plus foreigners Wouk, Solzhenitsyn, Garcia Marquez, and Graham Greene, for a sum of 12 titles. The Québecois already have a highly respected literary novel of their own, Anne Hébert's *Kamouraska,* in 4th place on the super-seller list, and approximately 20 canonical works in their 100 strongest sellers, of which half are from Québec. What should one make of those findings? That the smaller the nation, the fiercer its pride in its canonical literature? Of course one could challenge the comparability of the samples: *Publishers Weekly* selects according to the total number of copies printed, while the other two lists rely on information taken from bookstores, hence turning out somewhat different data. Still, one is left to wonder whether the American public, influenced by a national critical consensus, ever converges to buy a chosen few of its own literary masterworks. Canadians, and Québecois apparently even more so, do so not only for their own authors but also for foreigners. It appears that the massive strength of the American market works to the detriment of public literary recognition.

These broad remarks can of course give but a glimpse of the complexity and intricacy of the themes touched on in the texts included in the samples, especially the novels. Comparison according to main themes, generic plots, and literary value remains quite sweeping and shows very little of what goes on in the world of fiction; novels—and for that matter all narrative works, biographical or historical—rarely have as simple a theme as nonfiction works, which avoid the complexities of recreating life. They need to be properly understood, as literary research has amply shown, employing a type of close attention that delves deeper than the simple search for similarity of plot line and main themes.

For instance, *The Godfather*, the story of the rise of a Mafia capo, is a clear enough case of a theme of resistance to aggression centered on the power of money. Nonetheless, its relation to the world of crime gives it a moral overtone quite absent from its nonfiction financial "how to" counterparts. It is easy enough to tie it to the "endure and succeed" main topic of narrative best-sellers and classify it as typical "male" fare. But the simple fact that in *The Godfather* the hero is a villain, or more precisely that the character who wins in the end is a very dangerous gangster, creates a fascinating ambivalence of interpretation that the critics were quick to point out as soon as the work was released. This obvious tale of American success shows the rise of modern organized crime in a totally corrupt society, where nobody is either able or willing to even curb somewhat the greed and cruelty of thugs who like to pose as honorable feudal lords. Don Corleone, the main character, is both a savior for his endangered family and a ruthless mobster. Are we to understand that the "good" deed in terms of family values somehow redeems the career in crime of the hoodlum? As it is written, the plot ends positively—the protagonist wins. One should not be surprised that *The Godfather* fared well in Hollywood; they normally thrive on happy endings there.

Another interesting and tricky case is provided by *Trinity*, which relates the birth of the IRA and Sinn Fein and, as such, has to do with national resistance to oppression. But then, of course, it inevitably deals with class struggles and again with the sacrifices of individuals to common causes. Eventually, if read in that light, it also purports to show how riches can be milked out of a colonized land. But whatever perspective one takes on the main theme, a deceptive ethical point here lies in the appraisal of the virtuous defensive action carried out by the Irish terrorists who, in the end, after countless injustices, succeed in blowing up weapons stocked by the other side, thus killing nobody and even saving lives in the future. But is it really what the IRA had turned to when Uris wrote his book? History does tell another tale. Here once more the violent are shown as justified in performing acts of aggression that are nicely glamorized so as not to shock too much.

An interesting aside here is that while the Americans have pushed a novel on the Irish resistance to the top of their charts, the French have elected as their most-read American best-seller, in 6th position overall, Alex Haley's *Roots*. Their second-highest book, and first-ranked novel on the lists, *Louisiane,* from Maurice Denuzière, also deals with slaves of African origin in the United States. Of course, Louisiana was once French and many Irish have found a second homeland in the United States—it still seems that the sins of one's neighbors sell better at home than one's own. Does one find greener pastures on the other side, or juicier evils?

The Dead Zone provides yet another typical example of fictional justification of violence. The plot in this instance pits a hero who has acquired a paranormal power of foresight against a dangerous politician bound to become president of the United States; if that happens, the hero "knows" the new president will launch a world war. There is no stopping the villain, who cleverly and ruthlessly gathers ever more momentum. Nobody else sees the danger that looms ahead; alone, the hero must save his country and the world as he cannot, of course, show proof of what he only paranormally "knows." So he attends a political rally, where he takes a gun and fires at the candidate whom he cannot otherwise impede. It all ends well enough, as the targeted victim hides behind a child so the hero, not daring to hurt the innocent, stops shooting and ends up being the only person killed in the proceedings. Nevertheless, the politician fails in his bid for power, as proof of his cowardice is preserved on film and used effectively against him in the following course of events. There are at least two readings for this ending. One is that the generous sacrifice of one's life might in extreme cases save the world against very difficult odds; the other is that if you "know" that a politician will lead the country toward great evils, you have a duty to take a weapon, bring it to a political rally, and shoot this enemy of the people. A chilling thought—there is not always a handy child about to shield! To choose but one instance, was, then, Lee Harvey Oswald, who sacrificed his life in such circumstances, a hero after all?

On the Québec list, on the other hand, *Kamouraska* also has to do with violent crime, as its heroine is a murderess, using not the hand that kills, but rather the head that plots and guides those who act for her. While she succeeds in her crime, she is caught and severely punished. Not only does she lose her lover, she is forced to marry a man she despises. In this instance, violence seems to offer no redeeming characteristics. None of the other novels on the Québec shortlist either has to do with violent deeds or sanctions them favorably if they somehow appear. But one should not make too much of this disparity, as the longer list of 100, for instance, contains a good enough number of American action novels. However, the relative difference of emphasis tends to agree with our previous findings in this respect. In American culture violence is often valued as commendable not only in real life but also in the realm of fiction; in Québec's culture, such a tendency apparently matters less.

The overview given here purports to establish exploratory grounds for comparison and obviously much work remains to be done in the field. We have mainly tried to show with this rapid overview that in the general book trade in North America, where the only actual hindrances to the free circulation of goods are of a linguistic nature, national cultural differences resist up to a point the trend toward globalization, but of course far less so in the case where this obstacle does not exist. So, to briefly touch on the theme of NAFTA and its cultural impact on cultural industries, which we seem to have totally left aside up to now, it should be obvious that this neglect on our part is tied to the nearly complete lack of relevance of this agreement in the sector. The Canadian-English market is already largely dominated by the American editors and we see nothing that could change that situation. The Québec market is more autonomous, though dominated to a point by French editors, and NAFTA matters even less in this instance. Neither the push toward globalization of the cultural markets nor the nationalistic countermeasures created against this trend by smaller states should disappear very soon. In areas of trade where liberalization has nearly completely won the day, such as in the English-Canadian book industry, there is very little change left to anticipate from NAFTA, GATT, and such agreements. The barriers to free circulation that seem to carry most weight are of a quantitative or a linguistic character—the size and inertia of the American market, the different languages of the Québec and Mexican markets. And who would expect much change there?

NOTES

The authors wish to thank their colleague Claude Martin from Université de Montréal, also a member of this team studying best-sellers, as well as their research assistants: Caroline Bergeron, Izabela Greulich, Pierre Huard, Alain Poiri, and Nicolas Tremblay. Without their help, not only statistical data processing but also general interpretation would have been much more arduous. It should also be mentioned that the team studying best-sellers is only a part of a multidisciplinary research group studying cultural industries, of which Roger de la Garde and Line Grenier are also members.

1. This is to imply not that best-selling books did not exist in Québec before 1970, but rather that best-sellers gained much more visibility then than they had enjoyed previously, as a result of the following factors: the growth of book readership in the 1970s, following a substantial increase in the education level of the francophone Québecois population during the 1960s; the fact that publishers and bookstores began to use the term "best-seller" as an advertising or marketing device; and the fact that leading media started compiling best-seller lists on a regular basis.

2. At the time, we considered 1970 to be the starting point of such lists in Québec. However, we recently found an earlier list published at the beginning of the 1960s in Montréal's weekly *Le Petit Journal*.

3. Owing to translation or distribution delays, usually from the anglophone to the francophone markets, the U.S. list begins in 1968 and the English-Canadian one in 1969.

4. For a detailed methodological discussion of best-seller lists, see Martin (1994).

5. After 1990, *La Presse* divides Québec and foreign fiction and nonfiction into four separate lists; this makes it impossible to compare the relative performance of local and foreign top-sellers.

6. The total number of best-sellers should be 625 (25 books a year × 25 years), but there are a few missing data.

7. Jean Chrétien's *Straight From The Heart* (1986)—political memoirs of a Canadian Liberal Party politician, then out of office, who came back as prime minister of Canada in 1993; it ranked 108th.

8. Since biographies are "stories," like novels, their analysis can be done by using the same narratological methods as are used for novels; essays and practical books, however, need other approaches.

9. Even in the U.S. list (*Publishers Weekly*), where the presence of local authors is globally overwhelming (87%), U.S. writers fare better in nonfiction (91%) than in fiction (81%).

10. Thus it appears that best-selling English-Canadian authors rarely attain as big an audience as their U.S. competitors. Such a situation does not seem to exist in Québec and French Canada, since local writers' presence in the top 100 titles in *La Presse*'s list is similar to its global proportion in the whole data base of 451 titles.

11. Titles were first coded from data found in bibliological repertories such as *Books in Print* (United States) or *Livres d'ici* (Québec); this information, as well as

missing data, were then cross-checked during brainstorming sessions between members of the research team.

BIBLIOGRAPHY

Bonnassieux, Marie-Pierre. 1990. "Les best-sellers au Québec et l'internationalisation du marché du livre." Master's diss., Université de Montréal.

Bonnassieux, Marie-Pierre, Jacques Lemieux, Claude Martin, and Isabelle L'Italien. 1991. "Les best-sellers et leurs lecteurs." *Communication* 12(1): 75–99.

Dassas, Véronique, ed. 1992. *L'industrie de la publicité au Québec en 1991–92*. Montréal: Publicité-Club.

Grenier, Line. 1992. Can you Teach an Old Dog New Tricks? "Chanson" and the Québec Music Industry in the 1980s. Paper presented at the 18th Conference of the IAMCR, Guarujà, Brazil, August.

Grossberg, Lawrence, Cary Nelson, and Paula A. Treichler, eds. 1992. *Cultural Studies*, London: Routledge.

Krieling, A. 1978. "Towards a Cultural Studies Approach for the Sociology of Popular Culture." *Communication Research* 5(2): 240–263.

Lemieux, Jacques, and Claude Martin. 1993. "La lecture des revues et des livres au Québec." *Chiffres à l'appui* 7(4): 1–20.

Lemieux, Jacques, and Denis Saint-Jacques. 1990. "Un scénario motif dans le champ des best-sellers." *Voix et images* 44(Winter): 260–268.

Long, E. 1985. *The American Dream and the Popular Novel*. Boston: Routledge.

Martin, Claude. 1985. "Comme des petits pains chauds: Essai d'économie industrielle du best-seller en français au Québec." *Communication* 7(4): 107–127.

———. 1986. "L'économie politique des industries culturelles et la prise en compte des auditoires." *Communication* 9(3): 109–117.

———. 1994. "Ce que racontent les listes de best-sellers." In *Ces livres que vous avez aimés: Les best-sellers au Québec de 1970 à aujourd'hui*, ed. Denis Saint-Jacques, Jacques Lemieux, Claude Martin, and Vincent Nadeau, pp. 65–122. Québec: Editions Nuit Blanche.

Saint-Jacques, Denis. 1987. "La France, relais de l'américanité dans le marché du livre au Québec." *Cahiers pour la littérature populaire*. Fall: 57–63.

———. 1988. "Ce que racontent les best-sellers." In *Le risque de lire*, ed. Hans-Jurgens Greiff. Québec: Editions Nuit Blanche.

Saint-Jacques, Denis, Jacques Lemieux, Claude Martin, and Vincent Nadeau. 1994. *Ces livres que vous avez aimés: Les best-sellers au Québec de 1970 à aujourd'hui*. Québec: Editions Nuit Blanche.

13

Cultural Exemptionalism Revisited: Québec Music Industries in the Face of Free Trade

LINE GRENIER

COMPARED WITH THE Free Trade Agreement (FTA) between Canada and the United States and the large-scale debate as well as the intense political controversy that accompanied it, the North American Free Trade Agreement (NAFTA) went virtually unnoticed in Québec. The highs and lows of the negotiation round of this American-written document attracted little attention. In fact, what appears to have aroused people's interest was the ambivalence of Canada's newly elected Liberal prime minister, Jean Chrétien, about NAFTA; it remained unclear for a while whether Chrétien, having been a strong opponent of the agreements negotiated by his Conservative predecessor, Brian Mulroney, would sign NAFTA or even agree to observe Canada's engagements in the FTA.

The relatively low popular interest in NAFTA does not mean that the issue of free trade has been exhausted, but it certainly looked like an old story was being revived. Very few, if any, new arguments have been expressed, either in favor of or in opposition to the agreement. Most of the public statements made by businesspersons, local and provincial politicians, and community leaders had a sense of déjà vu. So too had the positions of the representatives and members of the various artistic and cultural milieus, whose active involvement in this kind of debate has been a mainstay of modern national politics in Québec. Musicmakers, artists, and their trade representatives and professional associations, together with provincial groups of affiliated trade unions, were among the most outspoken and vociferous critics of the FTA. If they have kept a relatively low profile in the debate surrounding NAFTA, they nevertheless maintained the same basic political credo: cultural industries must be exempted from free trade agreements.

This paper critically examines Québec music organizations' stand on the free trade agreements and the rationale of "cultural exemptionalism" underlying their discourse. By focusing on some of the key forces that came into play in the development of the Québécois popular music terrain over the last ten to fifteen years, I wish to show that their position is indicative of how a small cultural industry has adopted new production and marketing strategies in keeping with alternative ways of representing itself, its constituents, and its products, both within Québec and across its boundaries. It has done so by coming to terms with recent international developments (such as the increased market concentration of multinational record companies and the greater integration of major labels with international multimedia and entertainment conglomerates), as well as with long economic recession and nationwide political turmoil. These new production and marketing strategies and the representations they articulate form an integral part of an altered process of *mise en société* or societization of Québécois popular music which, I argue, constitutes the ideological background against which the discourse on free trade can best be understood.

▪ ▪ Music Organizations' Critical Stand on the FTA and NAFTA

Québécois artists and music producers, like most of their Canadian colleagues, have been critical of the FTA and NAFTA agreements. In their view, the accords further jeopardize the economic viability of local music production, diminish even more the political scope for public subsidies and interventions, and thus increase the threat to cultural sovereignty (Berland and Straw 1991). From the outset, music-related trade and professional associations[1] have also voiced their concerns about the impact of the liberalization of trade on the indigenous industry, and hence the local music culture it produces and promotes, and have made "exclude culture" their unanimous battle cry.

Like most supporters of the exemption-of-culture argument, their position tends to be based on a twofold assumption: that the future of national, regional, or local cultures should not be determined exclusively by market forces, and that state interventions should not be dictated only by economic concerns—arguments that have been used since the

1930s by many a Canadian politician and activist engaged in the ongoing quest for cultural sovereignty. Music people claim that protective measures with regard to culture are especially important for Québec, given its marginal position as the only official French-speaking society within the predominantly English-speaking North American context. They consider government support of the local music industry to be fundamental, given the minority position of Québécois artists and their products in both the national and the international scenes. Furthermore, given that what is at stake is Québécois music, seen as the very symbol of modern Québécois culture, and hence one of the main driving forces behind the survival and development of *le fait français* (the French factor) in the Americas, it has been argued that the collective advantages gained from the exemption of cultural industries would outweigh the disadvantages some individuals may suffer because of it.[2]

Having lobbied powerfully on this exemption issue, Québec's sole music trade organization, ADISQ, welcomed with relief the inclusion of the cultural-exemption clause and its accompanying "notwithstanding" clause in the FTA (Article 2005) and, more recently, their reproduction in full in NAFTA.[3] Insofar as these provisions allow the federal and provincial governments to continue to subsidize the recording of an album or the production of a live concert by a local artist, and the Canadian Radio-Television and Telecommunications Commission (CRTC) to continue to regulate the content of radio and television programs, ADISQ agrees that they offer some insurance against a further marginalization of indigenous musical products on both the markets and the airwaves. But it is not yet rejoicing. On the one hand, it takes issue with the definition of the term "cultural industry" used in the FTA and NAFTA, which establishes a distinction between artistic/intellectual and material sectors of cultural production, and thereby limits the application of the exemption clauses to the former. In a study on the impact of free trade commissioned by the federal ministry of communication in 1988, ADISQ representatives argued that the close and indissociable links between the artistic and material production of music make it effectively impossible to protect the recording, publishing, and promotion of music if, at the same time, the trading of compact discs, pressing of master tapes, and distribution of records is liberalized. Because the material activities by and through which artists produce music are left out, these free trade agreements cannot be said to adequately protect the indigenous music industry which relies heavily on adequate Québec-based nationwide distribution and pressing of master tapes to compete against its much larger and wealthier American competitors (ADISQ 1988). On the other hand, as a spokesperson pointed out in a telephone interview in March 1994, ADISQ is still very much concerned with the Canadian government's political will to effectively make use of the cultural-exemption clauses, and if need be, as agreed by the signing parties, to take "measures of equivalent effect" in response to actions inconsistent with NAFTA. In short, the inclusion of exemption clauses may represent a step in the right direction, but as long as the scope of such clauses is limited to artistic production and their enforcement is still uncertain, they remain an imperfect means with which to counterbalance what ADISQ and other music lobby groups view as the inevitable negative implications of a general liberalization of trade within North America.

How can we account for Québécois music organizations' stand on free trade? In whose interests do they so fiercely advocate the exemption of culture? Whose culture are they attempting to protect? Drawing from Michel Foucault's approach to discourse (Foucault 1991) as material "traces of practices, and accomplishments of projects" (Allor and Gagnon 1993), I argue that music-trade people's discourse on free trade and its underlying rationale of cultural exemptionalism[4] can best be understood in light of the "politics of truth" which works to regularize the production of statements on popular music in Québec, local versus foreign music, and Québécois music and, hence, accounts for its social and political effectiveness. I therefore wish to examine some of the developments that have marked the recent history of Québec's musical terrain in order to point out the particular social, economic, political, and cultural conditions that have rendered this particular discourse (as opposed to any other) possible.

■ ■ **The Changing Politics and Economics of Popular Music in Québec**

The 1980s have been extremely eventful years for an indigenous music industry still in the making. Left in the throes of crisis at the end of the 1970s, it managed to overcome what could well have spelled its doom, by means of a process through which, however, power relations within the music milieu have been altered, ideological and aesthetic divisions that were instrumental in making nationalism the key item on the agenda of popular music since the 1960s displaced, and hence the definition of Québec as a distinct musical entity transformed.[5]

Overcoming the Crisis: The Consolidation of the Local Industry

By the end of the 1970s there were unmistakable indications that the international music business, dominated by a small group of multinational companies, was facing its most severe crisis in thirty years. After having flourished steadily from 1973 to 1978, the industry was confronted with an unprecedented decrease in international record sales which accompanied the recession. Significant loss of revenue and profit induced the majors not only to lay off thousands of workers but also to significantly reduce the number of new releases and concentrate production and marketing resources on well-established artists and products.

Similar conservative strategies were adopted by Canadian affiliates, responsible at that time for more than 80% of the albums produced/released in the country. Between 1978 and 1979 the number of albums they released in Canada had already dropped by 33%. From 1980 to 1989 they produced an average of 2,191 albums annually, 17% less than the 2,645 albums produced in 1977 and 1978. Not surprisingly, their production of Canadian-content music[6] was more severely affected than that of foreign music albums—the former decreased by 47% and the latter by 15% (Leclerc et al. 1989). Moreover, in their attempt to minimize financial risks, and given the limited size of the market for French-language recordings, Canadian affiliates, that had invested heavily during the more prosperous early 1970s, withdrew almost completely from this sector. French-language vocal music represented 61% of their total production in 1978, but only 5.5% in 1987! Over the same nine-year period, however, the overall volume of record production by Canadian-owned record companies (mostly small or medium-sized businesses located mainly in Ontario and Québec) increased. Between 1977 and 1978, production grew by 32%. After a significant cutback in 1979 (−36%), activities picked up again in 1980–1981. Thereafter, Canadian labels produced an annual average of 764 albums—that is, there was a noticeable gain of 22% compared with the average of 627 albums produced in 1977, 1978, and 1979. Their participation in Canadian-content music, after having gone down by almost 25% at the end of the 1970s, remained relatively stable throughout the 1980s, at approximately 36% of their total production. They too were more cautious with regard to French-language recordings, and did not invest as much as they had in the past.

Despite a relatively good showing, Canadian-owned companies did not succeed in fully compensating for the disinterest of large foreign firms in Canadian-content music, and especially in French-language vocal music which, at the peak of the crisis in 1984, represented 22% and 2%, respectively, of the 4,665 new albums released in the country (Tremblay 1990).[7] This situation impacted seriously on Québec's music industry, whose indigenous sector, it should be noted, was not yet twenty years old. From 1978 to 1983, 54% fewer recordings by French-speaking artists were released in Québec (Blain and Cloutier 1986). The production of foreign French-language albums in Québec plummeted by 79% between 1980 and 1989. Furthermore, the production of albums by local artists, which account for three-quarters of total French-language record sales in the country, suffered a 53% drop in 1978–1979. It picked up gradually to approximately 75 albums per year in the years following, but still remains 10% lower than in 1978. The majors and their Canadian affiliates, which contributed to the release of 180 new Québécois albums in 1979, produced only 38 albums in 1987 (ADISQ 1989). The void their loss of interest created was progressively filled by new Québécois independent labels, which emerged in the very crux of the crisis and have controlled close to 85% of local popular music production since 1986.[8]

The structural crisis in the international record industry and the general economic recession that was aggravated by the escalation of interest rates in Canada were not, however, the only problems faced by Québec's music industry at that time. It also had to cope with the waning of popular interest in so-called nationalist music, hitherto a mainstay of popular music in the province: sales of albums by Québécois artists, which usually represent 18–20% of the total record sales in the province, had reached an unprecedented low of 10%.[9] The fervor of Québec's nationalist movement reached its peak with the 1976 election of a separatist party, the Parti Québécois, and this certainly played an important role in the commercial and cultural vitality of local French-language music throughout the decade. The frustration, disillusionment, and bitterness that followed the defeat of the referendum on the sovereignty of the province in 1980 likewise contributed to Québécois' loss of interest in local music. The constitutional turmoil created first by the unilateral repatriation of the Canadian constitution by Trudeau's Liberal government in 1982, and later by the failure of the negotiations surrounding the Mulroney-led Conservative government's new constitutional proposal (the Meech Lake Accord), have given a second wind to the nationalist movement and hence to nationalist music. In the fall of 1995, during another referendum campaign on sovereignty, the popularity of Québécois music was clearly on the upswing. While the defeat of this referendum has led some to fear once again for the future of local francophone popular music, the closeness of the results (49.4% in favor of sovereignty and 50.6% against) and the strong support of French-speaking voters for sovereignty have given others reason to remain optimistic.

The political turmoil did not only affect audiences' tastes and consumption patterns, it also affected, albeit to varying degrees, artists who were associated by the public with the nationalist movement. Considered to be among the few sure bets of the time by local record producers, some of these artists reacted by taking several years to release a new album. Given the scarcity of new local material and audiences' mixed reactions to it, others appeared in concert less frequently, did not take part in so many television programs, and modified their marketing strategies with regard to radio broadcasting in their attempt to avoid media overexposure. In fact, while the political turbulence made waves throughout Québec's artistic and cultural circles, it enjoyed a particular importance in music milieus, where it contributed to exacerbating ideo-logical conflicts and power struggles that dated back to the early 1960s—that is, to the very genesis of the local industry. These internal conflicts and divisions among music-trade people, which had long been raging behind the scenes, were taken up by the media and became matters of public debate in the early 1980s. The often-proclaimed two founding schools of thought regarding popular music in Québec engaged in a battle that lasted until the mid-1980s. As they portrayed each other, the battle opposed on the one hand a snobbish intellectual clique known not only for its more or less overt nationalist and leftist discourse but, more importantly, for its connections with the provincial government and its funding institutions—in short, for its close affiliation with the establishment; and on the other hand, a kitsch, tacky, populist clique, consisting of pragmatic and realistic advocates of mass culture and es-pecially of mass consumption, who claimed to be the real voice of the Québécois people, but who were primarily interested in defending their own commercial interests. What appeared to be an irreconcilable gulf between the two approaches to popular music production and, by cor-ollary, between musical traditions associated respectively with *chanson*[10] and pop-rock, has proved to be the divided yet dynamic terrain from which a renewed and consolidated local industry emerged.

Québec's music industry started to show clear signs of being on the upswing in 1986–1987. French-language music consumption had risen to over 55% and, perhaps more importantly, local firms had gained almost total control over record production in the province, being responsible for 90% of new releases by Canadian French-speaking artists (Brunet 1991). It had thus taken the industry approximately six years to recover from the crisis, a period marked by a twofold consolidation process that involved the strengthening of the industry's economic and commercial foundations as well as the sociopolitical amalgamation of its formerly scattered and conflicting corporate interests.

Locally owned independent labels have been key to the industry's commercial revitalization insofar as their emergence and rapid growth provoked a shift in the distribution of power between local and transnational firms in Québec and contributed to the economic reinforcement of the local industry as a whole. But they did not succeed in gaining control of the market simply because most of their operations are centered on French-language genres—that is, on markets that the transnational conglomerates no longer found sufficiently lucrative or attractive; they also achieved such a success because, despite their relatively small size, their almost chronic underfinancing, and the lack of appropriate industrial and commercial infrastructure, they played the cards of diversification and vertical integration well. Using similar strategies to those adopted by transnational firms, albeit on a much smaller scale, they were quick to form allied industry interests in artist management as well as in television, film, video, and stage production.

But perhaps most importantly, Québécois independent labels could also rely on an increasingly active network of locally owned national distributors. In fact, some of today's most successful independent labels developed out of distribution companies that decided to move into record production. Audiogram constitutes a perfect example of these new distributor-based companies that have played such a significant role in rejuvenating the local record industry. Created in 1982, it grew out of Distribution Select, owned by Archambault Musique, one of Québec's oldest music retailers, and also got involved in Spectra-Scène, already one of Québec's most influential concert-stage production firms. In the 1930s, control over record distribution had proved to be the trump card that enabled U.S.-owned record companies to gradually become economically dominant on the international music scene. In the 1980s Québec's trade people played the same trump card and it undoubtedly helped French-language music to get more adequate exposure than it had when the majors, which gave priority to their own English-language products, had the lead in this key sector. In gaining control over record distribution, they gave the local industry as a whole a clear advantage over its English-Canadian counterpart—most Canada-owned record companies still depend on transnational firms and their affiliates for distribution (as well as for the production of master tapes and pressing).

But as Audiogram director Michel Bélanger explained, the private sector would not have taken such a financial risk at such a difficult time without knowing that there would be government support: "At the time of the creation of the Audiogram association, we could feel there was going to be [government] support for the record industry over the next five years . . . Without it, Audiogram would not exist" (Blain and Cloutier 1986, p. 12 [my translation]). Bélanger refers to programs that were established in the early 1980s by both the provincial and federal governments in their common attempt to foster investment in the private sector, encourage domestic cultural production, and further build audiences for local products. These programs are symptomatic of the new orientation of Canadian policy in the 1980s, which emphasized the economic significance of cultural industries. Together with book publishing and film production, sound recording received increased direct support, since it was considered to be a type of cultural production "which could most easily be made self-sufficient in the present market" (Berland and Straw 1991, p. 278). Because these measures did not provide the means with which to modify the overall distribution, retail, and broadcast structure of music markets prevailing throughout English Canada, they may well have contributed to the growth of an independent, domestically owned recording sector, but they served, nevertheless, to strengthen the dominant position of transnational firms which already exerted control over most key sectors of the industry, including distribution (ibid., p. 282). Given, however, the specifics of Québec's industry and market structure, the decreasing interest of transnational affiliates in the French-language sector, and the increasing involvement of domestic interests in distribution activities, the implications of government programs for Québec's local music industry were not as paradoxical. At a time when local investors had the opportunity and the will to fill the void created by the majors' loss of interest in Québécois music, government support came in handy, but in the end, it was merely one of many forces contributing to the establishment and growth of several small independent labels.

In a similar vein, national broadcasting policies and regulations (such as the Canadian Content Regulations), which presumably provide further, albeit indirect, government support for domestic cultural production, were said to have also reinforced the dominance of transnational firms in Canada (ibid.). However, the CRTC's recent rulings, in particular with regard to French-language vocal music (FVM), were not inconsequential to the economic consolidation of the local industry in Québec. This highly controversial policy, which forces radio stations to devote at least 65% of their programming to French-language music, was introduced in accordance with the CRTC's ongoing attempts to provide French-speaking communities in Canada with programs that recognize their particular needs and concerns. While it has been the object of ongoing debate ever since its adoption in 1973, in Québec music milieus, it is viewed as an imperfect but essential means of protecting French-language culture, specifically Québécois music, and of ensuring its adequate diffusion (Grenier 1993b).

The debate over broadcasting policies is a particularly pointed example of the increasingly strong and well-organized lobby exerted by Québec's music industry which, as of approximately 1983, started to gain more visibility and credibility in various political arenas. A good part of this lobby has been executed by ADISQ, whose activities behind the scenes and in the media have increased significantly over the last decade. In the first few years following its creation in 1979, ADISQ concentrated most of its activities on the organization of the annual Félix Awards— the Québécois counterpart to the Juno Awards in English Canada and the United States' Grammy Awards. Designed to celebrate and promote commercial and musical achievements by local artists and music firms, in fact, for nearly five years, they proved a battleground that revealed the scope of the power struggles that were raging within the industry. As the media coverage of the televised awards ceremony indicates, the celebration of local music culture was indeed pushed into the background. There were harsh disputes over the nomination procedures, the definition of awards categories, and the composition of juries that were suggestive of the tensions between the industry's corporate and individual members around issues of, among other things, nationalism, copyright, and royalties.

The extent and exact nature of the changes that have occurred within ADISQ since the mid-1980s—that is, their underlying rationale, or the economic and political alliances upon which they rested—have yet to be fully grasped. But the immediately observable modifications pertain to nomination criteria that apparently allow a fairer distribution of Félix trophies between pop-rock and *chanson*-oriented artists, and to boards of directors whose composition perhaps more adequately reflects the different tendencies of producers and other corporate interests. However, the overall results of these changes are unmistakable. In the span of a few short years, the local industry transformed its public image from that of a highly divided group of Québec-minded semi-professionals to that of a united whole composed of accomplished, well-organized, and increasingly powerful trade people who voice their concerns, defend their interests, and take a stand on most national or international music-, media-, and entertainment-related issues, including broadcasting policies, copyright legislation, and free trade.

Displacing Internal Divisions: The Emergence of a Local Mainstream

There is no doubt that the economic and political consolidation of the local industry has not fully eradicated internal conflicts within Québec's music milieu. It appears, however, to have shelved or displaced some of the aesthetic, cultural, and genre-related divisions that were central only ten years ago. It has subjugated them to the imperative of economic survival of the industry which, in my view, called for the transmutation of how local popular music was produced, as well as what it stood for, both socially and culturally. I argue that the emergence of a new form of musical communication, the Québécois mainstream, has been instrumental in this unmistakable, albeit gradual, transmutation process.

I use the notion of mainstream to refer not to an aesthetic category or a musical genre/style but rather to a whole way of conceiving, making, and using popular music. The Québécois mainstream denotes a specific pattern of relationship between highly heterogeneous products enjoying great commercial success, and forming a diffused yet recognizable whole; these relationships link a number of songs that get both the widest exposure and broadcast diffusion and that come to stand, within the confines of Québec, for the ever-changing familiar, popular, common, and "middle of the road" in music. These social and economic relations that constitute the mainstream mediate a form of musical communication that evolves around single-song units rather than records, and is characterized by the mixing rather than the mere juxtaposition of musical genres and styles.

Since the 1930s and 1940s the popular record has been the predominant form of musical communication. Standing for what most people in North-Western societies know as "music," it represented much more than a particular technology (digital sound recording) and a specific commodity (vinyl records) associated with the rise of format radio as well as with the emergence of both the pop audience and the teen market. Rather, it has been the archetypal embodiment of music as the final product of an industrial process which, as Frith argues, "cannot be understood as something that happens *to* music" but rather as "a process in which music itself is made." He asserts that "twentieth-century popular music means twentieth-century popular record, not the record of something (a song? a singer? a performance?) which exists independently of the music industry, but a form of communication which determines what songs, singers, performances are and can be" (Frith 1988, p. 12). Built into the basic structure of the modern music industry is the idea, therefore, that the "popularity" of music can be measured and defined by record sales and radio airplay, and that "popular music" can be seen as a fixed performance (a recording) with acoustic, musical, and emotional qualities that musicians are somehow expected to reproduce in concert.

The structural changes in the international music business that followed the crisis of the 1980s have, however, defied the hegemonic status of the popular record form. Technological shifts such as the replacement of black vinyl by cassettes and compact discs as popular music's principal medium and commodities were among the most obvious changes. But they were inseparable from other, perhaps more significant, modifications, which included the move from record sales to copyright exploitation as the industry's basic source of income, the shift from radio to TV and video as the main promotional devices, and the substitution of individual record buyers by television, film, and advertisement audiences as target consumers. These diverse yet convergent changes reworked the relationship between recorded and live music, artists and fans, radio formats and musical genres, radio and television audiences. They threw the pivotal basis of the popular-record form into question and, as such, paved the way for the emergence of a new form of communication—the mainstream pop.

In Québec this new socioeconomic mode of organization of music surfaced in the mid-1980s. Québec's music-trade people started to put more emphasis on the permutation and sequencing of songs viewed as discrete, relatively homogeneous (the three-to-five-minute pop song), and independent, meaningful musical events in and by themselves, the raw material out of which albums, radio, and music television programs are fashioned. Although still concerned with maintaining an acceptable level of record production, they began to accord a great deal more attention to single-song units and their inclusion on radio and television. These new tactics jived with the local industry's attempt to diversify and broaden its market beyond radio listeners and record consumers in order to reach music video viewers, concertgoers, movie fans—in short, everyone exposed to individual song units, regardless of the medium or commodity involved.

In the wake of the song-oriented form of musical communication, music-related industries, which had once relied almost exclusively on the sustained interest of the public in a few well-known artists, their biography, career, and also—especially in the case of *chansonniers*— their political agenda, began to function on the basis of the success of individual songs by new star-performer figures, some of whom tended to be of the flash-in-the-pan variety. The presence of a new generation of artists contributed to the rejuvenation of a popular music terrain in Québec, which had been relatively stagnant since the end of the 1970s. The fact that many rising artists were women who, moreover, did not necessarily intend to build their careers solely on singing but also on music writing further accentuated their impact on what has been traditionally a predominantly male milieu. Furthermore, this new explosion of musical activity has been accompanied by an unprecedented blurring of genres and styles. None of the prevailing genre or style categories seemed to adequately describe and assess the performance, on both stage and record, of artists whose music could not readily be labeled as either *chanson* or pop-rock, hitherto the two pillars of popular music in Québec.

Along with the challenge to traditional genre distinctions came a threat to the superior status accorded to singer-songwriters (especially those of the *chansonnier* tradition) over other performing artists (mainly associated with the pop-rock tradition), from increasingly popular star interpreters and from relatively unknown rising stars whose hit songs were regularly included on Québec's record sales and radio charts. One of the most widely held assumptions of popular music in Québec— namely, that singer-songwriters are the very embodiment of fully accomplished musicianship and that, given that they perform strictly original, indigenous material, they are the only true Québécois artists singing the only authentic Québécois music—was put into question. As a corollary, and with only a few noticeable exceptions, pop-rock singers have often been considered second-rate artists who, like popular *yé-yé* groups of the 1960s who for the most part played translations of U.S.-inspired beebop and rock 'n' roll songs, did not have enough talent to write their own music, and had to rely on the creative labor of those whose foreign hit songs they chose to interpret. Both assumptions were put into question. Symptomatic of this significant change in the distribution of power/prestige between various types of practices that make up Québec's music milieu is the fact that over the last few years an increasing number of well-known local singers have released albums that contain new interpretations of some of the most famous Québécois songs. A phenomenon that a few years ago would have been considered a clear sign of an artist's lack of inspiration is now viewed as the revival of an emerging "classic" repertoire, and hence as a sign of the maturity and richness of Québécois popular music as a whole.

It is important to note, however, that the emergence of the mainstream did not eclipse the popular-record form so much as it complemented it. In fact, the industry appeared to want the best of both worlds, and did so, moreover, with good reason. While music-trade people aimed at keeping up with the most recent trends in the international music and entertainment business by making a move into the mainstream, they could not afford to completely dismantle the popular-record-oriented musical system out of which the indigenous industry grew. Furthermore, given its small size and relatively precarious financial situation, Québec's local industry could not run the risk of jeopardizing a socioeconomic mode of organization of music which, with the economic and legal support of policies designed to protect local products from foreign competition, had just begun to bear fruit on the economic, as well as the political, level.

▪ ▪ Contemporary Articulations of the Québécois Popular Music Terrain

All in all, in the wake of the recovery of the local industry and its two-pronged production and marketing strategies, Québec has experienced a gradual but unmistakable dismantling of most genre and artistic category hierarchical power/knowledge distinctions around which its trade and artistic milieus have been organized since the advent of an indigenous music industry in the early 1960s. These developments have contributed to altering the ways in which popular music is produced, distributed, promoted, and consumed locally. In fact, they have been instrumental in transforming the very process of *mise en société* (Hennion 1988), or societization of popular music in Québec—that is, its social construction through historically contingent linkages between discursive and institutional agencies.[11]

For close to thirty years, the province's musical field has been defined by and through the iterative opposition between two almost mutually exclusive systems. This founding opposition was based on a conflation of politics, musical genre, and performing styles that made other sites of differentiation (with the possible exception of language), such as age, gender, ethnicity, and region, appear secondary, if not completely irrelevant. Despite its severe and profound divisions, Québec undeniably showed the qualities associated with a musical community viewed or defined as "a population group whose composition is relatively stable . . . and whose involvement in music takes the form of an ongoing exploration of one or more musical idioms said to be rooted within a geographically specific historical heritage" (Straw 1991, p. 373). The sense of purpose articulated within this community depended on a strong affective link between, on the one hand, contemporary indigenous musical practices (especially those within the *chansonnier* movement and the pop-rock tradition), and on the other hand, the twofold musical heritage that rendered these musics appropriate to their particular sociohistorical context—that is, Québécois' heritage as a national group of French descent and as one of the few francophone minority groups in North America. Some of the ways in which Québec is currently constructed within its boundaries have similar attributes. Adapted to fit the contemporary soundscape, *chanson*-derived practices remain at the heart of this space against pop-rock forms which are now accepted as legitimate and indigenous. The *chanson* versus pop-rock hierarchical distinction is still a central feature of this musical community, but it no longer discriminates between the authentic "dyed-in-the-wool" Québécois and the foreign "disguised American." What persists is the golden rule, so obvious it remains unspoken—that all Québécois music is sung in French. The language acts, within this binary opposition, as the seal of authenticity that defines the community's sense of purpose. The defining characteristic is not the language proper, but, rather, the way in which the rubric of authenticity and the need to perpetuate the culture underline its use.

In reactivating the heritage of Québécois music, whether of France or the United States, the community, as defined along the boundaries, is still posed in strict opposition to these spaces. This opposition defines rigid bilateral relationships between Québec and France and between Québec and the United States, seen as the two primary reference points for the community. The complex and changing relationships between the Québécois and the French *chanson* and between the Québécois and the Anglo-American pop-rock combine respect, love, and admiration, as much as envy, frustration, and distrust—and are therefore reminiscent of the typical love-hate relationship that Québec has traditionally maintained, albeit in a different way, with both France and the United States. Within this space, Québec is therefore positioned not autonomously but only in negative relationship to the outside—that is, it is influenced by, but distinct from, its two most "meaningful Others."[12]

The mode of relationship characteristic of the musical community is not, however, the only one that currently operates in instituting Québec's musical terrain, its so-called indigenous products, and its audiences. As a result of the changes that occurred over the last eight years or so, Québec is also increasingly defined in terms of a musical scene—that is, in terms of "a cultural space within which a range of musical practices coexist, interacting with each other within a variety of processes of differentiation, and according to widely varying trajectories of changes and cross-fertilisation" (Straw 1991). In contrast to the sense of purpose of the Québécois musical community, that of its musical scene is articulated in terms of alliances rather than of binary opposition. The effervescent mainstream pop contributes not only to the blurring of previously pivotal genre-distinction hierarchies, but also to the hitherto nonexistent mingling of styles, both as musical and performance practices. In the same vein, alliances between traditionally scattered, if not feuding, industry camps form a defining trait of this space within which Québécois music gains its specificity not in strict terms of language, but in terms of ethnicity. From this perspective, Québécois music has to be not French but francophone, and this translates as music from Québec that is not ethnically Anglo. This conundrum was publicly discussed for the first time following the 1990 industry awards at which superstar Celine Dion, who enjoys success both in Québec and English-speaking North America, turned down the award for best anglophone artist for her first English-language album, *Unison*. She made an emotional speech in which she denounced the industry for insulting her, as well as her sympathetic fans, by labeling her an anglophone, thus driving home the point that Québec, within the musical scene, was facing the issue of language in popular music not in terms of poetic and non-poetic forms, *chanson* versus pop-rock, but in terms of culture and ethnicity.

The alliances through which this scene gains its sense of purpose also extend along the boundaries. Rather than being posed negatively in terms of bilateral exclusion, as is the case when the community is communicated along the boundaries, the musical scene is established in terms of multilateral inclusion. The Francophonie, a network of nations that have the use of the French language in common, represents a key point of reference for contemporary scene-oriented musical practices.[13] Musically speaking, it enables alliances between cultures the world over, but, moreover, between musics sung in innumerable languages, for while the French language is the raison d'être for the network, this by no means implies that it is either the first language or the language of choice for most musical performers. While the English language is not excluded out of hand, in practice it remains largely unheard. If the Francophonie proves to be an economically and culturally viable alternative, it could provide not only an international forum for Québécois music, as well as one where artists who sing in languages other than French (and English) are more than welcome, but also an opportunity to further explore, at the local level, musical idioms hitherto excluded from or marginalized within the sociomusical sphere in Québec.[14]

Given that these various patterns of relationships operate simultaneously, the local musical terrain can thus be said to be defined at the interplay of "other" cultural spaces considered to be different and exterior to Québec and distinct yet related concurrent spaces seen as being constitutive of Québec as a whole. Therefore, there no longer exists within this singular pluralistic space a single center from which guidelines for establishing the boundaries of popular music's local terrain are derived, just as there is no longer a clear, unambiguous set of criteria for defining *Québécois* music. While there is still a relatively high correlation between *chanson* and Québécois music, especially French-language music, the latter no longer has the same hierarchical or narrow political connotation. Used perhaps less frequently ever since it lost its emblematic character, *chanson* has become a kind of generic label for any popular music created/made in Québec, regardless of genre distinctions.[15] A particular musical genre that constituted the canon of Québécois music proper, it has become an all-encompassing, generic term that signifies what members of Québec's indigenous industry, and other cultural agents as well, deem a consolidated yet open musical space.[16] There would still be validity to the observation made by music composer Stéphane Venne some thirty years ago that "*chanson* has been loaded with an impossible burden: that of being [for Québécois] what jazz is for American Blacks, opera for the Italians, and so forth. A pivot of Québec culture; a passport to all the countries in the world" (cited in Roy 1992, p. 246); applied to Québec's musical terrain in the 1990s, however, it takes on a different meaning.

▪ ▪ "Cultural Exemptionalism" in Perspective

Music organizations' stand on FTA and NAFTA and their sustained discourse on the importance of exempting cultural industries from the agreements constitute, in my opinion, a particular articulation of the changing politics and economics of popular music in Québec that I have discussed in this paper. From this perspective, I wish to conclude this discussion by taking issue with both the view that cultural exemptionalism represents yet another case of abusive protectionism typically supported by an industrial-commercial logic conveniently wrapped in narrow-minded nationalism, and with the view that it is a typical example of long-standing and systematic anti-American bias.

Given the conflation of nationalism and music-related commercial issues as a key ideological springboard for the development of Québec's indigenous industry during the 1970s, it might be tempting to argue that the "cultural exemptionalism" argument used by music trade groups and organizations is merely a way of preying on nationalist sentiments to protect and promote their own economic and corporate interests. But as I have tried to show, the distinct yet concurrent ways in which industrial-commercial and political-nationalist logics have been articulated over the last ten years or so should not be overlooked.

In contrast to the somewhat "closing in on itself," self-centered tendency largely characteristic of the earliest period of its young but eventful history, the music industry in Québec has progressively put forward an "opening to the outside" approach. On the one hand, as the local music terrain is no longer defined exclusively in terms of a community whose rationale of authenticity is essentially derived from the ongoing exploration of *chanson*-oriented idioms, producing and promoting Québécois music as a whole appears to have become as important, if not more so, than fighting over its sites and modes of internal differentiation. The emergence of the mainstream and musical scene it contributed to establishing has thus been instrumental in initiating an important shift in the traditional link between politics and popular music; this shift has been signaled by, among other things, new promotion and marketing strategies that have ceased to represent Québécois popular music as the mere celebration of a somewhat essentialist form of nationalism. On the other hand, in a context in which Québec is increasingly defined at the cross-section of local and international articulations of musical activity, far from objecting to more extensive trade relations per se, including in cultural domains, actors in the local industry have come to see the establishment of production and distribution alliances and partnerships as a necessity rather than a luxury they presumably could not earlier afford.

It might be argued that the local industry could use to its advantage the liberalization of trade that agreements such as the FTA and NAFTA encourage, to foster and further develop alliances that inform the development of today's musical terrain in Québec, and hence to carve a niche for Québécois artists and products within the international music scene. But it could also be argued that the sociocultural as well as economic usefulness and effectiveness of this strategy depend on the ability of artists and trade people to produce a variety of musics whose potential international appeal lies in the very locality they articulate—that is, insofar as locality is not opposed to globality but is, rather, seen, as Cohen claims, as "a political strategy within a global, plural system" (Cohen 1994, p. 113). From this perspective, the exemption of culture and the protective measures this allows may perhaps constitute not only the sole viable foundation of equitable exchange, but the only condition under which musicmakers from Québec, as from other small or minority nations, can fully participate in today's intensifying global culture.

There is little doubt that in some of its most widely publicized articulations, Québec music industry's discourse on free trade bears traces of the anti–cultural imperialism crusades that, throughout the century, have made more than one Canadian (and some Québécois) politicians, intellectuals, and cultural activists famous. Combined with the fact that critical comments on NAFTA are directed at the music industries and products of the United States but not at those of Mexico, it could be tempting to view this discourse as a typical example of anti-American propaganda. But I think that this remains a much too simplistic and reductionist understanding of the complex issues at stake here. While it is beyond the scope of this paper to engage in an in-depth discussion of key issues such as those pertaining to identities as singular articulations of difference, and belongings (Probyn 1994) as conjunctural manners of being, I have attempted to show the partial and incomplete character of any representation of the cultural relationships between Québec and the United States in terms of a mere dual opposition. On the one hand, while Anglo-American musics have always been both a key pole of attraction and an object of antagonism that mediates the definition of the musical terrain in Québec, they have never been the only one; for historical, linguistic, and cultural reasons, musics associated with France have had a very similar status. On the other hand, consistent with the outward-looking orientation increasingly articulated by its local industry, Québec's way of presenting itself as comprising a distinct musical entity is changing as ethnicity, more than language alone, becomes the pivotal element in the process. Québécois music is therefore increasingly presented as a specifically North American manifestation of francophone music, and local musicmakers as actors who contribute to further developing an international heterogeneous but coherent francophone cultural space.

From this perspective, it could be argued that the stand taken by trade groups on free trade does not so much reflect a bias against the United States as it denotes an anti-anglophone or, more precisely, a pro-francophone America bias. To support the exemption of culture from the FTA and NAFTA may well mean to seek support and protection for various products and practices which, albeit typical of the North American social formation of which they are a product, are constitutive of a francophone space that remains marginalized in the predominantly anglophone-centered "New World Order." What further supports this interpretation is that Québec was among the forty-seven countries and communities whose representatives, gathered at the Fifth International Francophone Summit at Île Maurice in the fall of 1993, unanimously voted a resolution exempting culture from their trade relations within the General Agreement on Trade and Tariffs (GATT). Conceived in preparation for the Uruguay round of multilateral trade negotiations, this resolution acknowledges "the role of the State, of governments, as well as of public and territorial collectivities in the promotion, protection, and expansion of national and regional cultural industries within their respective countries and on the international level," and, in direct reference to NAFTA, describes the exemption of culture as an "effective means to maintain a strong Francophone cultural production" (AFP 1993: B-6 [my translation]).

Québec music organizations' discourse on free trade and its underlying rationale of cultural exemptionalism are undoubtedly highly debatable. But as I have tried to argue in this paper, given the conjunctural conditions under which it has been developed and maintained, it may well have been the only possible discourse these organizations could articulate.

NOTES

The author wishes to acknowledge the support of the Social Sciences and Humanities Research Council of Canada and Québec's Fonds FCAR for financing the research on which this chapter is based.

1. These organizations are ADISQ (*Association de l'industrie du disque, du spectacle et de la vidéo du Québec*), the sole trade organization that represents music producers; UDA (*Union des artistes*), a union whose members are singers, actors, dancers, and radio/television artists; SPACQ (*Société professionelle des auteurs et des compositeurs du Québec*), a professional association devoted to defending and promoting the rights of composers and songwriters; and the *Guilde des musiciens du Québec*, a union that negotiates musicians' working conditions and minimum fee with various employers.

2. Like other supporters of free trade, Lipsey (1988) has argued that the cultural community would not be gaining unambiguously. He views the absence of restriction on temporary entry to the United States, which the inclusion of culture would have made possible, as one of the key benefits of the FTA that musicians, actors, and dancers have denied themselves.

3. It is important to note, however, that these clauses apply only to trade relations between Canada and the United States, since the U.S. government has refused to extend to Mexico the concession it made to Canada.

4. I am borrowing the notion of exemptionalism from Graham Carr (1991), who uses it to describe Canada's overall strategy with regard to free trade negotiations.

5. The arguments articulated in this section have been presented in Grenier (1993a). The author wishes to thank Cambridge University Press for allowing her to reproduce parts of this article.

6. In order to meet CRTC's Canadian-content (CanCon) definition, the selection must have at least two of the following characteristics: music composed by a Canadian; lyrics written by a Canadian; instrumentation or lyrics performed by a Canadian; live performance wholly performed in Canada and broadcast live in Canada or recorded in Canada.

7. Transnationals and affiliates have recently renewed their interest in French-language music. They invested in compact-disc reeditions of Québécois music, a very lucrative market within which local record companies managed, however, to get a fair share.

8. In 1993 there were 80 locally owned record companies as well as 80 independent producers (Tremblay and Lacroix 1993).

9. A record high of 26% was reached in 1973 and 1974, during the often-called golden years of Québécois music. This was an especially good performance given that the supply of locally produced albums was—and still is—nine times lower than that of foreign albums (Tremblay 1990).

10. *Chanson* refers to a local lyric-oriented genre of mixed origins (Irish, French, and Scottish, among others), inspired mainly by France's rive-gauche tradition and the U.S. folk tradition, typically associated with the repertoire of singer-songwriters known for their leftist and/or nationalist political agenda.

11. The following analysis of the changing *mise en société* of popular music in Québec focuses, analytically, on the particular modes of relationships between diverse musical practices that coexist today at the local level (Straw 1991) and on the specific strategies of boundary management (Cohen 1985) of Québec as a distinct

cultural space. Val Morrison and I have developed this twofold analytical framework and have used it to account for the existence and popularity of Québec-born Native duo Kashtin on the Québécois popular music terrain (Grenier and Morrison 1995a, 1995b).

12. It is interesting to note that this equation excludes not only the U.K. as an influential center of Anglo popular music, but Canada as well—two entities which, however, embody the "Other" in political and institutional terms.

13. While there is an ongoing debate as to the centrality France should occupy in this space, the overwhelming majority of member-nations, in which Québec has a strong voice, are indeed working to preserve the multilateral character of the political, cultural, and economic relations of the network.

14. The ongoing popularity of Kashtin—who sing exclusively in their Native Innu, a language understood by some 10,000 people in Québec—and their acceptance as an indigenous musical act (Morrison, in press) typifies this new trend.

15. For example, the sole local magazine devoted entirely to popular music is entitled "Chansons"; numerous rock- and pop-oriented music festivals use the same term to describe their entire program; and Québec's oldest and internationally famous French-language popular music contest is called the Festival International de la Chanson de Granby.

16. This revised status has not, however, eclipsed the presence of *chanson* as a distinct genre. Still a very popular genre among songwriters and music composers, as well as among audiences, it continues to be acknowledged as a fundamental component of Québec's musical history. As a matter of fact, there has recently been an outburst of interest in this type of music, thanks to the emergence of artists who, by reworking the genre, contributed to its popularization with younger audiences who were not active cultural-products consumers when the *chansonnier* movement was at its peak, in the late 1960s and early 1970s.

BIBLIOGRAPHY

ADISQ. 1988. *L'impact du libre-échange sur l'industrie de la musique.* Montréal: ADISQ.

———. 1989. *Musique populaire de langue française.* Report presented at the CRTC hearing on French-language vocal music, Montréal, November.

AFP (Agence France-Presse). 1993. "Une résolution destinée à faire échec à la mainmise US." *La Presse,* October 10, p. B-6.

Allor, M., and M. Gagnon. 1993. *L'État de culture. Généalogie discursive des politiques culturelles québécoises.* Montréal: Groupe de recherche sur la citoyenneté culturelle (GRECC).

Berland, J., and W. Straw. 1991. "Getting Down to Business: Cultural Politics and Policies in Canada." In *Communications in Canadian Society,* ed. B. D. Singer, pp. 276–294. Toronto: Nelson.

Blain, F., and B. Cloutier. 1986. "En bonne compagnie avec Audiogramme." *Chansons d'aujourd'hui* 9(5): 11–13.

Brunet, A. 1991. "The Québécois sound: An expression of heterogeneity." *Billboard,* July 27, pp. F-8, F-24.

Carr, G. 1991. "Trade Liberalization and the Political Economy of Culture: An International Perspective on NAFTA." *Canadian-American Public Policy*, 6(June): 1–51.

Cohen, A. 1985. *The Symbolic Construction of Community*. London: Ellis Horwood, Tavistock Publications.

Cohen, S. 1994. "Identity, Place, and the 'Liverpool Sound.'" In *Ethnicity, Identity, and Music: The Musical Construction of Place*, ed. M. Stokes, pp. 117–134. Oxford and Providence: Berg.

Foucault, M. 1991. "Politics and the Study of Discourse." In *The Foucault Effect: Studies in Governmentality*, ed. Graham Burchell, Colin Gordon, and Peter Miller. Chicago: University of Chicago Press.

Frith, S. 1988. *Music for Pleasure*. London: Routledge.

Grenier, L. 1993a. "The Aftermath of a Crisis: Quebec Music Industries in the 1980s." *Popular Music* 12(3): 209–227.

———. 1993b. "Policing French-Language Music on Canadian Radio: The Twilight of the Popular Record Era?" In *Rock and Popular Music. Politics, Policies, Institutions*, ed. Tony Bennett, Simon Frith, Lawrence Grossberg, John Shepherd, and Graeme Turner, pp. 119–141. London: Routledge.

Grenier, L., and V. Morrison. (1995a). "Quebec Sings 'E Uassiuian': New Trends on a Local Popular Music Scene." In *Proceedings of the Seventh Conference of the International Association for the Study of Popular Music (IASPM)*, ed. W. Straw, held in July 1993 in Stockton, California.

———. 1995b. "Le terrain socio-musical populaire au Québec: 'Et dire qu'on ne comprend pas toujours les paroles. . . .'" *Études littéraires* 27(3): 75–98.

Hennion, A. 1988. *Comment la musique vient aux enfants*. Paris: Anthropos.

Leclerc, J., et al. 1989. *Disponibilité de la musique vocable de langue française au Canada: Le contexte économique et industriel*. Montréal: Média Culture and ADISQ.

Lipsey, R. G. 1988. "Sovereignty: Culturally, Economically, and Socially." In *Free Trade: The Real Story*, ed. J. Crispo, pp. 148–160. Toronto: Gage Educational Publishing.

Morrison, V. In press. "Mediating Identity: Kashtin, the Media and the Oka Crisis." In *Resituating Identity: Race, Ethnicity, and Culture*, ed. V. Amid-Talai and C. Knowles. Toronto: Broadview.

Probyn, E. 1994. *Love in a Cold Climate*. Montréal: Groupe de recherche sur la citoyenneté culturelle (GRECC).

Roy, B. 1992. "Chanson in Québec." In *Encyclopedia of Music in Canada*, ed. H. Kallman, G. Potvin, and K. Winters, pp. 246–247. Toronto: University of Toronto Press.

Straw, W. 1991. "Systems of Articulation, Logics of Change: Communities and Scenes in Popular Music." *Cultural Studies* 5(3): 358–367.

Tremblay, G., ed. 1990. *Les industries de la culture et de la communication au Québec et au Canada*. Montréal: Presses de l'Université du Québec.

Tremblay, G., and J.-G. Lacroix. 1993. *Portrait de l'industrie du disque au Québec: Étude réalisée pour le Ministère de la culture du Québec*. Montréal: Université du Québec à Montréal, Groupe de recherche sur les industries culturelles et l'informatisation sociale (GRICIS).

Part Five

Creativity and Control: Copyright and Contract

. . . .

Mass Communication, Intellectual Property Rights, International Trade, and the Popular Music Industry

STEVE JONES

POPULAR MUSIC IS OFTEN overlooked as the site of cultural struggle. This is in part because it is visual media (film and television particularly) that garner the most attention, and in part because popular music is often considered an even less "serious" cultural form than other types of popular culture. And yet it is in the arena of popular music that cultural policy, intellectual property, and other important issues are most visible. Popular music at least relies more than other media on the exploitation of copyrights for revenue. I will concentrate my analysis on popular music in this chapter.

Popular music in America in the 1980s and 1990s has been characterized by an increased awareness of non-Western music among musicians, music industry executives, and music fans. "World music" is the moniker for recordings employing non-Western instruments and/ or sounds, and it has become a recognized, institutionalized musical category through its use in publications from the industry standard *Billboard* to punk fanzines like *Maximum Rock 'n' Roll*.

Coincident with the birth of world music, the American music industry finds itself competing in a global, internationalized[1] popular music marketplace. Corporate acquisitions that place American record companies under foreign corporate control (for instance, Sony's purchase of Columbia's record and music-publishing interests and the fact that only one major label, Warner Brothers, is U.S.-owned) and stiff competition from foreign record labels whose acts dominate the charts (like Virgin Records' releases by Janet Jackson and Paula Abdul) are forcing a rethinking of the means by which popular music is exploited as an investment with global dividends. The investment is essentially the same as it ever was, represented by the "song" or "album." And the music business has always been international, insofar as licensing agreements (to exploit sales of those investments) existed between record companies in different countries. Popular music, though, especially in regard to rock 'n' roll, is symbolic of America, and though labels may have corporate roots outside the United States, it is American music that these labels continue to make the most of, and from.

The dividends on these investments (songs and albums) now come from a variety of sources, including the exploitation of copyrights in emerging and new markets and the revision of trade agreements. Threats to these dividends come from legislative activities and international agreements that affect the ability to exploit copyright, just as they also come from new technology. Digital media and digital sampling open up new areas for exploitation, by way of sales of new media and royalty options for copyright holders, and make it difficult to enforce copyright by making copying quick, easy, private, and easily concealed.

It is against this backdrop that American record and music-publishing companies (often owned by the same parent company), whether or not they are ultimately owned by corporations outside the United States, are partaking in a flurry of legal activity that leads to a kind of cultural policy by default. That is, as cases involving the music business, trade, copyright, and immigration law are decided, precedents are set which affect the quantity and quality of popular music entering and leaving the United States. The cases, as should probably be expected, are argued largely on the basis of their perceived impact on profit/loss margins of parties involved, or their effects on employment and labor, but rarely (maybe never) in regard to their impact on cultural production and consumption, a point to which I will return. Moreover, as ownership is problematized it is rarely asked whether owners are creators, authors, employers, and so on. This is an issue with great consequences for the discussion of moral rights in intellectual property on an international scale and it has clear connections to free trade agreements.

Additionally, corporate policies that affect the production, distribution, and promotion of popular music may likewise be viewed as formations of cultural policy. However, as with the legal issues to be discussed, they too form a fragmented, often somnambulistic cultural policy dictated by the economics of the music industry, an industry beset by challenges brought about both by its internationalization and by new media technologies. And, difficult as it is to unravel the interests represented in said legal issues, it is virtually impossible to penetrate to the levels necessary to determine and unravel corporate policies.

Thus far, legislation concerning intellectual property issues in international trade in the music industry has focused on three discrete, though related, fronts in the United States. As expected, one front is that of copyright law and another is that of trade law. A third, less-expected front is that of immigration law. I have examined these in greater detail elsewhere[2] and will only briefly go over them here to create a framework for further discussion.

▪ ▪ Popular Music and U.S. Immigration Law

During the 1980s changes in U.S. Immigration and Naturalization Service (INS) laws made it more difficult for non-U.S. musicians to enter America and perform their music. The issue revolves primarily around H-1 work permits for entertainers. In the past, the INS required applicants for H-1 work permits to make their way through a forest of paperwork and to include documentation (in the form of press clippings, recordings, etc.) that proved the entertainer's "distinguished merit."

The wording in the INS law has changed, however, so that the term "distinguished merit" has been replaced by "preeminence." If distinguished merit was difficult to document (the INS provided no definition of it), at least it had a vagueness to it that allowed broad interpretation. The implication of preeminence is that a performer must be popular—for all intents and purposes, a star. Among groups that have been affected by enactment of the new law are the U.K.'s Blow Monkeys, Membranes, and New Model Army, Germany's Bochumer Ensemble, Poland's Stary Teatr, East European folk-jazz ensembles, reggae group Third World, and countless African performers (among them guitarist Chief Commander Ebenezer Obey). The difficulty faced by those wishing to book those groups in the United States is tremendous, since tours must be booked well before the INS bureaucracy grinds out a visa (or grinds to a halt).

A *Village Voice* article correctly placed the origins of the H-1 work permit in a "union-conscious legislature bent on protecting American labor."[3] First drafted in 1952 to allow those with no intention of abandoning their own country to work temporarily in America, the H-1 permit was initially not difficult to obtain. But as the entertainment industry and its unions grew stronger, pressure on the INS to restrict H-1 permits mounted. The 1980s saw music industry pressure on several legislative fronts (the Recording Industry Association of America [RIAA] even moved its offices to Washington, D.C., to be closer to the source of its lobbying efforts). It is not surprising in light of such efforts by the industry that the INS has been subjected to industry pressure, especially when one considers the increase in record sales and radio play accompanying a concert tour. As Steven C. Bell, senior writer and editor of the *Immigration Law Review*, writes,

> the U.S. labor market is glutted with persons who seek careers
> in the various fields of the arts, most of whom are unemployed at
> any one time, and . . . no occupational field in the United States is
> more heavily unionized than the entertainment industry.[4]

Those accompanying an artist (roadies, sound mixers, etc.) are subject to the H-1 rules as well. A work permit category, H-2, exists that allows temporary entry to those who "perform temporary services of labor, if unemployed persons capable of performing such service or labor cannot be found in this country."[5] It is, of course, difficult to show that no one in the United States is capable of performing said service.

Since the musicians' union is exclusively consulted by the INS in these matters, ultimately it is the union that really runs the show, collapsing issues of artistic merit into ones of commercial control or, at the very least, equating issues of artistic merit with commercial success. Access to live performance before an American audience is determined by union executives whose experience of music (as performers and audience members) may bear no relation to the music of those seeking work permits. Moreover, these issues are further confused by quotas "limiting to 25,000 the number of annual visa applications from nonsuperstar musicians, athletes and dancers."[6] Making the limit more problematic is a revision requiring individual members of orchestras, dance troupes, ballet companies, and the like to file for visas. In the past, one visa admitted an entire ensemble. Whither artistic merit for application number 25,001?

The greatest fear among U.S. booking agencies and record companies is that the INS rules will provoke retaliation from other countries' unions and immigration services. The manager of several non-U.S. rock and reggae acts said, "The INS is going to create a cultural trade war. It could cut domestic rock musicians' income in half by preventing them from traveling outside of America to earn money. The Dutch, the French, and the Canadians are already upset about this."[7]

In an era characterized by the continuation of Reaganite and Thatcherite trade policy, it is not surprising to find that trade unions in the U.K. and the United States have a reciprocal agreement. Union officials from each country keep track of performers to ensure that equal numbers are "exchanged."[8]

In many recent cases the only means for a foreign artist to come to the United States is under the guise of a tourist visa. But it would not be surprising to find that modern recording techniques such as multitracking are being used to bypass the INS—it would be difficult to deny entry to a tape recording or a sample of an African singer, or a French horn section, for instance, sent to the United States for additional recording, or for use during a performance.

The musicians' union is also seeking to address the issues technology has muddled for it. It is now circulating a new contract to recording studios that requires that those who program drum machines, computers, sequencers, or any form of electronic equipment that produces music (or, for that matter, anyone who starts any such piece of equipment) belong to the union. The long-standing joke that goes, "Sure, I'm a musician. I play the stereo," may not be so funny. And I can foresee the day that my friends from other countries will need work permits to use my CD player.

Immigration issues are particularly important to attend to, as they affect the circulation of music. Unlike distribution issues, which are most greatly affected by copyright and are concerned with the broadcasting, importation, and commodification of music, the live performance of music can be understood in terms of circulation of sound and musical ideas that creates an opportunity for a different form of exchange. It may nevertheless be commodified exchange (via the purchase of concert tickets, at least), but it is distinguished from distribution insofar as the exchange is not one of goods but, perhaps, is one of services. In that context immigration laws can greatly affect the music of those who provide such a service, especially insofar as there are many, many performers who will not have their music commodified and thereby mass-mediated.

▪ ▪ Technology, Music, and Copyright

Authorship, uniqueness, reproducibility, and a host of other issues preoccupy the business and legal transactions in the music industry. Within that framework, copyright has traditionally been regarded as an author's protection against the copying and pirating of music. It has also been a means for record companies and music publishers, who usually own the copyrights to songs, to ensure income during periods of low sales, and to control the manufacture and distribution of recordings. Copyrights are bought, sold, and exploited via licensing fees and royalties. New technologies that enable a diffusion of authorship and ready reproduction are making traditional copyright protection obsolete.

The most recent and best-publicized controversy over copyright concerned home taping of records and compact discs when the recording industry sought a "tape tax" on blank audio media. Though beginning in the late 1970s, when the recording industry's sales slumped, copyright issues have taken on altogether new meanings with the development of digital recording and digital audio tape (DAT). The Electronics Industry Association's Consumer Electronics Group (EIA/CEG) was at the forefront of groups opposed to legislation sponsored by the RIAA in the United States Congress seeking a tax on blank tapes and audio recorders to make up for revenue allegedly lost due to home taping. The EIA/CEG has agreed, however, to jointly seek legislation with the RIAA "requiring the hardware companies to pay (record) labels a royalty on blank audio-tape and digital recording equipment to compensate for sales lost to home taping"[9] in exchange for the RIAA dropping its request for such a tax on analog media.

These issues obscure the larger concern record companies have about the pirating of recordings. It is, simply put, easier to tax audio media than it is to organize teams of law enforcement officials and attorneys to engage in anti-piracy efforts in various countries (though the latter is a practice the RIAA continues to pursue). Presumably, at some point in the chain of production, even pirates will pay a tax on the blank media they use! In any event, the recording industry's long-term goal is complete penetration of such anti-copying mechanisms as those the Serial Copying Management System (SCMS) built into DAT recorders inhibiting digital-to-digital copying. The RIAA is currently funding research to invent a system that will prevent analog-to-analog copying using digital recorders.

It is also necessary to consider the effects of digital sampling on the use of copyright law. At present recordings using sampled sounds are evaluated by attorneys (and sometimes musicologists) at the record company and clearances secured from copyright holders for a (usually small) licensing fee. Such a system operates informally and does not turn over large sums of money (except in the rare instance of a hit song such as M. C. Hammer's "U Can't Touch This" or Vanilla Ice's "Ice Ice Baby"). Still, this matter has not been solved in any routine, consistent fashion. The trend is toward following guidelines established for compulsory license. If a recording has been publicly released it can be re-recorded, with a mandatory mechanical royalty to the copyright holder. Mechanicals can add up to a large sum, as shown in the case of pre- and post-reunification Germany. Since reunification, all of Germany is covered by Western copyright conventions. The German authors' rights society, GEMA, reported a $53 million increase in revenue (for a 1990 total of $478 million) in the first year after reunification.[10]

The more significant issue in terms of international trade in the music industry concerns the use of samples outside the United States in areas whose culture provides little or no conceptual framework for the ownership of sound. Issues of labor and income are at play, as are cultural issues. Reggae groups, for instance, use backing tracks dozens of times for different songs. These forms of "versioning" are widespread. How should copyright be established in these cases? Wallis and Malm[11] note that in many third world countries musicians record backing tracks that are used by producers for overdubbing singers and other instrumentalists. David Toop suggests that part of the reason for the use of backing tracks is economic: "Versions are obviously a convenient way of making records, as most of the ideas have already been worked out in the original."[12] U.S. record companies argue that since they've paid for the original, which is now being reused, some licensing set-up is in order.

As copyright laws become more alike from country to country, and as new markets are exploited to their fullest, copyright holders will seek new means of exploiting rights. Copyright has less to do with authors' protection and the establishment of an "authentic" original and more to do with profit. New media such as DAT, digital compact cassette (DCC), and mini disc (MD) not only allow increased income from sales of existing product in new formats (as the compact disc did), they also generate income from mechanical royalties and soon also from royalty income derived from hardware taxation.

Record companies have long recognized the importance of copyright as a means of producing income, and the RIAA is very actively engaged in international lobbying to bring copyright legislation to as favorable a position as possible for copyright holders. In 1991 the RIAA was instrumental in passage of new legislation in Mexico that revised that country's copyright law and may earn record companies some $75 million a year.[13] And new legislation in Japan extends copyright protection in that country from thirty to fifty years, and prohibits rental of recordings for one year from their release. It is estimated that the new law may gain record companies up to $1 billion annually.[14] Copyright is clearly a high-stakes enterprise, and a source of income whose importance can rival that of record sales.

▪ ▪ The Import Blockade

With the discussion of sound and copyright as a background, two cases regarding importation of sound recordings will now be considered. U.S. copyright holders have blocked the availability of many recordings issued by non-U.S. labels. The cases set a precedent for blocking importation of recordings (legally licensed for manufacture and distribution abroad) whose copyrights are held by American record companies.

In the first of the two cases, *Columbia Broadcasting System, Inc., v. Scorpio Music Distributors, Inc.,* that was decided on August 17, 1983, the court held that

> phonorecords manufactured abroad and imported by a third party intermediary without the consent of the copyright owner constituted unlawful importation of phonorecords under section 602 of the U.S. Copyright Act. . . . [Such] "importation" infringed the plaintiff's copyright in the phonorecords.[15]

The second case, *Harms Music v. Jem Importers,* that was decided on March 26, 1987, upheld the copyright of a music publisher against the importation of sound recordings containing the publisher's copyrighted songs. Out-of-court settlements between major labels and import distributors followed both cases.

These cases deal with what is commonly referred to as "parallel imports," and the result has been chilling as far as U.S. importers are concerned. Lawyers advised importers that

> the prudent United States purchaser of phonorecords from abroad would have determined, before entering into a purchase agree-

ment, the nature and extent of any American copyright owner's rights to the phonorecords at issue. Since Scorpio Music, however, such a determination would be wise not only with respect to purchases from abroad but also purchases within the United States because of the possibility that the domestic purchaser would be found to be acting within the chain of importation and deemed a contributory infringer.[16]

Ostensibly, major labels and music publishers perceived a threat to their profit margin created by importation of recordings that had been manufactured more cheaply outside the United States. It is more likely, however, that they reasoned that U.S. consumers had a limited budget for their products, and that that budget was stretched too thinly when imports were available to consumers. Though unable to completely halt the importation of records into the United States, they damaged the importers sufficiently to convince most to cease import operations. Along the way they damaged the U.S. independent record label, as U.S. distributors (Caroline, Important, JEM, Rough Trade, Twin Cities) acted as importers but also generally stocked 50% independent label releases. U.S. independent labels have had a difficult enough time getting paid by distributors, and any financial difficulties placed on the distributors trickled down to the independent labels.

Importing records in the United States has never been an easy task to begin with. Import duties on records are relatively high, and unlike printed materials, records are not treated as perishable materials. It also takes some time for a shipment of records to clear customs. These factors, in a market in which timing may be all-important, create problems for the importer.

The implications are interesting for fans of hard-to-find American music that is released by European labels such as Charly, Ace, Demon, and Pathe-Marconi. In Europe there is a great appreciation for jazz and blues records that have long been deleted from the catalogs of U.S. record companies—but whose copyrights those companies still hold. Presumably, then, most Europeans will be able to buy records by American artists that are inaccessible to people in the United States.

Emphasizing the multinational nature of the record industry, Warner, Sony, and PolyGram have begun attempts to limit recordings exported by U.S. distributors out of America. A weaker dollar means that foreign wholesalers may purchase recordings from U.S. distributors and have them shipped overseas for less than it costs to purchase them from the international arms of major labels. Such a practice weakens the profit and position of the non-U.S. branch of the label. It is clearly a policy among the major record labels to monitor and ensure that their business is functional and profitable on a multinational level.

▪ ▪ Trading Music

Though the case of record imports has the clearest connections to NAFTA and GATT, intellectual property issues have the most long-term significance for international trade in popular music for two reasons. First, copyright exploitation has the greatest income-producing potential for the music industry; and second, popular music is used in many media, and as a result, music copyright creates a ripple effect in film, television, and multimedia productions that use music.

And yet there is a fundamental contradiction that the music industry faces—namely, in the definition of that which is copyrighted. On the one hand, it is recorded or, as U.S. copyright law has it, "fixed" sound that is copyrightable and thus it would seem that it is the material objects that contain music that are protected. On the other hand, however, it is the creative object that is of value and not the material object that contains it. This contradiction is embodied in copyright law itself, which states that ideas cannot be copyrighted, only their expression. To copyright a musical idea, then, one must record it, or "fix" it. And although the recording has intrinsic value (a recording of a Bob Dylan song can have value based on who recorded it, the quality of the performance, and so on), it is the musical content that is valuable and copyrighted (the law notwithstanding). There are two consequences. First, the creator of a song benefits more from copyright law than its performer does; and second, trade in its everyday sense of the exchange of commodities does not take place in the music industry. Although material objects (records, compact discs, cassettes) are indeed traded, what gives those commodities value is the abstracted object of copyright—namely, music.

In discussion of intellectual property issues in Chapter 17 of NAFTA, Article 1706 directly addresses sound recordings. It is clear from that discussion that NAFTA considers sound recordings as commodities, even though there is mention that "secondary uses" of sound recordings (such as for film or broadcasting) are understood as part of the agreement. There is little evidence that copyrights are themselves understood as commodities. In other words, exploitation of rights, it seems, occurs only when rights are "fixed" or "embedded" in material objects, such as compact discs or cassettes. The trading of rights, the use of rights for commercial purposes, and the relationship between performance rights and copyrights are not addressed in NAFTA (or, for that matter, sufficiently in GATT). Put another way, what NAFTA allows for is free trade in record albums but not necessarily in music. And regarding GATT, it would appear that record companies are quite the winners.[17]

Among the questions that thus need to be raised, the most important is: What room do these trade agreements leave for the definition of nonmaterial, but nevertheless copyrighted, information? It is easier to understand why NAFTA left such questions unanswered than it is to answer them. NAFTA is, ultimately, a conservative document that favors those with the wherewithal to mass-produce material objects within the legal limits available to them as copyright holders or licensees. There is no mention of income and labor related to authorship and creation. Indeed, there is no attempt to define the creation of intellectual property and rights associated with it. The goal of Article 1706 concerning sound recordings in particular is clearly to give producers of sound recordings protection against unauthorized (namely, unpaid) reproduction. Consequently, NAFTA continues the evolution of copyright as publisher's right and largely overlooks the author. The focus of discussion is the material object and not the creative subject, a dubious focal point, one that gives marketing preeminence and that disenfranchises creation.

▪ ▪ Copyright and Trade

I have addressed critical issues of copyright elsewhere[18] and do not wish to engage those here, except to say that although copyright may have use as an author's protection against unauthorized copying, copyright was initially enabled and engaged as a means of determining who had the right to publish. It was publishers who first used copyright law provisions to circumscribe the marketplace. Similarly, authors' organizations are defensive in nature and "are proud to be champions of the rights and economic interests of their members."[19] Particularly in the music industry, authors' organizations are closely linked to industry organizations and their interests, most commonly by way of Broadcast Music, Inc. (BMI) or the American Society of Composers and Publishers (ASCAP). Given that BMI and ASCAP are also *publishers'* associations, one finds little distinction between the interests of authors and those of publishers. Consequently, whether in the service of authors or publishers, copyright law must first and foremost be understood as law created to regulate trade and protect property, and as such it is antithetical to free trade. Copyright is a monopoly right ostensibly given to encourage creativity. The monopoly is generally justified by the desire to give economic benefits to the creator, but is often counterbalanced by "fair use," the clause in copyright law which permits free use of copyrighted materials for a variety of purposes (such as criticism), provided such use does not take away from the market value of the copyrighted work.

The issue of authorship therefore must be addressed. Article 1706 of NAFTA clearly gives "the producer of a sound recording the right to authorize or prohibit" a variety of the uses to which a recording is put. Lacking is any mention of a performer, creator, author—or even copyright holder. The NAFTA wording regarding the types of traded commodities understood as "music" (that is, compact discs, records, tapes, etc.) gives the clear impression that record companies—the ones that produce (manufacture) recordings—are the ones with "rights." In many, many instances it is undoubtedly the case that a record company's agreement with an artist gives the record company copyright in the artist's music (and this is particularly true in cases where the work-for-hire clause in copyright law gives the employer rights in employees' works). In other instances, however, the record company may indeed own the recording, but others (artists, publishers, investors) may control a variety of rights, further complicating matters owing to the variety of royalty mechanisms (mechanical, performance, and the like) generating income to rights holders. Though NAFTA and GATT make provision for trade, they do little, if anything, to address exploitation of copyright by way of such royalties. Granted, this may be a daunting task as it means that labor, broadcasting, and cultural issues and policies need to be addressed.

A significant symbol of these concerns is GATT and NAFTA's basis in economic rights. Moral rights have not been a segment of U.S. copyright law, but have been an important element of the Berne Convention and other countries' intellectual property legislation. Moral rights are inalienable and in a sense *not* commodifiable. They are, however, part of contract law, and thus play a substantive role in the negotiation of intellectual property issues. Technology in particular has made moral rights problematic as it has lessened the ability to protect those rights by making copying easier. On an international level, the United States' ability to refrain from recognizing moral rights causes great difficulty in relation to its dealings in intellectual property with those countries that do recognize such rights. In some countries, for instance, translating song lyrics from one language to another qualifies as a creative act and the translator is recognized as an author. To a degree, adherence to NAFTA and GATT may represent a significant weakening (if not dissolution) of moral rights. An exclusion of moral rights from these agreements represents the clearest indication that both represent a further industrialization of culture and are industry-driven. They also represent further support for the definition of "ownership" as being vested in producers and manufacturers, an outcome of such industrialization.

In the recording industry (whether U.S.-based or multinational), part of the reason for the emphasis on producers that is found in trade agreements is the focus on piracy and the profits it seems to siphon off and concomitant lobbying efforts by producers. To that end, NAFTA seems geared toward establishing boundaries within which legitimate recordings can be freely traded and piracy vigorously stamped out. The industry has defined several types of piracy (indeed, the RIAA considers parallel imports pirate recordings). To combat them, copyright law has most often been invoked. Consequently, for the recording industry, NAFTA establishes the bounds (national and transnational) within which copyright can be used as a means of legitimately selling recordings. In terms of the transnational component, it creates a definition of those who will be able to move recordings across borders; in terms of the national component, it creates an environment within which nonnational recordings will be given "national treatment." In both cases the interest is, as the RIAA's president Jason Berman has stated, to "[press] for the exclusive right of record companies to authorize or prohibit the reproduction and rental of their works for a period of at least 50 years."[20]

Of course, the interest is not only to protect rights but to exploit them. As Neal Turkewitz, the RIAA's vice-president, pointed out in regard to trade negotiations with China, record piracy losses there represent $16 million in lost revenue, but if China were to open its markets, yearly sales could be near a half billion dollars.[21]

Such interest also explains the recording industry's concentration on Mexico rather than Canada in the NAFTA negotiations. Canada has already been infiltrated by U.S.-based record labels and seems to have less market potential. Indeed, there is not a Canadian national distribution network operated by a Canadian record label—an indication that non-Canadian labels have a significant hold on the system. Canada also participates actively and directly with BMI and ASCAP. Mexico, however, represents both an untapped market and a site of piracy, and consequently NAFTA would appear to the RIAA as the stone that will kill both birds (protection and exploitation).

As mentioned before, complicating these matters is the difficulty of addressing a variety of issues concerning labor, broadcasting, and culture. The former two are, in some sense, already part of the NAFTA and GATT discourse. Culture, however, though it may be embedded in the "cultural products" exemption granted Canada in NAFTA, gives the recording industry more trouble. As Les Bider, chairman and CEO of Warner/Chappell Music, put it, "We're educating [people] about the concept of paying for music."[22] Whether others share a decidedly Western belief that music must be bought is beside the point.

▪ ▪ Protection, Exploitation, Enforcement

Each of the three issues discussed previously (immigration, copyright, parallel imports) and addressed by the U.S. recording industry (primarily via the RIAA) makes it clear that the industry is fundamentally protectionist. Given that the RIAA has been able to use legal means to enable protectionism, its current strategy seems to be one of establishing similar legal structures in other areas of the world it wishes to exploit. Consequently, as Gabriel Richerand points out, in terms of trade-related aspects of intellectual property (TRIPS), GATT seeks

> to do three things: (a) to ensure that contracting parties to GATT (or at least those who sign the new agreement, which must be a touchstone for international trading respectability) meet the substantive standards of the international copyright (and patent and trade mark) conventions, so establishing and reinforcing the requirements of the conventions as international standards; (b) [to] requir[e] contracting parties to provide effective administrative and judicial enforcement procedures under their legal systems; and (c) [to] provid[e] an international dispute-settlement procedure, backed by the availability of trading sanctions, when contracting parties fail to meet these obligations.[23]

Of course, such an effort has been under way in terms of intellectual property since organization of the Berne Convention. GATT gives teeth to the drive to not only establish intellectual property ownership but enforce rights on a global scale. However, as Richerand points out, the concept of an "open market" renders protection difficult. It has been the practice in the recording industry to grant individual exclusive licenses within specific territories. For instance, a U.S. record company may license a recording to a French record label for European release and distribution, and to a Japanese label for Asian release and distribution. Or, as Richerand puts it,

> it has normally been accepted that the [intellectual property] conventions require each of their contracting parties to grant separate exclusive rights within their separate territories, with the automatic consequence that copies licensed for other territories can be excluded. Indeed, it would be impractical to exercise the local exclusive reproduction or publishing right if imports from other territories could not be excluded.[24]

Until now, I have focused on music and rights associated therein. However, any discussion of the exploitation of rights via licensing is incomplete without a consideration of income from auxiliary sources, such as mass merchandising. The recording industry derives significant income from the sale of T-shirts, books, posters, and such. Estimates vary, but in the United States, T-shirt sales at concerts are said to gross over a half billion dollars a year. *Musician* magazine reported that New Kids on the Block "sold $30 million in merchandise at their shows" in 1990.[25] The U.K. industry is in a similar position, even at the level of the independent record label. Cow Records, for instance, reported that at one Inspiral Carpets performance in Manchester the label earned £25,000 solely from T-shirt sales.[26] As one reporter for the U.K. magazine *The Face* put it, "At times it seems—and bands will admit this—that T-shirts are as important if not more important than records themselves."[27]

The industry thus has as much interest in protecting merchandising rights as it does in protecting any rights associated directly with recordings, particularly as tie-ins to films, books, and the like are perceived as mutually beneficial—one promotes the other. Cross-marketing tie-ins of recorded products also highlight the fact that the recording industry (by now quite well integrated with media industries generally) gains less and less from the outright sales of recordings and more and more from what I would characterize as "trans-mediation"—that is, the placement of artist, music, merchandise, and so forth across a wide variety of media.

Consequently, NAFTA and GATT can be interpreted as guidelines structuring two elements of the global popular-music market. First, they are intended to establish a (near-) uniform legislative arena within which rights holders can enforce their rights; and second, they are intended to remove restrictions on the flow of commodities across borders. However, having overlooked (most likely deliberately) the commodification of music via copyright, neither agreement restricts or circumscribes the rights that the recording industry has generally enjoyed vis à vis copyright. Such restrictions could have come about had either agreement made clear the relationships between rights, labor, and control, for any such clarification would establish some force other than producers (manufacturers or publishers) as integral to the creation and performance of music (recorded or otherwise).

▪ ▪ Conclusion

Both NAFTA and GATT need to be viewed as documents that are preliminary to a comprehensive agreement on trade-related aspects of intellectual property rights (TRIPS). As Swiss observers have noted,

> GATT is concerned with tangible goods, while the subject-matter of the [intellectual property] conventions is intangible rights that can extend over both products and processes. GATT is concerned with the "dynamic" flow of goods, while the intellectual property conventions only deal with the "static" question of the protection of [intellectual property rights], rather than [with] their use or exercise.[28]

What, then, might be a next step in negotiations and clarification of these agreements? One likely direction is the establishment of an international performing rights organization. As one legal scholar noted in a discussion of the *Columbia Broadcasting System vs. ASCAP* case, the necessity for a performing rights organization is driven by "the difficulty of individual negotiation and the near impossibility of individual policing and enforcement."[29] Both NAFTA and GATT, as mentioned previously, represent a first step toward establishing a uniform legal structure for policing and enforcement. Negotiation will follow once that structure is in place, but a police force (or collection force) will still be necessary. After all, it is the performance of music that is valuable to the copyright holder, not just its sale. Cultural "content" policy, like Canada's "CanCon" and Australia's "music quotas," recognizes this, but there is a difficulty in determining not only where to draw the line when defining national origin, but also sufficient minimums—and sustaining the bureaucracy to do so.

It is instructive to note that the measure of success used by the recording industry when it releases figures to the public is unit sales of recordings, and that this is the measure used during discussions of the impact of international trade agreements on the industry. At best, statistical measures are used to determine the direction of a particular market, medium, or genre. Of course, it is difficult to imagine what other measures exist. Yet, Jocelyne Guilbault notes:

> statistics alone do not suffice here. As Wallis and Malm explained in their study of four small countries, few "hard facts" could be obtained by gathering statistics on cultural practices . . . It could be argued that an evaluation of . . . groups' or singers' popularity based on measurements of record sales, for example, can be misleading as it reifies what it is trying to prove. The categories on which the measurements are based are devised by the record promoters themselves to confirm the success of their own products and to achieve a specific goal, that is, to boost sales.[30]

Of course there are matters other than sales to be considered, matters having to do with culture, identity, consumption, and creation. Guilbault does a marvelous job attending to those matters in her study of zouk. How, though, will such issues be brought forward in an economistically driven neoconservative document such as NAFTA? It is clear that the audience is largely not conceptualized in these agreements, and if it is at all, it only serves to whet the appetites of industry by dint of its size and potential. Another way to view these agreements, then, is as geographer Edward Soja might—that is, as

> a continuous process of societal restructuring that is periodically accelerated to produce a significant recomposition of space-time-being in their concrete forms, a change in the nature and experience of modernity that arises primarily from the historical and geographical dynamics of modes of production.[31]

Soja points out that "capitalist development is geographically uneven," while "[at] the same time, there is also a persistent tendency toward increasing homogenization and reducing these geographical differences."[32] This is precisely the situation vis à vis the popular music industry. On the one hand, there need to exist untapped markets for consumption, reservoirs of labor for production, and cultural homogeneity for both consumption and production of the popular music product generated by the global popular music industry.

Some of the impetus for free trade agreements doubtlessly comes from the "information superhighway," the National Information Infrastructure in the United States (and elsewhere), which in actuality establishes the opportunity to upload and download cultural products (media content). That this can be done at great distances clearly problematizes the ability to maintain exclusion, national treatment, and a host of other issues that FTAs address. As Roger de la Garde has said, "free trade does not mean deregulation but regulation of another kind,"[33] and economies will find ways in which to regulate (and thereby institutionalize exploitation of) electronic media from cassettes[34] to digital samplers to computers. And yet, as Horace Newcomb has stated, "culture cannot be protected by treaty or agreement."[35] There is a kind of "will to market" that is operative not only in cultural industries but in culture itself that permeates our production and consumption of popular music in particular, but of culture generally. Kenichi Ohmae has observed this from the perspective of business:

> There are, for example, 600 million consumers in . . . Japan, the United States, the nations of the European Community . . . with strikingly similar needs and preferences. Gucci bags, Sony Walkmans, and McDonald's hamburger stands are seen on the streets of Tokyo, London, Paris, and New York.[36]

I can thus think of only one way in which the music industry understands the term "world music," and I assure you that it has nothing to do with music that is non-Western and everything to do with marketing particular music(s) to the world.

NOTES

1. I use the term "internationalized" to mean the inclusion of non-Western sounds and music in Western popular music, the growing popularity of non-Western music among fans of popular music, and the growth of the music business into an industry dominated by transnational corporate interests. It is not intended to mean the exportation to (and hence exploitation in) third world and other countries of Western popular music. The term "popular music" is taken to include forms such as pop, rock, rock 'n' roll, and so forth.

2. See Steve Jones, "Who Fought The Law? American Responses to Popular Music, Cultural Production and the International Popular Music Industry," in *Rock and Popular Music: Politics, Policies and Institutions,* ed. Tony Bennett, Larry Grossberg, Graeme Turner, and Simon Frith (London: Routledge, 1993).

3. L. Berman, "Foreigners Need Not Apply," *Village Voice,* December 30, 1986, p. 34.

4. S. C. Bell, "Special Procedures for the Entry of Alien Entertainers," in *1985 Entertainment, Publishing and the Arts Handbook,* ed. Alexander Lindey, p. 421 (New York: Clark Boardman Company, 1985).

5. All references to the U.S. Immigration Reform Act are from Section 101(a)(15)(H)(ii), the *United States Immigration Reform and Control Act of 1986* and subsequent congressional revisions.

6. Bill Holland, "Tighter Visa Rules Bad News for Biz," *Billboard,* June 8, 1991, p. 1.

7. P. Verna, "Fed Quota Law on Visas May Limit Overseas Acts," *Billboard,* June 15, 1991, p. 77.

8. H. D. Deutsch, *Employer's Complete Guide to Immigration* (Paramus, N.J.: Prentice-Hall Information Services, 1987), 213–214.

9. Bill Holland and S. Nunziata, "Duping Royalty Pact Signals New Era," *Billboard,* July 20, 1991, p. 1.

10. W. Spahr, "Mechanical-License Income Boosts GEMA to Record Year," *Billboard,* June 8, 1991, p. 2.

11. Roger Wallis and Krister Malm, *Big Sounds From Small Peoples* (New York: Pendragon Press, 1984).

12. David Toop, *Rap Attack* (Boston: South End Press, 1984), 111.

13. Bill Holland, "New Mexican Law Recognizes U.S. Copyrights," *Billboard,* July 20, 1991, p. 8.

14. J. Clark-Meads and Bill Holland, "Japan Boosts Copyright Protection," *Billboard,* May 11, 1991, p. 1.

15. O. J. Sloane and R. Thorne, "International Aspects of United States Copyright Law: The Music Business," in *1986 Entertainment, Publishing and the Arts Handbook,* ed. Alexander Lindey, p. 69 (New York: Clark Boardman Company, 1986).

16. Ibid., 73.

17. Thomas Cottier, "The Prospects for Intellectual Property in GATT," *Common Market Law Review,* 28(1991): 402.

18. Steve Jones, "Critical Legal Studies and Popular Music Studies," *Stanford Humanities Review,* 3(Autumn, 1993): 77–90.

19. William Klein II, "Authors and Creators: Up by Their Own Bootstraps," *Communications and the Law,* (September 1992): 49.

20. Jason Berman, "International Copyright Battle Persists," *Billboard,* December 21, 1991, p. 12.

21. Bill Holland, "China Hears U.S. Plea: Protect Copyrights," *Billboard,* January 25, 1992, p. 6.

22. Sal Manna, "For Les Bider, Success is Measured by More Than the Bottom Line," *BMI MusicWorld* (Summer 1993): 22.

23. Gabriel Richerand, "GATT, Intellectual Property Rights and the Developing Countries," *Copyright Bulletin,* 25, no. 3 (1991): 13.

24. Ibid., 14.

25. Thom Duffy, "The Rag Trade," *Musician,* January 1992, p. 42.

26. Amy Raphael, "Material Gains," *The Face,* June 1991, p. 50.

27. Ibid., 54.

28. Rajan Dhanjee and Laurence Boisson de Chazournes, "Trade Related Aspects of Intellectual Property Rights (TRIPS): Objectives, Approaches & Basic Principles of the GATT and of Intellectual Property Conventions," *Journal of World Trade,* 24, no. 5 (September 1990), p. 7.

29. Simon H. Rifkind, "Music Copyrights and Antitrust: A Turbulent Courtship," *Cardozo Arts and Entertainment Law Journal,* 4(1): 4.

30. Jocelyne Guilbault, *Zouk: World Music in the West Indies* (Chicago: University of Chicago Press, 1993), 177–178.

31. Edward Soja, *Postmodern Geographies* (London: Verso, 1989), 27.

32. Ibid., 107.

33. Roger de la Garde, remarks at the international conference, Media, Culture and Free Trade: NAFTA's Impact on Cultural Industries in Canada, Mexico and the United States, Austin, Texas, March 3–5, 1994.

34. Cassettes are a particularly interesting medium. Portable, easy to copy, easy to mail, the cassette has, in a sense, made the postal service a distribution system for music in much the same way that it is a distributor for magazines and newspapers.

35. Horace Newcomb, remarks at the international conference, Media, Culture and Free Trade: NAFTA's Impact on Cultural Industries in Canada, Mexico and the United States, Austin, Texas, March 3–5, 1994.

36. Kenichi Ohmae, *Triad Power* (New York: Free Press, 1985), 23.

15

Copyright, Contract, the Cultural Industries, and NAFTA

KEITH ACHESON AND CHRISTOPHER J. MAULE

▪ ▪ Introduction

The cultural industries[1] significantly affect the quality of our lives. On average, we spend an increasing amount of the day reading the newspaper, tuning in to the radio while commuting to work, purposefully searching for information on a data base, browsing on an electronic bulletin board, listening to recorded music, and watching television or seeing a film in the evening.

The Electronic Mall

Shopping is another activity that absorbs much of our time and is equally symbolic of the North American lifestyle. There are interesting parallels between developments in retailing and in the cultural industries. In the past twenty-five years shopping malls have grown to dominate North American retailing. In many cities the malls are urban parks in which locals and tourists gather. By locating stores conveniently and judiciously controlling the mix of local stores and a growing number of chain stores, a mall reduces the search and travel costs of the shopper.

What malls have done in consolidating shopping opportunities, cable television has done for viewing. Viewers browse among a mix of local stations and an expanding set of cable networks. As shopping malls have steadily got larger and extended their menu to include professional services, more eating opportunities, and a burgeoning set of entertainment options, so cable systems have grown in capacity and developed new nonentertainment services—burglary and fire alarm systems, data transmission, classified ads, and real estate channels. It is arguable that malls have reached the point of diminishing returns.[2] In contrast, cable appears to be on the threshold of a further dramatic expansion in capacity and services.

Ironically, one of these expansion opportunities is in retailing. The problems that have limited the size of conventional shopping centers— assembling land, providing parking, negotiating and accommodating public transportation connections, and obtaining regulatory approval— do not confront the developer of an electronic mall of shopping channels. The electronic shopping mall can be readily adjusted to demographic and economic changes. Channels can be allocated to other retail uses or to totally different purposes. No abandoned cement monuments will mark our limited ability to forecast and plan where cities would or would not sprawl.

The rise of the suburb and the growing dependency on the car accompanied and partly drove the revolution in shopping. City and town life were fundamentally altered by events that occurred over a relatively short period. Stores on main street and in the downtown core of many towns and cities were adversely affected. Over the same period, the advent of television, cable, and video had a similar effect on the fabric of life generally, and specifically on other parts of the cultural industries— newspapers, magazines, traditional broadcasting, and film and record distribution. The coming together on the electronic mall of the cultural industries promises to have an equivalent impact on where people live and how they learn and organize their work.

Impact of Content

Balance sheets and employment statistics can be examined to trace the impact of change on jobs and activity in the cultural industries. It is much more difficult to measure and interpret the effects on the customers of the content provided by the cultural industries. How content, processes of distribution, and terms of delivery join with our other experiences to shape and inform images of ourselves and our relationship with others is still largely a mystery. In some instances we—readers, listeners, and viewers—actively control content by choosing to read or watch A rather than B. At other times, our participation is more passive. We browse among late-night television shows or go to a jazz club offering "nightly entertainment." In these instances, a gatekeeper—the program

producer or night club entrepreneur—provides us with a novel variation on a theme rather than known material. Within bounds, we choose
to depend on the choices of others.

In North American countries, a complex set of commercial, com-
munity-based, and political processes determines what will appear on
the expanding menu of options. The mix of regulation and commerce
differs across media and countries. Within the relevant regulatory constraints, private, profit and not-for-profit groups, and government-
sponsored channels provide alternative sources of content and vie for
favorable treatment from whoever in the family controls the remote. As
television shifts more to a subscription and pay-per-view basis, regulatory constraints are diminishing and affordability is playing a larger role
in controlling what we can actually read, hear, or watch. If content is
more than a mirror of our lives, and actually conditions what we are as
individuals and as societies, how the menu of choices is determined is
important, as are the economic terms of our access to those choices.

With respect to cable television and content, the analogy of the
shopping center remains instructive. Originally department stores anchored many shopping centers and were crucial to their success. For
cable, the traditional networks played a similar role. Specialized chain
stores developed that exclusively sold their products in malls. Similarly,
cable networks have experienced a rapid development and were in the
1980s the most profitable segment of the American broadcasting business. Government broadcasters, either tax funded or pledge supported,
claim a diminishing share of North American cable viewers, in the same
way that government monopoly liquor stores and mail outlets take a
smaller and smaller share of mall space. The government players are on
the defensive against privatization in both systems. Community activities are relegated to charitable promotions in the aisles of the mall and
to badly funded community channels on cable. As malls have grown
larger, observers have criticized the sameness of the proliferating stores.
Parallel comments have been made of cable programming as channels
have multiplied.

Despite these similarities, new technologies promise to increase the
ability of electronic systems to deliver diversity. Digital transmission,
compression, fiber, lasers, and satellites are making it possible to deliver
to the home or office information and entertainment with a diversity
and range that is unprecedented. Scrambling technologies also provide
means of granting access that will encourage and finance more diversity
and experimentation. In our opinion, a mixture of advertising-based

television, evolving public television, cable networks, and pay channels will provide a diverse menu. The new technologies will permit more finely tuned subscription networks, pay networks, and video to be successful. The resulting domain of choice will resemble that of the magazine rack more than that offered by advertising-based radio or television. Since this diversity will be accompanied, indeed driven, by services that charge subscribers, access will be an issue.

North Americans take it for granted that the shelves of their shops will be filled with attractively presented and priced goods, and know little about how that is accomplished. An invisible network of contracts link the worker, often from some distant country, to the purchaser who carries it to the cashier in a North American town. To fill the expanding "shelves" of the electronic mall a similar network of contracts have to be drawn and enforced. For cultural products, copyright law is the basis of the contracting network. We first discuss in general terms the connection of copyright to how product is produced and distributed. Against this background, we describe and comment on the impact of the changes in copyright arising from the North American Free Trade Agreement (NAFTA).

▪ ▪ Copyright and Contracting

Copyright creates enforceable rights to "works" or "expressions." A copyright holder controls, for a prescribed time and subject to a number of constraints, the right to reproduce the work and license access to the copies under specified terms. The following example shows the interplay between contracts, the details of copyright law, and the costs of piracy.

Copyright, Trespass, Organization, and Contract: An Example

It is the beginning of term in a small liberal arts college. A teacher meets with a class and recommends that her students buy a specific textbook. The textbook is only available in hardback and a new edition has made second-hand copies imperfect substitutes. The new text sells for $90. Students either buy the book for $90 at the university bookstore, purchase an illegally photocopied version from a budding entrepreneur in the class, who sells it for $40, or make do with the previous edition, available used at $20. For the assigned readings, assume that the university library can legally photocopy the material and place it on reserve for the students. Some students join with their friends and photocopy the articles and share them; some with greater wealth or fewer friends make their own personal copy; some borrow the library copy. The university and commercial photocopiers in the area are required to pay into a reprography fund for each page of copyrighted material photocopied on their machines. The reprography fund does not pay anything to the authors of the articles assigned by the teacher, but finances cultural events in the state or province. After lecturing, the teacher relaxes in the evening by renting from a video store a video that is offered at half the normal charge. Unknowingly, she is watching a pirated copy of an original movie that the video store operator has bought from an underground manufacturer.

Focus on the share of revenue that the creators of information used by the teacher are able to garner. The textbook author, publisher, and bookseller do well if the $90 text sells to each student, but badly if only one copy is sold to the class "copying entrepreneur," and very badly if only second-hand books are purchased. For each new text sold, the creator, producer, and distributor receive contract-determined shares of the $90. The publisher will try and price the new text so that the revenue is as large as possible. The price will be higher the more imperfect the photocopy or the second-hand copy are as substitutes for the new edition. The publisher or organizations that represent publishers will also try and raise the costs of the pirated editions by exhorting the local authorities to enforce copyright law.

The teacher has assigned a number of articles, but each one appears in a journal issue in which there are also many articles not assigned. Moreover, the journals are sold in bundles (i.e., in yearly subscriptions), so the student will also be buying issues that contain no relevant articles. To raise revenue the publisher will ignore the student market and charge just below the maximum price that the library would be willing to pay for the journal. The library is less damaged by the forced purchase of articles not assigned, since they may be assigned in other courses or in future courses. Both the students and the library can "produce" copies of any articles in the journals purchased by the library at the relatively low cost of the reprography royalty. From the students' perspective, the situation is identical to that of the textbook if all students chose to buy photocopies. The only difference is that their copying is legal, while that of the class entrepreneur is not.

With respect to the pirated film, the video store receives payment. Unlike the university bookstore that unwittingly sells a text to the class "copying entrepreneur," the video store is knowingly part of the pirating group. The maker and distributor of the original film receive only the payment for the video that was used to manufacture the illegal copies. Like the publisher, the film producer will lobby directly or through a relevant association to curb piracy. Specific measures may be taken to help law enforcement by identifying rental outlets with pirated material. The journal publisher, however, has no legal recourse against the copying. He or she can experiment with discriminatory prices that maintain the single sale to the "institutional" buyer while charging a lower price to individuals, inducing an occasional subscription from an expert in the field or a particularly well-off student. The lobbying by journal interests might focus on narrowing or removing the special rights to copying given to educational institutions, although the existing arrangements may generate as much money as they could obtain under any feasible alternative.

The share of value earned by the creators, producers, and distributors will be greater in situations in which free access is granted in fewer instances, in which the work is more valuable to users, in which price discrimination is more effective, and in which illegal access is less viable. The strategies chosen by each party in the contracting chain linking the authors to the student or teacher who enjoys access to their work will be affected by the nature of copyright protection and the ability to enforce its provisions.

Effect of Technology on the Capture of Value Through Contract and Copyright

Each new type of work and related technology of distribution requires a number of copyright issues to be addressed. The elements of copyright protection—coverage, duration, exemptions, and who the initial owner is deemed to be—have to be adapted to the exigencies of the technology of distributing copies and the piracy potential. Law, commercial practice, and technology evolve together in an interconnected fashion. The pricing strategy of the journal publisher is an example of a commercial practice or strategy adopted when copyright protection is weak or nonexistent. In the nineteenth century, many English authors contracted with and were paid by publishers in the United States, despite the lack of copyright protection for foreign books. The following strategic practices gave the publishers certain advantages that allowed them to make and honor such contracts: being first in the field with the book; adhering to the "tacit understanding among the larger publishers in America that the books published by one should not be pirated by another" (Plant 1934, pp. 172–173); publishing "fighting editions" if another publisher brought out an edition; printing a large number of books; and setting relatively low prices. In eighteenth-century England, where English-authored works did have statutory protection, arrangements among publishers and strategies adopted by individual publishers augmented copyright protection substantially.

> Yet, one finds it recorded as late as 1813 that the copyright in Cowper's poems, which under the Act had but two years left to run and yielded its proprietor a mere £834 per annum, was put up for auction and sold in shares for the sum of £6,764. Evidently the purchasers were not spending that kind of money for the sake of the statutory protection. What they were really buying was the right to have their intangible property respected by the other members of the trade. For it was the long-standing custom that once the "copyright" was entered in Stationers' Hall in the name of one publisher, no other publisher would touch it. The same source mentions that the copyrights of Shakespeare, who of course had been dead over two hundred years by then, were still being bought and sold in the trade. (Prescott 1989, p. 454)

Copyright law creates rights that generally make contracts more effective. Courts can enforce the rights against illicit copying and these rights can be transferred by contract. The value to the trade of a copyright statute and its enforcement depends on the efficacy of cartel and other private arrangements to create "property" in the absence of legally enforceable rights.[3]

Copyright is adapted to technological differences along four main dimensions: original assignment, coverage, duration, and exemptions. The maxim that copyright originally vests with the creator requires interpretation since creativity is seldom an individual and isolated act. With some jointly produced works, such as a song composed by one creator with lyrics by another, the copyright will be held jointly.[4] Each of the creators can make contractual commitments for the work, subject to sharing the revenue with the other. The contracting freedom for each joint holder avoids a holdup problem for commercial development of the work, while making the coordinated exploitation of the right more difficult. One party may be negotiating the licensing of a right that is in the process of being alienated by the other. When valuable works (e.g., films) are created by a relatively large group of artists and technicians, uncoordinated selling of rights could be very expensive to the group. Granting the producer of the work sole copyright of the integrated work enhances the potential for commercial exploitation.

Production of software also involves teams of creators. Developing a coherent production, distribution, and marketing plan is facilitated by employment contracts making the employer owner of the copyright. A work may also be "presold" by an independent creator through contract. Music commissioned for a television program is often sold in this way. Copyright technically vests originally with the author, but it is transferred before the work is actually created.

Coverage is constantly being adjusted as a result of court decisions that have a direct application in the country of decision and an indirect one in other countries. In determining what is protected, courts examine the degree of novelty in the expression. For example, important cases on the style of presentation or "look and feel" of computer programs have been decided or are currently proceeding in many countries. It is the distinction between expression and idea that is supposed to determine the boundary of protection: the former is protected and the latter is not. The vagueness of this distinction means that the line may be drawn quite differently from country to country and from medium to medium, despite a similarity in the wording of the law being interpreted. With respect to different media, writers and composers generally receive greater protection than visual artists against nonliteral reproduction of works (Brownlee 1993).

In the music world the protection of style is one of many issues raised by the new technologies. Through digital sampling the sound of a vocalist, group, or instrumentalist can be reproduced and applied to different material. According to Spurgeon, a member of the Canadian collective representing composers, authors, and music publishers, this leads to "an insidious form of piracy, permitting the pirate to get at the essential 'genetic material' of the copyrighted sound recording, which may then be recast into new musical works" (1992, p. 8).

The duration of copyright is also important for contracting. Longer duration means more protection for producers and a more extended wait for users to obtain legally free access.[5] The duration of copyright varies across works and in some instances depends on the longevity of the author.[6] Of course, if copyright cannot be effectively enforced, its legal duration is irrelevant.

Copyright laws also generally provide for exemptions. Typically these are for specific uses, such as the dissemination of news, teaching, criticism, religious functions, or research. Fair use or fair dealing also provides a general defense of infringement for specific activities. In writing this paper, we quote sources that make a telling point, and we are permitted by copyright law to do so. In the recording business, borrowing small bits of one record and inserting them into another can be readily done with digital technology; adding a scream by James Brown may substantially enhance the commercial value of a record by a relatively unknown artist. Is such use legal by analogy to the practice allowed in print of limited quotation with attribution? If so, how can an attribution be made? If, on the other hand, such an analogy is not valid, would it be legal if the scream were shifted an octave in the new recording? Such questions are currently before the courts. Because of the difference in the two technologies in terms of the impact of such borrowing of small excerpts, we would expect that the law will evolve in a different manner for sound recordings than it has done for print.

Fair use in the United States or fair dealing in Canada is also being defined with respect to other technologies. In the American Betamax case, the Supreme Court denied a motion to ban the sale of video tape recorders. In presenting their client's case, the Sony lawyers argued that much of the taping done in the home was justified by the fair-use doctrine. The Court decided five to four in favor of the defendant, Sony.

Free access for research or education makes existing materials more widely available but reduces the incentive to create works.[7] Presumably free access is granted when access serves a broad social purpose.[8] Ironically it contributes to retarding the growth of the stock of information in an area that society has earmarked as being of particular importance. Another determinant on granting free access is the ability to contain the access for the prescribed purpose. The boundaries of an exemption have to be enforceable or access becomes free for all uses. As enforcement effectiveness differs among technologies, it may be rational not to offer an exemption for a particular use for every medium.

▪ ▪ Restrictions on Contracting

Contracting is regulated by general legal constraints operating on all contracts and by specific constraints imposed on particular contracts. The purpose of this regulation is to make contracts more effective and, in some instances, to alter the sharing of the gains from contracting.

Contract Law

Contracts are an enforceable exchange of promises. In traditional legal theory, the law covering contract was concerned with determining whether an enforceable agreement existed, as well as with the appropriate remedies for breach and the responsibilities of each party in case of unforeseen circumstances. Contract law was not concerned with the terms of the agreement, unless they were imposed under duress or were affected by the misrepresentation or withholding of important information.

In current law, courts may rule that a contract is invalid because either the terms or the process by which agreement to the terms was reached were "unconscionable." Four rules have been proposed by Eisenberg (1982) to guide the courts in interpreting this slippery concept. He suggests that a contract is void for unconscionability if a contractor was in a distressful state when the deal was made, if the transaction was so complex that a party, despite being of at least average competence, was at a transactional disadvantage, if unfair bargaining processes were adopted by a contractor, or if a party was ignorant of what the "going" price was for a service or good.

Statutory and Common Law Protection Against Unfair Trade Practices

In addition to contract law, competition or antitrust law also constrains contracting in the cultural industries. For example, in Canada, the abuse-of-dominance provisions in the Combines Investigation Act contain a limited exception for the exercise of intellectual property rights.[9] The common law also protects against unfair trading practices. A producer of material who apes a style or deceives as to who the author of transmitted material is may be found guilty of "passing off." Common law or statutory concerns with the right to privacy, libel, and defamation also restrict content that can be copyrighted and be the basis of contract.

In the United States, both the contractual and the institutional structure of distribution in the film industry were affected by a number of cases initiated under the Sherman Act.[10] The resulting consent decrees imposed significant constraints on contract and institutional arrangements in the film industry. Minimum-price clauses, block booking, and blind contracting were prohibited. Vertical integration was curtailed.

During the late 1970s in Canada, competition policy cases focused on the maintenance of minimum prices at theaters.[11] In late 1982 the system of allocating films to cinemas by the major distributors was referred to the Restrictive Trade Practices Commission. At issue was a complaint by Cineplex Corporation, at the time a relatively small theater chain, that it was not gaining the same access to pictures as the two major cinema chains. An agreement was reached during the following year to change the process of film distribution. Under this agreement, the distributors undertook not to grant any chain right of first refusal [12] and committed to a detailed set of restrictions on their contracting with cinemas.[13] On May 29, 1984 Cineplex Corporation bought Canadian Odeon Theatres Ltd., the second-largest cinematic chain in Canada. What was once a small interloper became a dominant player in exhibition. Organized agitation to regulate the system of distribution subsided.

A provision of copyright law that has had a much greater effect on contracting is the legal recognition of the right of collectives to represent the interests of groups of creators. Collectives representing publishers, composers, and lyricists have been important in the recording business of both the United States and Canada. The 1988 revision of the Canadian Copyright Act encouraged the development of further collectives. The act provided the societies with an exemption from the Competition Act for any privately negotiated agreement establishing rates and terms of access to the works of its members, as long as a copy of the agreement was filed with the Copyright Board of Canada.[14]

In the United States the two dominant collectives representing composers and lyricists, ASCAP and BMI,[15] traditionally contract through blanket licenses. A contracting user gains access to the entire repertory for a fee that may be revenue dependent. These licenses have been frequently challenged in the courts as anticompetitive restraints of trade. Consent decrees regulating the contracts of the societies have been entered.[16] Litigation in this field is common.[17] Under current arrangements in Canada, some collectives lack a regulatory shield. If an unregulated collective has assembled enough members to dominate the market, its contracting options may be restricted by competition policy considerations.[18]

Regulation and Contract

Competition or antitrust policy regulates industry as a whole. The details of its application differ from industry to industry, but the same law is applied. Specific regulatory structures constraining an activity or limited set of activities develop when generic regulation, such as competition policy, fails to cope adequately with perceived problems. Of the cultural industries in North America, broadcasting and cable are regulated in the most detail. A part of regulation consists of restrictions on contracts and institutional scope. For example, the American Cable Television Consumer Protection and Competition Act of 1992 prevents a cable network from signing an exclusive contract with traditional cable distributors.[19] The network must make its programming available to competitive modes of distribution such as direct broadcasting satellites and wireless cable systems. In television broadcasting, the financial-syndication rules governing network programming in the United States are an example of constraints that are being eroded by recent court challenges and regulatory decisions.

In Canada the contractual constraints in broadcasting are also extensive. The Canadian Radio-Television and Telecommunications Commission (CRTC) sets priority rules for carriage on cable companies and requires Canadian channels to be included in packages of pay television. Content requirements tailored to the specific broadcaster or cablecaster are also imposed at the time of license renewal. Regulatory guidelines for gender representation and the portrayal of violence have also been issued.

At an institutional level, regulatory concern with cross-ownership has resulted in restrictions of ownership by cable companies of broadcasting interests and vice versa. Where cross-ownership is allowed (e.g., cable networks may be owned by multiple system operators [MSOs]), monitoring and ensuring that networks not owned by the MSO have equal access to its cable franchises presents a difficult regulatory challenge. Previously viable boundaries of regulation are proving inadequate to cope with the issues raised when computers, telecommunications, and content banks are merged into massive informational systems. Pressure to abandon long-standing ownership restrictions across activities and limitations on foreign ownership will increase as commercial interests seek to reduce risk and the costs of coordinating responses to emerging market opportunities by integrating across old boundaries.

Contract Restrictions in Copyright Law

CONTRACT DURATION AND OTHER TERMS

Copyright law itself places restrictions on contracting. Historically, it was common to break the copyrighted term into two parts. For example, until the 1976 revision of the United States' Copyright Act, the copyright term was broken into two periods of twenty-eight years. To maintain protection, a work had to be registered for the second term.[20]

Default clauses that govern in the absence of contrary stipulations are often provided in the statute. These clauses can be specific. For example, with respect to publishing contracts for existing works, Mexico's Copyright Law requires any stock of books left over at the termination of the contract to be sold back to the author at cost plus 10%, unless otherwise specified. The same law also imposes a term of one year for the publisher to get a book to market unless the contract provides differently. With respect to a work consisting of music and words, the Mexican law provides that in the absence of a clause to the contrary, the copyright shall be owned in equal parts by the composer and the lyricist.

Compulsory licenses can also be imposed by copyright law. The statute either imposes rates for the contract directly or sets up a board that will set rates as a matter of course or in the contingency that negotiations are not successful. The United States' Copyright Act of 1976 introduced and set rates that have to be paid by American cable companies for retransmitting distant signals. The resulting pool of funds is distributed to producers of programming that appears on distant signals. The imposition of a regulated price of access for distant signals contrasts with the right to negotiate terms of access with cable companies that was recently granted to local stations under the Cable Television Consumer Protection and Competition Act.

In the music field, statutorily imposed rates are common. In Mexico, royalties negotiated by users and societies in accordance with the law are operative, but many of the rates for public performance are established by law.[21] In Canada the mechanical rights for records were set by statute until the revision of the act in 1988.[22] Under the current legislation, the Canadian Musical Reproduction Rights Agency (CMRRA) does not have to file and gain approval for the terms by which it disposes of the reproduction rights for its members' works. With respect to the public performance charges for the works of composers and lyricists, the users and the societies present their cases before the Copyright Board. The Board establishes the rates after hearing the evidence. In a recent decision, the rates for 1990–1993 were set for a number of tariff categories.[23]

Copyright law can also strengthen the ability of rights holders to raise more revenues from their rights by allowing them to constrain the economic options of subsequent holders of the rights. For example, a record or video may be given a rental right. The sales contract can specify that the record or video cannot be rented to others by the purchaser. A rental right permits price discrimination. It overrides the "first sale" or "exhaustion" principle in Anglo-American law that makes forbidding a buyer from renting the item after purchase unenforceable before the courts.

MORAL RIGHTS

Moral rights emerged in Europe in the nineteenth century. They reflect a "belief that an artist incorporates his spirit and personality in works of the artist's creation" (Bloom 1991, p. 8) and are the most discussed restriction on contract in copyright law. Of the moral rights, the right to integrity and paternity is required to be given protection by adherents to the Berne Convention. In North America, Mexico's Copyright Law explicitly granted such rights to an author long before Mexico joined Berne.[24]

Following British practice, Canada and the United States have traditionally relied on common law to protect the reputational interests of the creator. Although Canada did include a weak section addressing moral rights in the Copyright Act of 1924, effective statutory recognition of these rights did not occur until the 1988 revision of the act. With accession to Berne, the United States incurred an obligation to protect the right to integrity and paternity. To meet its commitment, the United States has relied mainly on common law. Federal statutory protection was granted only to visual artists.[25] The statutory integrity right of artists in Canada and of visual artists in the United States cannot be assigned but can be waived in writing. In some continental European countries the right cannot be assigned or waived. The restriction on contract is therefore more severe in Europe than in Canada or the United States.[26] In France creators have successfully invoked moral rights when the theme of a film was repellent to an artist providing a copyrightable input, such as music, and more recently with respect to the colorization of films. Less protection has been forthcoming in other jurisdictions.

In our opinion, the net effect of moral rights on business arrangements has to date been negligible in most countries. Historically most of the court cases involved a well-publicized alteration of a painting or sculpture.[27] Some intrusions on the integrity of a work are whimsical and banning them would create little harm. For example, the most celebrated case in Canada involved the tying of red ribbons around the necks of geese suspended from the ceiling as part of the Christmas decoration in a large Toronto mall.[28] However, there are other situations in which an inalienable integrity right has the potential to significantly disrupt current commercial practices. For example, films and programs shown on television are frequently time compressed and interrupted by commercials. If these factors are ruled to compromise the integrity of the works, the adjustments required in the television industry will be substantial and expensive. The implications of the right to integrity are currently being examined in the courts of a number of countries (Geller 1990, p. 426).

NEIGHBORING RIGHTS

The effectiveness of contracting depends on technology and the related costs of coordinating. In response to the view that copyright failed to provide an adequate contracting framework for reconciling the interests of performers, manufacturers of records, and broadcast undertakings, a number of countries negotiated the Rome treaty in 1961.[29] Signatory countries are obliged to protect the intertwined economic interests of these groups by creating neighboring rights.[30]

The implementation of national legislation typically creates an obligation to remunerate performers and/or record producers for public performances of their works. Users such as broadcasters have to pay a levy that is either negotiated or imposed by statute or a regulatory body. Mexico is a member of the Rome treaty, but neither the United States nor Canada belong. A member of Rome can require reciprocity of treatment before making payments to artists or producers from other member countries. The reciprocity clause effectively excludes performers from non-Rome countries from sharing in the income pool. The U.S. government actively opposes what it considers to be the discriminatory aspect of neighboring rights legislation and the suppression of negotiated contracts as the basis of remuneration for performers. In contrast, the previous Canadian government, before its defeat at the polls, planned to introduce a public performance right for performers and producers based on a blanket contract and requiring reciprocity for foreigners to share in the pot.

As a result of the introduction of digital audio tapes (DAT), piracy has become an even greater threat to the traditional revenue sources of recorded music and the flow through to performers based on contract. The legal environment has slowly been shifting to provide a compensating increase in protection. Many countries have introduced a rental right for tapes and discs. By being able to sell only recordings, which do not have a rental right attached, the industry can prevent the growth of a rental business that nourishes piracy. If the rental right is attached to sales by the industry, as would likely be the case for video, its exercise typically requires that a portion of the rental income be paid into a fund and distributed among composers and lyricists, performers, and producers. Presumably, private contracts in the industry will alter over time to reflect the existence of this source of remuneration. Similarly, reprography and blank-tape levies have been introduced or proposed in many countries. The funds that are collected are subsequently distributed to broad categories of artists. Since no one knows which works have been copied, the distribution tends to be a general subsidy to artists. A system that compensates those artists who have actually been damaged by copying requires better measurement systems of what is being copied than now exist. Many of these new funds, if not all of them, require reciprocity and are diplomatically opposed by countries whose performers and producers are excluded.

▪ ▪ Technology, the International Character of Works, and the International Harmonization of Copyright Law

Sections of the cultural industries have always had an international orientation. With the print media, international linkages followed linguistic boundaries. In the silent-film era, few natural barriers limited the market for a film. With sound, balkanization along language lines occurred, although dubbing and subtitles offered a partial offset. What differs today is the volume of business and the increased proportion of records, films, and books that are marketed internationally. The new technologies have increased capacity in existing distribution systems (e.g., compression techniques on a traditional cable system) and have allowed the creation of economical new means of distribution (e.g., direct broadcasting satellites). A further increase in the international flow of software to fill the new distributional pipelines can be expected. The greater demand for content, the cheaper costs of delivering it, and the new technological modes of delivery have also resulted in new contracting and institutional adaptation. International takeovers, mergers, strategic alliances, and co-productions are responsible for important changes in the institutional structure of the cultural industries.

A similar opportunity for adaptation and expansion has been created for pirates. In the current state of flux with powerful new players, such as HBO, CNN, and the large cable MSOs, cartel strategies are less potent in protecting commercial activities. Adapting and strengthening copyright and its enforcement has become an important issue for the legitimate cultural industries.

Because NAFTA addressed intellectual property issues in great detail, one might conclude that North American economic integration was the driving force behind the initiative to harmonize copyright laws. In our opinion, the dominant forces for harmonizing copyright were international and technological rather than regional and trade-policy related. The copyright sections of the Canada–U.S. Free Trade Agreement (FTA) and NAFTA were part of a worldwide set of initiatives taken to strengthen copyright.

At the national level, the United States drafted new copyright laws in 1976 and 1988. The later revision brought American legislation into conformity with the Berne Convention that the United States had decided to join. In the following year, Canada made major revisions to its Copyright Act. In 1991 Mexico implemented substantive changes of its federal law covering the author's rights. These revisions expanded the domain of copyright to include computer software and generally tightened copyright protection.

The flurry of legislative activity was not restricted to North America. The U.K. revised its act in the same period and the European Union (EU) has published a number of copyright directives.[31] The EU and the United States have not limited their efforts to transforming their own laws—they have also actively sought the tightening of copyright laws in other countries and vied with each other to influence the orientation of reforms in other countries.[32]

The recently concluded GATT round of negotiations included for the first time an agreement on trade-related intellectual property rights (TRIPS). Under TRIPS, each country commits to protective stipulations concerning a number of copyright issues—national treatment, duration, coverage of computer programs and recordings, and transparency of laws, regulations, and procedures. These commitments are made on a most-favored-nation basis.[33] Countries that do not belong to Berne or the Universal Copyright Convention (UCC) are thereby brought into a tight network of protection. In addition, the dispute settlement mechanisms of GATT are available to enforce these copyright commitments.[34]

▪ ▪ NAFTA

Copyright, Related Rights, and Contracting Implications

In the Canada–U.S. FTA, Canada exempted the cultural industries from the treaty with four exceptions,[35] only one of which concerned copyright. The one copyright condition is interesting. The United States, which traditionally has opposed compulsory licensing of intellectual property, asked Canada to make cable companies liable for a royalty on distant signals. The compulsory licensing part of the scheme is that broadcasters or the owners of the programming cannot deny a cable company the right to retransmit.

After hearings in 1990, the Copyright Board of Canada established a royalty rate of 70 cents per month per subscriber for large cable systems.[36] The rate did not depend on the number of distant signals received, as long as at least one was carried. A complicated two-tiered formula[37] divided the pool of approximately $50 million among collectives representing producers of programming. A subsequent decision has lowered the rate on francophone systems by 50%, because of the lower value of the distant signals to French-speaking viewers.[38] An irony of the FTA distant-signal condition is that Canada accepted a scheme that the United States then rejected with respect to establishing terms for the retransmission of local channels.

Although copyright was peripheral to the FTA, it was central to NAFTA. Chapter 17 of NAFTA reinforces the domain of coverage and the principles of national treatment and waiver of formal requirements for establishing copyright that are embodied in the Berne Convention, to which all three countries belong.[39] An important exception is that the moral rights of Berne are not incorporated into the agreement. NAFTA requires separability and transferability of rights. Any party who acquires copyrights by contract can exercise them and enjoy fully the benefits derived from them. While echoing the duration requirements of Berne, NAFTA clarifies that duration for a work owned by a corporation will be fifty years from the date of first publication. As well, the treaty confines copyright exceptions "to certain special cases that do not conflict with a normal exploitation of the work and do not unreasonably prejudice the legitimate interests of the right holder" (NAFTA 1992, Article 1705:5).

For recordings, existing rights are confirmed and new obligations created. Each party must establish a rental right for recordings and must prohibit the importation of records from a partner country unless the producer of the records approves. The duration of copyright for records must equal or exceed fifty years.

With respect to encrypted satellite programming, NAFTA requires that the manufacture, importation, or distribution of an unauthorized decoder be made a criminal offense, while unauthorized commercial use of an encrypted program—attracting customers to a pub to see an unauthorized signal while they imbibe, for example—must be made a civil offense.

Much of the detail of the copyright section in NAFTA concerns obligations and constraints on enforcement. The agreement calls for simplified and transparent civil procedures, for the disclosure of relevant information, for processes that protect confidential material, and for defendants to have the right to timely written notice of an alleged infringement. Each country must provide the courts with the power to issue injunctions, to seize and have destroyed infringing copies, to dispose of piracy tools seized in such a manner as to minimize the chances that they will be used for infringement in the future, and to order compensating damages, including court costs. Procedures for enforcing copyright at the time of clearance through customs have also been strengthened. Although it is unusual for a treaty to constrain the criminal law of other countries, the agreement calls for imprisonment or monetary fines, or both, to provide a deterrent "consistent with the level of penalties applied for crimes of a corresponding gravity" (NAFTA 1992, Article 1717).

NAFTA's process of harmonizing the copyright laws within North America is an ongoing one. The commitments to principles of national treatment reinforce existing obligations that each country has as a result of its Berne membership. NAFTA emphasizes national treatment at the more detailed level of process. Each country has committed to offering equal access to adjudication systems that will be more similar than before in process and in the structure of civil and criminal sanctions. At least implicit in the commitments is the prohibition of Catch 22 administrative procedures that deny in practice what was granted in principle. Combined with these affirmations of principle and openness of process are clauses that require specific responses. A number of these constraints apply to the recording industry. Others address new technologies, such as direct broadcasting satellites. Overall, the changes in copyright law supported by NAFTA reinforce the ability to forge effective contracts in the industry and enforce against piracy.

Canada's decision to exempt the cultural industries does not mean that it will end up with copyright law that differs drastically from that of the United States or Mexico.[40] Canadian law already provides for action against illegal decoders and provides complying protection for sound recordings. Canada adopted a rental right for recordings in early 1994. Canadian enforcement powers and procedures also appear to be in line with the NAFTA obligations. Therefore, as far as the specific provisions of NAFTA are concerned, Canada was largely exempted from provisions that it had already adopted or that it intends to adopt. Without the cultural exemption, Canada would have been constrained from adopting public performance rights for performers and producers on recordings, a measure that the previous government intended to enact. However, it presumably could have negotiated a specific exemption on this matter, as Mexico did.

Our overall impression of NAFTA's impact on copyright is that it homogenized the copyright environment and adopted rules that enhance the making of contracts in the context of the new technologies. For Mexico, the new regime differs markedly from its predecessor. The strong moral-rights orientation of Mexican copyright law has been muted and a number of Mexican measures, such as the compulsory licensing of translations of works not available in Spanish after seven years, appear to be in conflict with NAFTA (see the excellent discussion in Watts 1993). Watts laments this change. We believe it is largely technologically driven and that similar adaptations would have been made by Mexico, either in isolation or in other fora. A strict interpretation of the right to integrity would have major effects on the film and television industries—effects that no country, in our opinion, will accept.

Other Aspects of NAFTA and Contracting in the Cultural Industries

The investment and service chapters of NAFTA also impact on the cultural industries. The realignment of interests apparently required by the new technologies can be more easily realized in an open investment environment. Unfortunately, ownership restrictions in broadcasting in all three countries and in cable in Mexico and Canada have been preserved by exempting them from the national treatment requirements of the investment chapter. Any large investments in program distribution systems will have to work around existing limits on foreign ownership in both of these industries. For example, arrangements to share ownership in satellite broadcasting systems with a reach into more than one country will be more difficult to negotiate. In other sectors of the cultural industries explicit limitations are not imposed. However, both Mexico and Canada have maintained their programs of approval of foreign takeovers.[41]

▪ ▪ Conclusion

By all accounts, the simultaneous development of new technologies will dramatically increase the capacity of distribution systems to deliver programming to the home. Part, at least, of this increase will be filled by the cultural industries. The quality and diversity of content that will be delivered by these industries depends on the coordination of financial and creative resources by contract. Copyright is a legal structure that both enhances and regulates contracting. The law of copyright is in a constant state of change, as the courts and legislatures adapt legal practice to both the promise of new technologies and the threat they pose to maintaining existing desired levels of protection. Recently, the industries involved in developing the new technologies, on both the hardware and the software side, have promoted the adoption of more protective copyright codes domestically and internationally. Copyright reform and harmonization of generally tougher copyright laws is therefore occurring at a rapid rate. An arcane area of theory and law has become an important part of the international agenda of countries hoping to participate in the development of the new informational world.

Although we have used the term "tougher" to describe recent revisions of copyright law, judging the overall effect of copyright reform on the contracting environment is difficult. Copyright has always provided an uneven and somewhat unpredictable blanket of protection for creative commercial activities, and still does. Judges can modify an apparent increase in protection by extending the domain of exceptions. Longer duration may be accompanied by increased restrictions on contracting. An increase in flexibility in contracting permitted by copyright reform may be nullified by regulatory or competition policy constraints. Nevertheless, in our judgment, the trend has been to make copyright more protective.

Our discussion of the current legislative thrusts, regional agreements, and international initiatives has emphasized the industrial side of the picture. This may be an appropriate place to start. It is conceivable that within a more protective copyright environment private institutions will deliver an appropriate mixture of closed and open content for the electronic networks of the future. Think again of the shopping mall. In addition to an array of stores with a variety of goods from all over the world, a modern mall provides free parking and a commons in which people meet and socialize. A curious blend of open and priced access results. The innovativeness of the mall developer is visible, but the background laws that allow its realization are rarely appreciated. The contours of what will be private and public space on the emerging electronic mall are not yet clearly visible. Many experiments are under way. Some will be successful and many will fail. Governments can play a constructive role by developing guidelines for determining the rules governing access and for developing a favorable contracting environment for experimentation.

NOTES

For their comments and criticisms we thank and absolve of responsibility Rachel Michaux, Rick Michaux, Doug Smith, Jake Watts, and the conference participants. We are grateful for financial assistance from the Social Science and Humanities Research Council of Canada.

1. In Article 2107 of NAFTA cultural industries are defined as "persons engaged in any of the following activities: (a) the publication, distribution, or sale of books, magazines, periodicals or newspapers in print or machine readable form but not including the sole activity of printing or typesetting any of the foregoing; (b) the production, distribution, sale or exhibition of film or video recordings; (c) the production, distribution, sale or exhibition of audio or video music recordings; (d) the publication, distribution or sale of music in print or machine readable form; or (e) radio communication in which the transmissions are intended for direct reception by the general public, and all radio, television and cable broadcasting undertakings and all satellite programming and broadcast network services."

2. The press kit of the largest mall in the United States, the Mall of America, located in Minneapolis, reports: 140,000 hot dogs sold each week, 10,000 permanent jobs, 44 escalators and 17 elevators, 12,750 parking places, 13,300 short tons of steel, $1 million in cash disbursed weekly from 8 automatic-teller machines (as noted in Guterson 1993, p. 49).

3. Statutory law has generally granted the first ownership of copyright to the creator of the work, while cartel arrangements make the producers the original owners. Who owns the right will not alter what is done, since the author will typically transfer the copyright to a publisher by contract, but it may affect the distribution of income between the author and the publisher. If cartels could duplicate the effects of copyright they would essentially be first owners of a right the duration of which was not limited. Book publishers and producer-distributors for other media would therefore be expected to embrace and support politically the implementation or strengthening of copyright when their abilities to make a cartel effective are weak. They trade off the improvement in the ability of contract to generate wealth against the improved bargaining power of creators.

4. Other examples are novels with illustrations, and performance art in which the visual art and music are supplied by different artists. For the copyright to be issued jointly in American copyright law, the authors must intend that their separate contributions will form a unitary whole (Spyke 1993, p. 466).

5. With transactions that involve more than one country, the duration of rights can vary, with some odd results. For example, Porter (1991, p. 86) points out that if the interpretation of existing law held by the Commission of the European Community was accurate, the copyright duration of a television program broadcast from one country and picked up by a TV antenna in the home of a viewer in a different country would be different from the copyright duration for the same program deliv-

ered to the home by a cable company. In the first case, copyright duration would be determined by the law in the transmitting country, whereas in the second case, it would be determined by the law of the country of reception (i.e., the country in which the cable company operated).

6. For example, the English Copyright Designs and Patents Act of 1988 extended the term of copyright to Sir James Matthew Barrie's *Peter Pan* for an indefinite period in order to fund the Hospital for Sick Children, Great Ormond Street, London.

7. This fundamental tradeoff is faced when designing an educational exemption for a less-developed country. Free access makes foreign works readily available, but reduces the number of indigenous texts. The dependence on foreign texts, whose authors are rewarded by sales in other countries, is increased. The disincentive to create new educational works may be offset by other rewards for scholarly activity and by limiting the scope of the exemption.

8. Organizations representing the creators, whose income is affected by the exemptions, argue that these worthy purposes should be paid for out of general tax revenue and not out of the creators' pockets. The general public has seldom been persuaded of the wisdom of that course.

9. Exactly what the limitation means is yet to be defined with any precision. In the opinion of a former director of competition policy, the abuse of dominance continues to constrain effectively anticompetitive contracting based on patents, trademarks, and copyright. Section 32 of the act also allows the attorney-general to apply to the federal court for remedial measures when contracting based on copyright has "undue" anticompetitive effects, as long as the measures do not violate Canada's international commitments.

10. The Department of Justice originally prosecuted the eight major studios in 1938. A consent decree followed in 1940, addressing block booking, blind licensing, and expansions of theater holdings. In 1944 the department brought a suit asking for divestment of theater interests. A district court decision in 1946 made illegal the specification of a minimum price in contracts between a distributor and a cinema, and required competitive bidding. The district court also ordered the studios to divest their cinemas. In 1948 the Supreme Court rejected the competitive-bidding requirement and asked the district court to reconsider divestiture. In 1948 and 1949 RKO and Paramount agreed to sell their theaters. The district court on remand found that the vertical arrangements in the industry were part of a conspiracy to fix prices and ordered divestiture. In addition, all of the major studios were restricted in the clearances that could be granted. They were prevented from entering into franchise arrangements with the cinemas and had to license each theater individually. In 1950 Columbia, United Artists, and Universal signed the decree. Warner Brothers and 20th Century Fox signed in 1951 and Loew's Theaters signed the following year. De Vany and Eckert (1991) argue that the courts misunderstood the economic functions served by the contracting arrangements.

11. In 1977 Columbia Pictures Industries, Inc., pleaded guilty to not allowing a theater owner to reduce prices. Later in the same year, Warner Bros. Distributing (Canada) Limited was charged with "unlawfully attempting to discourage the re-

duction of the price of theater admissions" by entering into an agreement with Famous Players, Canada's largest chain of cinemas, to suspend the senior-citizen discount for a showing of *Barry Lyndon* at the Nelson Theatre in Ottawa. In 1979 United Artists Corporation was found guilty of requiring that Famous Players not provide discounts of any kind. Bellevue Film Distributors Limited, which distributed Disney films in Canada, was also convicted of prohibiting cinema owners from giving children discounts. In both instances a court order required the companies to discontinue the practice.

12. It was alleged that Paramount, United Artists, and Warner Bros. gave Famous Players cinemas a right of first refusal, while Columbia and Universal gave the same right to Odeon cinemas. Two-thirds of 20th Century Fox's films were made available to Famous Players on a first-refusal basis and the other one-third were made available to Odeon. (*Source:* Director of Investigation and Research, Combines Investigation Act, report to the Restrictive Trade Practices Commission on the operation of the undertakings given by six major motion picture distributors, March 1984, p. 35.)

13. All cinemas could submit offers to show films. Each offer was to be considered on its merits, with comparisons limited to theaters that were in substantial competition with each other. That an exhibitor could show the film in more than one cinema was not to be taken into account in accepting an offer among competing cinemas. Distributors were to provide all eligible bidders with estimates of the patterns and length of runs. Clearances would be limited to theaters that were in substantial competition with each other. They were also to forbear from agreeing not to grant another run of a film unless the new run would significantly reduce the expected audience of the film in the original run. New offers were to be entertained for any subsequent run. With respect to blind bidding, the distributors committed to making screenings available in more locations on as timely a basis as possible. The authorities also recognized the pro-competitive aspect of blind booking and did not ban it outright. "Day and dating" occur when two or more cinemas exhibit runs of film at the same time and in the same competitive location. An acceptance by a distributor of a clause ruling out day and dating in an offer by an exhibitor was a violation of the agreement. The agreement is reproduced in Director of Investigation and Research, Combines Investigation Act, Annual Report for the year ended March 31, 1984, Ottawa: Consumer and Corporate Affairs Canada, 1984.

14. The exemption is limited in the following sense: the director of competition can ask the Copyright Board to examine the agreement and amend clauses deemed to be anticompetitive.

15. American Society of Composers, Authors and Publishers, and Broadcast Music, Inc., respectively.

16. These consent judgments have been modified as technology changed and new problems emerged. With respect to the relations between a collective and its members, they prohibit contracts requiring members to transfer exclusive licensing authority to the society. In contracting with users, the societies have to offer broadcasters a per-program license as an alternative to the blanket license. The ASCAP consent judgment, but not the BMI decree, provides for judicial ratemaking to set a

"reasonable" blanket or per-program fee when negotiations are unable to achieve a voluntary agreement.

17. The film industry of the United States, as distinct from the television broadcasting industry, won the right to clear music rights at source at the time synchronization rights are negotiated, avoiding the need for each cinema to have a license with the societies. In contrast, in Canada, cinemas have to be licensed by the collective to play music from its repertory.

18. According to one legal opinion, offering *only* a blanket contract to users may be construed as a conspiracy to monopolize (illegal by Section 42 of the Competition Act). A blanket contract that discriminates among users, as most do, would also be in violation of Section 50 of the Competition Act (Grant 1989, p. 18). For a more detailed account of the work done by the Canadian collectives and the related policy issues, see Smith (1984, 1986, 1988).

19. Regulatory constraints in the broadcasting and cable field are currently in a state of flux. The United States, for example, has experimented with two fundamentally different approaches to cable regulation within a span of eight years. Experimentation does not seem to be at an end. Canadian regulation of broadcasting and cable is more comprehensive than that in the United States. The degree of freedom that the broadcaster has in choosing programming and that the cable operator has in deciding what services will be available on what tiers is more tightly constrained. More gradual adjustments to change have traditionally been orchestrated by the Canadian regulator. Whether the current imperatives for change can be accommodated while maintaining the viability of the old system is doubtful. In Mexico the structure of commercial television broadcasting has been more concentrated and cable has been a relatively minor force. With respect to distribution, Mexico has access to the same technologies as Canada and the United States. The Mexican response may rely more on spectrum systems as there is less coaxial cable in place. On the programming side, linguistic markets will remain important. In the same way that France is an important market and source of finance and partners for French-Canadian producers, Spain and Latin America will remain key markets for Mexican producers. However, the Spanish-speaking market is much larger than the French-speaking market in the United States. Many American Hispanics have close family and cultural ties with Mexico. Exploiting this market will be an important influence on Mexican regulation of broadcasting.

20. De Freitas (1977) argues that clever wording allowed an author to commit to a publisher in the second period.

21. For example, the music tariff, dated July 29, 1957, applicable to distributors of films, was 1.5% of net receipts. This 1.5% was broken down into 0.6% to authors, 0.5% to composers, 0.25% to directors, and 0.15% to performers. (*Source:* Official Spanish text published in "Diario Oficial," August 8, 1957.)

22. The royalty rate was set by statute at 2 cents for each playing surface of each record sold. Industry practice adapted to the long-playing record by paying 2 cents per side for singles and 1½–2 cents per selection on an album. The standard industry contract divided the royalty so that 50% went to the producer, while the other 50% was split between the lyricist and the composer. Payment depends on actual use.

23. The categories include: radio; commercial television; different provincial educational television services; cabarets, cafes, dining rooms; recorded music for dancing; karaoke bars; aircraft; public parks; theme parks; background music; and music on hold. Rates are sometimes tied to performance indices of the user; for example, the radio tariff is 3.2% of gross revenue. Rates within a category are often tiered. The radio tariff is 1.4% for "low use" stations that use protected music for less than 20% of the broadcasting time. (For details, see Copyright Board Canada, *Statement of Royalties to be Collected for the Performance in Canada of Dramatico-Musical or Musical Works in 1990, 1991, 1992 and 1993*, Ottawa, December 6, 1993.)

24. Inter alia, Article 2 provides that the law recognizes and protects in respect of the author: (i) the recognition of his or her quality as author; (ii) the right to oppose any deformation, mutilation, or modification of the author's work which takes place without his or her authority, as well as any action denigrating the same, or which is damaging to the honor, prestige, or reputation of the author.

25. The Visual Artists Rights Act (VARA) of 1990 creates a statutory right to integrity and paternity.

26. By 1991, eleven of the U.S. states had legislation that protected some aspect of moral rights (Tanenbaum 1991, p. 456).

27. In France, Bernard Buffet created a work in which six panels of a refrigerator were painted. One was signed. The work was given to a charity which auctioned it off. Later, a single panel was offered for sale in another auction. In another case, in the United States, Richard Serra created a sculpture for an American government office building site in New York. In response to a petition from those who worked in the building which claimed that the sculpture prevented them from enjoying the plaza, the sculpture was removed. And in a third case, the Venice Biennale selected works of Giorgio de Chirico to display in a retrospective. All three artists sued, arguing that their statutory or common law moral rights had been violated. Buffet was successful in France; Serra was unsuccessful in the American courts; and de Chirico's case was dismissed by the Venetian Court of Appeal. Bloom (1991) discusses these cases and provides citations. He argues that all three artists had a good chance of being successful under current Canadian law.

28. The sculptor, Michael Snow, successfully sued and won the right to prevent the owners of the mall from adding the ribbons (Snow v. The Eaton Centre Ltd. 1982. 70 C.P.R. [2d] 105. Ontario High Court).

29. International Convention for the Protection of Performers, Producers of Phonograms and Broadcasting Organisations (the "Rome" Convention), adopted in Rome, October 26, 1961.

30. A neighboring right protects those who make a similar contribution as the copyright holders to value, but who are not covered by copyright law.

31. European Union directives are not European laws; they are models to which national laws should conform.

32. The EU has negotiated an agreement in which the six European Free Trade Association (EFTA) countries (Sweden, Norway, Austria, Switzerland, Iceland, and Finland) have committed to adopting copyright legislation that complies with the

EU model. A similar agreement has been made with Poland, the Czech Republic, and Hungary, although these countries have been given a longer period in which to comply. A similar arrangement with the Baltic republics, Bulgaria, and Romania is in an advanced stage of negotiation.

33. Rights granted to performers, producers of records, and broadcasters under the Rome treaty do not have to be extended to others as a result of TRIPS.

34. The only mechanism available to discipline a noncomplying member of Berne is to bring suit in the World Court. No country has ever done that, although few members of Berne are in total compliance with their obligations.

35. First, inputs to cultural industries—cameras, tapes, musical instruments, studio equipment, and so forth—enter duty free. Second, if, in a takeover or merger, a subsidiary operating in a cultural industry has to be disinvested because of ownership restrictions, the Canadian government ensures that fair market value will be paid. Third, a Canadian restriction that magazines must be typeset and printed in Canada for a company to be able to deduct advertising in the magazine as a business expense for Canadian corporate tax calculations was canceled.

36. Cable systems with less than 6,000 subscribers are charged a lower royalty, according to a tapered schedule.

37. First, the viewership of programs was measured during a three-week period in November 1988. The proportion of viewership of a program was adjusted by a factor reflecting the extent to which it was carried on Canadian rather than American distant signals. Some minor adjustments were then made to compensate seasonal programming that would not have been fairly represented in the November sweeps.

38. "The figures advanced by various parties may differ; however, they all confirm that whether one looks at prime time, off-prime or full time, distant signal viewing as a percentage of hours tuned to cable is between 14.9 and 17.7 per cent for Canada, 18.3 and 21.5 per cent for Canada excluding Quebec, and only between 4.4 and 5.2 per cent in Quebec" (Copyright Board of Canada, January 14, 1993, p. 48).

39. NAFTA does not extend this principle of national treatment to neighboring rights. Specifically, performers from other member countries are denied national treatment with respect to public performances of sound recordings. In this case, each party to the treaty is obliged to grant rights to performers from the other country only to the extent that they have rights in their own country.

40. A change in the definition of cultural industries from the FTA to NAFTA makes it clearer that the copyright provisions of NAFTA do not apply to the cultural industries in Canada. The definition of cultural industries in the FTA referred to any enterprise engaged in the specified activities. In NAFTA the definition refers to the broader concept of any legal or natural person.

41. In Mexico, the Comisión Nacional de Inversiones Extranjeras will review acquisitions of more than 49% of the ownership interest in a Mexican enterprise in an unrestricted sector, that is directly or indirectly owned or controlled by Mexican nationals. In Canada, under the Investment Canada Act, acquisitions of Canadian businesses in designated sectors by non-Canadians are subject to review by Invest-

ment Canada. In both countries, takeovers are vetted only if they exceed specified threshold values.

REFERENCES

Acheson, Keith, and Christopher Maule. 1991. Shadows Behind the Scenes: Political Exchange and the Film Industry. *Millennium* 20(2): 287–307.

Bloom, Glen. 1991. "Copyright in the Visual Arts." In *Copyright: New Developments, New Costs*. Mississauga, Ontario: Insight Press.

Brownlee, Michelle. 1993. "Safeguarding Style: What Protection is Afforded to Visual Artists by the Copyright and Trademark Laws?" *Columbia Law Review* 93: 1157–1184.

Copyright Board of Canada. 1990. *Statements of Royalties to be Paid for the Retransmission of Distant Radio and Television Signals*. Copyright Board of Canada. Decision of the Board File 1989-1.

de Freitas, Denis. 1977. "Authors' Contracts and the Public Interest." In *Copyright Contracts*, ed. H. C. Jehoram, pp. 29–51. Amsterdam: Sijthoff.

De Vany, Arthur, and Ross D. Eckert. 1991. "Motion Picture Antitrust: The Paramount Cases Revisited." *Research in Law and Economics* 14: 51–112.

Eisenberg, Melvin Aron. 1982. "The Bargain Principle and its Limits." *Harvard Law Review* 95(4): 741–801.

Fox, Harold G. 1945–1946. "Some Points of Interest in the Law of Copyright." *University of Toronto Law Journal* 6: 100–144.

Geller, Paul Edward. 1990. "Can the GATT Incorporate Berne Whole?" *European Intellectual Property Review* 11: 423–428.

Grant, Peter. 1989. "Competition and the Collectives in Canada: New Developments in the Relationship between Copyright and Antitrust Law." Paper presented at Law Society of Upper Canada Conference on Entertainment, Advertising and Media Law, April 15, Osgoode Hall, Toronto.

Guterson, David. 1993. "Enclosed. Encyclopedic. Endured: One Week at the Mall of America." *Harper's*, August, 49–56.

North American Free Trade Agreement, legal text. October 7, 1992.

Plant, A. 1934. "The Economic Aspects of Copyright in Books." *Economica* 1: 167–195.

Porter, Vincent. 1991. *Beyond the Berne Convention*. London: John Libbey.

Prescott, Peter. 1989. "The Origins of Copyright: A Debunking View." *European Intellectual Property Review* 12: 453–455.

Smith, Douglas A. 1984. *Collective Agencies for the Administration of Copyright*. Ottawa: Supply and Services.

———. 1986. "Collective Administration of Copyright: An Economic Analysis." *Research in Law and Economics* 8: 137–152.

———. 1988. "Recent Proposals for Copyright Revision: An Evaluation." *Canadian Public Policy* 14(2): 175–185.

Spurgeon, C.P. 1992. "Digital sampling: Some legal considerations." *Copyright Bulletin* 26(2): 7–19.

Spyke, Nancy Perkins. 1993. "The Joint Work Dilemma: The Separately Copyright Contribution Requirement and Coownership Principles." *Journal of the Copyright Society of America* 40(4): 463–493.

Tanenbaum, William A. 1991. "US Copyright Law After the Berne, Moral Rights and 1990 Amendments." *European Intellectual Property Review* 12: 449–459.

Watts, Tom Jake. 1993. "'El Derecho de Autor': Mexican Copyright Law and the North American Free Trade Agreement." Ph.D. diss., University of Alabama.

Appendixes

- -

■ ■ Editors' Comment on Appendixes A and B

As we mentioned in the foreword, an important goal in organizing the conference at which the preceding chapters of this book were presented was to include participation by representatives of two other influential groups in the cultural industries. Policymakers had direct input in the FTA and NAFTA agreements by representing their respective countries' positions in the negotiations vis à vis cultural industries. Representatives from the cultural industries themselves have knowledge of media markets and the power to influence their day-to-day characteristics and future development. We invited the policymakers' and industry representatives' contributions as a means of grounding the symposium in the give and take of policy negotiations and market competition. Given the practical aspects of the free trade/cultural industries question, it made little sense to engage in a dialog strictly among academics.

The policymakers and industry representatives were asked to give a 10-to-15-minute statement, then discuss the more salient issues among themselves and with members of the audience. (The different presentation and discussion format accounts for these sessions' inclusion as appendixes rather than chapters.) As the following pages demonstrate, the participants' positions were sometimes at odds, and the discussion of their ideas was often vigorous. The two appendixes that follow provide an overview of the participants' central arguments in the policymaker and industry-representative roundtable sessions and discussions.

. . . .

The Policymakers' Roundtable Discussion Session

(MARCH 3, 1994)

MODERATOR
Sharon Strover, Department of Radio Television Film,
University of Texas at Austin

PANEL PARTICIPANTS [1]
Emery Simon—former cultural industries negotiator,
U.S. Trade Representative

Emmy Verdun—Industry, Science and Technology Canada

Bernard Miyet—former Manager of Culture Relations,
Ministry of Foreign Affairs, France

THIS SESSION BEGAN WITH Emery Simon's intentionally (and success-fully) provocative question, "Why is it that when a television program of Miles Davis playing his trumpet is aired [in a non-U.S. city] it is con-sidered a good thing, but a one-hour broadcast of the series 'L.A. Law' is considered American cultural imperialism?" The question goes di-rectly to several issues that came to dominate the policymakers' discus-sion, and that have concerned government officials, international com-munication researchers, and some others for a number of years. Is international cultural product flow more an economic or a cultural is-sue? Should free market competition be left to order international re-gimes of cultural production and export? Should the public or private sector have the power to decide what constitutes audience preferences and/or necessities for cultural products? How far should governments go in imposing barriers to imported cultural products and in subsidizing their national cultural industries? What will the impact be of new distri-bution technologies on the flow issue? We were unable, of course, to adequately answer these complex questions, but by discussing them among people of differing orientations and opinions, we defined the ter-rain more clearly. These questions were addressed in the policymakers' statements, as well as in the discussions that followed; both are summa-rized in the following pages.

Emery Simon's answer to his own question was that we are reluctant to give the consumer a free choice to watch "L.A. Law," but do not hesitate to offer the same consumer Miles Davis. This has implications in several areas. It is a censorship issue because if quotas are set to protect local cultural industries, consumers are not given the freedom to choose among various options. It is an economic issue in that local producers are less threatened by the prospect of competing against Miles Davis than of competing against "L.A. Law"—the local industry's profitability is at stake. It is a trade issue in that other countries try to protect their domestic markets from U.S. cultural products which enjoy a number of competitive advantages. (It is important to note that these arguments assume that the U.S. produces higher quality cultural products than other nations.)

Mr. Simon also defined terms important in understanding the negotiations concerning cultural industries. Whereas an "exemption" excludes certain items brought to the negotiating table, a "derogation" excludes those items from the list of items to be negotiated. In the U.S./Canadian FTA negotiations, the cultural industries were derogated, not exempted. This occurred because, according to Mr. Simon, it was important to the Canadian negotiators to appear to the U.S. cultural industries to be recalcitrant.[2] Thus, the cultural provision in the FTA and later in NAFTA was symbolically important but economically irrelevant. Economics were very relevant, however, in the actual negotiations—more so than culture itself.

Emmy Verdun described the Canadian context as a backdrop to outlining her government's position vis à vis cultural industries and free trade. Canada's market for cultural products is approximately one-tenth that of the United States. Canada commits less public funding to cultural production than do most European nations, but spends more than the United States, which is commercially oriented. U.S. cultural products dominate Canadian markets: of films, 90% are American, 5% Canadian, and 5% other; of music recordings, 84% are American, 11% Canadian, and 5% other; and of books, 31% are Canadian and 69% other. Clearly, Canadian artists have difficulty reaching their domestic audience, and the government has intervened to assist them.

One type of assistance has been financial, in the form of grants to individuals and groups. Another important facet has been closer regulation of such elements as cultural product imports (especially films and books), cultural industry ownership, and the protection of Canadian artists' intellectual property. The 1988 FTA carried four provisions concerning the cultural industries. First, tariffs were removed on cultural products; second, the government agreed to pay fair market value when it forced divestiture of a company found to be under illegal foreign control; third, requirements to print in Canada were eliminated; and fourth, Canada agreed to pay U.S. broadcasters for program retransmissions.

Ms. Verdun pointed out that the cultural industry status quo had not changed with the FTA and NAFTA and was unlikely to do so in the near future. The Canadian film industry had experienced an upswing in the first half of the 1990s, partly due to co-productions which had some success in export markets. In spite of this development, a vigorous debate persisted in Canada concerning "good" (i.e., local) versus "bad" (i.e., U.S.) culture. Ms. Verdun concluded her remarks by surmising that the qualitative debate over culture will be rendered largely irrelevant by new technologies that will transform present methods of cultural production and distribution.

Bernard Miyet participated not as a representative of a NAFTA nation, but rather as an important negotiator for France in the GATT discussions which stalled just before the agreement was to be signed in December 1993 due to the cultural industries issue. He began by stressing the close links between cultural sovereignty and national politics in France. He also emphasized the importance of cultural production to the maintenance of national culture over the long term. The power of self-expression in the audiovisual sector was being lost, Mr. Miyet argued, to U.S. competition.

Directing his comments to Emery Simon, Mr. Miyet argued that consumers did not have the power of choice in television because broadcasters decide which programs will air, basing those decisions on the contradictory objectives of earning more advertising revenues through higher ratings and of making economical program purchases. The higher ratings obtained by purchasing expensive local productions are usually insufficient to generate more revenue than the purchase of a less popular but much less expensive U.S. series.[3]

In reference to the GATT negotiations that reached a widely reported deadlock over the cultural industries and agriculture in December 1993, Mr. Miyet claimed although the FTA and NAFTA negotiations were important precedents, the terms of the GATT agreement are different, and include such provisions as Most Favored Nation status and subsidies for cultural production. While it will be difficult for the United States to take unilateral sanctions against other countries in the audiovisual sector, American companies will increase their revenues from the

European market. The regional fragmentation that facilitates U.S. penetration is manifested through in-fighting between the EU and the Council of Europe, the concentration of regulatory power at the national level, and the fact that in telecommunication Europe has had limited input to computer hardware and software industries.

Like the other policymakers, Mr. Miyet finished his statement with a reference to new technologies. He ascribed to them an emancipatory function—as the number of channels multiplies, so will the difficulty of applying quotas. This deepens the process of transnationalization which favors the continued flow of cultural products from the U.S. to Europe. The coming interactive technologies will cripple traditional broadcasting that foments national identity through common interests and values shared through television.

As many of the comments during the discussion session were directed toward Emery Simon, we present those in order before overviewing more general themes. The first comment suggested that only those destinations of U.S. cultural products that share the United States' worldview could justifiably be considered in an "exchange." Denis St. Jacques stated that the central problem was not whether U.S. cultural products had access to international markets or not, but whether any space was left for locally produced products. Mr. Simon responded that a market player should not be constrained simply because he has a good product and markets it well. This provoked another audience member's response that this theory of "if it's American it's better" is what others resent. Eduardo Barrera commented that the issue should be less the quality of the final product, and more the trade practices used to dominate the market (e.g., the U.S. Motion Picture Export Association amortizing costs of film production in the wealthy U.S. market, giving it competitive advantages internationally). Barrera also suggested that too much emphasis was placed on "Americanization" and not enough on the transnationalization of cultural industries and the concentration of their ownership in fewer hands. Emery Simon responded that Europeans and Japanese have become corporate owners of U.S. sound recording and film/television studios, but the management and on- and off-screen talent remains American. The issue is more about employment than culture. An audience member expressed concern that the cultural identity issue might become lost in the discussion of employment, trade practices, and the like. Mr. Simon responded that culture is a dynamic process which we cannot control or protect.

An audience member's question concerning the relationship between international news reporting on such networks as CNN and U.S. foreign policy prompted a short response by Emery Simon that it is unclear whether news reports beget policy or vice versa. Bernard Miyet provided a longer response. He questioned the importance of international audiences knowing about the problems of the Kennedy (or, for that matter, Bobbitt) family. The change in news media agendas was intertwined with changed foci of international organizations. In the 1970s the problems of the developing nations were at the forefront as organizations such as UNCTAD (whatever their limitations) took a long-term view. In the 1990s, we have GATT as the principal international economic forum, and the news agenda is organized around shorter term problems of the developed nations. The news media's "polluting the international system" could have serious consequences on our ability to manage the planet in the future, according to Mr. Miyet.

Mr. Miyet also clarified the subsidy issue. GATT does not prevent subsidization of cultural production which, in Mr. Miyet's view, does not create competitive inequalities in any case. Even with subsidies by the government, the average cost of producing a film in France is between three and four million U.S. dollars. The average cost for a Hollywood film is twenty million dollars. It is difficult for these products to compete, so mechanisms are necessary to render local productions more competitive. This is not only for cultural reasons but also to provide employment. Emmy Verdun commented that ownership is another important consideration in this regard. Following debate of the issue, Canada decided that in many sectors ownership was of little consequence. Regulation in other areas such as technology, however, is critical in identifying and reaching niche markets for locally produced products.

NOTES

1. Unfortunately, Mexico's Secretariat of Commerce was understaffed at the time of the conference and therefore unable to send a representative.

2. Mr. Simon claims that certain intellectual property provisions were "buried" in the NAFTA agreement because Prime Minister Mulroney did not want it to appear that his position in the previous FTA with the United States had changed.

3. According to Mr. Miyet, an original French program would cost one million dollars whereas a U.S. series costs around fifty thousand dollars.

. . . .

The Industry Representatives' Roundtable Discussion Session

(MARCH 4, 1994)

MODERATOR
Ira Abrams, Department of Radio Television Film,
University of Texas at Austin

PANEL PARTICIPANTS
Charlotte Leonard—Senior Vice President of Turner Network Television
(TNT) International and Manager of Turner's Cartoon Network

Patricio Luna—Assistant Director, Instituto Mexicano de Cinematografía
(IMCINE, "Mexican Film Institute," a government agency)

Pedro Galindo—President of Silverstone Productions, a film production
company based in South Texas and specializing in the Spanish-language
market

Bernard Miyet[1]—former Manager of Culture Relations,
Ministry of Foreign Affairs, France

THIS ROUNDTABLE DISCUSSION FOCUSED principally on audiovisual
market conditions and the real and potential impacts of regulatory en-
vironments and free trade in two regions: Europe and Latin America.
Canada was not represented on this panel because a confirmed participant was forced to cancel at the last minute.[2]

Charlotte Leonard began her talk by describing the growth of Ted Turner's media empire from a small independent TV station in Atlanta to a
communications giant of five domestic and three international networks. CNN entered Latin America in 1985 and initiated a region-
specific newscast in 1991. TNT Latin America was also launched in 1991
as a regional pay-TV service offering films, series, sports and entertainment specials, and awards shows. The Cartoon Network began transmissions in Spanish and Portuguese in 1993.

Ms. Leonard outlined the central features of the Mexican television
market. A population of approximately 90 million people have a per
capita annual income of $2,000–$3,000. Between 13 and 15 million

households have television. In 1977 there were 45 cable operators, with approximately 180,000 subscribing households. By 1990 the number had grown to 97 operators with 680,000 subscribing households. Of Mexico's total advertising expenditures, 65% are on television; 15% growth, or an increase of 2.3 billion dollars, was projected for Mexican advertising in 1994. The growth in television outlets and advertising is what attracted Turner and other U.S.-based companies to the Latin American market during the first half of the 1990s.

Ms. Leonard mentioned four principal regulations on foreign television imports to Mexico—concerning language (the government is concerned about preserving Spanish), moral standards, maintenance of public order, and restrictions on quantities of advertising time dedicated to alcohol and cigarettes. Some unofficial agreements resulted from the NAFTA regulations: networks should dedicate 5% of daily programming to health, culture, and educational programs, and there should be self-censorship of violent, sexual, and drug-related messages.

Apart from the changed regulatory environment, Ms. Leonard identified four effects of NAFTA in the audiovisual cultural industries: 1. unified windows of release for theatrical films, pay-per-view, television, and video rentals in the three NAFTA nations will transform the syndication business; 2. more Spanish-language newcasts will enter Mexico from outside the country; 3. improved relations will be sought between U.S., Canadian, and Mexican advertising agencies so the smaller agencies, particularly in Mexico, do not feel they are being displaced; and 4. permissible foreign ownership of Mexican broadcast outlets will be increased to 49%.[3]

According to Pedro Galindo of Silverstone Productions in Brownsville, Texas, the principal issue in the Mexican film industry for NAFTA has been screen time for Mexican versus non-Mexican productions. Before NAFTA, Mexican law required that 50% of screen time be devoted to Mexican films; Mr. Galindo understood that this will drop to 20% over the next two or three years. This provision has created controversy within the industry. Silverstone Productions' view is that the change is positive, since it will pressure Mexico to produce better films. Further, having more American competitors in Mexico will also open new channels of distribution for Mexican products. In the past, film distribution was limited to two companies, one owned by the government, and the other by Televisa; it was very difficult to negotiate adequate distribution contracts. Mr. Galindo hoped that with new players such as Turner and

HBO in the market he would be able to co-produce or at least secure better distribution.

Along with the obvious disadvantages of competing in the same market with a giant like Televisa, there can be advantages as well. With Televisa in so many international markets, Mexican Spanish may become the standard much as American English is in the anglophone world. Establishing this linguistic standard is important to Silverstone Productions because it opens markets to their products. As interest in U.S. Latino culture and the U.S. Spanish-language market has increased, so has the interest in producing films and videos that appeal to that market. Some companies based in Spain have expressed interest in co-producing with Silverstone. In the past, they co-produced a number of successful films with Televisa, but it is very difficult for independent producers to break through, partly because Televisa's productions are very family oriented.

Patricio Luna of IMCINE described the challenges facing the Mexican film industry under the short timetable for economic modernization drawn up by the federal government. In the pre-NAFTA era Mexican filmmaking suffered from structural problems, limited investment, the weakening of distribution systems, failure to maintain cinemas, and a lack of adequate means of stimulating investment in the industry. These problems negatively impacted the creative quality of Mexican films, and the industry lost much of the audience and international market position it previously enjoyed. In 1989 IMCINE was placed in the sector of fine arts and was given two mandates: to conceive of film as an artistic medium much like music and literature, and to stimulate the creation of higher quality productions that would improve Mexico's international image.

To meet these challenges, IMCINE developed two policies—first, to cease producing and instead support promising independent productions, and second, to promote Mexican films at international festivals and assist Mexican companies in securing co-productions, distribution agreements, and other important contracts. This international effort is being complemented by a domestic initiative to facilitate distribution, reduce customs barriers, and streamline the bureaucracy related to film production.

As regards NAFTA, Sr. Luna foresees the continuation of national policymaking in the film industries. Some of the tariff reductions on audiovisual equipment will facilitate the modernization of Mexico's film production infrastructure. Mexico will continue to encourage and accept foreign investment in production, distribution, and exhibition. Mexicans understand that an open economy is the proper development path, offering opportunities for change: the Mexican film industry will respond to the challenge.

Bernard Miyet began his statement by reflecting on transformations in European film industries over the past ten to twenty years. The national industries in the U.K., Italy, Germany, and other countries weakened considerably. Only France and to a lesser extent Spain remained productive, due not to quotas but rather to subsidies and other means of financing and reinvesting in films. These programs are necessary because the U.S. invests larger amounts of capital in its productions than other countries are able to. Since the wealthy U.S. audiovisual market is closed to imports, other countries cannot benefit from exporting to it, even when the productions are in English.

Mr. Miyet stated his preference for subsidies to support local and national production over quotas to impede imports. The limited efficacy of quotas was demonstrated in Europe's pay-TV industry, where there was a large increase in the number of channels during the 1980s and early 1990s, causing U.S. program imports to increase exponentially *after* restrictions were imposed by the EU directive on television (passed in October 1989). Quotas can also have the opposite effect of that intended by driving down the cost of imports and thus making them more difficult to compete against. Despite these problems, however, the quotas helped demonstrate that audiences preferred local programming.

Recognition of local program popularity stimulated the recent trend in European broadcasting away from voluminous imports from the U.S. and toward balancing local and imported programming.[4] Notwithstanding privatization, the public service broadcasting tradition in many European nations has also hindered the wholesale adoption of commercial television: public television has become more commercial, but there are limits on how commercial private broadcasters can be. These factors have been more effective in protecting the European television market than has the imposition of quotas. Future strategies will not be protectionist, but rather will be aimed at encouraging European nations' creative and productive capacity through greater penetration of their products in non-European markets, increased investment, and other forms of support for local production.

Such programs would conflict with the strategy of American majors to integrate their activities on a global scale by controlling production, distribution, and dissemination not only for over-the-air television but also for pay-TV services such as cable, pay-per-view, and direct broadcasting satellites. It is precisely this that Turner is attempting to achieve by amortizing the cost of acquiring its MGM film library in markets worldwide. The effect of such a strategy would be to reduce broadcasters' revenues earned from advertising and thus their financial capacity to support local program production. Although it is impossible to know the future balances of power and how local channels will react, it is a problem we should begin to consider.

The first question for the panelists was from Emile McAnany and was directed to Mr. Miyet: How are the big broadcast companies handling the dilemma of lower-cost imported programs attracting insufficient audiences for prime time while local fiction programs are often prohibitively expensive? Mr. Miyet responded that the answer depends on the number and wealth of channels in a market. A contradiction exists between the number of channels and the capacity to produce fiction programs. For example, in the U.S. four major networks share revenues representing approximately 50% of total world television revenues (including the Canadian anglophone market); Europe represents 25% of world television revenues, but divides them among 25–30 networks. The essential parameter in financing television drama—how many dollars you have to spend per hour of programming—is unbalanced between the U.S. and Europe. This is why European governments, and the French in particular, have been seeking means of obliging broadcasters to finance local production. One method has been to levy a 6% tax which goes to a program-production fund at the National Center for Cinematography—the broadcaster gets the tax back if it produces or co-produces with a local partner. The quotas have also stimulated more airing of programs from neighboring countries. It used to be that all imported programs were purchased in packages from U.S. distributors; now, however, there is more knowledge of and interest in programs produced in other European nations.

Charlotte Leonard commented that the regulatory environment in France was less open than it appeared to be, causing Turner some problems there. When Turner planned to launch the Cartoon Network in Europe it had a different interpretation than European regulators had of what it meant to include European productions "where practicable." Turner's plan to dub its existing libraries was unacceptable to the regulators, and investing several hundred million dollars to acquire European films in order to satisfy EU rules was unacceptable to Turner.

Ms. Leonard also referred to a system in France requiring that two-thirds of the input to a co-production be French in order for it to be classified as a "national" product; such requirements, she said, discourage co-production. An incentive offered by the French government (and with which Turner tried to comply) is favorable treatment in France in exchange for the airing of French productions in the U.S. market. Turner aired a French program in a Saturday night slot for six weeks, after which it was forced to cancel for lack of sponsors. U.S. audiences show little interest in imported films and television programs.

Bernard Miyet responded that the EU directive reads that European programs be aired not only "where practicable" but also "when possible." From the EU's point of view, the problem was not Cartoon Network's content in ethical terms, but the high percentage of programs originating from outside the region. If one cable service not conforming with the guidelines was accepted, the problem would spill over into all channels in all countries. As regards co-production, Mr. Miyet pointed out that it could be executed with any country in the EU system in order to gain "national" status.

An audience member commented that the NAFTA agreement would likely accelerate an already favorable investment trend in Latin American broadcasting and pay-TV, and asked what Turner's strategy would have been had NAFTA not been adopted. Ms. Leonard responded that NAFTA's effect would be minimal in broadcasting but substantial in advertising. First, Mexican law used to prohibit the airing of commercials originating from outside the country; now they can be uplinked to Mexico's Morelos satellite for subsequent distribution. Second, as more goods are shipped to Mexico, the demand for advertising will increase. Thus, TNT Latin America leaves 20–25% of its commercial time for local companies to sell to advertisers or to use to promote their own channels.

A first question directed to Patricio Luna concerned authors' rights in Mexico and whether they were likely to change under NAFTA. Sr. Luna responded that he was unaware of any plans to change the existing legislation, and reminded the audience that cultural industries were included in the agreements between the U.S. and Mexico and Canada and Mexico, but not between Canada and the U.S. He maintained that any change in existing law would have to preserve Mexico's values and cultural identity as well as the creative style of its artists. A second question for Sr. Luna requested clarification of his comment that "devious competition" existed in the film trade between the NAFTA nations and of how the reforms he outlined in his statement might address the problem. Sr. Luna responded that NAFTA was promoted as a balanced, equitable agreement, but that in reality it may not offer equal participation and mutual benefits to all participants. IMCINE planned to build up the Mexican film industry gradually through investment from the public and private sectors, with the goal of developing an industry that would be self-sufficient or at least able to attract funding through co-production.

Pedro Galindo was asked whether his experience in Brownsville represented a viable alternative for the Mexican film industry. Mr. Galindo answered that Brownsville is "the most Mexican city in the U.S.," with a wealth of stories concerning the border and interracial activity. This strategic position offers his company an advantage in international markets, especially Spanish-language markets.

Charlotte Leonard was asked to elaborate on TNT Latin America's programming strategy and acceptance among audiences. She responded that region-wide ratings are not conducted in Latin America, and it is difficult to find metropolitan ratings that compare cable and non-cable homes. However, a number of companies with interests in pay-TV were organizing a group ("LatTap") to gather better data to present to advertisers. TNT Latin America is, along with HBO Olé, typically among the top three cable services in the ratings. Ms. Leonard's network has produced some cultural programming in Spanish and Portuguese, and is looking for Spanish-language co-producers.

NOTES

1. Before becoming a trade negotiator Mr. Miyet was chairman and CEO of the Societé Financier de Radiodiffusion (Broadcast Financing Company) and Counsel General of France in Los Angeles.

2. Airport closures due to a snowstorm in the eastern U.S. prevented another confirmed participant, Larry Loeb of ABC/Capital Cities, from attending. Nevertheless, we appreciate Mr. Loeb's agreeing to participate.

3. The U.S. cable giant TCI negotiated to purchase 49% of Cablevision, the cable television subsidiary of the Mexican communications conglomerate Televisa. The deal fell through in early 1994.

4. Mexico's Televisa has been following this strategy almost from its inception. See John Sinclair (1986), "Dependent development and broadcasting: 'The Mexican formula,'" *Media, Culture & Society*, 8(1), 81–101.

Index

····················

can adolescents' media preferences, 168–183; in Mexico, 197; passive, 164–165, 189; preference for local productions, 119, 162; Russians view telenovelas, 110; segmentation, 14, 123; for serial narratives, 113; and soap opera characters, 114; talk among viewers, 113, 273; television viewing in Canada, 265–275; youth, 102–103; mentioned, 8, 11, 16, 25, 35, 49, 54, 72, 82, 84, 95, 101, 105, 108, 109, 112, 116, 120, 123, 158, 160, 163, 166, 209, 227, 238, 246, 269, 281, 290, 294, 298, 312, 314, 316, 317, 321, 352, 381, 383, 385, 387, 391, 393, 394
Audiovisual industries. *See* Cultural industries
Audiovisual products. *See* Cultural products
Audley, Paul, 7
Austin Project, 105, 108; described, 97; goals of, 99
Australia: state support for ethnic media, 40; mentioned, 18, 34, 45, 51, 52, 72, 80, 85, 112, 113, 122, 125, 346
Authors: in Québec book market, 283–286; Québecois and English Canadian, 288–289; mentioned, 25, 73, 98, 102, 104, 106, 107, 116, 279, 282, 287, 290, 291, 293, 294, 297, 300, 341–342, 355, 356, 358, 360, 383
Authorship, 341-342

Bartra, Roger, 196
Basilica of Guadalupe, 137, 139
BBC (British Broadcasting Corporation), 69, 79
BBM (Bureau of Broadcast Measurement), 247, 250–251, 257
Bélanger, Michel, 314
Belgium, 16
Bell, Steven C., 334
Bell Atlantic, 15
Bennett, Tony, 198
Berman, Jason, 343

Berne Convention, 342, 344, 364, 367, 368. *See also* Intellectual property
Best-seller genres and topics: affective success, 290–294; biography, 287–288, 290–293; class, 292–293; crime, 292–293; cultural success, 290–294; environment, 292–293; essays, 287–288, 289, 290, 292–293; ethnic/race relations, 292–293; fiction, 287–288, 289, 290–291, 292–293; fictional violence, 301–303; freedom, 292–293; gender, 292–293; generations, 292–293; interpersonal relations, 292-293; non-fiction, 287–288, 289; novels, 289, 292–293; politics, 292–293; practical books, 287–288, 289, 290; psychological success, 290–294; religion, 292–293; romance, 299; science, 292–293; social or economic success/failure, 290–294. *See also* Best-sellers; Book genres; Books
Best-sellers, 25, 233, 298; central elements, 281; defined, 281; fiction *v.* non-fiction, 294; "private" *v.* "public," 290–293; and readers' gender, 299–300; scholars' recognition of, 279–280; super-sellers in Québec, English Canada, and U.S., 289, 294, 295; in U.S., 290. *See also* Best-seller genres and topics; Book genres; Books
Bider, Les, 344
Billboard magazine, 331
Bill C-58 (Canada), 76
Blair Television, 199
Blank-tape levies, 366
Blockbuster Video, 10
BMI (Broadcast Music, Inc.), 341, 343, 361
Bonfil, Guillermo, 140
Bonnassieux, Marie-Pierre, 289
Book genres: biography, 280, 281; crime, 279; fiction, 238, 282, 296, 301; narrative, 282; non-fiction, 238, 282, 296, 301; non-narrative, 282; novel, 280,

Horizontal integration, 37, 191; in cultural industries, 34. *See also* Competitive strategy
Horkheimer, Max, 30, 31, 32
Hoskins, Colin, 18, 43, 44, 68, 70, 71
Human rights, 137

Identity: and audience exposure to imported films, 182–183; and broadcasting in Montréal, 274; conditions for change, 160; and free trade, 155; issues in defining, 148; in Mexico, 143, 153, 157, 160; notions and study of, 144–145; in Nuevo Laredo, 176–184; and otherness, 190; and public culture, 245; and television in Mexico, 158; and television in Québec, 274; mentioned, 12, 23–24, 114, 189, 192, 243, 347, 386, 394. *See also* Mexicanidad; National identity
Ideology: in media content, 164–166; in U.S. cultural products, 166; mentioned, 3, 31, 115, 132, 136, 175, 181, 183, 226, 247, 280, 290, 309, 312
Imagined communities, 56
IMAX theaters, 85
IMCINE (National Cinematography Institute), 389, 391, 395; policies to improve Mexican film industry, 391
Immigration, 187, 335
Immigration law, 332, 333, 334; distinguished merit *v.* preeminence, 333. *See also* H-1 work permits
Immigration Law Review, 334
Independent film producers, 80, 88, 391. *See also* Producers
India, 48, 52, 110
Industrialization, 343; of culture, 30, 32
Industry representatives, 381
Industry, Science and Technology Canada, 383
Information superhighway. *See* National Information Infrastructure
INS (U.S. Immigration and Naturalization Service), 333, 334, 335

Intellectual property: agreements favor U.S., 52; in Canada, 384; moral rights, 332, 342–343; mentioned, 9, 10, 26, 331, 333, 340, 345, 360, 365, 366, 367. *See also* Berne Convention; Copyright; Copyright law; Intellectual property law; Rome Treaty
Intellectual property law: in Mexico, 394; under NAFTA, 9
Intellectuals, 134, 137, 243, 312
INTELSAT, 5, 13
Interactive technologies, 26, 386. *See also* New technologies
Internationalization: of television, 49; of television in Québec, 252; of U.S. cultural industries, 14–15; mentioned, 56, 144, 164, 198, 265, 331, 333, 386. *See also* Globalization
Intertextuality, 193
Investment, 7, 13, 148, 151, 155, 310, 314, 332, 392, 394, 395
Ireland, 301–302
Italy, 47, 63, 71, 120, 151, 152, 392

Jameson, Frederic, 194
Japan, 51, 71, 134, 154, 196, 268, 338, 345, 348, 386
Jhally, Sut, 206
Joint-consumption good. *See* Public good
Journalism, 253–254
Juárez. *See* Ciudad Juárez
Juno Awards, 315

Kantor, Mickey, 3, 7
Kennedy, Paul, 64
Knight-Ridder, 199
Korea, 120

L'Express, 282
La Jornada, 131
La Presse, 281, 289, 290, 304 nn.5, 10
Labor, 332, 334, 342, 344
Language: advantages to productions in English, 72; and book industry, 233;

and broadcast policy in Canada, 252; as community's defining characteristic, 320; as comparative advantage, 42; as cultural defense, 286; and cultural discount, 18, 68, 72; and cultural imperialism, 272; and cultural product flow, 273–275; distinguished from culture, 45; English Canada similar to northern U.S., 83; in European regional market, 15–16; and international media markets, 366; issue in Québec music industry, 321; knowledge of English and media exposure, 180–181; and market advantage, 42–43, 45; multiple audio tracks, 14; and music, 322; national accents in international markets, 391; as protective barrier, 11, 12, 46; in Québec, 237–238, 239, 242–244, 247, 268; role in media markets, 15–21, 42–46, 55–56, 72; and television advertising in Ciudad Juárez, El Paso and Harlingen, 206; and television viewing in Canada, 265–275; as trade barrier, 44–46, 298, 303; and U.S./Canadian book trade, 289; and U.S. television, 124; U.S. audiences reject foreign accents, 125; mentioned, 70, 93, 107, 131, 246, 250, 253, 324, 325, 390

Language transfer: and closed U.S. market, 66, 73–75; and cultural discount, 68; in cultural linguistic markets, 15–17; and cultural resistance, 273; dubbed programs in Canada, 263–264; in Europe, 16–17; in francophone market, 18; in Latin America, 19; for Québec, 236; and reception, 273; of TV Globo programs, 47; U.S. audiences' resistance to, 44, 125; mentioned, 85, 110, 155, 158, 163, 225, 235, 279, 366, 393. *See also* Translation

Laredo (Texas), 167, 168, 171

Latin America: concerns over U.S. influences, 158; film attendance, 150; film industry, 153; media system, 11;

pay television, 15; television import/export, 19; television production and export advantages, 120–121; television production and flow, 48; and U.S. films, 183; VCRs and video rental, 153; mentioned, 7, 10, 13, 16, 17, 19, 21, 40, 46, 52, 112, 120, 121, 122, 136, 141–143, 152, 154, 155, 161, 165, 171, 193, 389, 394

LatTap, 395

Law, 332, 356; antitrust, 360–361; common, 360, 364; compulsory licenses, 363; and music industry, 332–344; passing off, 360; performance rights, 340–341; statutory, 372 n.3. *See also* Trade law; Copyright; Copyright law; Immigration law

Lazarsfeld, Paul, 33

Le fait français, 308

Legislation, 371; impact on music industry, 332, 333, 336, 338, 345

Le Monde, 65

Levitt, Theodore, 14

Licensing, 332, 336, 337, 357

Like Water for Chocolate, 154, 161

Literacy, 224

Literature, 105, 136; cultural influences in 19th c., 94–95. *See also* Bestsellers; Books

Literature studies, 279–280

Lobbying, 76, 308, 315, 334, 338, 343, 356. *See also* Politics

López Portillo, José, 133

Lorimar, 117, 119, 121

Lyricists. *See* Music artists

Magazines: in Québec, 224, 234; mentioned, 34, 157, 160, 228–229, 232, 237, 238, 243, 352

Malm, Krister, 337, 347

Maquiladoras, 24, 167, 187, 195–196, 199

Market strategy. *See* Competitive strategy

Marketing, 15, 34, 194, 341, 358; across different media, 191, 345; of best-